W9-BSC-147

America's War on Same-Sex Couples and Their Families

America's War on Same-Sex Couples and Their Families is a legal, political, and social history of constitutional amendments in twenty American states (with 43 percent of the nation's population) that prohibited government recognition of all forms of relationship rights (marriage, civil unions, and domestic partnerships) for same-sex couples. Based on 175 interviews with gay and lesbian pairs in Georgia, Michigan, North Carolina, Ohio, Texas, and Wisconsin, the volume has great human-interest value and chronicles how same-sex couples and their children coped within harsh legal environments. The work ends with a lively explanation of how the federal judiciary rescued these families from their own governments. In addition, the book provides a model of the grassroots circumstances under which harassed minority groups migrate out of oppressive state regimes, together with an estimate of the economic and other costs (to the refugees and their governments) of the flight from persecution.

Daniel R. Pinello is a professor of political science at John Jay College of Criminal Justice of the City University of New York and was educated at Williams College (B.A.), New York University (J.D.), and Yale University (Ph.D., political science). His scholarship includes *America's Struggle for Same-Sex Marriage* (2006), *Gay Rights and American Law* (2003), "Linking Party to Judicial Ideology in American Courts: A Meta-Analysis," in *Justice System Journal* (1999), and *The Impact of Judicial-Selection Method on State-Supreme-Court Policy: Innovation, Reaction, and Atrophy* (1995).

America's War on Same-Sex Couples and Their Families

And How the Courts Rescued Them

DANIEL R. PINELLO

John Jay College of Criminal Justice of the City University of New York

CAMBRIDGE
UNIVERSITY PRESS

CAMBRIDGE
UNIVERSITY PRESS

One Liberty Plaza, New York, NY 10006, USA

Cambridge University Press is part of the University of Cambridge.

It furthers the University's mission by disseminating knowledge in the pursuit of education, learning, and research at the highest international levels of excellence.

www.cambridge.org
Information on this title: www.cambridge.org/9781107559004

© Daniel R. Pinello 2017

First published 2017

Printed in the United States of America by Sheridan Books, Inc.

A catalogue record for this publication is available from the British Library.

Library of Congress Cataloging-in-Publication Data
Names: Pinello, Daniel R., author.
Title: America's war on same-sex couples and their families : and how the courts rescued them / Daniel R. Pinello.
Description: New York : Cambridge University Press, 2017. |
Includes bibliographical references and index.
Identifiers: LCCN 2016000899| ISBN 9781107123595 (hardback) |
ISBN 9781107559004 (paper back)
Subjects: LCSH: Same-sex marriage–United States. | Same-sex marriage–Law and legislation–United States.
Classification: LCC HQ1034.U5 P556   2017 | DDC 306.84/80973 – dc23
LC record available at http://lccn.loc.gov/2016000899

ISBN 978-1-107-12359-5 Hardback
ISBN 978-1-107-55900-4 Paperback

For Lee

Contents

Acknowledgments   *page* xi

1   Introduction   1
    Declarations of War   3
    The Book's Research Methods   9
    A Description of the Couples Sample   12
    Contemplating Super-DOMA Effects   15
    The Motivations of Amendment Sponsors and of Voters   17
    Ohio   25

2   State Judicial Interpretations of Super-DOMAs   34
    Ohio State-Court Action regarding Issue 1   36
    Michigan State-Court Action regarding Proposal 2   43
    Wisconsin State-Court Action regarding Referendum 1   50
    Other State-Court Action   53
    Understanding the Lack of Further State-Court Super-DOMA
        Litigation   54
    Conclusion   58

3   The Effects of Super-DOMAs on Same-Sex Couples   59
    The Initial Shock: Personal Devastation and Isolation   60
    Positive Effects   62
    Super-DOMAs as Impediments to Change   66
    Health Care   69
    The Limitations of Legal Paperwork   77
    Employment Discrimination   80
    Housing Discrimination   81
    Public Hazing When Changing Names   82

Tax Penalties   84
Alienation from Family, Friends, and Associates   86
Fear, Insecurity, and Emotional Loss   89
Little Things   94
Wisconsin's Domestic-Partner Registry as a Rights Touchstone   96
Inability to Divorce or Otherwise Access Legal Remedies   101
Conclusion   104

4   The Effects of Super-DOMAs on Families with Children
    Being Raised by Same-Sex Couples   107
    Michigan and Ohio   111
    North Carolina   111
    Wisconsin   112
    Texas   115
    Georgia   118
    The Value of Having Two Legal Parents Raising Children in
        Households Headed by Same-Sex Couples   126
    The Added Costs of Raising Children in LGBT Families   134
    The Message to Children   135
    Marrying out of State to Solidify and Clarify Intrafamily
        Relationships   136
    When Parents Were Separated   137
    Other Challenges for Same-Sex Couples Raising Children   144
    Conclusion   147

5   Super-DOMAs and LGBT Migration: Fight or Flight?   149
    An Estimate of LGBT Emigrants from Super-DOMA States   150
    Other Relevant Migrations   152
    Knowledge and Appreciation of the Threat to Well-Being   153
    Loyalty to Country or State   155
    The Bubble Effect   156
    Family Ties   160
    An Expectation of Legal or Political Redemption   162
    Economic Issues   163
    The Impact of Traditionally Gendered Relationship Roles   165
    Internalized Homophobic Social Stigma   168
    The Ability to Pass as Members of the Majority or Otherwise
        Play the System   173
    Same-Sex Couples Who Left Super-DOMA States Partially or
        Temporarily   177
    Same-Sex Couples Who Did Emigrate Permanently   181
    Super-DOMA Effects on Immigration into Super-DOMA
        States   199
    Conclusion   222

6   How the Federal Courts Rescued Same-Sex Couples and
    Their Families   224
    The Impact of Lower Federal Courts   225
    The Legal Precedents   226
    The Lower Federal Courts' Lopsided Interpretations of
        Windsor   232
    The Impacts of Good Fortune and Political Party   234
    The Importance of Precedent   236
    Justice Scalia as a Double Agent   237
    The Alternative to Judicial Action: The Roberts-Scalia-Alito
        Thesis of Waiting, and Waiting, and Waiting for the
        Democratic Process   241
    Other Difficulties with the Roberts-Scalia-Alito
        Democratic-Process Thesis   249
7   Conclusion   253
    Did Super-DOMAs in Fact Defend and Protect Marriage?   258
    The Economic Losses to Super-DOMA States   260
    Sponsor Motivations for Super-DOMAs: Bigotry or Not?   267
    Judicial Efficacy   279

Appendix A: The Texts of Super-DOMAs   285
Appendix B: Protocol of Interview Questions for Same-Sex
    Couples   287
Case References   291
References   295
Index   309

Acknowledgments

This book would not have been possible without the unsparing generosity of the people who invited me into their homes and offices to conduct the 203 in-depth interviews on which the volume is based. They have my particular gratitude.

A variety of professionals, community leaders, and interest group representatives graciously gave me their time and attention. They were, in Georgia, Dr. Frank A. Anania of Emory University School of Medicine; Michael L. Baker, aide to former Atlanta mayor Shirley Franklin; Daniel A. Bloom, Esq.; Douglas L. Brooks, Esq.; Jason A. Cecil of Atlanta Stonewall Democrats; Deepali Gokhale, co-chair of the Atlanta steering committee opposing referendum Question 1 of 2004; Jeff Graham, Georgia Equality's executive director; Barbara E. Katz, Esq.; Gregory R. Nevins, supervising senior staff attorney of the southern regional office of Lambda Legal; Debbie Seagraves, executive director of the ACLU of Georgia; and John F. Szabo, director of the Atlanta-Fulton Public Library. In Michigan, I spoke with Mary A. Ferguson, diversity officer of the Michigan State University College of Law; Jay Kaplan, staff attorney for the LGBT Project of the ACLU of Michigan; and Dr. Eric P. Skye of the University of Michigan Medical School.

In North Carolina, Maxine Eichner of the University of North Carolina School of Law in Chapel Hill; Tracy L. Hollister, a Democratic political operative in Raleigh; Paula A. Kohut, Esq.; Jaye J. Kreller, a Chapel Hill real estate agent; and Terri Lynn Phoenix, director of the LGBTQ Center at the University of North Carolina in Chapel Hill, shared valuable information and opinion with me. In Ohio, I spoke with Michael D. Bonasera, Esq.; A. Lynne Bowman, founding executive director of Equality Ohio; Phil Burress, president of Citizens for Community Values; Carrie L. Davis, staff counsel of the ACLU of Ohio; Susan Doerfer, executive director of Equality Ohio; Timothy J. Downing, Esq.; Carol Ann Fey, Esq.; Mellissia Fuhrmann, president of Stonewall Democrats of

Central Ohio; LeeAnn M. Massucci, Esq.; and Marc Spindelman of the Ohio State University College of Law.

In Texas, Phillip D. Archer, contender for Martha Stewart of Dallas; Lorie L. Burch, Esq.; Patrick J. Tester, a Dallas real estate agent; and Chad West, Esq., met with me. In Wisconsin, I spoke with Katie Belanger, executive director of Fair Wisconsin, and the Rev. Wendy R. Woodruff, pastor of the Metropolitan Community Church of Milwaukee.

Equally crucial to the book's empirical foundation were interviews with 325 people in 175 same-sex relationships in Georgia, Michigan, North Carolina, Ohio, Texas, and Wisconsin. As the introductory chapter explains, I am not at liberty here to divulge their real names. These couples' participation in the volume occurs under pseudonyms to protect against sexual-orientation discrimination in employment, housing, and public accommodations within five of those jurisdictions (Wisconsin being the exception), which have no statewide policies prohibiting such behavior. For Chapter 5, I had conversations with Michael L. Falk, formerly of Ann Arbor, Michigan, and other Super-DOMA refugees in their new places of residence.

Many of the interviews for this volume and my 2006 book, *America's Struggle for Same-Sex Marriage*, are preserved for posterity at the Department of Manuscripts and Archives at Yale University's Sterling Memorial Library. I am very grateful to Yale for accepting the gift of my collection and raising the resources necessary for its preservation. Yale historian George Chauncey presented my data to William Massa, Head of the Collection Development, and Christine Weideman, the Director of Manuscripts and Archives at the Sterling Library. Their positive assessments of the interviews' historical value were most gratifying.

I also appreciate the funding received from the City University of New York for four of this project's seven field trips. John Jay College of Criminal Justice provided a Research Support Grant of $3,500 for equipment and travel to conduct interviews in Michigan in January 2009, and then a Research Assistance Grant of $2,000 to go to Georgia in January 2010. The Research Grant program of CUNY's Professional Staff Congress awarded a total of $3,700 for journeys to Columbus, Ohio in June 2010, and to Texas in January 2011. I bore the expense of the field trips to Cleveland, Ohio in July 2010, Wisconsin in July 2011, and North Carolina in July 2012.

I presented preliminary findings at the 2010 Annual Meeting of the American Political Science Association in Washington, DC. John J. Dinan and Keith E. Whittington were discussants and provided helpful appraisals. In February 2013, I delivered a precursor of Chapter 5 at a Human Rights Seminar held at the CUNY Graduate Center and sponsored by the Center for International Human Rights of John Jay College of Criminal Justice. George Andreopoulos and Kenneth Sherrill supplied useful insights and guidance there. Other friends in academe – Ellen Ann Andersen, H. N. Hirsch, and Charles Anthony Smith – also gave generous commentary to shape the project.

I owe special gratitude to Jack Jacobs, my colleague at John Jay College of Criminal Justice, for introducing me to the scholarship of historian Marion A. Kaplan during a departmental research colloquium. John Jay political scientists Samantha Ann Majic and Andrew H. Sidman also provided helpful advice at the forum. My other John Jay colleagues – George Andreopoulos, Brian K. Arbour, Janice Bockmeyer, James Bowen, Jean Carmalt, James N. G. Cauthen, Susan L. Kang, Maxwell H. H. Mak, G. Roger McDonald, Verónica Michel, Jill Norgren, Peter Romaniuk, Jennifer Geist Rutledge, Monica W. Varsanyi, and Michael W. Yarbrough – supplied steadfast encouragement and support.

Robert Dreesen at Cambridge University Press is an indulgent editor as any author could hope to work with. Indeed, my experience over three titles with Cambridge taught me well that its editorial staff is uniformly among the finest in academic publishing. Gail Naron Chalew, the copy editor, provided the most sure-handed guidance transforming the manuscript into a book.

My husband, Lee Nissensohn, nurtured this endeavor in every way. He has been my rock for more than twenty precious years.

Introduction

[C]oncerns...about the preservation of minority rights...are particularly pronounced with regard to proposed legislation that targets homosexual rights. On many such matters, the ballot has proved a fertile *battleground* to restrict and repeal protections.

> – Daniel R. Biggers, *Morality at the Ballot: Direct Democracy and Political Engagement in the United States* (2014, 172, emphasis added)

Q: What did the passage of Michigan's 2004 marriage amendment mean to you?

LINDA: It was totally demoralizing. I spent so much time trying to educate the students, faculty, and staff at my university about how such antigay campaigns give people permission to act out their disapproval. I tried to prepare my work community for the potential bias, harassment, and hate crimes that might and, in fact, did occur. My attempts on campus were first met with skepticism. Then things started to happen.

People were intimidated and assaulted. Knives were pulled, and beer bottles thrown. People were knocked down, including a faculty member and a blind, older, returning student. So the amendment really meant we didn't have the same rights as other people.

My partner Patricia, who has a chronic illness, wasn't included on the health insurance from my job. And the amendment would make getting coverage for her a lot harder. We were concerned about who would make the health care choices if one of us had to go to the hospital.

PATRICIA: The amendment really increased the number of people who helped us because they wanted to, but not because they had to. They made it clear to us, really clear, that they were just being kind.

LINDA: Because of the amendment, I started looking for jobs elsewhere. In January 2005, I began applying at universities in other, more welcoming places. The amendment was the last straw. We were going to leave Michigan.

PATRICIA: Actually, the last straw was Elizabeth.

LINDA: Elizabeth and Jennifer were our friends, because Elizabeth was a professor I knew through the state university system. In June 2005, her car was hit by a drunk driver, and Elizabeth died in the wreck. Then we watched Jennifer, in tremendous grief, suffer further because of the marriage amendment. The coroner's office wouldn't tell Jennifer, who knew something had happened, that her partner had died. Instead, the officials had to wait five hours for Elizabeth's blood relative to drive there from another city. Jennifer couldn't claim the body or have it moved to a funeral home. There was nothing Jennifer could do without Elizabeth's brother being there to sign the papers. And without the brother, Jennifer would've been completely lost. She had no legal rights. She had no control over any decision making.

Elizabeth had been teaching that summer. Generally what happens when somebody dies in the middle of a semester or other teaching period is that their sick time covers the remainder of their salary, and the spouse gets paid the balance. But the university didn't pay Jennifer, because she wasn't legally married to Elizabeth. So she didn't get any income from the salary.

PATRICIA: And Jennifer didn't get Elizabeth's pension, which was hard. Jennifer worked only part-time as a freelance writer and editor.

LINDA: The pension was just lost, and Jennifer was really struggling financially. She couldn't even sue the drunk driver for wrongful death. Under the marriage amendment, Jennifer had no legal standing to do so, even though she had lived with Elizabeth for twenty years.

PATRICIA: So the shock of her partner's death was compounded by being set down and told, over and over again, "You have no protections. You might have thought you had. But you don't."

LINDA: Patricia and I just couldn't imagine ourselves in the same position as Jennifer, if something were to happen to either one of us. It would be awful to be in that helpless place. And my biological family wouldn't be supportive of Patricia, if something were to happen to me. I worried that they would challenge our will under the marriage amendment.

So in July 2005, we decided to move to Canada. A friend of mine at the university was originally from Winnipeg, and had moved back to Canada the year before. The firm where I'm at now is where she worked. They had an opening for a manager. So she called me about it. I applied and got the job in March 2006.

PATRICIA: Bear in mind here that we're talking about Winnipeg. [They laugh. Winnipeg is about sixty-five miles north of the Canada–U.S. border, just above where the states of Minnesota and North Dakota meet.]

LINDA: Not Vancouver, which is much more temperate.

PATRICIA: Winnipeg is really frigid. People told me that it was going to be cold in the winter. But it was actually worse than what they said it would be: −50 degrees.

LINDA: But you know what?

PATRICIA: *It was still better than living in Michigan.*

LINDA: Because it was just the elements in Winnipeg that we had to deal with. You play with them and get cold, and then you do what you need to to warm up. But we could be legally married in Canada, and my company's extended health benefits covered Patricia. There was no condescension or hostility at getting service in the medical or legal communities or anywhere else. Canadians just took for granted that we were a married couple.

This striking story introduces the serious challenges faced by same-sex couples in American states that prohibited *any* legal or political recognition of their relationships. Thus, despite a twenty-year commitment with Elizabeth,[1] Jennifer had no binding right to receive official notice of her partner's death, nor to direct the disposition of Elizabeth's remains or estate, nor to receive employer-sponsored death benefits from her salary or pension, nor to sue the person responsible for Elizabeth's death. Confronted with their friends' tragic experience, Linda, age fifty-two,[2] and Patricia, forty-nine, came to grips with the difficult choice of whether to remain in a state and country that did not support their relationship. In addition, both couples had to rely on the good will of third parties (such as Elizabeth's brother in Jennifer's case, and health care personnel with regard to Linda and Patricia) to achieve kinship goals that married pairs take for granted as legal rights. These motifs and other themes infuse the oral histories that are the empirical foundation of this book, which documents how doors painfully slammed shut on same-sex couples and their families throughout much of the United States in the first decade and a half of the twenty-first century. This volume is the bookend to my 2006 work, *America's Struggle for Same-Sex Marriage*, which chronicled how doors in other parts of the country opened wide to welcome lesbian and gay pairs during the same era.

But before offering further narrative or commentary, some legal and political background is appropriate.

DECLARATIONS OF WAR

Congress

During the first term of the presidency of William Jefferson Clinton, Congress twice declared war, but not on a nation or other foreign entity. Rather, the hostilities were directed at just under 4 percent of the American population (Gates and Newport 2012; Lee 2014). In 1993, Congress passed, and President Clinton signed, the "Don't Ask, Don't Tell" (DADT) policy, which prohibited people who "demonstrate[d] a propensity or intent to engage in homosexual acts" from serving in the Armed Forces of the United States, because their presence "would [have] create[d] an unacceptable risk to the high standards of morale, good order and discipline, and unit cohesion that are the essence of

---

[1] All first names initially unaccompanied by surnames in this volume are pseudonyms. Since most of the states where the book's narratives take place had no legal protections against sexual-orientation discrimination in employment, housing, and public accommodations at the time this study was published (Eckholm 2015b; Wolfson 2015; cf. Scheiber 2015), I protect the identities of the people whose tales appear here. Indeed, when necessary to conceal information that could be used to identify individuals, I have changed salient facts of stories to shield the privacy of my sources.

[2] Unless otherwise indicated, I report the ages of interviewees at the time I met them.

military capability." During the seventeen years in which DADT was the law of the land, the Pentagon processed involuntary discharges for more than 14,000 service members because they were perceived to be lesbian or gay ("261 DADT Discharges in 2010" 2011).[3]

The other congressional war declaration against homosexual citizens was more consequential than DADT, because this second pronouncement was not limited to people who volunteered to serve in the military. Rather, two main provisions of the federal Defense of Marriage Act (DOMA) of 1996 potentially affected all gay Americans. First, DOMA defined civil marriage for the purposes of federal law as only a union between one man and one woman. Second, the statute authorized states to refuse to recognize civil marriages granted to same-sex couples under the law of other jurisdictions (cf. Liptak 2004).

But the worst was yet to come for queer folk. Because under the American federalist system of dividing powers between the national government and the states, the latter were granted primary authority to regulate domestic relations. Thus, states traditionally have defined the most basic terms and conditions of civil marriage for their citizens, including eligibility to enter and depart the institution. Accordingly, the most consequential proclamations of aggression against lesbian and gay pairs and their children would appear at the state level.

Super-DOMAs

Between 2000 and 2012, voters in twenty American states containing 43 percent of the nation's population ratified amendments to state constitutions banning recognition of all forms of relationship rights (i.e., marriage, civil unions, domestic partnerships, reciprocal benefits, etc.) for same-sex couples: Alabama, Arkansas, Florida, Georgia, Idaho, Kansas, Kentucky, Louisiana, Michigan, Nebraska, North Carolina, North Dakota, Ohio, Oklahoma, South Carolina, South Dakota, Texas, Utah, Virginia, and Wisconsin.

These state measures were dubbed "Super-DOMAs." The nickname derived from the federal legislation that preceded them. In 2006, for example, 57 percent of Virginia voters authorized this amendment to their state constitution:

Only a union between one man and one woman may be a marriage valid in or recognized by this Commonwealth and its political subdivisions. This Commonwealth and its political subdivisions shall not create or recognize a legal status for relationships of unmarried individuals that intends to approximate the design, qualities, significance, or effects of marriage. Nor shall this Commonwealth or its political subdivisions create or recognize another union, partnership, or other legal status to which is assigned the rights, benefits, obligations, qualities, or effects of marriage.

---

[3] As many as 100,000 gay and lesbian service members were discharged between World War II and the repeal of DADT (Philipps 2015). See D'Amico (2000) and Engel (2015) for historical overviews of the adoption and repeal of DADT.

More comprehensive language designed to limit the relationship options of lesbian and gays pairs would be difficult to imagine.[4]

The Virginia provision was far more ambitious than the constitutions of ten other states (Alaska, Arizona, California, Colorado, Mississippi, Missouri, Montana, Nevada, Oregon, and Tennessee) that were amended in the same time period to include "Mini-DOMAs" (i.e., just limiting marriage to one man and one woman and doing nothing more). For instance, California's notorious Proposition 8 of 2008 (which federal courts invalidated in 2013) said, "Only marriage between a man and a woman is valid or recognized in California." This language left intact the comprehensive statutory system of domestic partnerships that granted virtually all of the rights and responsibilities of civil marriage to same-sex couples in the Golden State. Likewise, despite the passage of Measure 36 ("It is the policy of Oregon, and its political subdivisions, that only a marriage between one man and one woman shall be valid or legally recognized as a marriage") in 2004, the Oregon legislature three years later enacted full civil unions for gay and lesbian couples.

Thus, the objectives of Super-DOMAs were substantially greater than those of Mini-DOMAs such as Proposition 8 and Measure 36. Whereas the latter spoke just to marriage and were silent about relationship arrangements such as civil unions, domestic partnerships, and reciprocal benefits, the former aspired to ensure that same-sex pairs could be nothing other than complete legal strangers to one another. In short, the goal of Super-DOMAs was to restrict the word *and all of its attributes* to heterosexual pairs.[5] In contrast, Mini-DOMAs preserved the word "marriage" exclusively for opposite-sex couples, but not necessarily the attributes of civil marriage. Thus, lesbian and gay couples who were in California domestic partnerships or in Oregon civil unions could inherit from each other under state intestacy law, could adopt or sue for custody of or visitation with minor children of the couple, and enjoyed a plethora of other rights comparable to those of civil marriage, regardless of the constitutional Mini-DOMAs. Yet same-sex pairs in Super-DOMA jurisdictions such as Virginia could not benefit from any such attributes of marriage. As a result, the variation in rights between gay-marriage-mecca Massachusetts and Measure-36 Oregon was minuscule compared with the difference between Super-DOMA states such as Virginia and many Mini-DOMA jurisdictions (cf. Conley 2007).

How Super-DOMAs Were Added to State Constitutions

American states typically amend their constitutions in one of two ways: through initiatives or referenda. The former involve the circulation among voters of

---

[4] The full texts of all state constitutional Super-DOMAs discussed in this volume appear in Appendix A.

[5] In addition to legal and social benefits, marriage also brings better health ("Married People Are Healthier, Study Finds" 2004).

petitions containing the proposed constitutional language, and if a legally speci-fied threshold amount of signatures is obtained within a designated time period, the measure goes to a statewide ballot. In contrast, referenda originate in state legislatures and appear on the ballot as a result of the action of elected offi-cials. Thus, initiatives bypass legislatures and are usually the product of interest groups having the organizational capacity to gather tens of thousands or more (depending on the size of the state) voter signatures, whereas referenda are the brainchild of political elites. Although every state embraces the option of leg-islative referenda, not all permit citizen initiatives.[6] Accordingly, referenda are more common nationwide. But initiatives as the mechanism of constitutional change can be important when grassroots movements are unable or unwilling to persuade political leaders to embrace their policy agendas.

Among the six states studied here, the legislatures in Georgia, North Car-olina, Texas, and Wisconsin sponsored their Super-DOMAs. In Michigan, the state's Christian Citizens Alliance formed a committee called Citizens for the Protection of Marriage that crafted and supported the passage of the Wolverine State's initiative (known as Proposal 2). Likewise, Cincinnati-based Citizens for Community Values promoted Ohio's Issue 1. Both Michigan's Democratic gov-ernor Jennifer Granholm and Ohio's Republican governor Bob Taft (as well as both of the Buckeye State's Republican U.S. senators, Mike DeWine and George Voinovich, and Republican attorney general Jim Petro) publicly opposed their states' ballot measures against same-sex marriage (Witkowski 2004; Salvato 2004; "Marriage and Politics" 2004), thus demonstrating how initiatives can be used to flaunt the policy preferences of state political elites (cf. Rivkin and Casey 2006).[7]

The popular majorities garnered by the Super-DOMAs were 59 percent in Michigan and Wisconsin, 60 in North Carolina, 62 in Ohio, and 76 in Georgia and Texas.

A casual political observer might have expected the process by which the legislatures in Georgia, North Carolina, Texas, and Wisconsin decided to place Super-DOMA referenda on the ballot to have been more deliberative than what occurred in Michigan and Ohio with their citizen initiatives. After all, a basic tenet of Political Science 101 is that examination, discussion, and care-ful thought characterize the legislative action through which important public policies are adopted. Bills introduced with the prospect of becoming new laws are allocated to committees with specialized subject-matter jurisdiction. In turn, committees hold public hearings at which all potentially interested parties have

---

[6] "In 15 states, citizens can place a potential constitutional amendment on the ballot without leg-islative participation or approval.... In all other states except Delaware, constitutional amend-ments must be placed on the ballot by the legislature" (Lupia et al. 2010, 1225).

[7] Even President George W. Bush publicly disagreed with GOP opposition to civil unions for same-sex couples (Bumiller 2004; cf. Burger 2014), as did Vice President Dick Cheney (Toner 2004) and other Republicans in the U.S. Senate (Hulse 2004).

an opportunity to be heard on the prospective policy, and then committee members reasonably consider the evidence before them before voting bills out for consideration by the full legislative chamber. Public debate meant to persuade colleagues, as well as constituents, toward particular points of view on bills is expected throughout the entire time-consuming and contemplative legislative process. Such might have been a bystander's expectation of what happened in Atlanta (the capital of Georgia), Raleigh (NC), Austin (TX), and Madison (WI).

But what actually took place in Raleigh would certainly disappoint political science students, as reported by Maxine Eichner, a professor at the University of North Carolina School of Law in Chapel Hill and the lead author of a forty-page 2011 memorandum titled "Potential Legal Impact of the Proposed Same-Sex Marriage Amendment to the North Carolina Constitution."

EICHNER: On a Friday afternoon in September, the leadership of the relevant state senate committee took a bill that I believe was on term limits for legislators and stripped out its content. And in its place, they put the language of the Super-DOMA bill. Then they noticed it for a hearing on Monday. It looked to folks who are familiar with how things work in Raleigh that perhaps the committee was trying to prevent the public from learning about it in advance. So unless you pulled up the content of the bill, you wouldn't have understood that this was the marriage amendment being considered.

At the same time, the House committee chair announced there would be no public testimony or other hearing taken in that chamber. At which point, Democrats who opposed the bill said this was absolutely wrong. But apparently, failing to hold hearings wasn't a violation of House rules, although it certainly was an infraction of the spirit of democracy. So some of the legislators opposed to the bill said that this procedure was horrific, that a constitutional amendment was an incredibly important event, that the public needed to participate, and that experts like myself were there ready to testify.

The Republican leaders' response was that the public was going to get a chance to testify at the polls. So the House passed the referendum very expeditiously.

The Senate rules provided that, if one of its committees took up the same language of a bill passed in a House committee, then the Senate didn't have to hold a hearing of its own. So there was no public hearing on the Senate side either.

That was the process by which the bill passed the North Carolina General Assembly.

Q: So all of the legislative action essentially happened overnight then?

EICHNER: That's right. It happened very quickly. My coauthors and I sent our legal memorandum off to legislators in June, and months went by without a word. Then all of a sudden, boom, this thing moved right through the General Assembly without any public hearing.

Florence, a forty-eight-year-old Raleigh jeweler, characterized the action of North Carolina lawmakers this way:

When the legislature was considering Amendment 1, there should have been equal time for each chamber to discuss it and have questions and answers. The issue should have been placed on the legislative calendar just like any other bill, as is the case with fracking right now [2012].

But Amendment 1 was shoved under the rug, as though the lawmakers didn't want to get caught addressing it. They behaved in such a shady, behind-the-scenes way, as if the topic itself were dirty. So the legislative process sent folks a message like "We just don't think this topic should be debated in public, because it's so unsavory."

Yet even legislatures that appeared to follow the PoliSci 101 procedural outline did not really engage in careful deliberation when considering Super-DOMAs. A psychology professor at a distinguished Georgia university shared this experience of what happened in the Peach State in 2004:

I'm a board member of the Georgia Psychological Association. Our organization attempted to work with the legislature when it considered the marriage amendment. We lobbied at the State Capitol, hoping to give legislators accurate information about statistics concerning same-sex couples' relationships and also about what the amendment's impact on children might be.

Professionally, our involvement was a big loss. We accumulated and presented published, bonafide research of empirical information, which was completely overwhelmed by people's religious fervor. Legislators were blinded by their own viewpoint, but had no factually based foundation for it.

As a scientist and a scholar, I think that's very disappointing. And as professionals, we in the Association knew the amendment was going to be a tremendous loss for clients and their families, who were going to feel this whether they were gay or lesbian themselves, or whether they had children or other family members who were gay or lesbian.

The legislature seemed to believe there'd only be a small group of people affected by the amendment. And that wasn't true.

In addition, a potentially very influential voice in public policy making – the business community – was largely absent in the nation's Super-DOMA debates (cf. McKinnon 2015). In July 2012, for instance, a twenty-seven-year-old New York–based private-equity banker born in North Carolina and a graduate of the university in Chapel Hill described what happened earlier that year in his home state during the nation's last Super-DOMA campaign:

I was really disappointed in the reaction to the marriage amendment from medium- to large-sized businesses in North Carolina, in that there was essentially none. Compare that to what we're seeing in Minnesota now. General Mills and other large companies there are publicly coming out against Minnesota's proposed amendment [which was defeated in the November 2012 general election].

Jim Rogers, the Duke Power CEO, spoke out in very strong words against Amendment 1. But if I think about the other companies that, frankly, I'm really very close with ... like Bank of America, whose CEO I saw three weeks before the vote. He was pushed to act, but chose not to do anything.

For the amount of LGBT [lesbian, gay, bisexual, and transgendered] advocacy that those businesses do in New York, around recruiting – they're incredibly active with

LGBT recruiting organizations – and then for them not to take a stand in their home state, I thought was very disappointing.

I believe it showed a lack of values. I was just coming out of business school at the time, where I had a leadership and ethics class. So I felt what happened down in North Carolina was a big failure. I don't think public opposition would have cost the companies much, and their participation might have had a big political impact.[8]

THE BOOK'S RESEARCH METHODS

The first state to add a Super-DOMA to its constitution was Nebraska in 2000. One virtue of examining its implementation and effects is the long time in which they had to develop. However, the Cornhusker State is among the fifteen least populous in the nation, and identifying sufficient interview subjects there would have been especially daunting, as explained later.

The next states to adopt constitutional Super-DOMAs, in 2004, were Arkansas, Georgia, Kentucky, Louisiana, Michigan, North Dakota, Ohio, Oklahoma, and Utah. I chose the three most populous among these – Georgia, Michigan, and Ohio – to begin a national study. I also included Texas, which joined the Super-DOMA fold in 2005, Wisconsin (2006), and North Carolina (2012).

There is no way to document the grassroots effects of constitutionally based state policies without direct observation on the ground. Accordingly, to track the implementation and impact of Super-DOMAs (cf. Eskridge 1994; Fenno 1986), I set out in 2009 to conduct in-depth interviews (typically lasting between forty-five minutes and an hour) of same-sex couples and members of other relevant groups (such as the sponsors of the constitutional amendments, attorneys and law professors with expertise on Super-DOMAs, and officials with state LGBT organizations) in the most populous adopting jurisdictions, while choosing at the same time a sample of states that was geographically diverse. Thus, five of the six states studied here (with Wisconsin the exception[9]) are among the ten most populous in the country, and three states each are in the North and South.

I made a total of seven trips to the largest metropolitan areas of each state. I arrived at a destination on a Friday and departed on the second Monday thereafter. That way, I had two full weekends to get together with people who

---

[8] See also Davey (2015).

[9] A significant virtue of including Wisconsin in the study is that it was the sole Super-DOMA state to pass (in 2009) a limited domestic-partner registry for same-sex couples, despite the adoption of its constitutional amendment three years earlier.

   To boot, another Badger State oddity is that Wisconsin has a criminal marriage-evasion statute, with a potential fine of up to $10,000 and/or nine months in prison for "any person residing and intending to continue to reside in this state who goes outside the state and there contracts a marriage prohibited or declared void under the laws of this state." In other words, lesbian and gay couples living, say, in Milwaukee or Madison (the state's largest cities) who went to Massachusetts, Canada, or elsewhere to get legally married would have been guilty of crimes upon return to their Wisconsin homes.

worked on weekdays. Moreover, interviewees typically had the option of meeting me at my hotel suite or of having me drive to their homes or businesses. The maximum number of interviews I conducted in a single day was six.

In January 2009, I drove to Detroit and its suburbs, as well as Ann Arbor and Lansing/East Lansing, in Michigan.[10] The next January, I went to Atlanta and the surrounding area in Georgia. In June and July 2010, I made separate journeys to Columbus and Cleveland and their respective environs because Ohio was of particular interest, as I explain at the end of this chapter. Then, in January 2011, I flew to the Dallas-Fort Worth metroplex. Six months later, I was in Milwaukee, Madison, and Appleton in Wisconsin. Finally, in July 2012, I drove to Charlotte, the Research Triangle (Chapel Hill, Durham, and Raleigh), Greensboro, and Winston-Salem in North Carolina.[11]

Hence, all of the book's 203 interviews were completed before there was any significant federal-court intervention in the same-sex-marriage policy arena. In other words, before 2013, there was no good reason to believe that the country's Super-DOMAs would go away any time soon. Rather, the couples and other people I spoke with accepted as fate that their states' marriage amendments would be in place for years to come. Time and again, in fact, gay people volunteered to me that they did not expect to be able to get legally married in their home states during their lifetimes.

Nearly 90 percent of the interviews here – 175 – were with same-sex couples,[12] because recognizing and documenting the grassroots effects of

---

[10] I chose the Wolverine State for the first field trip because, less than a year earlier, the Michigan Supreme Court interpreted its Super-DOMA more broadly than any other state court of last resort, as discussed in Chapter 2.

Note to field researchers: *never* go to Michigan in January, unless you really like to ski cross-country. It snowed nearly continuously for the entire ten days I was in the Wolverine State. Plus, my car's external thermometer in the mornings registered as low as 10 degrees below zero, and I had to cross my fingers that the engine would turn over. One day, moreover, as I was creeping along to within a half-block from my destination in a suburb north of Detroit, my otherwise dextrous front-wheel-drive vehicle got stuck in a snowdrift, and the couple I was scheduled to interview had to rescue me. I will never forget the sight of what initially appeared to be a small blizzard heading in my direction, but which turned out to be the spray from their gigantic snowblower. Michiganders are truly hardy souls.

[11] I made the North Carolina trip then because I was able to interview people within just two months of the May 8, 2012, popular vote on its Super-DOMA, while memories of the plebiscite were still very fresh. In contrast, I spoke with interviewees in the other states more than five years after the passage of their constitutional amendments. Indeed, my original plan was to select Florida (whose Super-DOMA passed in 2008) as the sixth state for my sample. But when the North Carolina referendum was scheduled for May 2012, I jettisoned going to the Sunshine State (in January) in favor of the upcoming Tar Heel referendum.

Note to field researchers: *never* go to the American South in July. My vehicle's thermometer registered as high as 112 degrees – while the car was in motion, not still.

[12] In a total of twenty-five instances, one partner in a couple was unavailable to talk with me. Sometimes travel or illness was the reason for their absence. So although I actually spoke with just one person, I still count those interviews as with a couple.

Likewise, I met some people whose partners had died, as well as still others whose relationships had ended due to incompatibility. But because my conversations in all cases substantially

Super-DOMAs in the LGBT community are fundamental to the project.[13] The most likely population for a researcher to target in analyzing the impact of state constitutional provisions is the same group those words concern and touch.

Yet sampling same-sex pairs is a challenging task for any study because the gay and lesbian population is, in a sense, invisible. "Whether a researcher meets someone face to face, makes phone contact, or gives out anonymous confidential questionnaires, that researcher remains at the mercy of the participant to self-identify as lesbian or gay" (Riggle and Tadlock 1999, 6).

Nonetheless, I developed a satisfactory process for finding same-sex couples for the investigation. The *Gayellow Pages* (gayellowpages.com) is a geographically arranged directory of American organizations, businesses, and other resources for the LGBT community. Begun in 1973 and published continuously ever since, the *Gayellow Pages* is as comprehensive a reference as one can find for LGBT contact information in the United States. Accordingly, about a month before each of my seven trips, I sent an introductory email message to every relevant source – listed under *Gayellow Pages* categories such as "Organizations/Resources: Family and Supporters," "Organizations/Resources: Political/Legislative," "Organizations/Resources: Social, Recreational, Support," and "Religious Organizations, Publications, Resources" – with an email address in the metropolitan area of interest. Then, I interviewed every couple who responded to the electronic solicitation and volunteered to meet with me. Also, as I discovered when conducting eighty-five interviews in five states for my 2006 book, *America's Struggle for Same-Sex Marriage*, word-of-mouth introductions supplemented the search for interview subjects once on location.

Strictly speaking, the distribution of couples here is not a random one, as that term is commonly understood in social-scientific research. In truth, no large interview sample can be random in the precise sense of the word, because a consequential amount of self-selection necessarily occurs in the process of people agreeing to be interviewed. Those individuals who want to tell their stories, and who think they have something of importance to say, will likely dominate the distribution. Others who do not believe that their experiences are especially noteworthy are more likely to opt out of the discussion. Thus, my findings cannot necessarily be generalized to all lesbian and gay pairs in the twenty Super-DOMA states. However, the sample here is certainly large enough to provide ample justification to believe that what appears in these pages does represent what transpired with far, far more than just the 325 coupled people with whom I spoke across six states.[14]

---

involved what had occurred when the interviewees were together as a couple, I also consider those discussions as with pairs.

[13] The interview protocol for lesbian and gay pairs appears in Appendix B.

[14] As the commentary by Linda and Patricia introducing this chapter indicates, a few of the people I interviewed had relocated from the state of interest by the time of our conversation. Most of those discussions (seven in all) come up in Chapter 5.

A DESCRIPTION OF THE COUPLES SAMPLE

I conducted twenty-four interviews of same-sex couples in Georgia during my trip there and then later spoke by telephone with another pair who formerly lived there. The same sequence of events was true with twenty-five and then three couples involving Michigan; thirty-seven/one for North Carolina; twenty-eight/one for Texas; and twenty-five/one for Wisconsin. All twenty-nine interviews with Ohio couples occurred in the Buckeye State itself.

Ninety-four (or 53.7 percent) of the 175 couple interviews were with lesbian pairs. In contrast, Gates and Cooke (2011b) determined that 51 percent of all American same-sex couples were female. So my sample has a slightly larger distribution of lesbians over gay men.

The mean age of the 325 coupled individuals in my sample was 46.7 years, whereas the median was 47.[15] The youngest person was twenty-four and the oldest, seventy-nine.

Most of my interviewees were in relationships of considerable duration. The mean for the number of years couples had been together at the time of interview was 13.0, while the median was ten. The shortest relationship was just one year, and the longest, forty-eight.

Fifty-five (31.4 percent) of the 175 couples were raising minor children. Among those with kids, thirty-eight (69.1 percent) were lesbian pairs. So more than twice as many female couples had children than male pairs.[16] Thirty-three couples had one child; fifteen had two; five had three; and two couples had four. Among lesbian pairs, twenty-one had a single child; ten had two; five had three; and two had four children, whereas for male couples, twelve had one kid, and five had two. So not only were substantially more female pairs raising children, but they also had larger families than the men.[17]

---

[15] In statistics, the mean refers to the "average" value of a variable in a population. So the ages of all 325 people in my couples sample were added together, and then that total number of years was divided by 325 to come up with the figure of 46.7 years of age. Mean values as measures of the central tendency of variables, however, can be skewed by outliers. So if a researcher were looking at a sample of, say, just twenty-five people and wanted to know what their average income was, the mean would not be a good measure if twenty-four were middle-class individuals, and the twenty-fifth was a billionaire. Her vastly larger income would artificially increase the value of the mean. In that circumstance, the median – referring to the number that is in the exact middle when all of the values of a variable are incrementally arrayed from the smallest to the largest – might be a better measure of central tendency, because outliers do not affect median values.

   As sample size becomes larger, mean and median values tend to converge. That occurrence in this sample suggests that it is big enough not to worry about which approach for measuring central tendency is best.

[16] Gates (2013) documented that 48 percent of LGBT women nationwide were raising minor children, compared to 20 percent of LGBT men. In my sample, 41.2 percent of the women had minor children, whereas 23.0 percent of the men did.

[17] Gates (2013) found that 50 percent of children under eighteen years old living with same-sex couples were nonwhite. Although I did not meet all of the children being raised among the fifty-five pairs with children in my sample, my observations of those I did see are in line with the Gates finding. In particular, a significant proportion of the white lesbian and gay couples I interviewed were raising adopted children of color. See also Tavernise (2011).

The people in my sample had substantial roots in their communities, as measured by the length of time they had lived in their states, with fully one-third (107) having been born and raised there.[18] The mean number of years that individuals had resided in home states at the time of interview was 25.4, with the mode at 23. The shortest stay was six months, whereas the longest was seventy-nine years. Excluding the native-born folks from the analysis reduces those figures to a mean of 16.1 years of residence in their adopted home states and a median of 15. The longest stay of a nonnative was fifty-four years. Thus, even among those people who had not been raised in the states where I met them, most had resided there for quite a while.

I asked all couples whether they had had a ceremony celebrating their relationship. At the time of interview, fifty-nine pairs (33.7 percent) said they had been married in a jurisdiction (Canada, Massachusetts, etc.) where it was legal to do so. Another forty-one couples (23.4 percent) had had some public ceremony in their home states, including church weddings and other commitment ceremonies, but did not later travel elsewhere to tie the knot legally. Even among the pairs who were legally married, eighteen (30.5 percent) of them had had a

---

One lesbian couple – Dorothy, fifty-seven, and Lisa, fifty-four – deserves special mention. During the late 1980s and early '90s, large American cities experienced a crisis with what became known as "boarder babies" (Brennan 1989; Kusserow 1990). These were children born to women addicted to crack cocaine and who were abandoned by their mothers or otherwise removed from their custody because of parental unfitness. There were so many such infants during the crack-cocaine epidemic of the era that foster-care systems ran out of foster homes in which to place the babies. As a result, the children were boarded at public hospitals until they were old enough to be moved to group homes.

At forty and thirty-seven, Dorothy and Lisa adopted three such boarder babies over a period of fourteen months. The infants had been prenatally exposed to alcohol and cocaine. The oldest child has Down syndrome and developed cerebral palsy after three spinal-fusion surgeries. The middle child was born premature, weighing only one pound, ten ounces. She also acquired cerebral palsy and is legally blind. When the women adopted her at twenty-six months, the little girl could not walk, crawl, sit up, or turn over by herself. The youngest child was also born prematurly and has significant learning disabilities, requiring his attendance as a teenager at boarding schools for students with special needs.

I met Dorothy and Lisa's two oldest children, who were eighteen and nineteen in 2010, and can attest they were thriving in spite of their many physical and other disabilities. The middle child's progress was especially noteworthy. After numerous operations, she walks entirely unaided and is otherwise independent. Once I discovered we share a passion for classical music, she and I carried on a lengthy conversation about Beethoven and Mozart.

I write this book at the age of sixty-five and have known many noteworthy individuals during a long life. If I were given the opportunity to nominate just two people for sainthood, the choice would be easy: Dorothy and Lisa.

[18] I observed an interesting regional difference regarding native-born interviewees. The proportion of the Ohio coupled individuals I met who were born and raised in the Buckeye State was 46.3 percent. In Wisconsin, the figure was 40.4 percent and in Michigan, 35.8 percent. Thus, among the three Midwestern states in my study, more than a third of interviewees were natives.

In contrast, 29.0 percent of my North Carolina interviewees grew up in the Tar Heel State, whereas the figures for Texas and Georgia were 25.5 percent and 21.3 percent, respectively. In other words, southern states appeared to have greater influxes of adult gay people than their northern counterparts.

prior public ceremony in their home states. So by July 2012, a total of fifty-nine couples (33.7) had publicly celebrated their relationships at home among friends and family.

More importantly, virtually everyone I spoke with expressed interest in obtaining some or all of the legal benefits that would flow from government recognition of their relationships, such as Social Security survivor benefits or the right to inherit property tax free or to be the legal next of kin for a hospitalized partner. In effect, no one said to me, "Oh, no. We're not concerned about *any* of the rights and benefits of marriage or civil unions or domestic partnerships." Even the handful of ardent feminists who inveighed against the patriarchal history of the institution of marriage – when pressed about whether they wanted the option to receive their partners' Social Security benefits or public pension, or not to pay state and federal estate taxes on property inherited from deceased partners – typically admitted they were not averse to the economic benefits coming from government recognition of their relationships (cf. Hirsch 2005). Dollars and cents usually prevailed over principled opposition, especially as the age of interviewees increased and the sense of their own mortality grew.

Thus, the reason more couples in my sample had not been legally married somewhere else is that they thought it was futile to do so. Over and over, interviewees said to me something like the following: "What's the point of going off to Massachusetts or Canada when the marriage certificates from those places would be meaningless once we got back home? Why go through the expense and bother of such travel, and only be more frustrated on our return?"

In any event, despite the statistics just reported, I must acknowledge that my couples sample is not fully representative of the population of American same-sex pairs. Consider, for example, ethnicity and race. Just fourteen (4.3 percent) of the coupled individuals in my distribution were people of color, whereas another eight (2.5 percent) were self-identified Latinos/as. Of course, the proportion of those two groups in the American population is much larger. The disparity arose from my sampling technique.

Yet, I did seek minority respondents for interviews. Whenever I found a *Gayellow Pages* listing of an organization catering to black or Hispanic LGBT folks in the geographic areas I traveled to, I made special efforts to contact them. In Georgia, for instance, there was a listing for "In the Life Atlanta," a group for people of color. On November 30, 2009, I emailed the three addresses for the organization's officers provided on their website, explaining the nature of my research and that I would be in Atlanta for interviews in mid-January, closing with this request: "I'm especially interested in meeting with lesbian and gay couples of color. Can you introduce me to such pairs?" Only the group's president responded to my message, saying "I would be glad to assist you, just give me a call two weeks before you are in town." On December 31, 2009, I contacted him again as requested. Five days later, he indicated he was still interested. But (long story short), I was never able to obtain an interview with him or anyone he could introduce me to. Similarly, frustrating experiences occurred in other states as well. In short, I learned that identifying minority members of a minority population that is itself potentially invisible to investigators at a distance is an exceptionally difficult research challenge. So the fourteen people of color and eight Latinos/as who ended up in my sample appeared entirely by chance, despite my best efforts to find more minority respondents.[19]

There is a second important way in which my couples sample was not representative of the population of American same-sex pairs. Among the coupled individuals I interviewed, forty-six (or 14.2 percent) were full-time members of college and university faculties, nineteen (5.8 percent) were attorneys, ten (3.1 percent) were clergy, and eight (2.5 percent) were physicians. Yet, each of these professions constitutes less than 1 percent of the adult American population. Another thirty-five individuals (10.8 percent) were otherwise involved in the health care field, such as nurses, physician assistants, and social workers. In other words, the couples here represented a better educated and more prosperous distribution than that of the full population of interest. Without doubt, the people who agreed to speak with me were among the best suited to advocate for, and protect, their own interests.

As a result, these individuals were optimally situated to test for Super-DOMA effects. If such constitutional provisions could touch this set of well educated and politically sophisticated gay people, then the amendments certainly must have affected individuals who were less well prepared to look out for themselves.

CONTEMPLATING SUPER-DOMA EFFECTS

The impact of Super-DOMAs on LGBT communities and beyond was likely to be quite extensive. American history teaches, for instance, that state consensual-sodomy statutes had broad civil effects (Pinello 2003, 54). Such criminal sanctions touched the home, with courts citing the laws as good reason to refuse lesbian and gay parents custody of, and visitation with, their children. The statutes also encroached on the workplace, with the federal ban on gay and lesbian service members being the most conspicuous example. At the state level, the denial of employment to otherwise qualified lesbian and gay employees was upheld in part because of sodomy laws. Accordingly, the wide-ranging prohibitions against same-sex relationship rights contained in Super-DOMAs may well have had profound consequences on the daily lives of coupled LGBT Americans.

Although a substantial social-scientific literature has investigated the effects of civil marriage on lesbian and gay couples (e.g., Hull 2006; Pinello 2006; Taylor et al. 2009), no large systematic inquiry has yet occurred into the

---

[19] Three couples accounted for six people of color, whereas the other eight African Americans were in interracial pairs. All eight Hispanic individuals were partnered with someone of a different ethnicity or race.

practical consequences of affirmative state denials of all relationship recognition to same-sex pairs and their families. Likewise, the legal literature on Super-DOMAs lacks empirical studies, because the existing books and law review articles on the topic are either theoretical, track the relevant case law, or only speculate about the grassroots effects of the constitutional amendments (e.g., Koppelman 2006; Strasser 2007; Neely 2008).

The primary goal of this study, then, is a comprehensive documentation of Super-DOMA impact. And since the federal courts have invalidated all federal and state proscriptions against same-sex marriage, as elaborated in Chapter 6, the book thus is a *history* of the implementation and effects of these state constitutional amendments.

I am mindful of the need to distinguish between state-law effects that arose merely from the denial of civil marriage to same-sex couples, which Mini-DOMAs such as California's Proposition 8 and Oregon's Measure 36 might have fostered, and those that sprang from a denial of *all* relationship recognition between such pairs pursuant to Super-DOMAs.[20] Thus, the relevant inquiry for research in these Super-DOMA states was to ask whether an observed impact there would also have occurred in either California or Oregon with their systems of civil unions and domestic partnerships. If so, then the perceived effect did not arise from a Super-DOMA as such.[21]

Furthermore, I kept the prospect of a null set of effects in mind. As a lesbian attorney in Atlanta told me,

The Georgia legislature may regularly burn gay people in effigy. But in terms of dealing with actual Georgians on a daily basis, things here have been fine. In our kids' schools,

---

[20] As discussed in Chapter 6, the federal government treated all gay and lesbian couples (whether legally married in their home states, or having civil unions or domestic partnerships there, or nothing at all) in the same way – by denying them all federal marriage benefits – until 2013, when the U.S. Supreme Court struck down the Defense of Marriage Act in *United States* v. *Windsor*.

[21] In truth, I found very few instances where a same-sex couple's state-law dilemma would have occurred in *both* Super-DOMA and Mini-DOMA jurisdictions. The clearest example involved a Michigan lesbian couple in which one of the partners was heir to a family trust fund, along with two siblings of the lesbian woman. The trust language, specified by a grandmother who was aware of her granddaughter's sexual orientation, required that fund payments could go only to the three grandchildren and their *legally married* spouses as determined *by Michigan law*. Hence, among the six parties who survived the grandmother's death – the female couple and the lesbian heir's two siblings and their married opposite-sex spouses – only the same-sex partner of the heir was unable to receive trust-fund payments, even though none of the other five survivors objected to her getting the money.

    Moreover, although the lesbian couple could have been legally married in Massachusetts (because they owned a vacation home on Nantucket Island), the lesbian heir's partner still would not receive payment because the trust language stipulated that Michigan law controlled who qualified as a legally married spouse.

    Thus, *either* a Super-DOMA *or* a Mini-DOMA in Michigan would have accomplished the same outcome for this couple. However, in virtually every other story in these pages, full civil unions or domestic partnerships would have supplied remedies for the legal disabilities at issue.

in the hospitals we go to, people don't bat an eye at us. The Georgians who deal with lesbians and gays don't reflect the values of the state's political culture.

THE MOTIVATIONS OF AMENDMENT SPONSORS AND OF VOTERS

Advocating for the adoption of such broad, constitutionally based measures, Super-DOMA proponents argued that their comprehensive approaches were essential to the protection and defense of the institution of marriage. At the same time, they denied that any antigay animus motivated their actions or the amendments they advanced.

In May 2012, for example, at the end of the very last Super-DOMA campaign, Tami Fitzgerald, chairwoman of and spokesperson for Vote for Marriage NC, which promoted North Carolina's amendment, said, "We are not antigay; we are pro-marriage. And the point – the whole point – is simply that you don't rewrite the nature of God's design for marriage based on the demands of a group of adults" (Karimi 2012).

Likewise, Phil Burress, president of Cincinnati-based Citizens for Community Values, which initiated and promoted Ohio's Issue 1 of 2004, justified his group's actions this way during our interview:

Marriage is for a man and a woman. The nuclear family is about raising children. Protecting the institution of marriage is my first line of defense. So we didn't want people to say, "We're going to call it marriage" over here, and "We're going to call it pseudo-marriage" over there, with all the people in both parts getting the same benefits. In the end, that approach destroys the institution of marriage as well. My purpose in why I did what I did was to protect the institution of marriage. It wasn't to be anti-anything.

In the end, we felt that granting homosexuals quasi-minority-class status was wrong. We do believe that these are people made in God's image like us. We don't dislike them. It's about public policy. You'll not find any place where I've ever disparaged them, because I don't do that. Rather, we just disagree about public policy and the law.

What is more, numerous states, including populous ones such as Florida, Ohio, Texas, and Virginia, enacted statutory Super-DOMAs prior to their adoption of similar constitutional prohibitions. Indeed, Virginia had adopted both narrow and broad statutory marriage bans in addition to the constitutional amendment quoted earlier. That they sponsored constitutional Super-DOMAs even though laws were already on the books to that effect disclosed these advocates' belief that embedding the language in a state charter was more authoritative and effective than legislative action by itself.

I make a distinction between sponsors' motives and those of the voters who approved the ballot measures, especially because the average voter was likely to have substantially less information about the purpose and likely effects of Super-DOMAs than the people who crafted and promoted them (Wilcox et al. 2007; Lofton and Haider-Markel 2007). And that difference may have been particularly pronounced in states like Georgia, where the complete language of the proposed amendment never appeared on the ballot. As a Peach State political operative informed me,

The state legislature gets to tell Georgians what the question is on the ballot. They don't print the actual amendment there. So ours had two parts. One addressed the definition of marriage. The second was the Super-DOMA portion. Yet the question on the ballot was merely, "Shall marriage in the state be defined as a union between one man and one woman?" End of story.

Hence, the following language from Georgia's constitutional amendment, approved by 76 percent of voters in 2004, did not appear on the ballot itself:

Marriages between persons of the same sex are prohibited in this state. No union between persons of the same sex shall be recognized by this state as entitled to the benefits of marriage. This state shall not give effect to any public act, record or judicial proceeding of any other state or jurisdiction respecting a relationship between persons of the same sex that is treated as a marriage under the laws of such other state or jurisdiction. The courts of this state shall have no jurisdiction to grant a divorce or separate maintenance with respect to any such relationship or otherwise to consider or rule on any of the parties' respective rights arising as a result of or in connection with such relationship.

As Jeff Graham, executive director of Georgia Equality, the state's leading LGBT organization, observed in 2010,

Since all that appeared on the ballot was the definition of marriage as a union between one man and one woman, and because the referendum was not all that much discussed in the mainstream media here, I honestly believe that many people who took the time to vote for it didn't necessarily see it as an antigay position. Many saw it as words that just made sense to them, because that's exactly how they'd always thought of marriage.

So I don't think the vast majority of voters really appreciated what they were voting for. They had not thought through the positions and their consequences at all.

As the issue of same-sex marriage evolved into mainstream discourse in more recent years, the vote margins have been closer. But in 2004, the matter was so new that most people didn't know what was involved.

Even in the fieldwork that we did that year, the door-to-door canvassing, as well as the leafleting and the passing out of flyers and the holding of rallies – especially on the day of the election itself, in almost all of the precincts I oversaw that day – people came up to our volunteers and said, "There's no possible way that this can pass, right?" These were well-informed individuals who understood what they were voting on. And I'm talking about straight couples here, who couldn't believe that the amendment was going to win.

In contrast to Georgia, the entirety of Michigan's Super-DOMA amendment appeared on the Wolverine State ballot in 2004. But unlike the lengthy referenda in states like Georgia and Virginia, the Michigan initiative was succinct, a mere forty-two words: "To secure and preserve the benefits of marriage for our society and for future generations of children, the union of one man and one woman in marriage shall be the only agreement recognized as a marriage or similar union for any purpose." Indeed, the first seventeen words were just introductory. The heart of the measure took up just twenty-five words, with the last six encompassing all of the Super-DOMA portion.

As an informed Wolverine State observer told me,

> The really cynical political part of Proposal 2 was its wording, with that last phrase of "or similar union for any purpose." I know just exactly what the two authors of that passage were thinking. They were aware that public-opinion polling in Michigan showed that, if the initiative were viewed as wiping out partnership benefits for same-sex couples in the state, the measure wouldn't be popular enough to pass. But they really wanted comprehensive language like that in Ohio or Virginia. So they tried to have their cake and eat it too.
>
> First, they lied throughout the campaign leading up to the vote, saying that the amendment simply concerned the definition of marriage and would not at all affect the ability of the same-sex partners of public employees to get health-insurance benefits. Then, literally the day after the election, they filed a state-court lawsuit to get the larger objective they really sought. And the Michigan Supreme Court ultimately obliged, with a very expansive judicial interpretation of the amendment's last six words that eliminated all state-sponsored benefits for the partners of lesbian and gay employees.

Polling data taken during that campaign lend credence to this perspective. According to an October 2004 canvass by the Glengariff Group of Chicago that was commissioned by the *Detroit Free Press*, just 24 percent of Michiganders supported civil marriage rights for same-sex couples, whereas 42 percent – nearly twice as many people – backed legal recognition of civil unions (Bell 2009). Accordingly, average Michigan voters in 2004, just like their Georgian counterparts the same year, would not have substantial reason to believe on Election Day that they were voting on anything other than a simple, and familiar, definition of marriage.

Voters in Wisconsin two years later would have believed similarly, as explained by Katie Belanger, executive director of Fair Wisconsin, the Badger State's principal LGBT interest group:

> BELANGER: From the proponents' communications, the 2006 referendum was a very general campaign about protecting marriage. According to them, it wasn't supposed to be about hurting gay or lesbian people. It was about protecting the institution of marriage in our state. We did have a statute defining marriage as between a husband and a wife. But that wasn't enough. They needed to go a step further and put in our state constitution that it's a man and a woman.
>
> Wisconsin Family Action and State Senator Scott Fitzgerald, who was then the Senate Majority Leader, said that the amendment would not prohibit limited legal protections for same-sex couples. That it was really about marriage and things that were everything like marriage but by a different name, such as a Vermont-style civil union. But not a limited domestic-partner registry. Scott Fitzgerald literally said, "Could a legislator put together a package of fifty things and call it a domestic partnership? Absolutely."
>
> That is what was told to the voters during the 2006 campaign. That it was really about marriage and not about discriminating against gay or lesbian people. Obviously,

we here at Fair Wisconsin believe that any type of limitation on the rights of LGBT people is discrimination. But that's what was told to the general public.

Q: So as far as what the average voter in Wisconsin knew in 2006, Referendum 1 was just about marriage?

BELANGER: Yes, that's right. Besides, what the amendment campaign was able to do in 2006, I think, was scare enough people into believing that something was going to change. We all hear those talking points from the antiequality folks, about how the equality movement is trying to change the definition of marriage. And I think that for a while, that tactic really worked with people. And it was enough to scare the middle folks, who really didn't know what it meant – to frighten them away from doing the fair thing and voting against discrimination.

The nation's last Super-DOMA campaign, in North Carolina in 2012, had a similar emphasis, as recounted by Greensboro attorney Andrew Spainhour:

I served on the steering committee for the public campaign against Amendment 1. Day to day, I saw a lot of Tami Fitzgerald and her organization [Vote for Marriage NC]. They were very, very cautious as an entity not to come across as antigay.

Tami Fitzgerald's a professional, and is paid well to do so. The campaign here did take some pains not to be antigay in their public comments. I think their conduct was an interesting little marker that they didn't feel they could get away with that publicly in North Carolina.

A lesbian couple in Charlotte elaborated on Vote for Marriage NC's campaign approach.

MARIA: "We're not antigay. We're pro-marriage" was their whole strategy the entire time. It was such a clever tactical move for them. It's all everyone saw in their advertisements. "Vote *for* marriage." Well, who wouldn't vote in favor of marriage?
MARGARET: Yes, that was very smart, to be pro-marriage.
MARIA: *Well, we are, too.* We're pro-marriage.

As a gay man who is a native North Carolinian and graduate of the University of North Carolina at Chapel Hill told me, "Pulling back the politics on the 2012 popular vote, I think it wasn't that people hated my partner and me. Rather, I think it was that they just didn't understand the idea of same-sex marriage. And that ignorance didn't make them bad people."

Moreover, there was little organized opposition to the initiatives and referenda in most states. Had such countervailing forces been well coordinated and funded, they could have educated voters about the broad scope of the ballot measures before them. As Jeff Graham observed,

Many people felt that the fight in Georgia was over before it had begun. No national funders were willing to put money into our campaign against the referendum. Despite our best efforts, I don't believe we broke $100,000 in fundraising, for a statewide ballot measure in such a populous place.

Truthfully, we really focused on just a few very specific precincts within the state, in Athens [home of the University of Georgia], and some here in Atlanta. The vote was much closer within the districts that were targeted. In fact, in a couple, the vote went our way. So there was some good work done where we were able to get out door to door and speak with people.

But we didn't have nearly the capacity to make it statewide. There was no money for advertising. So the Christian Coalition of Georgia didn't have much work to do, other than just sitting back and letting the vote happen.

Furthermore, publicly opposing the ballot measures could have come at a very high personal price in those areas where countermobilization was most needed, as a North Carolina couple explained:

JAMES: Our local coalition in Raleigh against Amendment 1 was effective. Where opponents had the greatest impact, in fact, was where the largest number of people could be involved in staffing phone banks. So the amendment was defeated in all of the urban counties around the state.

But in the rural counties, gay people faced the problem of not having employment protection against sexual-orientation discrimination if they had lobbied in opposition to Amendment 1. There was no guarantee that such lesbians and gay men would not lose their jobs, whether they were at churches, or schools, or wherever.

JOHN: That's right. They simply couldn't take the risk of being visible.

Increasing visibility has always been a substantial personal and political obstacle for gay people to overcome, as Robert, a forty-seven-year-old Michigan interviewee explained.

Q: Do you see important differences between the history against interracial marriage in America and what's happening today [2009] with regard to same-sex couples?

A: When you're considering the race of people, there's a built-in solidarity that's generational. So if you're from an African American family, you have relatives who are people of color to turn to who understand what it's like to be black in a predominantly white society.

For gay people, by comparison, we're almost always born into straight families. And even if our relatives end up being supportive and welcoming of us, there's typically a long path they have to take to get there. And even then, they aren't automatically knowing and empathetic.

So the gay community has to be built from the ground up with each lesbian and gay man over time, instead of being transmitted familially. That's a really big difference for us as a minority group, and it creates organizational challenges that others don't necessarily have to contend with.

As an example of how same-sex couples who were free to be open about themselves might have affected local opinion, consider the experience of

Dorothy and Lisa (introduced earlier in Footnote 17), who live in a conservative Georgia suburb thirty miles outside of Atlanta. Dorothy is retired with a stable pension, and Lisa is an attorney at a progressive law firm.

DOROTHY: The people we deal with on a regular basis are fine, by and large. Like the folks in our neighborhood. There's a family across the street that's not particularly friendly to anybody. They're very devout Christians. But they love us. We are their favorite people in the neighborhood. They are very open with us.

We had folks in the neighborhood who stopped by to say, "Hey. We voted against Question 1 because of you guys." They absolutely did. They just volunteered that information.[22]

LISA: They were so proud of themselves.

When our disabled son was sick throughout several surgeries, our neighbors did a rotating supper thing.

DOROTHY: The neighborhood fed us for six months.

LISA: We had a big ramp for his wheelchair. When it came time for the ramp to come down, we had a ramp-busting party. And if you get men together with power tools, nothing is better. These men kept rushing home to get more equipment. That ramp was gone in less than three hours.

A final colossal force persuading citizens to vote in favor of the Super-DOMAs was organized religion. As Wald (2000, 17) observed,

Gays begin [referenda and initiative] campaigns with the disadvantage of popular antipathy and can only overcome it by turning out in huge numbers and inducing allies from other groups to do the same. To pass antigay initiatives or to repeal gay rights laws by referendum, the church-based opponents of gay rights can draw upon the natural organizing capacity of religious communities – their physical meeting places, telephone networks, regular gatherings, paid leadership, and moral credibility. By contrast, the gay community has to create political structures from scratch. There is simply no standing organizational equivalent within the gay community.[23]

Time and again, the people I spoke with in the six states brought up the power of churches in getting the marriage amendments approved at the polls. Take, for example, what Roman Catholic interviewees in Wisconsin told me about their church officials.

The bishop of our Madison diocese sent out either a DVD of a video, or a CD of an audio, that all priests were to play at mass on Sunday before the election. And the priests didn't have the choice not to play it. And they couldn't preach against it either.

The bishop's message was simple: Vote yes on Referendum 1. It was overtly political.

So when you ask what people thought of when they were going to the polls, many believed they were doing the right thing religiously.

---

[22] See also Barth, Overby, and Huffmon (2009) and Reynolds (2013).

[23] See also Green (2000); Kirkpatrick (2004); Sherkat, De Vries, and Creek (2010); Whitehead (2010); Ellison, Acevedo, and Ramos-Wada (2011); Beyerlein and Eberle (2014); Biggers (2014, 58–61); and Paulson (2015). Cf. Hinch (2014); Bruni (2015); and Eskridge (2015).

Each of the Catholic bishops in North Carolina, for the Western and Eastern dioceses, donated $100,000 to the Amendment 1 campaign. And all of the local newspapers reported that event the Thursday before the vote.

And besides the dollar total, the bishops sent out a postcard to all registered parishioners, that came in the mail the Friday before the vote, explicitly saying that good Catholics should vote in favor of this amendment.

A last empirical source on which to base a belief that animus toward gay people did not necessarily motivate voters who approved Super-DOMAs is found in polling data. LeeAnn M. Massucci, a family-law attorney in Columbus, Ohio, elaborated on the point in this way in 2010:

For so many people, marriage is a religious institution.

Super-DOMAs missed the boat because marriage is also a contract between two people. And anybody ought to have the right to enter into a contract.

Where the country is struggling with gay marriage is from a religious, or philosophical, or spiritual perspective. Because when pollsters ask whether same-sex couples ought to have the same legal rights as others, the majority of respondents say "Yes." For example: "Should a surviving same-sex partner have the right to a deceased partner's estate?" Sixty or 70 percent of respondents answer that question with "Yes."

And these are Ohio polls I'm talking about, not ones from California or New York. Folks here are coming back and saying, "Yes. We think that's okay."

So when you point out the real disadvantages to couples without the benefit of marriage...when you actually say, "Do you understand that, if my partner's in a car accident and is in the hospital, do you appreciate that, if I'm not married to her, I'm not her immediate family? Hospital staff could stop me from spending time with her." And people will say, "That doesn't make sense." "So it's okay with you if I have that right?" "Yeah, that's fine."

I think if you went through a series of those kinds of questions about the things that married couples never even have to encounter, most people in Ohio are in favor of same-sex pairs having the same rights.

It's the marriage issue that turns them off, given the underlying religious perspective of what marriage is in this country. I don't believe anyone is really concerned about whether we can file our income taxes jointly. Nor do I think anybody cares if I can visit my partner in the hospital. Or that I can inherit from her without estate taxes. People don't worry about those things, when it comes down to it.

Rather, they have a philosophical or emotional disconnect when it comes to the word "marriage."[24]

Polling data from other Super-DOMA states supported Massucci's claim. In June 2009, for instance, the Glengariff Group found that 63.7 percent of Michiganders approved of civil unions for same-sex couples. Moreover, 57.5 percent of respondents in the Wolverine State backed adoption rights for gay people; 65.5 percent supported domestic-partner benefits for government employees; and 70.9 percent were in favor of inheritance rights for same-sex partners (Bell 2009).

---

[24] Cf. Metz (2010).

In addition, Wisconsin's unique experience of being the only Super-DOMA state that subsequently adopted a limited set of domestic-partnership rights for same-sex couples bolsters an interpretation that a majority of voters were not overtly hostile to the rights of gay people, as explained by Katie Belanger of Fair Wisconsin.

In 2009, we passed a domestic-partner registry that provides forty-three different protections to same-sex couples. The registry supplies a quarter of what marriage gives to opposite-sex couples, which is a substantial difference. It furnishes what lesbian and gay couples need to take care of each other, such as hospital visitation and family medical leave. It's not about the taxes. It's not about joint property. It's not about children and adoption. It just concerns two people in a committed relationship who need some extra legal protections in order to be there in times of need.

The registry was a pretty noncontroversial bill when it was passed, during a time when the Democrats were in control of the legislature and the governor's office. But even the Republicans who were there, together with the conservative Democrats – because not all Democrats were pro-LGBT – everyone was pretty calm about the registry itself.

That experience is a testament to the fact that some of the people during the 2006 amendment campaign actually believed what they said about what the referendum would and wouldn't do. Because the proponents of the amendment went on record, and we were able to hold them accountable to that.

Plus, the registry's a really common sense thing that most people agree with. We saw it in our polling and research, where 77 percent of Wisconsin citizens thought that a domestic-partner registry for same-sex pairs was a good thing and the right step forward. So there hasn't been a lot of resistance. It's not the lightning rod that marriage or civil unions are.

I also think part of the reason for that attitude is that we have a constitutional amendment in place. If people are on the fence, or not supportive of marriage equality, they know that marriage is "protected." So they understood what we were trying to do with the domestic-partner registry wasn't marriage. Because they had already voted on that one.

Thus, separating voters' motives from the objectives of Super-DOMA sponsors, this book, which closely examines the daily experiences of lesbian and gay couples and their families living in six Super-DOMA states while their marriage amendments were in force, in effect tests the Burress-Fitzgerald claim that they and their interest groups were concerned merely with protecting and defending the institution of marriage through public-policy making and not with disadvantaging the LGBT community in the process.

Having interviewed numerous leaders in DOMA campaigns across Massachusetts, Ohio, and Oregon, I am convinced that they genuinely believed what they said, both publicly and to me in private, about their motivations. They truly thought they were honorable public servants abiding by God's will. Indeed, my observations while conducting seven in-depth interviews with such individuals for two books[25] on same-sex marriage were that virtually all of

---

[25] This one and *America's Struggle for Same-Sex Marriage*.

their zeal sprang from fervent fundamentalist religious beliefs. Hence, I do not question the authenticity of the justifications articulated for their actions.

Nonetheless, what happened on the ground should have conformed in broad measure with their professed goals if the Burress-Fitzgerald theory matched empirical reality. Heterosexual marriage should have been significantly fortified as a civil, legal, and social institution in Super-DOMA states, with just incidental and at most modest effects on their LGBT citizens. Without observed evidence of both such outcomes, a researcher can only conclude that other, less benevolent motives prompted the adoption of the constitutional provisions.

OHIO

Two days after the 2004 presidential election, the *New York Times* reported,

Proposed state constitutional amendments banning same-sex marriage increased the turnout of socially conservative voters in many of the 11 states where the measures appeared on the ballot on Tuesday, political analysts say, providing crucial assistance to Republican candidates including President Bush in Ohio....

[T]he ballot measures...appear to have acted like magnets for thousands of socially conservative voters in rural and suburban communities who might not otherwise have voted, even in this heated campaign, political analysts said. And in tight races, those voters – who historically have leaned heavily Republican – may have tipped the balance.

In Ohio, for instance, political analysts credit the ballot measure with increasing turnout in Republican bastions in the south and west, while also pushing swing voters in the Appalachian region of the southeast toward Mr. Bush. (Dao 2004a)

Matt Bai, in a November 21, 2004, *New York Times Magazine* article, "Who Lost Ohio?", about the last twenty-four hours of the presidential campaign, summed up the conventional political wisdom on what happened in the Buckeye State:

For Democrats,...Election Day felt like some kind of horror movie, with conservative voters rising up out of the hills and condo communities in numbers the Kerry forces never knew existed. "They just came in droves," Jennifer Palmieri [the Kerry campaign's Ohio spokeswoman] told me two days after the election. "We didn't know they had that room to grow. It's like, [no matter what we do,] ...[t]hey just make more Republicans." (Bai 2004)

Finally, the lead article – "Flush with Victory, Grass-Roots Crusader against Same-Sex Marriage Thinks Big" – in the "National Report" section of a late November 2004 edition of the *New York Times* profiled Phil Burress, observing,

Mr. Burress's organization...helped turn out thousands of conservative voters on Election Day. Their support is widely viewed as having been crucial to President Bush's narrow victory in that swing state. "In 21 years of organizing, I've never seen anything like this," Mr. Burress, 62, said in an interview. "It's a forest fire with a 100 mile-per-hour wind behind it." (Dao 2004b)

Unlike the conventional political wisdom reported in the *New York Times*, political scientists and others have debated at length in the scholarly literature whether Issue 1 was solely responsible for putting George W. Bush over the top in Ohio, thereby guaranteeing his second term as president.[26] It may well be possible that, without the ballot measure's prodding of conservative voters to turn out in the Buckeye State, John Kerry would have become America's forty-fourth president. The most that nearly everyone in the discipline of political science can agree on is that they do not know for certain whether Phil Burress was indeed a kingmaker, even though most American politicians believed he did anoint George W. Bush for another four years in the Oval Office.[27]

Regardless of the scholarly dispute, the widely held political perception that the Issue I campaign in Ohio was utterly crucial to the 2004 presidential election results provides the opportunity to focus on the Buckeye State as an archetype for the nation.[28] Accordingly, as an introduction to what happened in numerous states across the union, I offer here a précis of events leading up to the passage of Ohio's Ballot Issue 1.[29]

The LGBT Community in 2004

"Ohio was not a happy place for gay people in 2004," A. Lynne Bowman acknowledged. As the founding executive director of Equality Ohio – the first important statewide LGBT interest group there, established in 2005 – Bowman should know. "We got walked on. We got walked on big time."

Helen, age forty-nine, and Lee, fifty-one, a lesbian couple in Columbus (the state capital), who told me their story in 2010, epitomized the level of political sophistication within the Ohio LGBT community as of 2004.

LEE: We were the first Ohio couple to get a civil union in Vermont, in July 2000. That was the first day it was legal anywhere in the country, where a state officially recognized same-sex relationships. Then three years later, we went to Canada to get an upgrade. So we've been married since 2003. But in Ohio, we're "good friends."
HELEN: But not next of kin.

---

[26] See Cahill (2005); Klein (2005): Sherrill (2005); Smith, DeSantis, and Kassel (2006); Campbell and Monson (2008); Rosenberg (2008, 377–82); Klarman (2013, 111–13); and Biggers (2014, 56–57) for instances and summaries of the give-and-take in academe on the 2004 election. Garretson (2014) investigated how same-sex marriage ballot measures affected the 2008 and 2012 presidential elections. Cf. Grummel (2008).

[27] See Murphy (2004) and Gilgoff (2007, 173). Cf. Hulse (2006) and Ensley and Bucy (2010).

[28] Excellent comprehensive histories of the American struggle over same-sex marriage are plentiful and include Klarman (2013), Pierceson (2013), and Gash (2015, 51–88).

[29] "Only a union between one man and one woman may be a marriage valid in or recognized by this state and its political subdivisions. This state and its political subdivisions shall not create or recognize a legal status for relationships of unmarried individuals that intends to approximate the design, qualities, significance or effect of marriage."

LEE: It was kind of weird back then. We had gotten our civil union. And a few months later, George W. Bush was elected for his first term as president. So we woke up, and there was nobody representing us at either the federal or state level who we had voted for. We were like, "How can they represent us if we don't talk to them?" So we went and spoke with our state representative, and then with an aide to our state senator.

HELEN: The senate aide said, "If we get five letters on an issue, we have to start a file." And we thought, "We can get five people to write letters. How hard can it be?"

LEE: So we wanted to start talking with *all* of the legislators in the state capitol. And they would ask, "Are you a constituent?" "No." "Well, what organization do you represent?"

HELEN: Oh, crap.

LEE: So we started Ohio Freedom to Marry...

HELEN: ...in order to talk to more people.

LEE: Two dykes and an iMac. [They laugh.] After that, we could make appointments to go talk to more state officials, because we now represented an organization. Then the legislative DOMA came down, in late 2003, early 2004...

HELEN: ...after we started Ohio Freedom to Marry.

LEE: We arranged for a meeting at the Stonewall community center in Columbus to get organized. The announcement was in all the gay papers, and a bunch of people were there. And when DOMA hit, we were, like, *experts*. And we thought to ourselves, "What's the difference between Congress and..." [They laugh again.] Quick, let's brush up on Political Science 101. So we became sought-out experts. And we really were not. But we learned quickly and became part of the bucket brigade that was trying to put out this fire. Because there really was no organized effort.

HELEN: There certainly was no organization to speak of.

LEE: That's right. Except for Ohio Freedom to Marry. [More laughter.] There were the local Stonewall community centers and those kinds of things at the municipal level. By mid-2004, we had a statewide organization. I was on its board and knew it was never going to make it, because it was a top-down, Republican model, instead of a grassroots-up version. I was only on the board because of Ohio Freedom to Marry and our involvement with the legislative DOMA. I was the token poor Democrat.

No statewide Ohio organization had ever had paid staff. Prior to the 2004 election, HRC [the Human Rights Campaign, a prominent national LGBT interest group] held a planning session that brought in people from all the states that were facing DOMAs that year. Matt Foreman and other high-powered national leaders were there. And the only person from Ohio who could go was me, the kindergarten teacher, because I was off work then. When the representative from GLAD [Gay and Lesbian Advocates and Defenders, a Boston-based LGBT legal powerhouse] realized that Ohio didn't have paid staff, her jaw hit the table. It was ridiculous that I was the one person representing Ohio. I did what I could do, bringing back all of the information. But we had no full-time staff.

Lynne Bowman, the leader of Equality Ohio from 2005 to 2010, elaborated on the organizational and political environment in Ohio during 2004.

The LGBT community was so fractured that there were local leaders in Cleveland who, when brought together for an initial statewide meeting, had no idea there was even a campaign against Issue 1. That's how poorly the campaign was run. But it's also indicative of how clueless we all were as a community, having no idea then of what was coming at us.

There were battles from the very beginning about who would make decisions for the campaign against Issue 1, including fights just purely around the hiring of a campaign manager. HRC gave $100,000 for the resistance to Issue 1. At that point, after the campaign hired its manager, we were told as volunteer leaders on the ground to stay out of the way of the campaign, to let the campaign run the campaign. Some of that had to do with a lack of understanding by everyone about how big and bad this was going to be. And part of it had to do with the disagreement about the selection of the campaign manager.

There were two schools of thought about how the campaign should be handled. Whether it was an upper tier approach, with legal challenges and all of that, or whether it was a grassroots, ground-level campaign. The upper tier plan of action won out.

So in August, after CCV [Citizens for Community Values] turned the petition signatures in, the group that formed to oppose the measure decided that their focus would be on trying to keep Issue 1 off the ballot through contesting the validity of voter signatures. That was the first thing they did.

Once the signatures were certified, then they turned to the legal requirement that Ohio ballot initiatives must address only a single issue. LGBT advocates argued that Issue 1 concerned more than one subject since its first sentence limited marriage to one man and one woman, while a second sentence appeared to prohibit arrangements like civil unions and domestic partnerships. But that argument failed in the courts.

There are seven media markets in Ohio. It's one of the more expensive states to run a campaign in. But CCV and its allies had tons of money. I don't know what the final total was. But they had millions of dollars in order to do this, and were extremely visible. Of course, they were in all of the churches, too.

At the same time, very few people around Ohio knew about the campaign against Issue 1. There was no ground game. Anything that happened at the grassroots across the state really was from local activists doing it themselves. Whatever advertising there was played at, like, 1:00 and 5:00 in the morning on cable channels. It was a very, very limited run of cable ads in the last week before the election. There were one or two print pieces that were done. Most of the effort was spent on getting endorsements from people who said that Issue 1 was a bad idea for the state – the whole notion of leadership voices speaking out against the amendment.

There was no knocking on doors that I was aware of. There was no voter identification. We did a literature drop in one neighborhood on one weekend here in Columbus that I organized. Yet, as far as I know, it was the only lit drop in central Ohio. There were no bumper stickers. There was no online media campaign really. Even the campaign's website wasn't very good.

So the political contest was really bad for us. The battle over gay marriage in Ohio was extremely lopsided. There was no fight on our side really, that anybody could see. And by the weekend before the vote, our campaign was down to one or two staff people, because of internal fighting.

I just don't think that many people in the LGBT community took Issue 1 seriously. Because we didn't know. There had never been this type of social-issue amendment before in Ohio, at least that any of us were aware of or impacted by. And it was the first nationwide round of constitutional amendments against marriage equality. The people on our side simply didn't believe Issue 1 would really pass.

Even potential allies of same-sex couples in Ohio were ill informed about the ballot measure, as explained in 2010 by a lesbian attorney who was a student at a Columbus law school in 2004:

Many people in the straight community weren't particularly well informed about what the effects of the Super-DOMA might mean for them. One of my best friends in law school, who is straight, came to me one Monday, saying that she'd been in church the day before, and her minister was actually talking about Issue 1. He was speaking out against it, telling his congregation that it could have far-reaching effects, and not just for gay couples, but for straight pairs as well. And for elderly people.

My friend said she was surprised to learn this. And that shocked me. Because this was someone who was very close to me and extremely well educated. Yet she'd come to know these things by way of a minister at her church.

What I took away from the incident was, if this person – who was so well educated and gay friendly – if this was news to her, then there had to be a whole population of people out there, who were less well educated, that didn't appreciate the far-reaching effects of the Super-DOMA, not just on gay folks, but on straights as well.

The Opposition

In stark contrast to the LGBT community and its supporters, the people in Ohio who fought state recognition of same-sex relationships had been well organized for a long time. Phil Burress, president of Citizens for Community Values, was their leader. As early as 1993, CCV spearheaded a successful ballot measure to repeal an ordinance that the Cincinnati City Council had passed against sexual-orientation discrimination. A few years later, Burress turned his attention to gay marriage.

During the [Cincinnati charter-amendment] campaign, I met a fellow from Hawaii, named Mike Gabbard. He was dealing with an issue in Hawaii that I really didn't understand at the time. Mike was speaking out against same-sex marriage and special rights based on someone's sexual behavior. Today [2010], he's a senator in Hawaii.

In December 1995, Mike called me to ask, "Are you not concerned about what's going on in Hawaii with same-sex marriage?" I said that I had no idea what he meant. "How does that affect us?" He said, "Because of full faith and credit. If you don't do something about it, and if we lose here, all the other forty-nine states are going to have to accept same-sex marriage, if this goes down in Hawaii." I called some lawyers and verified that what Mike told me was correct. Prior to that, I never realized what threat we were under from the Hawaii case.

So on January 18, 1996, I held a meeting in Memphis, Tennessee, to discuss this. I brought in all the pro-family leaders from across the country to say that we needed to talk about same-sex marriage. As a result of the Memphis meeting, we came up with six action steps. One was to pass what later was called DOMA. Before the end of 1996, all the pro-family groups were working together, and we got the bill through Congress, and President Clinton signed it into law.

We then realized that this was going to be much bigger and that we had to pass DOMAs in the states themselves. So I hired a full-time person here at CCV. And the

Alliance Defense Fund was critical in this, too.[30] They're based in Phoenix and have lawyers in every state. They donate 400 hours to people like us to work on pro-family issues.

The Alliance Defense Fund helped write the DOMAs, because the bills were different depending on the state. In some places, you could only get through that marriage was between one man and one woman. In other states, we could go a lot further and restrict any government agency from emulating marriage through domestic partnerships or civil unions or whatever you want to call it. We were the first ones to go that far. [Ohio governor Bob Taft signed the statutory DOMA into law on February 4, 2004.]

I'm a member of the Family Policy Councils, which are associated with Focus on the Family. I worked with Tony Perkins and the Family Research Council. All these groups got together, including the American Family Association and Concerned Women for America. We kept meeting on a regular basis. In fact, since Memphis, we've been meeting every three months. So for 14 years [as of 2010], we've met quarterly to discuss the issue of marriage and the homosexual agenda.

We coordinated the nationwide effort, which took off like wildfire. People understood the threat. Thirty-eight states passed DOMAs. Most of them were quite easy. Citizens understood what the threat was, and that we had to establish a strong public policy to justify not having to accept marriages from other states. So we had all those state legislatures pass DOMAs.

The next fight was Vermont [in 1999–2000]. Out of this office [CCV], we actually sent a letter to every household in Vermont, signed by Democrats and Republicans from Hawaii, saying basically, "Don't be fooled. It's not about equality. It's forcing homosexuality and homosexual acts upon the people."

These grass fires went on all around the country. And everyone now knew about same-sex marriage and what the activists were trying to do. I've been to all fifty states in the last ten years, and not one group I've ever spoken to thought this was about marriage. Defending the institution of marriage was the right thing to do. But it wasn't about marriage for the homosexual activists. It was about destroying the institution of marriage and forcing their lifestyle on everybody else, whether you like it or not. And if you don't like it through public policy, then the courts will force it upon you. And that was quite obviously their plan.

So we knew we had to move into the realm of state constitutions. Because state statutes weren't enough in light of activist judges.[31]

On May 17, 2004, same-sex couples started getting married in Massachusetts, which absolutely shocked me. I did not think that would happen.

I commissioned a poll from Market Strategies, because there was a presidential election in 2004 and the marriage issue could affect it. My poll asked the question, "If this marriage amendment was on the ballot, would it affect the presidential vote?" The poll came back that it would help President Bush by three to five percentage points in Ohio. Undecideds would break six to one for Bush.[32]

---

[30] See also Crampton (2004).

[31] See also Hume (2013, 170–72)

[32] "[W]hile other salient or controversial matters may occasionally excite those who can be mobilized to the polls above normal voting levels, moral issue propositions [such as bans on same-sex marriage] possess an unparalleled capacity to do so" (Biggers 2014, 86). Cf. Powell (2013).

So the Family Policy Councils ended up putting eleven constitutional amendments on the November ballot in 2004 because of what happened in Massachusetts. [Statutory] DOMAs weren't strong enough. And that's why we had to campaign to pass constitutional amendments.

When our lawyer David Langdon wrote the language [of Issue 1], I said, "I don't want just to protect marriage. I want to make sure that domestic partnerships or nothing else at the taxpayers' expense is used in the state of Ohio to emulate marriage or to copy marriage."

The grassroots just absolutely exploded. We ended up collecting 557,000 signatures and, in the process, also delivered 55,000 new voter-registration forms to the Ohio Secretary of State's office. When we were circulating our petitions, we asked people whether they were registered to vote.

Once it looked like Issue 1 was going to the ballot, then the [Democratic presidential nominee John] Kerry people did everything they could to keep it off the ballot, because they knew it could impact the presidential election as well. We ended up being sued forty-two times in thirty-eight different counties to keep this off the ballot. We didn't expect all these lawsuits. They challenged our signatures. But we blew them out of the water with numbers. Our rate of good signatures was about 67 percent. They sued us on every count – that we did this wrong, and that wrong. But we did it all right. We knew exactly what to do, because the lawyers were telling us all along. We trained our volunteers. We had explicit instructions for them on our website. The web was a savior for us, because people could go there, download the petitions, and read the instructions.

Once Issue 1 was on the ballot, the campaign was easier than what I thought it would be. Every major newspaper in the state was against us. And they ended up being our biggest ally, and didn't know it. Because the papers titled Issue 1 as "anti-same-sex marriage." And that played into about 70 percent of the people. Going in, we knew that that many people were opposed to same-sex marriage. So when the newspapers titled it "anti-same-sex marriage," 70 percent of the people that looked at it said, "I agree with that." So the title that the newspapers used helped us.[33]

Churches had been our primary source for signatures, and so obviously, they would be our primary source for getting the vote out as well. I came up with the idea to have a church bulletin insert [saying "vote yes on Issue 1 on November 2"] that we would send out to thousands of churches statewide, eventually, 2.75 million bulletin inserts.

There were days that my phone started ringing at 6:00 in the morning and went to midnight. Interview after interview after interview. Especially when the media started thinking that this might impact the presidential election. So that part of the campaign took a life of its own.

We had our talking points and we stuck to them. We repeated the same thing over and over again. That this was not antigay marriage. This was about protecting the institution of marriage. To keep it the way it is. We called it the Ohio Campaign to Protect Marriage.

We were way ahead in the polls. I was asked to travel all over the state and debate this issue. I refused. I didn't debate it one time. I said, "Why should I do that? Why should I get up there on a stage, with somebody that opposes me, when I'm way ahead in the polls? My job is to get my people to the polls, to spend every minute of the day doing that. Why should I spend my time debating and taking attention away from what I really want to do?" I did talk to the press. I never denied an interview with the press.

[33] See also Oliphant (2004).

Our whole campaign was to get out the vote. We printed more than 2.5 million bulletin inserts, and passed them out in about 4,000 churches all across Ohio, telling congregations to vote yes on Issue 1.

We decided not to target the major cities, because we'd probably lose there anyway. The major cities in Ohio are very liberal and mostly Democrat now. We decided to go to rural Ohio. The interesting thing about the 2004 election was that the exit polling showed that Kerry would win Ohio. The largest cities are Cleveland, Columbus, and Cincinnati. Typically, if you lose two of those, you lose the election. Bush lost five of the six major cities in Ohio, and he still won the state. And that's because rural Ohio showed up en masse.

We didn't have to worry much about voter turnout. Because the newspapers were doing it for us. We were front page on every paper every day. Everybody knew that marriage was on the ballot. It wasn't a typical campaign where you have to spend a lot of money educating people. We spent most of our time in courts and talking to the press, because we realized that no matter what we did, we were not going to reach the people the way the media do.

We found 39,000 Amish who weren't registered to vote. They said, "We never vote. But we're not going to sit this one out." They did register, and they voted.

We hired a company that made robocalls and asked Ken Blackwell [Ohio's incumbent Republican Secretary of State] to record a call that went into 850,000 homes that we identified. We called every home that had a telephone with this robocall three times. That was the one thing we did do to turn out the vote – telling people that the marriage amendment was on the ballot, asking them to vote yes.

The money [for the Issue 1 campaign] came from the Family Research Council. They provided us between $1.5 million and $2 million, and were involved with the marriage amendments everywhere else, too. We appealed to them for help, and that's where the vast majority of money came from.

Issue 1 passed 62 percent to 38 percent. And Bush ended up winning Ohio by two percent, with a margin of fewer than 120,000 votes [among 5.6 million cast]. 3,239,250 Ohio citizens, many of whom had not voted for years, showed up at the polls to vote yes on Issue 1.

Yet we got only 62 percent of the vote, when we should've gotten 70, because the other side just basically started lying. They came out with a campaign that said, "Stop same-sex marriage. Vote no." So we lost a lot of people that we learned later were confused because they heard those type of messages.

Similar stories about the passage of Super-DOMAs played out in eight other states during the 2004 elections. LGBT communities – challenged either by citizen initiatives championed by long-established, religiously based conservative interest groups, such as Citizens for Community Values, or by referenda from Republican-controlled state legislatures – were caught politically flat-footed, with no effective statewide organizations to rebuff the proposed constitutional amendments (Rimmerman 2000; Dorf and Tarrow 2014; cf. Johnson 2006; Rich 2006). The single difference between Ohio's Issue 1 and most of those other 2004 ballot measures was that the latter garnered larger statewide popular majorities: 78 percent in Louisiana, 76 percent in Georgia and Oklahoma,

75 percent in Arkansas and Kentucky, 73 percent in North Dakota, 66 percent in Utah, and 59 percent in Michigan. And four other states adopted Mini-DOMAs: Mississippi (with 86 percent of the vote), Missouri (71 percent), Montana (66 percent), and Oregon (57 percent). Indeed, the battle over Oregon's Measure 36 was the most closely contested that year (Pinello 2006).

Be that as it may, this book is not primarily about what happened in 2004. Rather, the volume speaks to what occurred with same-sex couples and their families in Super-DOMA jurisdictions afterward. And there is much to tell.[34]

---

[34] Comprehensive analyses of how LGBT rights issues played out in state and local referenda and initiatives are available in Gamble (1997), Stone (2012), Lewis (2013), and Biggers (2014).

2

State Judicial Interpretations of Super-DOMAs

My book *Gay Rights and American Law* (2003) analyzed how federal and state appellate courts treated the civil rights claims of lesbians and gay men between 1981 and 2000, examining 1,439 votes by 849 appellate judges in 398 decisions and opinions from 87 courts in all federal jurisdictions and 47 states. In the final chapter, I concluded the following:

[L]esbian and gay litigants experienced substantially greater success in state courts than in federal fora, with the former deciding sexual minority rights cases more than twice as favorably, on average, as the latter. In particular, state appellate courts interpreting their own state constitutions enhanced the rights and liberties of lesbians and gay men far more than federal and state decisions construing the federal Constitution, with a state supreme court rate two and a half times more favorable than that of the U.S. Supreme Court. The results provide empirical support for the notion that a new judicial federalism has been at work in the nation. Accordingly, those interest groups pursuing litigative campaigns to secure rights – for either homosexuals or other beleaguered minorities – are best advised to work at the state level, in great contrast to the best strategies during the civil rights era of the 1960s and '70s. (Pinello 2003, 145)

Accordingly, I begin this investigation into the implementation and effects of Super-DOMAs – the sine qua nons of America's war on same-sex couples and their families – by surveying how state courts interpreted and applied these constitutional amendments. In truth, both state supreme courts and intermediate appellate courts serve as consequential implementation agents for state constitutions, permitting judges the opportunity to flesh out the meanings of these foundational government documents through the resolution of discrete factual disputes, in the same way that federal appellate courts apply the U.S. Constitution. This chapter examines how state appellate courts made sense of Super-DOMAs and thereby ascertains the evolving legal frameworks that regulated the daily lives of same-sex couples and their families.

I canvassed appellate-court decisions construing marriage amendments in the study's six states, as well as in Alabama, Florida, Louisiana, South Carolina, and Virginia, which complete the group of Super-DOMA jurisdictions within the nation's twenty-five most populous states. Two general findings emerged from the inquiry.

First, few state appellate-court decisions comprehensively and conclusively interpreted the meanings of Super-DOMAs as applied to same-sex pairs and their children. Relevant courts of last resort issued a total of just three pertinent rulings. Notably, these state supreme courts, from Michigan, Ohio, and Wisconsin, have justices chosen through nonpartisan popular elections.[1]

Second, despite the limited number of decisions, the variety of state judicial readings of the constitutional amendments was remarkable. Although courts across all jurisdictions found that gay and lesbian pairs could not enter the institution of civil marriage, the tribunals reached a hodgepodge of outcomes over what the balance of the Super-DOMAs required.

For example, the Supreme Court of Wisconsin, in *Appling v. Walker* (2014), unanimously ruled that the Badger State's Super-DOMA,[2] adopted by Wisconsin voters in November 2006, did not prohibit a system of domestic partnerships, passed by the state legislature in 2009, awarding same-sex couples forty-three enumerated rights, such as inheriting a partner's estate in the absence of a will, visiting a partner admitted to a hospital, and accessing family medical leave to care for a sick partner.

In contrast, the Supreme Court of Michigan, by a five-to-two vote in *National Pride at Work, Inc. v. Governor of Michigan* (2008), held that the last six words of the Wolverine State's Super-DOMA[3] required the denial of employer-provided health insurance benefits to the same-sex partners of all public employees – a much more restrictive judicial interpretation than that reached in Wisconsin. Thus, judicial mediation in the Badger State made the lives of lesbian and gay pairs far better there than in Michigan.

Equally noteworthy is how some courts in Super-DOMA states dealt with the issue of gay divorce. Two branches of the Texas Court of Appeals, for instance, reached opposite conclusions. In *In the Matter of the Marriage of J.B. and H.B.* (2010), the Dallas arm of the intermediate appellate tribunal ruled

---

[1] The judicial selection is nonpartisan in the sense that candidates' political-party affiliations do not appear on the ballot. Nonpartisan elections, however, do not necessarily mean that parties have no influence in the choice of judges. In Michigan, for example, supreme-court candidates may be nominated at political-party conventions. In Ohio, judicial candidates are put forward in partisan primary elections and are endorsed by political parties.

[2] "Only a marriage between one man and one woman shall be valid or recognized as a marriage in this state. A legal status identical or substantially similar to that of marriage for unmarried individuals shall not be valid or recognized in this state."

[3] "To secure and preserve the benefits of marriage for our society and for future generations of children, the union of one man and one woman in marriage shall be the only agreement recognized as a marriage or similar union for any purpose."

that the Lone Star State's constitutional amendment[4] prevented judges from granting divorces to lesbian or gay couples who were legally married elsewhere, because to do so would force judicial recognition of such marriages in the first place. Yet, in *In re Divorce of Naylor and Daly* (2011), the Austin branch of the same court awarded a divorce to a lesbian couple married in Massachusetts. In June 2015, the Texas Supreme Court dismissed the attempt by the State of Texas to intervene in the *Naylor and Daly* proceeding because the state's attorneys had waited too long to step in and contest the trial judge's divorce action (*Texas v. Naylor and Daly*). Consequently, the Lone Star State's court of last resort never addressed the merits of whether same-sex pairs legally married elsewhere could divorce in Texas.

I next discuss the substantive state-supreme-court actions in chronological order, drawing on interview commentary to supplement the analysis.

OHIO STATE-COURT ACTION REGARDING ISSUE I

Once the November 2004 popular vote added Issue 1 to the Ohio Constitution as Article 15, Section 11, both the immediate and enduring question for same-sex couples and their families in the state became: What did it mean? The first sentence, unambiguously defining marriage as "[o]nly a union between one man and one woman," made it abundantly clear that lesbian and gay couples were excluded from the civil institution. But what about the amendment's second sentence?[5] What did it signify?

Carol Ann Fey is an attorney who has served the greater Columbus LGBT community for more than a quarter-century. She is one of the best known gay-friendly lawyers in Ohio. When asked about the meaning of Issue 1's second sentence, Fey offered this opinion:

Ohio doesn't recognize common-law marriage. So unless a couple's gone through a formal marriage ceremony and obtained a marriage certificate from the state, they're not married. There isn't any approximation of marriage to be had.

Couples can do things to protect the relationship they have through executing various legal documents like wills and powers of attorney, and thereby set up circumstances to take them partway to the kinds of rights and responsibilities they would receive if they could get married and were married. But there's nothing about that process that approximates marriage.

It's like pregnancy. You're either pregnant or you're not. In similar fashion, you're either married or you're not, for purposes of that relationship.

---

[4] "Marriage in this state shall consist only of the union of one man and one woman. This state or a political subdivision of this state may not create or recognize any legal status identical or similar to marriage."

[5] "This state and its political subdivisions shall not create or recognize a legal status for relationships of unmarried individuals that intends to approximate the design, qualities, significance or effect of marriage."

We asked the drafters of Issue 1 about its second sentence at the time they wrote it, and they never provided a clear answer. I think its sponsors were concerned about getting language out there, really, that was political, that got people out to vote.

I understand our community's concern since 2004. There's a constitutional provision that appears to affect us, and we have to give it some kind of significance. So what does the second sentence mean? Well, I'm at a loss to know.

Phil Burress of Citizens for Community Values addressed the same issue this way:

Q: What is your understanding of the meaning of that second sentence?

A: It did exactly what I told our lawyers to do. When we were sitting here [at the CCV office], I told them what I meant. I wanted the institution of marriage protected, and also intended to make sure that nothing was done that emulated marriage, whether it be domestic partnerships or anything else. Taxpayer money should not be used to do an end run around the marriage amendment, and just call it marriage by a different name. That's what I told them. They're the ones that came up with the language.

I thought it was pretty clear. But a lot of people tried to say it was confusing. Obviously, and because of the court cases, city councils and everyone else are not doing anything about domestic partnerships in Ohio now.

As Burress's comments suggest, state courts would be in the best position to interpret Issue 1's meaning in actual disputes that came before such tribunals. Thus, a good way to begin teasing out the impact of the Buckeye State's Super-DOMA is through a review of Ohio court rulings about its application to specific factual settings.

However, because Article 15, Section 11 of the Ohio Constitution was the brainchild of an interest group, and not the product of the state legislature (as Ohio's statutory DOMA of 2003 was), judges faced a serious interpretive challenge: no public record existed concerning the process by which the words of Issue 1 were developed. For legislatively crafted statutes and referenda, there is typically a record of public hearings and debates that lead up to the legislative action. As a result, courts can subsequently draw on such accounts to seek guidance on what ends the creative body intended its language to achieve. In short, there is no "legislative history" for citizen initiatives like Issue 1. Rather, the primary indication of what the constitutional amendment meant were its words alone.

State v. Carswell

Remarkably, in the eleven years after the passage of Issue 1, the Buckeye State's court of last resort, the Ohio Supreme Court, authoritatively adjudicated the meaning of Article 15, Section 11 just once, and in a dispute having no LGBT parties. Instead, *State v. Carswell* (2007) involved the criminal prosecution of a man who was indicted for violation of a domestic violence statute, which provided, "No person shall knowingly cause or attempt to cause physical harm to a family or household member." The alleged victim was a woman to whom Carswell was not married. The state intended to present evidence that Carswell's alleged victim had been "living as a spouse" with Carswell and that she was therefore a "family or household member" under the statute. Carswell's attorney argued that the Ohio domestic violence law was illegally applied to his client because the statute recognized a legal status similar to marriage for unmarried persons, in violation of Article 15, Section 11.

In a six-to-one vote among the justices, the state supreme court rejected the defendant's claim and held that the domestic violence statute did not violate the state constitution. The majority concluded,

[T]he second sentence of the amendment means that the state cannot create or recognize a legal status for unmarried persons that bears all of the attributes of marriage – a marriage substitute....

It is clear that the purpose of Issue 1 was to prevent the state, either through legislative, executive, or judicial action, from creating or recognizing a legal status deemed to be the equivalent of a marriage of a man and a woman. The first sentence of the amendment prohibits the recognition of marriage between persons other than one man and one woman. The second sentence of the amendment prohibits the state and its political subdivisions from circumventing the mandate of the first sentence by recognizing a legal status similar to marriage (for example, a civil union). (114 Ohio St. 3d at 213)

Yet, as the *Carswell* dissent pointed out quite convincingly,

[Bearing all of the attributes of marriage – a marriage substitute] is not what the disputed [constitutional] sentence says. The legal status prohibited [there] is a legal status "that intends to approximate" *any one* of four attributes – "the design, qualities, significance *or* effect" of marriage. The series is disjunctive, not conjunctive....

Using the term "living as a spouse" within the definition of "family or household member" clearly expresses an intent to give an unmarried relationship a legal status that approximates the "effect of marriage." The constitutional problem in this case does not arise because cohabiting unmarried persons are included as one of the several groups to whom the domestic violence statutes apply. Instead, the problem is definitional: by using the term "living as a spouse" to identify persons whom the statutes protect and against whom prosecution may be instituted, the General Assembly inherently equates cohabiting unmarried persons with those who are married and extends the domestic violence statutes to persons because their relationship approximates the significance or effect of marriage....

[W]e must interpret [Issue 1] according to its text, not as we speculate it may have been intended. Insofar as [the domestic violence statute] recognizes as a "family or household member" a person not married to the offender but "living as a spouse" with the offender, it is, in my view, unconstitutional beyond a reasonable doubt. (114 Ohio St. 3d at 217, 219–220; emphasis in original)

Hence, despite what the actual words of Issue 1 signified, the *Carswell* majority took the practical approach that the voters who approved the amendment could not have intended to invalidate the state's otherwise constitutionally sound domestic violence laws, at least as they were applied to cohabiting unmarried opposite-sex couples. Men who assaulted the women with whom they lived, but to whom they were not married, would not walk scot free on a legal technicality in Ohio.

Thus, the *Carswell* decision appeared to limit the meaning of Issue 1 to something less expansive than what its own words suggested, and this judicially implied restriction would have seemed to be a blessing for the LGBT community in Ohio. But even this simple point was not necessarily true, as explained by Timothy J. Downing, a prominent Cleveland attorney and gay-rights activist.

DOWNING: *Carswell* was a totally results-oriented decision, where the Ohio Supreme Court tied itself in knots to get to the outcome it wanted, by claiming that it gleaned from a vote what the intent of the voters was.

I don't know how they do that without legislative history, for which there was none. The language of the amendment is clear, and that's all anyone could look at.

The majority said, "Well, in the domestic violence circumstance, we're going to have this carve-out of the amendment, because we don't want to have a situation where a victim of domestic violence who's not married can't go to a prosecutor to get help." They looked at the case from the position of its result, not from what logic required. The judge who wrote the dissent talked about that. I think the *Carswell* majority was simply wrong in the way they interpreted Issue 1.

Had the state supreme court not decided the case the way it did, had it upheld Issue 1 as written, that outcome could have led to a groundswell whereby people would say, "Wait a minute. We didn't ever expect this to be the result of Issue 1. We need to do something, at least to change that second part, the benefits-of-marriage section."

And that was a big disappointment. Everyone else believed it was great the court decided the case the way it did. I thought just the opposite. *Carswell* cemented Issue 1 politically, and the gay community got really screwed in the process.

Q: I interviewed a professor at the Ohio State University College of Law who believes *Carswell* limited the second sentence of Issue 1 to apply only to a prohibition of Vermont-style civil unions, but nothing short of that.

DOWNING: I disagree. The case concerned a domestic violence statute, and that's all it was about. Anyone who says *Carswell* goes beyond its own specific factual setting hasn't read the majority opinion carefully enough. It had nothing to do with civil unions. It was about whether Issue 1 prohibited prosecutions under domestic violence statutes that apply to more than married couples. That's plain and simple what it was about. Nothing else.

Echoing Downing's assessment, CCV's Phil Burress offered this comment about the *Carswell* precedent:

Q: Do you agree with the outcome of the Ohio Supreme Court's *Carswell* decision?

A: It's a double-edged sword. David Langdon [CCV's principal attorney and the author of Issue 1] told me that he thinks the outcome of the case could weaken Issue 1.

But the way it came down sounded pretty good to me. I didn't want this guy to go free. He beat this woman, and that made me angry.

I've never really understood the argument that this ruling somehow weakened Issue 1. I just wanted this guy to go to jail.

So when it came down the way it did, I was happy. But the lawyers weren't.

Accordingly, whether the solitary Issue 1 interpretation by Ohio's court of last resort indeed constrained the application of that constitutional amendment to same-sex couples and their families was an open question.

The Legal View in Ohio from Below

Perhaps more instructive of Issue 1's legal impact on gay and lesbian pairs and their children was the perspective on the ground of attorneys who represent LGBT litigants regularly in the trial courts of the Buckeye State, where most actual legal disputes there are resolved. Again, Carol Ann Fey:

FEY: I've practiced law for over twenty-five years. Long ago, when I first started, if I were working a divorce with a litigant who decided that they were lesbian or gay, the other side would frequently come into court thinking that they could yell, "But that person is a lesbian!" or "That person is a gay man!" They thought their clients would get custody of children and would get child support and could walk away and not have to work very hard.

Now that isn't any longer the case. It wasn't even very much the case then. But there were lots and lots of litigants and opposing counsel who really believed they could do that and it would be just that simple.

Today [2010] I think Issue 1 is a similar matter. It's not whether or not Issue 1 is relevant, but whether or not counsel can throw it in with the kitchen sink of their arguments, to color them as though it were, and say, "How can you possibly allow these women to share child custody? After all, we have Issue 1, and don't you know, judge, that gay people have no rights?" There are otherwise intelligent and learned attorneys who will say that kind of thing.

Q: How have the courts responded to those arguments?

FEY: So far, they haven't followed them. We've not had any such outcomes.

But these Issue 1 arguments make the cases tremendously more expensive and highly contentious.

If Carol Ann Fey represented the first generation of gay-friendly attorneys in central Ohio, LeeAnn M. Massucci was among the second such cohort. Indeed,

Massucci had served as co-counsel with Fey and elaborated on Fey's comment about the expense of litigation:

Child-custody litigation can be horrendously expensive. I estimate that in one case, both parties' attorney's fees have been somewhere around a quarter of a million dollars so far. And this case went up to the Ohio Court of Appeals and down twice before I got involved.

The biological mother is herself an attorney. She hired David Langdon – the lawyer who wrote Issue 1 – to represent her. Langdon has now [2010] brought what's called a writ of prohibition in the Ohio Supreme Court, saying in essence that the Franklin County Court of Common Pleas [in Columbus] doesn't have the basic jurisdiction to rule on these cases at all. He's saying that the trial court doesn't have authority over the children who are the subject of the disputes.

Langdon is a very smart attorney, but he's misstating the law. Langdon sued the trial court, saying that those judges don't have authority to put temporary child-custody orders in place. Langdon always figures out a way to thread in, first, the statutory DOMA [of 2003], saying that the Ohio legislature never intended for this kind of relationship to be recognized. Then he brings in the constitutional amendment as further proof of his argument. So, "Your honors, not only the legislature, but also the citizens of Ohio strongly voted that language in."

We continue to say in reply that, as problematic as the DOMAs are, they don't affect these cases. Because DOMAs involve only adults, while child custody concerns a relationship between a child and an adult.[6]

Massucci also offered an interesting commentary on a judicial trend involving same-sex couples that was emerging in 2010.

MASSUCCI: We're now starting to file for the divorces of same-sex couples. Trial courts here [in Columbus] have said that, if lesbian and gay couples have been married in another state, and they come here and want a dissolution, we will divorce them. Because, jurisdictionally, people have a right as Ohio citizens to have access to the courts. So we can divorce you, although we can't marry you.

Q: There are rulings to that effect?

MASSUCCI: Those of us who practice in this area have taken an informal poll of trial judges, and have said to them, "If we present you with a divorce, will you do it?" And they've said that they think they have to. Local judges believe that Franklin County citizens should have access to their own courts.

However, I don't think that would happen if it were a disputed divorce. I'm not sure our judges would actually allow a contested divorce to go forward.

But would they sign off on an uncontested divorce or dissolution? I believe so. To my knowledge, so far there are two that have been filed, and I'm preparing a third one right now. Although I didn't file the first two myself, I'm told that they're being signed off on.

---

[6] The Ohio Supreme Court ultimately rejected Langdon's argument and determined that Buckeye State trial courts did have authority to issue temporary custody orders pending final judgments (*Rowell* v. *Smith* 2012).

Q: So there will be divorce decrees?

MASSUCCI: Yes.

Location, Location, Location

Michael D. Bonasera is a distinguished Columbus attorney who specializes in estate planning and wealth management. In a lengthy interview, he addressed how Issue 1 did not greatly much affect his legal advocacy on behalf of gay and lesbian clients. One exchange from that conversation is especially noteworthy.

Q: Let me play the devil's advocate. You have clients who are a same-sex couple, with children or not, as the case may be. They've done everything you've asked them to do in terms of estate and financial planning. And some catastrophe happens. So they have to rely upon the legal documents you've created for them.

Imagine further that there's an antagonist out there who wants to attack your clients for whatever personal motivation he or she may have. This adversary makes the following argument to an Ohio court: "Article 15, Section 11 of the Ohio Constitution reads in relevant part, 'This state and its political subdivisions shall not create or recognize any status or relationship of unmarried individuals that intends to approximate the design, quality, significance, or effect of marriage.' And you know, judge, what happened here? This couple went to a fancy lawyer, and he put all these documents together for them. And what occurred here was an intention to approximate the effect of marriage! And that, Your Honor, *violates* the Ohio Constitution."

How do you respond to that argument?

A: It's total crap. And I'm highly confident about that response. With trust planning, the law doesn't contemplate to require any type of legal relationship at all among the various parties: fiduciaries, beneficiaries, or otherwise. And it happens frequently among non-LGBT families that trusts are used to care and pass money to and from other family members, but as often, nonfamily members, too.

To construe a trust as an instrument that in any way seeks to include certain definitional relationships, such as a class of married persons, is false on its face. Total strangers at arm's length can create legal trusts.

So my answer to the adversary's argument would be, "Judge, Issue 1 is a red herring here. It's completely immaterial to the dispositional wishes of the individuals involved. Article 15, Section 11 is totally irrelevant to this case."

And I'm very confident that our judges in Franklin County [Columbus] would not bat an eye.

Q: What about outside Franklin County?

A: I don't know. I don't know.

Q: Have you had any LGBT clients from elsewhere in Ohio?

A: No. None. I'm aware of them and frankly am amazed they live out there. I don't know how they do it. They have to be stronger folk than I am.

Because it's not pretty, even within some of the state's urban areas, like down in Cincinnati, which is affectionately referred to as the northern-most southern city. Opinions regarding gay and lesbian marriages might have changed since 2004, but I tell you what, the Mason-Dixon line has come a lot farther north. That city is not very gay friendly, despite being an urban environment. You'd think that it would be more progressive. But, man, you might as well be in the Deep South down there.[7]

So, I don't know. The legal argument regarding Issue 1 would go the same way. And while I'm 100 percent sure that my answer is the right one, I've seen crazier things done by judges.

So I'm not as confident outside Franklin County and its contiguous counties: Licking, Delaware, Madison, Morrow. I'm not as certain outside that small blue island that your hypothetical antagonist's argument might not carry more weight.

In fact, the other Ohio attorneys I interviewed for this study were also less sanguine about the success of their legal arguments on behalf of same-sex clients in courts outside the greater Cleveland and Columbus metropolitan areas. Thus, the three most important factors for determining the legal rights of same-sex couples and their families in Ohio may well have been "location, location, location."

In sum, the Ohio court of last resort mediated Issue 1 effects only at the margins of legal and political activity within the Buckeye State, quite unlike much more dramatic high-court interventions in other Super-DOMA jurisdictions such as Michigan and Wisconsin, as the next sections explain.

At the same time, Ohio's trial courts largely reflected their local legal and political cultures, with significant judicial resistance to Article 15, Section 11's apparent mandate occurring within some urban environments and more dutiful observance of the constitutional provision in suburban and rural venues.

MICHIGAN STATE-COURT ACTION REGARDING PROPOSAL 2

National Pride at Work was the nation's first unequivocally authoritative court-of-last-resort interpretation of a Super-DOMA that affirmed and documented a specific grassroots impact on lesbian and gay couples. In that ruling, the Michigan Supreme Court interpreted the words "or similar union for any purpose"

---

[7] Cf. Stolberg (2015).

of Proposal 2 to require the denial of health insurance benefits to the same-sex partners of state employees. The high court's five-member majority opinion determined that the constitutional language was unambiguous and thus prevailed:

The trial court held that providing health-insurance benefits to domestic partners does not violate the marriage amendment because public employers are not recognizing domestic partnerships as unions similar to marriage, given the significant distinctions between the legal effects accorded to these two unions. However, given that the marriage amendment prohibits the recognition of unions similar to marriage "for any purpose," the pertinent question is not whether these unions give rise to all of the same legal effects; rather, it is whether these unions are being recognized as unions similar to marriage "for any purpose." Recognizing this and concluding that these unions are indeed being recognized as similar unions "for any purpose," the Court of Appeals reversed. We affirm its judgment. That is, we conclude that the marriage amendment, which states that "the union of one man and one woman in marriage shall be the only agreement recognized as a marriage or similar union for any purpose," prohibits public employers from providing health-insurance benefits to their employees' qualified same-sex domestic partners. (481 Mich. at 86–87)

In short, the Michigan Supreme Court applied the Super-DOMA's language literally. Indeed, the bulk of the ruling parsed the constitutional amendment into individual words or word groups and then used a 1991 edition of *Webster's Dictionary* to define each such word or word set. What is more, the Michigan majority explicitly rejected consideration of any extrinsic evidence of what might have happened in the voters' minds when they approved Proposal 2 in 2004: "When the language of a constitutional provision is unambiguous, resort to extrinsic evidence is prohibited, and, as discussed earlier, the language of the marriage amendment is unambiguous" (481 Mich. at 80).

Thus, what the Michigan Supreme Court majority did in *National Pride at Work* was diametrically opposed to the Ohio Supreme Court's approach in *Carswell*. In the latter decision, the majority did not apply Issue 1's words literally. Only the sole dissenting Ohio justice advocated that formulation. Instead, the Ohio majority in effect invoked extrinsic evidence they presumed existed (but which the justices never produced in their opinion) that indicated the voters never intended the result explicitly required by the constitutional language they approved.

What is even more remarkable when comparing the Michigan and Ohio high-court rulings is the quantity and quality of extrinsic evidence that the *National Pride at Work* majority chose to ignore. As the two dissenting Michigan justices explained,

[T]he Michigan Christian Citizens Alliance commenced an initiative to amend the Michigan Constitution to bar same-sex marriage. The alliance formed the Citizens for the Protection of Marriage committee (CPM) "in response to the debate taking place across the country over the definition of marriage." The committee's stated goal was to place the issue of same-sex marriage on the ballot so that Michigan voters would have the ultimate say in the matter.

During CPM's campaign, concerns arose regarding exactly what the amendment would prohibit. CPM attempted to address these concerns at an August 2004 public certification hearing before the Board of State Canvassers. Specifically, CPM addressed whether the amendment, which it had petitioned to place on the ballot, would bar public employers from providing benefits to their employees' same-sex domestic partners. CPM's representative, attorney Eric E. Doster, assured the board that it would not. Mr. Doster stated:

> [T]here would certainly be nothing to preclude [a] public employer from extending [healthcare] benefits, if they so chose, as a matter of contract between employer and employee, to say domestic dependent benefits . . . [to any] person, and it could be your cat. So they certainly could extend it as a matter of contract. . . .
>
> [A]n employer, as a matter of contract between employer and employee, can offer benefits to whomever the employer wants to. And if it wants to be my spouse, if it wants to be my domestic partner – however that's defined under the terms of your contract or my cat, the employer can do that. . . .

Mr. Doster reiterated this point several times throughout the proceedings.

> I'd hate to be repetitive, but again, that's a matter of contract between an employer and employee. And if the employer wanted to do that, offer those benefits, I don't see how this language affects that. If the language just said "marriage" or "spouse," then I would agree with you. But there's nothing in this language that I would interpret that would say that that somehow would go beyond that.

In its campaign to win over voters, CPM made a number of additional public statements that were consistent with Mr. Doster's testimony before the Board of State Canvassers. For example, Marlene Elwell, the campaign director for CPM, was quoted in *USA Today* as stating that "[t]his has nothing to do with taking benefits away. This is about marriage between a man and a woman." Similarly, CPM communications director Kristina Hemphill was quoted as stating that "[t]his Amendment has nothing to do with benefits. . . . It's just a diversion from the real issue."

CPM also made clear on its webpage that it was "not against anyone, [CPM is] *for* defining *marriage as the union of one man and one woman. Period.*" Instead, CPM contended that its reason for proposing the amendment was its belief that "[n]o one has the right to redefine marriage, to change it for everyone else. Proposal 2 will keep things as they are and as they've been. And by amending Michigan's constitution, we can settle this question once and for all."

CPM even distributed a brochure that asserted that the amendment would not affect any employer health-benefit plan already in place. The brochure stated:

> Proposal 2 is *Only* about Marriage
> Marriage is a union between a husband and wife. Proposal 2 will keep it that way. This is not about rights or benefits or how people choose to live their life. This has to do with family, children and the way people are. It merely settles the question once and for all what marriage is – for families today and future generations.

It can be assumed that the clarifications offered by CPM, the organization that successfully petitioned to place the proposal on the ballot, carried considerable weight with the public. Its statements certainly encouraged voters who did not favor a wide-ranging ban to vote for what they were promised was a very specific ban on same-sex marriage.

And a poll conducted shortly before the election indicates that CPM's public position was in line with public opinion. The poll results indicated that, whereas the public was in favor of banning same-sex marriage, it was not opposed to employer programs granting benefits to same-sex domestic partners.

In an August 2004 poll of 705 likely voters, 50 percent of respondents favored the amendment while only 41 percent planned to vote against it. But 70 percent specifically disapproved of making domestic partnerships and civil unions illegal. Sixty-five percent disapproved of barring cities and counties from providing domestic-partner benefits. And 63 percent disapproved of prohibiting state universities from offering domestic-partner benefits.

Accordingly, the circumstances surrounding the adoption of the amendment indicate that the lead proponents of the amendment worked hard to convince voters to adopt it. CPM told voters that the "marriage amendment" would bar same-sex marriage but would not prohibit public employers from providing the benefits at issue. It is reasonable to conclude that these statements led the ratifiers to understand that the amendment's purpose was limited to preserving the traditional definition of marriage. And it seems that a majority of likely voters favored an amendment that would bar same-sex marriage but would go no further. Therefore, this Court's majority errs by holding that the amendment not only bars same-sex marriage but also prohibits the benefits at issue. (481 Mich. at 91–96; emphasis in original)

The dissenting Michigan justices concluded their analysis by excoriating the prevailing opinion's effect:

[B]y proceeding as it does, the majority condones and even encourages the use of misleading tactics in ballot campaigns by ignoring the extrinsic evidence available to it. CPM petitioned to place the "marriage amendment" on the ballot, telling the public that the amendment would not prohibit public employers from offering health benefits to their employees' same-sex domestic partners. Yet CPM argued to this Court that the "plain language of Michigan's Marriage Amendment" prohibits public employers from granting the benefits at issue. Either CPM misrepresented the meaning of the amendment to the State Board of Canvassers and to the people before the election or it misrepresents the meaning to us now. Whichever is true, this Court should not allow CPM to succeed using such antics. The result of the majority's disregard of CPM's preelection statements is that, in the future, organizations may be encouraged to use lies and deception to win over voters or the Court. This should be a discomforting thought for us all. (481 Mich. at 102)

Thus, a substantial majority of the Michigan Supreme Court bent over backward to apply the language of Proposal 2 literally, while every bit as large a number of Ohio Supreme Court justices went out of their way to avoid an equally exact usage of Issue 1's words. Why the striking differences in judicial approach to constitutional amendments whose ultimate policy goals seemed so similar? I think the most satisfying way to harmonize the Michigan and Ohio cases is to look at their outcomes politically, rather than legally or logically.

As Timothy Downing observed, the *Carswell* majority opinion made Issue 1 palatable to most Ohioans when the Buckeye State Super-DOMA was applied to opposite-sex couples. Had the Ohio Supreme Court espoused the dissenting justice's literal analysis of the marriage amendment, the high tribunal would have invalidated domestic violence statutes en masse, at least with regard to abuse among unmarried heterosexual pairs. Downing surmised that, had the dissenting opinion's approach won the day, the resulting disruption to domestic violence law would have prompted a backlash against Issue 1. But an equally, if not more, plausible public reaction would have been political repercussions against the justices themselves. Indeed, disturbing domestic relations statutes for opposite-sex couples so dramatically would have placed the Ohio judges in an untenable political posture, especially given that Chio jurists are elected to six-year terms of office, the shortest in the nation for courts of last resort.

In contrast, the Michigan Supreme Court majority faced no comparable public outcry in utilizing Proposal 2 word for word against the best interests of same-sex pairs and their families. The Wolverine State jurists were politically free to follow wherever *Webster's Dictionary* led them.

In any event, the clearest example of an actual, tangible, Super-DOMA-based *statewide* loss for gay and lesbian couples was that, as a result of the *National Pride at Work* precedent, the same-sex partners of public employees could not receive domestic-partner benefits in Michigan. This development was particularly troublesome for such partners who did not themselves have jobs providing comparable health-insurance coverage.

Of even greater concern was the circumstance where partners were the biological or adoptive parents of minor children being raised by the couples, because Proposal 2 also effectively eliminated the availability of second-parent adoptions for same-sex pairs in the Wolverine State. Trial-court judges who had been willing to grant such adoptions before passage of the Super-DOMA declined to do so afterward. Consequently, lesbian and gay public employees in that setting were not even able to provide health coverage for their children.

Further, in March 2009, Blue Cross/Blue Shield of Michigan announced that, because of the *National Pride at Work* ruling, it was withdrawing same-sex partner benefits from public-employee health plans that it underwrote in Michigan; this action principally touched smaller employers with non-self-funded plans ("Court Decision Prompts Domestic Partner Policy Revision" 2009).

However, as a result of the *National Pride at Work* litigation, some large public employers with self-funded health plans, including the University of Michigan and Michigan State University, revised personnel programs to eliminate partnership status for employment benefits and to replace it with "Other Designated Beneficiary" or similar alternative eligibility criteria (Smith 2011). In other words, these employers substantially enlarged the categories of employees receiving benefits to include virtually all unmarried couples, the considerable portion of whom were heterosexual. This expansion of the eligibility pool significantly increased such employers' health-insurance costs.

A Litigator's Perspective

Yet, the ultimate *National Pride at Work* impact might have been far more substantial for Michigan's lesbian and gay pairs and their families, as Jay Kaplan, the staff attorney for the LGBT Project of the ACLU of Michigan, noted in January 2009:

Michigan's highest court has interpreted Proposal 2 as broadly as possible.

The Michigan Supreme Court is an incredibly political and conservative bench. The majority in the *National Pride at Work* decision clearly wanted to reach a certain result, and they were going to go about it anyway they could. This court doesn't like same-sex relationships or anything else they consider to constitute alternative families.

In terms of legal reasoning, the *National Pride at Work* decision was so flawed. The majority consists of justices who are members of the Federalist Society.[8] They're strict constructionists of the law. But there's no mention of domestic-partnership benefits or anything like them in the body of Proposal 2. So the judges had to find a 1991 dictionary definition of the word "similar" to fit what they wanted to achieve in rendering that decision.

What does it say about our democratic process when the court majority held that lying to voters in an initiative election doesn't mean anything? We want citizens to be well informed. And if some apparently authoritative person says, "You're voting for the color black," when in fact the proponent's purpose is for the intended color to be white, and after the ambiguous language passes, the author says, "Now it means white" – to believe all of that doesn't mean anything as a legal matter is a very sad state of affairs.

But the really scary aspect is that we don't know how far the *National Pride at Work* decision will be interpreted. What's its reach going to be? Consider a last will and testament that refers to a beneficiary as a "domestic partner" or "partner for life." If the decedent's legal next of kin disputes the will as violating Proposal 2, will Michigan courts now invalidate the otherwise legal will?

---

[8] The website of the Federalist Society describes the organization's purpose as follows:

The Federalist Society for Law and Public Policy Studies is a group of conservatives and libertarians interested in the current state of the legal order. It is founded on the principles that the state exists to preserve freedom, that the separation of governmental powers is central to our Constitution, and that it is emphatically the province and duty of the judiciary to say what the law is, not what it should be. The Society seeks both to promote an awareness of these principles and to further their application through its activities.

This entails reordering priorities within the legal system to place a premium on individual liberty, traditional values, and the rule of law. It also requires restoring the recognition of the importance of these norms among lawyers, judges, law students and professors. In working to achieve these goals, the Society has created a conservative and libertarian intellectual network that extends to all levels of the legal community.

After all, the constitutional amendment is in the passive voice ["the union of one man and one woman in marriage shall be the only agreement recognized as a marriage or similar union for any purpose"]. It doesn't talk about *who* is doing the recognizing. So not only government is swept up into Proposal 2's prohibition, but third parties could be too. Thus, the ban might also cover private agreements between same-sex couples. We just don't know how far it's going to go. *National Pride at Work* is one of those precedents that depend entirely upon the goodwill of judges who later interpret it.

The ACLU of Michigan is involved in a case now between two formerly coupled lesbian women. They broke up and are disputing child custody, including bouts of abduction of the kids. The mom we're representing went into court and filed for custody. This was in a small, rural county, in western Michigan, where the trial court in effect said this:

> We'll recognize the fact that the women adopted these three children. We'll give full faith and credit to the adoptions.
>
> But their relationship to the children involved the nature of the women's relationship to each other when they lived together at the time. So we can't allow them to use Michigan law to enforce their rights as parents, because that would violate the marriage amendment.
>
> Therefore, we're dismissing the petition for custody. The two women cannot use Michigan state courts and will have to settle the dispute privately between themselves.

Neither woman was a birth mother. So both parents were out of luck. Neither one could utilize Michigan statutory law to enforce their rights as parents. It's an outrageous judicial result.

There's another case we heard about where a Michigan judge refused to enforce a business agreement between two people who at one time had been in a personal relationship. But this was explicitly an agreement about commercial business. The judge said she couldn't enforce it because at the time they signed the document, they were a couple. So to recognize the business agreement would violate the marriage amendment.

Thus, who knows how far this is going to go? Look at what the Michigan Supreme Court opinion said was in common with marriage. The fact that people have to be of certain genders, the fact that they can't be related by blood – all of that was enough for the court to say that such circumstances were "similar" to marriage in the meaning of the Proposal 2 ban. That's how far these judges were willing to go to reach their desired outcome.

So I worry that challenges to estate-planning or other documents between same-sex couples might be successful under this amendment as interpreted by the state supreme court. *National Pride at Work* did a great deal of damage.

A Michigan Couple's View

Michael, age forty-two, and Robert, forty-seven, have been together for fifteen years and have executed all the legal documents they thought necessary to protect themselves as a couple.

Q: In light of Proposal 2, with which you're so familiar, how confident are you that your documents will be honored when needed?

ROBERT: I have to be honest with you. I've never even thought of that issue before. And you're scaring me as I contemplate it. I'm amazed I hadn't addressed it earlier.

MICHAEL: I feel confident. It's all legally binding stuff. It's not based on anything except us saying, "This is the person I want to have this responsibility or power." I don't feel apprehensive about it at all.

ROBERT: One difference between Michael and me is that I really followed the court case thoroughly. I've read all of the opinions, and followed the reasoning very carefully.

What scares me about the *National Pride at Work* decision is, as I read it, I'm not sure what the judges were thinking about when they reached to make those last six words of Proposal 2 mean so much. One doesn't have to do a stretch any greater than that to start questioning things, perhaps like some of these legal documents we have.

For instance, we have health care powers of attorney that say each of us has decision-making authority for the other. But a Michigan hospital could respond that acknowledging such a right would recognize an agreement similar to marriage.

So I can imagine things getting bad enough that even well-meaning nurses and doctors might think, "Oh well, we don't want to get sued. Maybe we're better off with just the legal next of kin getting to make medical-care decisions for our patients."

I think that approach is definitely possible in some parts of this state, although not where we live in Ann Arbor, which is pretty progressive on LGBT rights.

WISCONSIN STATE-COURT ACTION REGARDING REFERENDUM 1

As the chapter introduction indicated, in *Appling* v. *Walker*, the Wisconsin Supreme Court unanimously upheld the constitutionality of the statewide domestic-partner registry, which was a significant boon to same-sex couples. The Badger State case is a stark contrast to *National Pride at Work*.

Two factors explain the disparate rulings. First, unlike Proposal 2 – an initiative of the Citizens for the Protection of Marriage committee that began with its circulation of petitions to collect voter signatures to place the matter on the Michigan ballot – Referendum 1 was the progeny of the Wisconsin legislature itself and therefore had a legislative history to guide justices as to the amendment's intended meaning. In fact, the Wisconsin Supreme Court opinion has an entire section labeled "What Information Was Given to Voters during the Constitutional Debates and Ratification Process?" which included this discussion:

We ... examine the relevant public statements made by the Amendment's framers and other proponents that were intended to persuade voters during the ratification process. During the process, the question of the effect on the rights of same-sex couples was a matter of intense debate. A newspaper article dated July 30, 2006, stated, "Although there's not much dispute that the proposed constitutional amendment on marriage in Wisconsin would bar same-sex unions, there is deep disagreement about what the wording might mean for civil unions and domestic-partner benefits." In one letter to the editor of the *Milwaukee Journal Sentinel,* taking issue with an opponent's statements, Rep. Mark D. Gundrum characterized opponents as "continu[ing] the effort...to deceive people about the impact the man-woman marriage constitutional amendment will have in Wisconsin" and flatly rejected the notion that it would "seriously jeopardize any legal protections for unmarried couples – gay or straight." Proponents made numerous statements on that issue as the following facts demonstrate.

A January 28, 2004, press release on the letterhead of the Wisconsin Legislature by legislative sponsors who spearheaded the effort to pass the Amendment, Rep. Mark D. Gundrum and Sen. Scott Fitzgerald, stated:

> The proposed amendment, while preserving marriage as one man-one woman unions, would also preclude the creation of unions which are substantially similar to marriage. "Creating a technical 'marriage,' but just using a different name, to massage public opinion doesn't cut it," Gundrum said.... Significantly though, the language does not prohibit the legislature [and other entities]...from extending particular benefits to same-sex partners as those legal entities might choose to do.

In December 2005, Sen. Scott Fitzgerald was quoted as follows in media accounts of legislative debates when the Senate was preparing to vote: "The second [sentence] sets the parameters for civil unions. Could a legislator put together a pack of 50 specific things they would like to give to gay couples? Yeah, they could."

A November 2006 statement issued by the office of Sen. Scott Fitzgerald struck back at opponents of the Amendment and said they were "intentionally mislead[ing] the public about the amendment." Contrary to those "misleading" representations, the statement said,

> Nothing in the proposed constitutional amendment would affect the ability of same-sex individuals from visiting a sick partner in the hospital or mak[ing] medical decisions for their partners as [prescribed] by a medical power of attorney. The non-partisan Legislative Council has written that the proposed amendment does not ban civil unions, only a Vermont-style system that is simply marriage by another name. If the amendment is approved by the voters...the legislature will still be free to pass legislation creating civil unions if it so desires.

An article written by Sen. Scott Fitzgerald and published in the *Wisconsin State Journal* stated, "Contrary to claims from...liberal activists, the proposed constitutional amendment would not prohibit state or local governments...from setting up a legal construct to provide privileges or benefits such as health insurance benefits, pension benefits, joint tax return filing or hospital visitation to same-sex or unmarried couples."

The Family Research Institute of Wisconsin, a group that advocated for the Amendment (it defined itself as seeking to preserve "traditional one-man/one-woman marriage in Wisconsin"), issued a six-page publication dated August 2006, listing 13 questions and answers about the meaning of the Amendment. In that publication, the organization stated, "The second sentence [of the Amendment] doesn't even prevent the state legislature from taking up a bill that gives a limited number of benefits to people in sexual relationships outside of marriage, should the legislature want to do so."

An article authored by Julaine Appling, a named plaintiff in this case, published Dec. 13, 2005, stated, "Contrary to the message being consistently given by opponents of the amendment, the second phrase does not 'ban civil unions.'...Nor does this phrase threaten benefits already given to people in domestic partnership registries by companies or local units of government."

In an Associated Press article dated Dec. 7, 2005, Julaine Appling was quoted as saying, "Nothing in the second sentence prohibits [legislative grants of adoption or inheritance rights]. Nor does it in any way affect existing benefits given by local governments or the private sector."

This representative sampling of messages, publicized by some of the most prominent and prolific advocates of the Amendment, makes clear that in response to concerns about what exactly the Amendment would prohibit, such advocates answered directly that the Amendment would not preclude a legislative decision to create a legal mechanism giving unmarried couples in intimate relationships specific sets of rights and benefits. The message was also clearly given that the Amendment would not diminish rights in existing domestic partnerships. Same-sex partners were specifically included in such answers. (358 Wis.2d at 157–160)

In other words, exactly the same kind of extrinsic evidence that the Michigan Supreme Court rejected out of hand as unworthy of consideration in *National Pride at Work*, the Wisconsin Supreme Court welcomed to guide its understanding of Referendum 1's meaning in *Appling*. But the fact that the nature of the proof in the latter case was legislative history, as opposed to the oral and published statements of the interest-group sponsors of Proposal 2, made all the difference.

A second important reason for the disparate outcomes of the two judicial decisions had to do with timing. In 2008, when the Michigan high court acted, there was absolutely no indication anywhere in the nation that state courts would not be the final arbiters of Super-DOMA-based disputes for the foreseeable future. However, by July 31, 2014, when the Wisconsin Supreme Court rendered *Appling*, the national legal landscape on who might have the final say over state marriage amendments had changed radically, as discussed at length in Chapter 6. By then, in fact, astute judicial observers clearly saw the writing on the wall. Federal judges were invalidating state gay-marriage bans from coast to coast. In Wisconsin itself, a federal district judge struck down Referendum 1 in June 2014, more than a month before the *Appling* decision came down; one of the state supreme court's concurring opinions made specific reference to that ruling. Thus, there was little, if any, practical incentive for the Wisconsin justices to take the kind of hard line against same-sex couples that their Michigan counterparts had done six years earlier.

In any event, the Wisconsin Supreme Court had no consistent history as a Midwestern bulwark against antigay action. In *Angel Lace M. v. Terry M.* (1994), for example, the Badger State high court denied second-parent adoptions to same-sex couples, a precedent that plagued lesbian and gay parents until the federal judiciary stepped in twenty years later. In contrast, at roughly the same time the Wisconsin bench rendered *Angel Lace*, other state courts of last resort, such as the Massachusetts Supreme Judicial Court (in

Adoption of Tammy 1993) and the New York Court of Appeals (*Matter of Jacob* 1995), authorized either joint adoptions or second-parent adoptions for families headed by same-sex partners.

OTHER STATE-COURT ACTION

The only other Super-DOMA-related litigation to reach state supreme courts involved whether the initiatives and referenda addressed multiple subject matters and thereby violated the common state constitutional rule that amendments could speak to just a single topic. Super-DOMA opponents argued that the proposed bans touched marriage and civil unions and domestic partnerships, as well as the respective benefits to same-sex couples from each relationship-recognition form. However, no court of last resort among the twenty-five most populous states upheld such a challenge. Each permitted the measures to proceed. (*Advisory Opinion to the Attorney General re: Florida Marriage Protection Amendment*, Florida 2006; *Perdue* v. *O'Kelley*, Georgia 2006; *McConkey* v. *Van Hollen*, Wisconsin 2010).

State intermediate appellate courts, however, did make some important Super-DOMA interpretations, most notably surrounding disputes involving children. The Michigan Court of Appeals, for instance, held that parents who were not biologically related to the children they helped raise and who had not formally adopted such children had no legal standing to seek child custody once same-sex couples separated and disputed the issue (*Harmon* v. *Davis* 2010; *Stankevich* v. *Milliron* 2013). In contrast, the Florida Court of Appeals suggested that the best interests of the child, and not standing rules, should be dispositive in such a case (*T.M.H.* v. *D.M.T.* 2011). The liberally minded Austin branch of the Texas Court of Appeals refused to invalidate an adoption jointly granted to a same-sex pair (*Goodson* v. *Castellanos* 2007), whereas the Alabama Court of Civil Appeals prevented second-parent adoptions in that state (*In re Adoption of K.R.S.* 2012).

With regard to property rights, the Houston branch of the Texas Court of Appeals held that the surviving same-sex partner of a decedent was not entitled to any part of the latter's estate without a specific bequest in a valid will (*Ross* v. *Goldstein* 2006).

Both the Louisiana Court of Appeal (*Ralph* v. *City of New Orleans* 2009) and the Ohio Court of Appeals (*Cleveland Taxpayers* v. *Cleveland* 2010) upheld municipal domestic-partner registries that did not confer consequential legal rights to gay and lesbian couples.

Lastly, adding to the confusion referenced at the chapter's start over whether same-sex pairs legally married in other places might seek divorce in Texas, the Ohio Court of Appeals turned down that option for such couples (*McKettrick* v. *McKettrick* 2015), while the Florida Court of Appeals gave a thumbs up (*Brandon-Thomas* v. *Brandon-Thomas* 2015).

UNDERSTANDING THE LACK OF FURTHER STATE-COURT
SUPER-DOMA LITIGATION

As the preceding case inventory indicates, three substantive and three procedural rulings from courts of last resort and another dozen holdings from intermediate appellate courts constitute the entire corpus of state appellate decisions implementing the eleven Super-DOMAs among the twenty-five most populous American states. Thus, the supreme courts of three jurisdictions in this study (Georgia, North Carolina, and Texas) rendered no opinions on the fundamental meanings of their marriage amendments.[9] And as suggested earlier, Ohio's *State* v. *Carswell* may not really have been about what rights, if any, LGBT people had under Issue 1. Moreover, Wisconsin's *Appling* v. *Walker* arrived very late in the event chronology. Accordingly, only Michigan's *National Pride at Work* can truly be considered a meaningful and enduring state-supreme-court Super-DOMA implementation.

I was aware of this legal scenario when my interview field trips began in January 2009. Indeed, I chose Michigan for the first of my seven journeys because of *National Pride at Work*'s prominence.

My second field trip was to Georgia in 2010, where I discovered that, unlike in the Wolverine State, at least six or seven counties and municipalities did in fact explicitly provide benefits to the same-sex partners of their employees. In other words, I learned that some lesbian and gay pairs were substantially better off legally in the Deep South than their counterparts in the Midwest, which struck me as counterintuitive.

Jeff Graham, executive director of Georgia Equality, the leading LGBT interest group in the Peach State, emphasized the absence of Question 1's practical impact on the extension of benefits to the domestic partners of public and quasi-public employees.

Grady Health Systems, a nonprofit health care organization that had been a governmental authority up until about a year and a half ago, recently adopted domestic-partner benefits with no conversation or controversy whatsoever.

Georgia Equality went to them with some Grady employees, and made our case about why this was fair, and how other hospital systems in the metro Atlanta area had implemented domestic-partner benefits. They had some key employees who were gay or lesbian, and so they felt it was the right thing to do. And they did it.

Grady isn't technically now a governmental or municipal agency. But it's a huge entity that's very much tied into the politics of both the metro area and the state legislature, where so much of their funding does come from.

But none of their board members or administrators ever raised a legal question when we went to them with this. In fact, the only concern that has ever come up with municipalities and the like is whether the change would cause a financial strain on their budgets. That's the only pushback we get.

---

[9] In fairness, I note that North Carolina's Amendment 1 was in effect for less than two years, thus not permitting sufficient opportunity for appeals to reach the Tar Heel high bench.

No one has ever brought up Question 1. And all of this has occurred during the last two years.

Accordingly, I pointedly asked the most knowledgeable people in Atlanta why some judgment like *National Pride at Work* had not occurred in Georgia. After all, the Peach State Super-DOMA passed at the same time as Proposal 2 in Michigan and had more than three times the number of words (136 vs. 42). So Question 1's language was arguably more limiting on its face.

Jeff Graham of Georgia Equality was the first person to offer an explanation for the absence of consequential judicial action in the Peach State.

GRAHAM: There haven't been any court cases addressing Question 1's significance that I'm aware of. So from that perspective, I don't know there's a lot of meaning to it from a practical point of view.

Two or three years ago, we addressed civil unions. In a statewide poll, 60 percent of respondents favored them. We've also done local polling in specific jurisdictions around employment nondiscrimination.

Georgia Equality's concern is not allowing our actions to inadvertently set off legal proceedings we may not be prepared to fight. So we react very cautiously, not reporting any of our poll findings in the media as an intentional choice.

Our worry has been that, say, if a municipality limited domestic benefits only to the unmarried partners of homosexuals, its action would spark litigation under Question 1. We try to avoid triggering lawsuits in the work we do.

Q: Yet Question 1 neither negated the existing county and municipal domestic-partner programs nor the creation of new ones in other places?

GRAHAM: Yes, that's correct.

Q: And apparently no one has seriously made the argument that these public employers are violating Question 1?

GRAHAM: No.

Q: Not even any conservative interest groups like the Georgia Christian Coalition?

GRAHAM: No.

Q: Why is that, do you think?

GRAHAM: That's a good question.

At the end of the day, I think the real motivation for the amendment was political. It was intended to facilitate Republican control of both the House and Senate in the state legislature, which they did. So the politics were about getting out the vote for the Republican Party, and securing a win for George W. Bush in his second term. I believe that was the true motive, more so than trying to disrupt families.

So in one sense, thank goodness for that.

It may also be that the thought hasn't occurred to them.

To be honest, although I'm happy to talk with you, as I'm sure everyone else in the Atlanta LGBT community is, frankly, there's a part of me that gets a little nervous bringing up this issue. I don't want anyone to give our opposition any ideas. "Oh my goodness, we can actually file lawsuits and overturn things?"

So we may have just been lucky.

My conversation with Debbie Seagraves, the executive director of the ACLU of Georgia, reinforced Jeff Graham's comments. After introducing Michigan's Super-DOMA implementation story, I asked Seagraves, "Why hasn't the same kind of judicial action happened in Georgia, in terms of test cases being brought against the City of Atlanta or Fulton County or whatever the circumstance may be?" In response, she raised a finger to her mouth and went, "*Sshhh,*" to halt the question. "I don't know. Maybe they just don't want a court case."

Next came Gregory Nevins, the supervising senior staff attorney of the southern regional office of Lambda Legal, a national LGBT legal, education, and advocacy organization:

NEVINS: Question 1 put a chill on the prospect for any broad-based domestic partnership legislation anywhere in Georgia. So it has the effect of taking some things off of the table.

But as a practical matter in a state that doesn't have any nondiscrimination laws or even hate-crimes prohibitions, I don't know how realistic it would have been to get any relationship rights off the ground in the first place.

Yet the really outlandish Super-DOMA enforcement effects have come to pass only in places like Michigan and Ohio.

Q: So Question 1 served mainly as a preemptive strike against future benefits?

NEVINS: Correct. I don't know the whole impetus of where the Michigan decision came from, but it's always been my thought that the full ugliness of these amendments hasn't appeared yet because the idea is to get as many of them passed as can be. Proponents don't want people thinking about what other negative effects might occur.

In Virginia, there was a long-standing attorney general's opinion that said same-sex couples weren't protected by domestic violence statutes. Then when the marriage amendment was proposed and people started talking about domestic violence issues in Ohio, the Virginia attorney general's opinion shifted 180 degrees. And all of a sudden, those couples were covered by it.

Q: I find it interesting that so many counties and municipalities here offer domestic-partner benefits to the same-sex partners of their employees.

In Michigan, as you know, the state supreme court in 2008 became the first one nationally to authoritatively interpret the meaning of a Super-DOMA as applied to same-sex couples. It ruled that the public employees of the state cannot receive benefits for their same-sex domestic partners.

So there's a disconnect here in Georgia in terms of the constitutional language and what's really happening on the ground across various local jurisdictions.

NEVINS: So far, I think there's a handy legal answer for that discrepancy. Georgia went through that cycle before 2004. There were two decisions by the Georgia Supreme Court, one in 1995, and the other in 1997, about Atlanta's ability to offer domestic-partner benefits.

So the concept of providing for one's dependents seems to been addressed by the Georgia Supreme Court. No further challenge has been launched since 2004.

Nevins was absolutely correct about *City of Atlanta v. McKinney* (1995) and *City of Atlanta v. Morgan* (1997), in which the Georgia Supreme Court ultimately adjudicated that Atlanta's Domestic Partnership Benefits Ordinance of 1996 was consistent with state law. Nonetheless, a highly motivated attorney like David Langdon, the author and protector of Ohio's Issue 1, could have made a compelling legal argument that, by authorizing the adoption of Georgia's Question 1, Peach State voters in 2004 intended to overturn any prior state-court precedent to the contrary. To be sure, amendments to the federal constitution for the purpose of overriding U.S. Supreme Court precedents have occurred. So why not at the state level as well?

At any rate, no sweeping high-court judgments like *National Pride at Work* came up in Georgia and the other Super-DOMA states. I think the key to understanding the variation in this state judicial landscape is the role of interest groups. As Gregory Nevins pointed out, "[T]he really outlandish Super-DOMA enforcement effects have come to pass only in places like Michigan and Ohio." And what common denominator did those two Midwestern states have that other jurisdictions did not? The answer: vigorous, well-funded private organizations with vested policy interests in protecting and implementing the Super-DOMAs they had struggled long and hard to place on the ballot and had catapulted to popular approval. This and other chapters chronicle the tenacity of Ohio's Citizens for Community Values in using Issue 1 in state court whenever possible. CCV's lead attorney, David Langdon, a highly experienced litigator,[10] was always available to invoke the Buckeye State's marriage amendment before the Ohio bench. A similar story of dogged enforcement of Proposal 2 by the American Family Association of Michigan and its Wolverine State legal affiliates could be recounted.

In contrast, the Super-DOMAs in Georgia, North Carolina, Texas, and Wisconsin were all referenda placed on the ballot by state legislatures. Thus, the authors and sponsors of Question 1, Amendment 1, Proposition 2, and Referendum 1 were state legislators primarily motivated by local politics and a desire to increase the turnout of conservative voters (Biggers 2014, 86–87). Accordingly, once their referenda passed on Election Day, lawmakers went on to address other matters on their political agendas and were not concerned

---

[10] A 2015 search of the LexisNexis legal database from 2004 onward revealed that David Langdon appeared as counsel of record in more than thirty Ohio state-court decisions. He did not represent Citizens for Community Values in all such cases, nor did those judicial rulings necessarily address Issue 1. Instead, this datum confirms Langdon's extensive experience as a litigator.

about enforcing their constitutional progeny in state court the way that the Michigan and Ohio amendment proponents were. The adage "out of sight, out of mind" pertained to Super-DOMA implementation in Georgia, North Carolina, Texas, and Wisconsin, whereas Proposal 2 and Issue 1 were always in the consciousness of their Michigan and Ohio interest-group guardians. Moreover, these citizen-initiative champions had the legal resources to seek judicial protection of their constitutional offspring.

CONCLUSION

Wisconsin's court of last resort was the only high bench to alleviate unambiguously the legal disabilities inflicted by Super-DOMAs, but only near the very end of America's war on same-sex couples and their families, when federal salvation from the state-law onslaught appeared manifestly on the horizon. In contrast, early in the country's campaign of hostility against LGBT communities, the Michigan Supreme Court strove mightily to exacerbate the constitutionally based deprivations levied on gay and lesbian pairs, despite clear and convincing evidence that most Michiganders did not intend such a harsh result. No other state supreme courts, however, took decisive measures one way or the other.

When state intermediate appellate courts acted, most of their decisions failed as well to ease the heavy legal burdens placed on the shoulders of same-sex couples. Typically, only judges who owed political allegiance to local bastions of social tolerance, such as in the Austin branch of the Texas Court of Appeals or the Franklin County trial courts in Ohio, offered any legal respite to lesbian and gay families.

In short, in contrast to *Gay Rights and American Law*'s findings for the last two decades of the twentieth century, the judicial officials who followed and were selected in large measure by the same local forces that chose state lawmakers were generally no more disposed to treat beleaguered sexual minorities with compassion than the proponents who put Super-DOMAs on the books in the first place.[11]

---

[11] See also Hume (2013) and Lewis, Wood, and Jacobsmeier (2014).

3

The Effects of Super-DOMAs on Same-Sex Couples

This chapter is a comprehensive survey of the legal, economic, social, and psychological effects that Super-DOMAs had on gay and lesbian couples across the six states in the study. The next chapter expands the investigation into issues involving the parenting and care of children in such families.

Atlanta attorney Douglas L. Brooks surmised the meta-impacts of the anti-gay constitutional amendments.

Question 1 means everything. And it means nothing.

Georgia's referendum was political action inspired exclusively by animus toward, and fear of, gay people. It's intended to keep us in our place.

On the other hand, from a legal perspective, the amendment accomplished nothing more than a codification of what existed by statute and case law at the time it was passed. I don't think anything here has happened or not happened by virtue of Question 1, at least not in a legal sense.

The couples I spoke with similarly acknowledged that the adoption of Super-DOMAs typically took away no legal rights they already possessed. In Georgia, Michigan, North Carolina, Ohio, Texas, and Wisconsin, gay and lesbian pairs had no statewide rights to marry or enter into civil unions or domestic partnerships before passage of the ballot measures that enshrined those prohibitions in constitutions. Thus, as a technical legal matter, the initiatives and referenda were nothing more than surplusage.

Nonetheless, the very public and often acrimonious political campaigns that preceded the adoption of Super-DOMAs exacted emotional and psychological tolls that were enduring, manifold, and widespread. Campaign media barrages minimally cost hundreds of thousands of dollars, whereas budgets in more populous states capped in the millions. In America's war on same-sex couples, all of that cumulative messaging had profound effects on those pairs.

THE INITIAL SHOCK: PERSONAL DEVASTATION AND ISOLATION

I visited North Carolina in July 2012, just two months after the passage of its constitutional amendment. So the immediate consequences of the political campaign were still vivid, having little opportunity to fade with time.

A lesbian University of North Carolina graduate student reported one way in which the fight leading up to the May 8 vote had affected her:

I live in a working-class, mixed-race vicinity of Durham. There were a lot of African American churches organizing against Amendment 1, and there were some having posters in favor of the amendment. I saw them when I went running in my neighborhood.

Those signs triggered a sense of self-protectiveness, that I had to be careful because somebody might want to hurt me. So the public markers made the event more stark. "Oh, inside that church I'm running by right now, there are people who are more likely to want to hurt me."

Whereas threats to well-being had been diffuse in the past, the Amendment 1 political experience made the menace more immediate and known. Where the risks, as well as the welcomes, were became clear and identifiable in my own neighborhood.

A second Durham lesbian offered another example of the impact the referendum's passage had on gay North Carolinians, even before the ballot measure went into effect on January 1, 2013:

Q: What did the passage of Amendment 1 mean to you in the broadest sense of the word?

A: Just your asking that question makes me tear up. It was devastating, absolutely devastating.

On election night, and the next morning, and really since then, I've felt overwhelmed by my state's betrayal of its LGBT citizens. Even though I know I'm valuable, I still feel devalued. The citizens of our state who voted for the referendum were somehow able to reconcile in their minds a worldview in which, because we're gay or lesbian, we're not as equally entitled to rights as they are. That is fairly incomprehensible to me.

That someone would be able to feel comfortable and resolved about seeing other human beings who are in relationships with people of the same sex as subhuman, and less entitled than they are to the same rights and privileges of citizenship.... We've failed somewhere as a society in terms of how we're raising our children and teaching people what it means to be human and members of the world.

I went into work the morning after the vote, and we started our unit meeting. No one acknowledged the passage of Amendment 1. It was like coming in with a major death, like losing a dear, close, loved family member, and people not saying anything to you.

Even when people did acknowledge it later, the event was so personally devastating to me and my family that I had to walk away from a couple of those conversations. Although I knew what they were saying was heartfelt, it was like someone who had never lost a loved one, after I just had, saying, "It's so hard to lose your mom." "But you really don't know. I'm grieving and can't hear you say that right now."

I wanted their support, but was almost beyond words. I could talk about it with other queer friends who felt similarly. But for a while, I really couldn't talk to straight friends.

And I didn't blame them. I knew they were very supportive. It just felt that profound, and still is. It's hard to do something with the depth of those feelings, and not feel isolated.

Although my conversations with North Carolinians were the closest in time in any state to the passage of its Super-DOMA, interviewees in other states also had vivid memories of how deeply and intimately affronted they were by the plebiscites against their legal and social interests.[1] Time and again, I heard stories about how, right after a Super-DOMA election, queer folk wondered, "Did my father/mother/brother/sister/neighbor/friend/co-worker vote against me?"

"When Issue 1 passed," Lee (introduced in Chapter 1) recalled, "there was a depression that just swept over Ohio. Gay people were so hurt their neighbors voted that way." Added Helen, "There was a sense of hopelessness. Just bleak despair."

Michelle and Sharon, both age forty-nine, live in Milwaukee and described the initial blow:

Q: What did the passage of the 2006 referendum mean to you in the broadest sense of the word?

MICHELLE: We'd both been very involved fighting the ballot measure, making phone calls, organizing fundraisers. We donated money we couldn't afford to give. We telephoned areas where people were so mean to us I couldn't even believe it.

But I still held on to an optimistic view that Wisconsin would do the right thing. So when Referendum 1 passed with such a landslide [59 percent], I cried for four days straight.

SHARON: It was really, really hard on her.

I'm from Michigan. So I'd already gone through the trauma in 2004 of feeling that your own people stabbed you in the back. I grew up in a part of Michigan that's really conservative. So the outcome there didn't surprise me as much.

But it hit Michelle harder, because Wisconsin had a tradition of being so progressive, and she had a hopeful, optimistic view of fellow Wisconsinites.

MICHELLE: I really felt like my state had broken up with me. That's what it seemed like. I'd been dumped in such a cruel way.

My family was supportive all the way through. But I don't think even they really understood how devastated I was. They just didn't get it. Some of my siblings were like, "Can we not talk about politics?"

---

[1] See also Maisel and Fingerhut (2011).

Q: Did the passage of Referendum 1 affect your senses of security or well-being in any way?

MICHELLE: Yes. I've always been a little cautious going out to rural areas, like western Waukesha County, where my mom lives and you see lots of ignorant signs. So the referendum made me very alert to the fact there were more of those people than what I'd thought.

SHARON: I saw the referendum as a means to get people to the polls who otherwise wouldn't vote. Legislators and other powerful politicians don't really care one way or another about whether we get married. They just use these devices to get ignorant, fearful people out to vote. That's the ultimate reason why such things happen. So I don't feel as much that it's a personal attack.

But I am scared to death of rural areas, where both of our parents live. In Milwaukee, we're completely out as lesbians. But when we go up there, we feel so conspicuous just walking around.

MICHELLE: People stare at us.

I think the conservative ads, and the talk radio, and the way that gays and lesbians were presented in the campaign got everyone fired up into a mob mentality. So the public hysteria made me nervous. I thought, "My God. Things could really get worse than what they are."

Referendum 1 caused me to worry that the future could be grim.

SHARON: I remember when these referenda first started happening, in Colorado and Oregon, back in the 1990s. Before those events, queer folk used to be able to go into public places, and people just wouldn't notice us. We could stop at gas stations and get snacks, or drop into little diners, and for the most part, people were friendly and didn't care who we were.

But after all those referenda occurred, I took a drive out West. And it was remarkable, particularly in Oregon,[2] how different it had become to venture into public spaces in rural settings.

All of these folks for whom I'd never before been on their radar had learned they were supposed to hate me. They were told to do so on television.

So when that fire gets stoked again and again to scare people to the polls, attitudes against us change for the worse, and that's especially true with older people.

POSITIVE EFFECTS

Although most outcomes of Super-DOMAs that gay and lesbian pairs reported across six states were deleterious, there were some notably positive consequences for the LGBT community from the passage of these constitutional amendments. Most prominently, the blatant electoral losses prompted lesbians and gay men to organize politically in a manner that had never occurred before. In the Buckeye State, for example, Equality Ohio emerged like a phoenix from the ashes of the November 2004 defeat and became a statewide political interest group with full-time paid staff and an annual budget in the hundreds of

[2] Between 1988 and 2004, Oregon had five statewide initiatives and in excess of twenty-five local ones directed at gay and lesbian rights, more than any state in the nation (Pinello 2006, 103).

thousands of dollars. The days of solely relying on the happenstance organizational efforts of self-motivated same-sex couples like Helen and Lee of Columbus were over. Instead, time-honored twentieth-century political lobbying and influencing techniques finally surfaced statewide in LGBT communities.

In addition to such overt political organizing, the initiatives and referenda motivated countless lesbian and gay Americans to be much more radically out on a personal level as members of a sexual minority.[3] Numerous interviewees reported the multifaceted measures, large and small, they took to increase their visibility among family, friends, co-workers, and acquaintances. So after the initial dismay, the ultimate response of same-sex pairs often was to steel themselves for more open lives as proudly lesbian and gay citizens of their state, as a twenty-eight-year-old journalist in Winston-Salem, North Carolina, proclaimed:

Ever since Amendment 1 passed, it's become my duty to be perceptibly gay, simply because some people feel they can vote us out of their state, that they can legislate us out of existence.

Well, guess what. I'm not going anywhere. I'll still be a lesbian who shows up at church on Sunday in a dress. It's just happening that way.

For me, Amendment 1's lesson was about being more visible. Although I won't have a rainbow-colored label pasted across my forehead shouting, "Big Fat Dyke," I will be, short of such a banner, as conspicuous as possible.

Brett, age fifty-one, and Lloyd, forty-five, who had been together for twenty years, provided another especially vivid instance of this phenomenon:

BRETT: Issue 1 really did change our lives in ways I wasn't anticipating. At the time [in 2004], even Ohio's Republican governor [Bob Taft] was saying, "Don't vote for this constitutional amendment." So I was very surprised when it then passed. My first reaction was just abject shock. I couldn't believe it.

Yet the real result for me – and I think for both of us – is that Issue 1 politicized me in a way I hadn't been prior to that point. Obviously, for a gay man of my age, I've lived through an awful lot of horror in the gay history of the United States. So I've always felt somewhat political. But this particular moment really galvanized me in a way that nothing else had.

---

[3] See Lannutti (2011). Bellafante (2006) reported how the passage of the 2005 Kansas Super-DOMA galvanized LGBT Kansans to come out of the closet in large numbers (cf. Zernike 2004).

   Indeed, LGBT Americans in droves took to heart the prophetic admonition posted on Andrew Sullivan's blog the day after the 2004 national elections:

STAND TALL: ...Being gay is a blessing. The minute we let [heterosexual] fear and ignorance enter into our own souls, we lose. We have gained too much and come through too much to let ourselves be defined by others. We must turn hurt back into pride. Cheap, easy victories based on untruth and fear and cynicism are pyrrhic ones. In time, they will fall. So hold your heads up high. Do not give in to despair. Do not let the Republican party rob you of your hopes. This is America. Equality will win in the end. (Sullivan 2004)

As a result, a number of things happened. A few months after Issue 1 passed, we made an appointment with an attorney, which we'd never done before. We made sure that all of our legal affairs were spelled out and resolved in documents.

LLOYD: Any document that we could legally do, we did.

BRETT: We did them all. Part of that was because, of course, our standing as second-class citizens became really obvious to us on Election Day in 2004. But I also think there were some personal issues.... A lot of Lloyd's family lives in Ohio....

LLOYD: And I'll speak to that.

BRETT: There was some real tension with blood relatives.... So we both went, "Wow. Maybe we had better take care of this, to make sure that it's all documented in the way we want it to be."

Then, we decided to get married, which for me was truly a political act. Of course, there are many good reasons to wed. But it was primarily a political statement on my part. Because I'd never really given a lot of thought to marriage prior to 2004. Yet Issue 1 certainly upped the ante. All of a sudden, marriage became mighty important to me. I felt like, "By God, if they're going to take this right away from me so publicly, then I'm going to fight for it." And I have to say now, having been married for four years, I still, politically speaking, harbor a certain ambivalence about it. Gay men of my generation weren't fighting for inclusion into a heteronormative construct. Rather, we were saying, "To hell with you. We don't want to be part of your oppressive institutions."

But the moment that the right was absolutely taken away from me, I was like, "Oh yeah! I'm going to do it." So I definitely think Issue 1 made getting married a much more urgent matter.

LLOYD: One of the reasons marriage was important to me is that it was a way to bring my family, my immediate blood relatives, to the idea that my getting married wasn't something "other," that it wasn't strange. I come from a large family, with nine children. And I was the last to be married. Some of them have had several marriages, either through divorce or death. And my family splits on how they view it all. Certainly, my initial coming out to them as a gay man brought a whole worldview they'd never had before. Then the next evolutionary step with my family was the idea of Brett and me actually getting married. And its being a legal event, just as they've had.

Now I have family over several states. But I have two brothers and a sister who live here in Ohio. Prior to Election Day in 2004, I emailed them to encourage votes against Issue 1. "If you support me in any way.... You know me. You know my life together with Brett. This amendment will have a directly negative impact on us." One sibling said that she'd vote for it, because she thought marriage should be limited to one man and one woman. But she hoped this wouldn't cause the family to fracture. She asked me to respect that and not to fight.

BRETT: The rationalization for her position was, "I'm a conservative, and you know how I'm going to vote."

LLOYD: It wasn't based on religious belief, but politics. So on a personal level, her rejection just shocked me.

Then, when Brett and I decided to get married in Canada, we wanted to have a celebration here in Ohio, to which we invited friends and family. I didn't intend to send an invitation to that sister. But she wanted to come. Brett said, "Let's think about your family more carefully. If you extend invitations to them, then the ball's in their court. And they have to make the decision. And if they come, maybe they'll see the friends and family who support us, with no qualms at all about it. And maybe that experience will sow a seed." My father was one of those people, as well as my other brother, who's a born-again Christian, and this sister here in Ohio. So they were all extended invitations, and two of the three showed up.

But who knows? Who knows? They certainly saw many people giving us a lot of support. So the sister was here. I don't know how she would vote on Issue 1 today, if it were on the ballot. That would be an interesting question.

BRETT: I feel like I gained something from the passage of Issue 1 that has nothing to do with either physical or fiscal sorts of benefits. Because the older I get, the more convinced I become that my status as "other" is my greatest strength. Every time I'm forced to recognize that the majority culture doesn't view me as their equal – or doesn't recognize a right of entitlement – I think it makes me a stronger person. I become more determined to be myself. Honestly.

So although there's not been a direct, tangible loss of any kind for us, I do feel I've attained a certain lucidity about my own sense of self as a gay man in the culture. If indeed the intention of Issue 1's sponsors was to prevent me from having the life that people around me might have, then the plan backfired. Because I benefited from it with a strength and clarity that I otherwise wouldn't have had.

Moreover, some couples I spoke with did not necessarily condemn the motivations of the voters who approved of Super-DOMAs. Angela, age thirty-two, is a minister who lives in a rural community outside of Cleveland with her partner of eight years and infant son Tucker. She told me,

There's a general sense within Ohio's LGBT community that neighbors and friends betrayed people they know and love by voting for Issue 1. And I wonder whether that perception's accurate.

We've had numerous conversations with people like our own neighbors. We have this really nice straight couple who've lived in the house behind ours for twenty-five years. They're like fifty-five or sixty, and raised their son here. We trade plants back and forth every year. Remember, we live in the country. They're wonderful people, and think of us as friends.

We were talking to them, when I was pregnant, about the fact that Jessica and I cannot both be legal parents to Tucker, and they were appalled. It never crossed their minds that Issue 1 would result in that kind of outcome. It never occurred to them that that was even a possibility.

So I think there was a lot of ignorance in 2004. I don't believe people were out to get anyone. They just didn't know better. They didn't realize these kinds of outcomes were on the horizon. It's not because they weren't decent, good people. They didn't appreciate who was going to get hurt.

Like Brett and Lloyd, most couples I met could not identify specific, concrete sacrifices they sustained from the addition of the initiatives and referenda to state constitutions, if only, again, because those political events simply did not change their marital status as a legal matter. Instead, Super-DOMAs just cemented their unmarried state. If one partner did not already benefit from the health insurance the other received from an employer, that loss continued. And if a couple indeed had the good fortune to enjoy such joint coverage, it also endured after the popular votes. Whatever their position, the status quo persisted as a general rule.

SUPER-DOMAS AS IMPEDIMENTS TO CHANGE

Nonetheless, the constitutional amendments constituted enormous preemptive strikes against future improvements in the circumstances of gay and lesbian couples and their families. Michigan's Proposal 2, for example, scuttled the introduction of domestic-partnership provisions into statewide collective bargaining agreements. At the time of the Super-DOMA's passage, major state employee unions had negotiated new contracts that included provisions for partnership benefits for same-sex couples. Shortly after November 2004, however, Democratic governor Jennifer Granholm initiated a moratorium on such benefits ("Gay state workers in Michigan lose DP benefits" 2004); this stoppage was ultimately ratified in the *National Pride at Work* decision.

Likewise, Referendum 1 created problems for Wisconsin public-sector unions, as Eric, a thirty-two-year-old higher education administrator, and Scott, a thirty-three-year-old school teacher, who live in Appleton, explained.

ERIC: Since my job offers domestic-partner benefits, I've registered Scott as my partner at work.

Conversely, he hasn't listed me with his union, the Wisconsin Education Association Council, because they don't support domestic partners. And that's unfortunate, since Scott's insurance is better than mine.

Referendum 1 is blocking the union's action.

SCOTT: There are a lot of LGBT union members. Yet they can't include their own families on their insurance coverage or in their retirement plans.

ERIC: But when my father died, Scott's principal let him out on a family leave. Although technically, he didn't have to do that, because according to the union, we aren't partners.

Q: The union leadership has said the constitutional amendment prevents them from making those opportunities available?

SCOTT: It's too much of a political hot potato. The bottom line is that extending benefits can't happen right now [July 2011].

When [Democrat Jim] Doyle was governor, the lid was starting to open. Some school districts thought about including LGBT people for domestic partnerships.

But the state's movement from one end of the political spectrum to the other in recent years nixed any improvements.

Q: So there's no public school district in Wisconsin providing domestic-partner benefits?

SCOTT: Madison may be the only one, although I don't know for sure even there. That's as far as we're aware right now.

ERIC: The constitutional amendment is a huge obstacle to progress.

As Super-DOMA proponents such as Phil Burress intended, their constitutional progeny made state government, and even the private sector, think twice about instituting change. What is more, the post-amendment-adoption strategy of interest-group sponsors like Citizens for Community Values was to sue or otherwise threaten legal action against public entities that might shift their attitudes in favor of same-sex pairs.

For example, in Ohio in 2005, former state representative Thomas E. Brinkman Jr., a Republican from Cincinnati and a Phil Burress confidant, sued Miami University, a public institution in Oxford, Ohio, near Cincinnati, because it began offering health insurance and other benefits to the same-sex partners of faculty and staff members in July 2004. Brinkman's lawsuit claimed that such action "created and recognized a legal status for relationships of unmarried individuals that intends to approximate the design, qualities, significance or effect of marriage" in violation of Issue 1.

Although Ohio courts ultimately dismissed the litigation, holding that Brinkman himself did not have sufficient legal standing to bring it (*Brinkman* v. *Miami University* 2007), the larger, enduring message was clear: "If government entities do anything to violate Issue 1, they'll be sued. So be prepared to defend any such change in court."

Likewise, when the city of Cleveland created a domestic-partner registry for same-sex couples in 2009 – where such pairs' signing up was entirely symbolic, producing absolutely no tangible benefits for them – CCV's ally, the Alliance Defense Fund, in August of the same year filed suit against Cleveland, arguing that the City Council's action breached the state constitution. Although the case again was eventually dismissed (*Cleveland Taxpayers* v. *Cleveland* 2010), the suit reinforced the *Brinkman* v. *Miami University* implication: "We'll confront each and every government shift away from Issue 1. Be sure to hesitate while pondering any such act carefully."

As Phil Burress said to me in June 2010,

BURRESS: Obviously, Issue 1 has had a major impact. Because there's not one City Council or anyone else that did the things they were doing prior to 2004. The state constitutional amendment trumps anything a City Council can do. So the Cincinnati City Council has never gone back to revisit the issue since 1992. If any government agency tries to use taxpayers' money to give people marriage benefits when they're not married, that violates our constitution now.

You know, we've been studying these people for twelve years, the people behind the homosexual agenda, behind the activism. It's a step-by-step incremental thing to get where they want to go. Because then if you have a registry, and you leave that in place for five years, or something like that, you go to court, and they say, "We've had the registry for five years and nobody complained."

Q: So it has to be nipped in the bud?

BURRESS: When they're trying to emulate marriage, yeah.

Evidence of Issue 1's deterrent effect appeared repeatedly throughout the thirty-seven Ohio interviews. The most comprehensive statement came from Sue Doerfer, who succeeded Lynne Bowman as executive director of Equality Ohio.

Ohio has no protection against sexual-orientation discrimination in employment, housing or public accommodations. So the political environment here hasn't been very supportive of LGBT employees.

In Cuyahoga County [in which Cleveland is located], we tried working with the county commissioners to pass sexual-orientation nondiscrimination laws, especially an ordinance involving employment protection, not just for county workers, but for all employees in the county. What the commissioners said to us in reply, however, was, "We can't do this because of Issue 1."

In other words, lots of employers have used the constitutional amendment as a reason for not being able to offer benefits. Sometimes that's legitimate, and sometimes it's not. Too frequently, it's just an easy out. Also, under Ohio's last [Republican] administration, the attorney general rendered a formal opinion saying that no government subdivision could offer domestic-partner benefits because of Issue 1. Now our current [Democratic] attorney general has issued a different opinion. But too many people still rely on the old view.

So I think Issue 1 definitely short-circuited the collective-bargaining process for LGBT union members and prevented other businesses from offering benefits that might have been forthcoming by now. Sadly, the constitutional amendment sent an unambiguous message that both government and the private sector didn't need to be fair to LGBT people in Ohio. And if an LGBT employee were to challenge that posture, employers could always fall back on Issue 1 for cover.

Nearly every lesbian and gay couple I spoke with in the Buckeye State was familiar with the Brinkman and Cleveland lawsuits and their preemptive value. Again and again, interviewees volunteered information about the litigation because the court cases were common knowledge, saturating everyone's awareness. CCV's enforcement strategy was well known and effective.

For instance, someone who works for the Columbus public schools told me this story:

Issue 1 created an overarching legal barrier to reform. So whenever there's been discussion, in our union or elsewhere, about domestic-partner benefits, the debate has always returned to, "Well, we're going to have to check this out with our attorneys, because of Issue 1."

Once the Columbus school system finally agreed in principle to provide health care benefits to the same-sex partners of its employees, we decided to test the mechanism that was created to administer the improvement, because we coordinate the LGBT teachers' caucus for the Columbus Education Association. So we went down to see how it played out, and it wasn't fun.

Initially, nobody knew about the new benefits arrangement, and some of the people were downright rude. Then they said we had to have certain kinds of forms. But since we'd been directly involved in the bargaining, we knew what had been intended. And the documents that were being demanded of applicants weren't what had been in mind during the negotiations.

So there had to be another round of bargaining. And the matter went back again to the attorneys, to check the new outcome against Issue 1. It was just bizarre.

Helen and Lee offered a far more blunt opinion of Issue 1's preemptive effect:

Q: What if one of you were incapacitated and couldn't make health care decisions for yourself?

LEE: Well, we have health care powers of attorney for that situation.
HELEN: So long as David Langdon didn't catch whiff of it, we'd be okay.
LEE: Because CCV is *mean*.
HELEN: They look for fights. They look for exactly that kind of thing, to make a case out of. And the supreme court in Ohio isn't leaning toward us.

HEALTH CARE

Unequivocal disabilities did occur nationwide with regard to the provision of health care to same-sex couples in Super-DOMA jurisdictions. Such impediments to families' medical well-being were often the most conspicuous handicaps arising from the anitgay initiatives and referenda.

Denial of Domestic-Partner Health Insurance

As discussed earlier, one of the first varieties of fallout from these constitutional amendments was the denial of health insurance to the same-sex partners of public employees.[4] Couples I spoke with around the country said the minimum out-of-pocket cost for privately procured health insurance was $400 per month. For some pairs, that expense required their choosing between a partner's either having health insurance or a car to drive, but not both.

Another aspect of such insurance denials that was not as widely understood is that the health benefit was unavailable not only during active employment but also in retirement, as recounted by Cheryl, age sixty-six, and Mildred, seventy, together for twenty-three years.

MILDRED: I worked for a Michigan county, and the health insurance from my job covered Cheryl while I remained an employee. Fortunately, we had a county director who was very understanding. He changed the qualifications for health-insurance coverage, putting in place that another adult living with a county employee for a period of years would be included.
CHERYL: The University of Michigan did something similar.
MILDRED: So I was really grateful that Cheryl was covered while I worked.

---

[4] Gossett (2009) provides a comprehensive overview of legal challenges to local domestic-partner-benefit programs.

But if we'd been able to marry, Cheryl could've also gotten medical insurance when I retired. Yet she didn't get that as a result of Proposal 2, although legally married spouses benefit that way from retirement packages in the state.

Q: So what do the two of you do now?

CHERYL: We're both on Medicare and have our own separate supplements.

MILDRED: I have Blue Cross and Blue Shield, and Cheryl has a plan she has to pay for. She missed out on the complimentary Blue Cross and Blue Shield from my retirement program.

CHERYL: Retirement coverage would've affected just eleven couples in the county.

MILDRED: It was such a small group.

CHERYL: And leadership voted against it.

MILDRED: The county couldn't justify the retirement part because of Proposal 2.

Q: [to Mildred:] So the Michigan amendment removed the option for Cheryl's health-insurance coverage once you retired?

MILDRED: Yes. Exactly.

Some private-sector employers were willing to extend benefits to the same-sex partners of their employees. Yet Super-DOMAs even potentially barred them from doing so, as Barbara E. Katz, an Atlanta attorney who specializes in helping gay and lesbians families protect themselves, explained:

I've had clients contact me to say their employer would give them health benefits for both parties if they could do a civil union or register for a domestic partnership. In other words, the pair didn't have to be married to get workplace benefits, but there had to be some document proving their relationship. And it couldn't just be a partnership agreement between the two. Rather, it had to have some force of law.

But there's no place to do that here in Georgia.

With some research, I discovered there are a couple of states, including Oregon, that will let couples register as domestic partners, even if they're not resident there. People can download forms online, send them in, and not have to be there in person. So I was able to get these clients a legal document by which they both could get health benefits.

Yet that circumstance is one in particular that Question 1 made harder. Because if it were just marriage that was prohibited, I know Fulton and DeKalb Counties, and the City of Atlanta would be allowing couples to register easily for civil unions or domestic partnerships right now.

Other attempts to make the same-sex partners of employees eligible for company benefits were not resolved favorably. A forty-year-old graphic designer at a regional planning organization in Atlanta reported on his experience:

We had a wide-ranging discussion of creating domestic-partner benefits at my office. Among the six people in leadership, two voted in favor of the move, while four said no.

Apparently there'd be no cost increase, except for the number of people covered. Yet some co-workers were like, "Why do we want to open ourselves up to more risk by increasing the number in the pool?"

We have some morbidly obese people in our office. If the organization is so concerned about cost and risk, why doesn't it consider them as an added hazard? Or why don't they ask everyone they're about to hire, "Tell us about the health of your family?" Sometimes the marriage amendment gives people cover to be discriminatory.

Hospital Denials of the Authority of Same-Sex Partners and of Their Visitation

An additional index of Proposal 2's impact in Michigan is how hospitals treated patients' same-sex partners after its passage. In a 2009 national survey, the Gay and Lesbian Medical Association sent questionnaires to every hospital in the Wolverine State inquiring about six measures of nondiscrimination involving LGBT patients (Healthcare Equality Index 2009). All nineteen institutions replying to the survey indicated that their visitation policies allowed lesbian and gay partners the same visitation access to patients as opposite-sex spouses and next of kin. However, seventeen of the responding facilities were located in or near Ann Arbor, home of the University of Michigan and the most socially progressive area in the state. Not one hospital in any of Michigan's six largest cities (Detroit, Grand Rapids, Warren, Flint, Lansing, and Sterling Heights) answered the questionnaire. This result confirmed what Wolverine State same-sex pairs repeatedly told me in the 2009 interviews: They would be afraid to be hospitalized anywhere in Michigan except Ann Arbor.

Lorie L. Burch, a Dallas attorney who specializes in helping same-sex couples draw up legal documents to protect their relationships and families, reported her own experience with a local Texas hospital:

My wife had to have surgery, and while she was under anesthesia, the doctor came in, when my in-laws were waiting with me. He'd found a mole he wanted to biopsy and needed permission to do so.

The doctor understood my relationship to the patient and knew I had her power of attorney. But he really didn't look at me to ask whether he should biopsy the mole.

Luckily, the in-laws nodded in my direction and allowed me to make the choice.

Yet if they'd wanted to make the decision themselves, or otherwise were inclined to cause problems for me, how successful would they have been? I can't tell you, because I don't know. It's a crapshoot.

A licensed professional counselor who worked in Georgia hospitals provided an insider perspective on the provision of health care to same-sex couples in the Peach State:

Q: You've worked in local hospitals. If someone wanted to visit a same-sex partner who was a patient, would she or he, be permitted to do so?

A: I was employed at a state psychiatric hospital. I did have some folks on the unit who were gay or lesbian. There was a woman who had a partner who was regularly admitted, and they did allow visitation by the partner. But even friends can come in and visit.

In terms of medical care, however, I'd say no. If I were admitted, they wouldn't allow my partner to come in and say, "These medications aren't good for her. Let's try something else." Absolutely not in that environment.

Yet if someone ended up in the Emory Healthcare system, there'd be a much better likelihood of such respect.

But where I worked, staff who clearly were in same-sex relationships themselves weren't even out of the closet on the job. There was a gay psychologist, and a woman on the unit who was clearly struggling with domestic violence in her same-sex relationship. But he wouldn't help her. So I did.

In my current position, I handle records every day from state-run behavioral health service institutions. I recently saw one document that said, "Resident was involved in inappropriate same-sex relationships." And this was under clinical information, where they'd put "engaging in self-harm" or depression. I delete that information when transferring data to my own records. I'm not going anywhere near that.

Q: What if your partner had an accident and were hospitalized and weren't alert enough to make medical decisions for herself? Would you be permitted in the local hospital to do that?

A: Probably not. But she has blood relatives here who'd turn to me and say, "Do you know what she'd want?" I think they'd follow what I'd tell them.

But if something happened to me, I'd be totally screwed. Because there's nobody here to advocate on my behalf other than her.

Q: Let's say you had health care powers of attorney and other legal documents in order. Would you feel confident that those papers would be honored when needed?

A: I think it would be a crapshoot, depending on where we ended up. If it were at a hospital in the Atlanta midtown area, say Emory or Piedmont, we'd have a much better chance of the paperwork being honored. The physicians and staff there are probably more sophisticated and better educated.

At Grady, no. They're too busy to care about anything. If we ended up at a facility in the Georgia mountains, absolutely not. And in rural areas like Valdosta or Tifton, forget about it.

Although many couples apprehended the precarious status of their legal documents, they nonetheless clutched onto such paperwork. Barbara, age forty-nine, and Jane, sixty-four, a Columbus couple raising two teenage boys, explained their worries surrounding health care, because Jane has a serious medical condition:

BARBARA: How many people going to hospitals and other health care facilities have to make sure they bring the proper file of legal paperwork with them? How many couples must be certain they have their wills with them for surgery?

JANE: We heard the story of what happened to the lesbian couple in Miami.

BARBARA: The worry leading up to health care episodes is draining, because of what's happened to same-sex pairs elsewhere, and because Ohio law wouldn't support us if there were a challenge to our relationship. So that fear greatly increases the stress of medical procedures that are nerve-racking to begin with.

We have medical powers of attorney. But I don't know whether they'd be honored. The women in Florida had paperwork, and they were denied access to each other.

JANE: We've done everything we can. But we don't know if that's enough. And it's a *huge* worry. Just terrible.

BARBARA: Knowing that the law is not on our side, even with the legal documents we've been able to cobble together to cover health care issues.... The fear is always there.

JANE: It's *always* there.

BARBARA: I carry the medical powers of attorney in the glove box of my car in case we're in an accident. So the paperwork's always there. It lives in the car. *Who else* has to worry about that kind of thing?

JANE: So in the glove box are road maps, a foldable cup if we need water, and our legal documents.

In their forties and vigorous at the time of interview, Rachel and Veronica fretted about what would happen to them when they would be older and more fragile:

RACHEL: Since we don't have kids to take care of us in later life, I worry about whether we might be stuck in a nursing home in single rooms or even in entirely different institutions. Are we going to be taken away from each other?[5] After all, with Issue 1, we can never be a married couple who could fight to be in the same room.

Those things scare me. I don't want to be separated from the person I love.

VERONICA: News reports suggest such failures to honor gay relationships happen often.

RACHEL: What special precautions can we perform now to make sure our aging and end-of-life care occur in a way that's respectful to us?

VERONICA: When I saw *If These Walls Could Talk* 2, I cried like a baby over the scene where the woman died alone while her partner waited in the lobby. I thought something like that could happen so easily.

RACHEL: It does still happen now.

VERONICA: And the deceased partner's biological family came in and took all their possessions away. They nullified everything that the couple created together. It's like the women's lives were erased. All gone!

Indeed, similar apprehensions over variations in health care provision came up everywhere I visited. As the interview protocol in Appendix B reveals, I asked whether couples had legal papers to protect their relationships. Fully 80 percent told me they had executed complete sets of documents between themselves to approximate the legal status of marriage: wills, living wills, durable powers of

---

[5] See Kendall (2010).

attorney, health care proxies, hospital visitation authorizations, and so on. Most couples who had not secured these legal arrangements either were together just a short time or could not afford the legal fees to obtain them.[6]

Among the pairs who did have all the legal documents, only 32 percent felt fully confident that the papers would be honored wherever and whenever needed. However, most of the roughly two-thirds who lacked such absolute confidence did believe that hospitals and other care providers in their immediate neighborhoods would reliably abide by visitation authorizations and medical powers of attorney between same-sex couples. Their primary wariness involved institutions elsewhere in the state, especially those in rural areas or those that were religiously affiliated.

Surprisingly, Equality Ohio executive director Sue Doerfer supplied – from her own personal experience – one of the most alarming examples of what happened within the Buckeye State LGBT community as a result of the popular vote in favor of Issue 1:

Some Ohio hospitals have adopted policies whereby they say they don't discriminate against LGBT folks. These institutions permit hospital visitation by same-sex partners and even allow them to make medical-care decisions for incapacitated patients, as long as the appropriate legal paperwork is in place.

But other hospitals don't have such policies. And I've heard horror story upon horror story about people who.... Well, it actually happened to me.

The year after Issue 1 passed [2005], I received a telephone call at work from the office of our family doctor. "Your partner's here, and something's really wrong. She may be having a stroke. You need to come by right now." I left immediately for the doctor's office, where I met and followed the ambulance taking my partner to a local Cleveland hospital. At the entrance to the emergency room, the admissions officer asked me what my relationship to the patient was. "I'm her partner!" I blurted out. I was terrified. It never occurred to me to lie about who I was. "Sorry," the admissions officer said, "You're not the patient's next of kin or other relative. So you can't go in."

Panic stricken, I pulled out my cell phone to call a friend who worked at the hospital to see if she could help. But the ER has a rule against the use of cell phones, and hospital security guards escorted me out of the building.

Fortunately, the ambulance driver who drove my partner to the hospital took pity on me and snuck me into the ER through the ambulance bay. Once inside, everything was all right. No one in the ER itself asked me who I was. But if they had, I'd have said, "I'm her sister." And my partner didn't have a stroke after all. Just a very bad migraine headache.

I hear stories like mine all the time. Unfortunately, they don't always have happy endings, like when someone is dying, and their partner is kept from them. I know of people who've died alone because their partners were blocked from seeing them.

Sometimes, the biological families of patients come in and take over the medical decision-making process. It's up to each hospital, and the personnel in each institution, how to apply the rules, if there are any.

---

[6] See Riggle, Rostosky, and Prather (2006).

The hospital where I was denied access in fact had a nondiscrimination policy. But this particular admissions officer either didn't know about the policy or didn't agree with it, and decided that I couldn't go back there.

Issue 1 legitimized discrimination. It said that our families aren't as valuable or legitimate as those of opposite-sex couples. Therefore, everybody gets to decide on their own whether they're going to recognize our family relationships. Gay people must trust others to be decent more than we should have to.

And especially in hospitals, which can be such stressful and emotional environments. We don't always think clearly there, and our defense mechanisms may be down. So if I'd had the presence of mind in my own situation, I could've said that I was her sister. But of course, that didn't occur to me at the time. And even if I'd lied, if her biological family had shown up, I'd have been thrown out anyway. Because they would've come in and said, "Who's that? She's not her sister." And I would've been out the door.

Doerfer's story is especially noteworthy because, before becoming Equality Ohio's executive director, she served in the same capacity for the LGBT Community Center of Greater Cleveland from 2004 to 2009. Accordingly, Doerfer was one of the most visible and politically active gay people in northeast Ohio at the time. So if the refusal of access to a partner in an emergency room befell someone like Doerfer, such overt denial of relationship recognition could certainly have happened in Super-DOMA states to any other lesbian or gay man, no matter how knowledgeable or well connected.

Of course, in 2010, under instruction from the Obama administration, the federal Department of Health and Human Services issued regulations mandating that all American hospitals receiving Medicare or Medicaid funding must extend visitation rights to the partners of gay men and lesbians and otherwise respect patients' choices about who may make critical health care decisions for them (Stolberg 2010; Sack 2010). As a practical matter, therefore, Doerfer's emergency-room-access dilemma ought never to have recurred, either to her or anyone else in a same-sex relationship.

But some people I spoke with had serious doubts that hospitals in small towns, or even religiously affiliated ones in urban areas, would willingly follow the Obama directive, as one interviewee quipped: "The feds in Washington, DC say 'Listen up! You treat gay folks with respect now!' And their message effectively penetrates the rural areas of the state, where our constitutional amendment passed with 80 or 90 percent of the vote? You gotta be kidding me."[7]

Other Health Care Consequences

Often Super-DOMA health care effects were far more subtle than being physically blocked from entering an emergency room. Two quite different stories offer a perspective on the more intangible consequences of these initiatives and referenda.

---

[7] Cf. Parker-Pope (2010).

Bertie, age fifty, and Olive, forty-seven, have been together for seven years. In the comfortable den of their suburban Ohio home, Olive confessed to an abiding fear:

I really worry about what would happen if Bertie had a medical emergency. She has a twenty-two-year-old biological son, Caleb, who's very accepting of our relationship, and I can't easily see anything bad happening with him. But the reality is, Issue 1's still there in our constitution.

Caleb's got a girlfriend that he's pretty serious about. And other people in your life affect how you make decisions. Would Caleb be able to be swayed by a girlfriend, or wife, who had a different opinion from him? You know what I mean? Aware of who he is, right now, I'd say no. But that thought is always there in my mind. Because, as a legal matter, he's Bertie's next of kin, and he's an adult. So in our state, under Issue 1, Caleb has more rights regarding Bertie than I do.

Richard and Tim had been partnered since 1990. Both appeared to be in good health and expected a long life and retirement together in a Columbus suburb. But Tim came down with a debilitating disease that slowly sapped his energy and spirit over many years, resulting in his death at age fifty-eight in 2006. Richard, age fifty-seven at the time of our interview, lamented how Ohio's constitutional prohibition of any government-recognized relationship with Tim affected them:

If I'd had the financial security of a legal spouse, or even family-medical-leave benefits, I could've probably stayed at home from my nine-to-five job and taken better care of Tim when he was disabled from illness for so many months. But instead, I had to worry about my own future, with my work and retirement, because I'd get no pension from Tim's employment after he died. [Tim held a prominent position in a state agency.]

During Tim's long illness, I carried this portfolio with me that contained all of our legal documents, in case anybody questioned my being his legal guardian with medical power of attorney. Nobody was outright hostile to me. But at the funeral home, where we did preplanning, a woman presented a lot of questions to Tim in order to prepare his obituary, which would include a list of blood relatives. So I had to speak up, "And name me, Richard Moore, his partner of seventeen years." She wasn't going to ask that. So I had to be very assertive.

She must've thought that I was his chauffeur or valet. Because when she sought out relatives, she didn't inquire into who I was at all, even though I'd been there with Tim all along. She wasn't rude to me, yet acted as though I were invisible. Sometimes people don't want to see two gay men together when dealing with a delicate issue like that. So she was polite, but uncomfortable. Nonetheless, I wanted my name to appear in his obituary.

Restricting Employment Options

A corollary of couples' inability to secure employer-sponsored domestic-partner benefits and thus affordable health care for all family members was a limitation on the partners' job opportunities. A thirty-six-year-old lesbian in an Atlanta suburb lamented Question 1's impact on her work options:

The constitutional amendment has affected me professionally. I used to work in public service, at community health centers or state-funded hospitals. But there's no access to domestic-partner benefits with such jobs in Georgia.

Two weeks ago, somebody called me up with a great offer, an ideal job for me, because I miss working in a clinic with people. I asked, "Can I get domestic-partner benefits?" "No." So I had to decline this wonderful opportunity.

Because I carry the benefits for our family. So no benefits, no job.

Another corollary of the lack of access to a partner's employment-sponsored benefits was reduced work flexibility, as was the case with a forty-eight-year-old lesbian at the Centers for Disease Control in Atlanta:

A: I'd probably have changed jobs if I could've been on my partner's health insurance. But I've declined to look for other kinds of work because of that inability to get on her coverage. It's too risky to venture out in new ways without those sorts of basic protections in place.

Q: What kind of a career change might you have made?

A: I would've been more aggressive in seeking out opportunities in the high-tech field, which is an area of specialty for me. I'd have looked for other potential executive positions.

Once upon a time, I was a freelance writer, and might have considered returning there. Or I'd just have gone into business for myself, if I could've been on her insurance.

So Question 1 has really had a big impact on me.

A thirty-seven-year-old mother of a three-year-old and a six-year-old supplied a final take on the issue:

Since my partner's employment doesn't provide domestic-partner benefits, I have to put in twenty hours per week, the minimum number to get health care coverage from my job. It would be much better for our family, in terms of child care, for me to work just twelve hours a week. But when all the factors come into play, it doesn't make financial sense to do so.

THE LIMITATIONS OF LEGAL PAPERWORK

Legal documents such as wills and powers of attorney offered same-sex couples in Super-DOMA states the promise of securing as many rights and responsibilities as they could in potentially hostile legal, political, and social environments. In truth, any paperwork evidencing their dedication to one another was often invaluable for the psychological well-being of lesbian and gay pairs because no official proof of their relationships would ever be available or honored in their home states. Over and over, interviewees shared with me their pursuit of documents demonstrating their commitment, as a thirty-seven-year-old lesbian from suburban Georgia declared when discussing the prospect of going somewhere else to marry:

I don't know that a Vermont marriage certificate would produce anything really concrete for us at the moment here. Yet I want to put as many papers in place to formalize and cement our relationship together. That's the reasoning for the trip up North, not that it would necessarily produce anything immediate.

But we want to have as many things as we can to show we have that commitment for each other.

An even more frequently expressed concern was a worry about the futility of planning to prevent or diminish family catastrophes. And that anxiety was epitomized for so many interviewees by what happened to a lesbian couple in Miami, alluded to by Barbara and Jane earlier in the chapter. In February 2007, Janice Langbehn, Lisa Pond, and their three jointly adopted children with special needs left their home in Lacey, Washington, for Florida. The family was planning a cruise to celebrate the couple's eighteen years together. Just as they boarded the ship, the thirty-nine-year-old Pond suddenly collapsed and was rushed to Jackson Memorial Hospital in Miami, with Langbehn and children close behind.

Hospital staff refused to accept information from Langbehn regarding Pond's medical history, informing her that she was in an antigay city and state and that she could expect to receive no information or recognition as family. A physician finally spoke with Langbehn, telling her that there was no chance for Pond's recovery (because of a massive stroke). Other than one five-minute visit (orchestrated by a Catholic priest at Langbehn's request to perform last rites), and despite the doctor's acknowledgment that no medical reason existed to prevent visitation, neither Langbehn nor the three children were allowed to see Pond until nearly eight hours after their arrival, even after Pond's power of attorney to Langbehn was faxed to the hospital from Washington State (Parker-Pope 2009).

Soon after Pond's death, Langbehn attempted to obtain her death certificate in order to get life insurance and Social Security benefits for the children. Both the State of Florida and the Dade County Medical Examiner denied her request.

A federal lawsuit against the hospital, doctors, and staff was dismissed. The court held that, although the defendants exhibited a lack of compassion and sensitivity, there was no relief available to plaintiff Langbehn and her children under Florida law (*Langbehn* v. *Public Health Trust of Miami-Dade County* 2009).[8]

The impact of this notorious story on the LGBT community was summed up by a thirty-year-old Durham, North Carolina, lesbian:

---

[8] Hospital-visitation denials occurred in Alabama as late as 2011 (Brekke 2014; Cason 2014).

What it means to be gay and coupled in America right now is that we get legal documentation, and there's no guarantee it will have any teeth. The women in Florida had paperwork from their own home state, but those documents didn't prevent the tragedy that occurred in Miami. So we're very much at the mercy of the power of individual nurses and doctors and other hospital staff.

Nonetheless, Terri Phoenix, the director of the LGBTQ Center at the University of North Carolina at Chapel Hill, still believed there was value in paperwork, regardless of its legality:

Even with all the documentation my partner and I have, you can still get things like the nationally broadcast story about the lesbian couple in Miami, Florida. And that's just one of hundreds I've heard through my job running the LGBTQ Center.

However, my partner and I still carry a set of documents with us when we travel. Even though we know some of them may not be considered valid, when we're driving somewhere, we count on the fact that other people may not be as up to date on such things.

So we can show our second-parent-adoption decree, and it will be respected, even though state courts subsequently invalidated such adoptions.

In any event, Super-DOMAs made legal instruments between same-sex couples more fragile because the constitutional amendments guaranteed that someone other than a gay or lesbian partner would be the next of kin, with the legal standing to contest wills and such. Atlanta attorney Barbara E. Katz elaborated:

Same-sex pairs can run into problems regarding wills. Georgia case law creates a rebuttable presumption that people leave their property to legal heirs at law. When the presumption isn't followed, that variation from the law's expectation creates the opportunity for an argument that a partner exerted undue influence.

So the wills of some queer folks may be at particular risk, especially for those living in outlying counties, where people tend to be more closeted. And not being out means that fewer friends and family know about personal relationships, which in turn implies that when someone dies, the family may have no idea, or were never explicitly told, about the same-sex relationship. Accordingly, a family may genuinely believe their relative had no desire to leave anything to the alleged partner. Thus arises the undue-influence claim.

Moreover, as a practical matter, when couples sign wills, they often see the lawyer together. And that fact doesn't help later on in a will contest.

If in initial interviews with clients, there are any red flags with regard to how a family of origin considers a partner, I have them come in to sign wills on different days, just so I don't have the partner in the room. Because that could be a piece of evidence used against the partner in a will contest.

Thus, gay people in urban counties like Fulton and Dekalb, where folks usually are far more out of the closet, can have a greater sense of security than their counterparts elsewhere.

The couples I spoke with repeatedly expressed awareness of this vulnerability of documents to legal attack. In Dallas, for instance, Christopher, age fifty-five, worried about the potential actions of the blood relatives of his partner of twenty-one years, Juan, age fifty-seven:

CHRISTOPHER: Juan has a brother and a sister from his birth parents. But he wasn't raised with those siblings.

JUAN: At three days of age, I was adopted by an uncle, my biological father's brother. I've seen my brother and sister on maybe five occasions in my lifetime. The last occurrence was in January 1994, at my biological father's funeral.

So my sibling are total strangers to me as a practical matter.

CHRISTOPHER: I have this horrible concern that if something happened to Juan, his brother and sister would step in to contest the will. And Proposition 2 leaves me more exposed, since the amendment ensures their role as Juan's next of kin.

In Raleigh, North Carolina, James, age fifty-seven, and John, fifty-nine, a couple for twenty-three years, expressed a similar fear:

Q: Let's say you get all of your legal papers in order. They're up to date, with all of the "t's" crossed and the "i's" dotted. You get the best legal advice possible.

How confident would you be that those papers will be honored when needed?

JOHN: Not a lot. Not anymore.

I have family members who have issues with me. If I were to predecease James, they could challenge a will. They'd say, "I'm the next of kin." I think this kind of thing is possible.

JAMES: I don't believe it would occur with my family. But you never know.

JOHN: And it may never happen. But the possibility is always in my head.

At our ages, we're ready to plan the rest of our lives.

JAMES: And how do you do that with this amendment?

JOHN: We've been thrown a curveball that we don't know how to deal with.

EMPLOYMENT DISCRIMINATION

Wisconsin was the only Super-DOMA jurisdiction to have a statewide statute prohibiting sexual-orientation discrimination in employment, housing, and public accommodations. Indeed, the Badger State has the distinction of being the first in the nation to enact such a law. Among the nineteen other states, however, no such legal protections existed for LGBT citizens statewide, although county and municipal ordinances to that effect existed in some jurisdictions (Eckholm 2015b; Wolfson 2015; cf. Scheiber 2015).

In any event, many employers in Georgia, Michigan, North Carolina, Ohio, and Texas were legally free both not to hire gay people because of their sexual orientation and to dismiss them without further cause once their orientation became known.

Yet, the inability of same-sex couples to marry or otherwise have their relationships recognized in Super-DOMA states also rendered more subtle forms of employment discrimination, as a tenured professor at the University of North Carolina in Chapel Hill told me:

I have a lot of discomfort with the university's employment guidelines. For many years, UNC has had a policy of trying to hire the spouses of its own faculty members. In fact, UNC and Duke University [in Durham, North Carolina] have a reciprocal agreement to that effect. So Duke will pay part of the salary for a spouse who's hired at UNC, and vice versa. Administratively, there's kind of a free faculty line for spouses.

I came up against the policy when I was hired here, because I was in competition for my position with a woman who was married to a Duke faculty member. Ultimately, both of us were employed at UNC, with me getting a job first. But I'd have been very pissed off if I'd been passed over because a straight, married woman had a special financial benefit by which Duke was paying UNC to hire her. Oh my God, I'd have been so unhappy. It would've seemed so unfair.

But the fact of the matter is that UNC has had a long-standing policy of spousal hires. The last time I checked, 20 percent of the faculty members in my department were brought in as spouses or had their spouses hired on their behalf. So that's a fairly large skew of the employment pool.

For many years, I've said this rule isn't fair to single people or gay folks. In UNC's entire history, for instance, the school has engaged only one queer couple as a joint hire under the policy.

So there's one gay man in the faculty of social sciences at UNC. In that entire division, just one. And there's no out gay man in any of the natural sciences.[9] Accordingly, outside of the humanities, there's one gay man in the faculty of the college, which accounts for between 750 and 800 people. And there's never been more than a total of a dozen openly gay men among the 800, which is a stunning statistic in higher education today [July 2012].

So 20 percent of our department consists of straight, married people who have had this incredible spousal benefit.

Please don't misunderstand. I'm not saying they're bad people or that the hires were of an inferior quality. Rather, it's just not a fair criterion for employment. The policy blatantly discriminates against the other categories.

The result is that there are very few gay male faculty on campus, and Amendment 1 will make it unconstitutional for UNC to hire the partners of queer faculty. I'm so discouraged by that prospect.

Thus, there's a long history of the university's not according gay people the same benefits as married straight couples. Even though my colleagues and UNC administrators tend to be fairly gay friendly, this hiring problem has been invisible to them. People here take their civil privileges for granted.

One of the few good things to come from Amendment 1 is that numerous people finally realized how many privileges marriage brings.

HOUSING DISCRIMINATION

As with the Amendment-1-related employment favoritism at UNC, Super-DOMAs prompted insidious forms of housing discrimination against same-sex couples too.

[9] See Suri (2015).

Oakland University is a public institution in the northern Detroit suburbs that provides employee housing near campus. Oakland faculty or administration members and their families can purchase homes in the designated area that have restrictive covenants limiting transfers of the properties to people affiliated with the school. Should the faculty member or administrator die, his or her spouse may continue to live in the house until the spouse's death.

Emma, age sixty-two, is a tenured full professor at the university and has been a faculty member there for more than twenty-five years. After a year-long search for a home in faculty housing, she and Joan, her partner of fifteen years, made an offer on a house and secured a mortgage to finance it. Then Oakland informed the couple that, because of Michigan's Proposal 2, Joan would have to leave the home before the end of the calendar year in which Emma died, or otherwise Joan would be evicted. Since Emma is fifteen years older than Joan, the survivorship limitation forced the pair to abandon their dream of moving to a new home.

Dawn, age forty-six, and Rita, fifty-three, pointed out another housing problem in North Carolina:

RITA: Chapel Hill has a zoning law prohibiting more than four unrelated people from living together.
DAWN: It's a college town. So they don't want five or six students rooming together off campus.
RITA: Yet we have friends who've adopted three or four children. So there are five or six people in a house who aren't all legally related to one another. Thus, Amendment 1 could result in families being denied housing here.

PUBLIC HAZING WHEN CHANGING NAMES

Having a common surname can be important for families. A single last name can bind people together in significant ways, both legally and socially. That thought occurred to Helen and Lee when they were getting documents to protect their relationship during the onslaught of the Ohio DOMAs.

HELEN: We went to see our attorney, and a staff member of the law office came out and asked, "Are you the Johnsons?" At that instant, I thought, "You know, I'd like for us to be the Somebodies." So that launched the effort to change our last names.
LEE: At the time, David Langdon, on behalf of Citizens for Community Values, had instituted a lawsuit down in Hamilton County [Cincinnati] around name changes for gay and lesbian couples. A judge wouldn't let two women change their names, and the case went all the way to the Ohio Supreme Court.

And this pair had been through hell. They'd had a multiple birth, and only one of the kids pulled through. So they wanted to have a common family name, and give the surviving child that last name. When they were getting their own names changed, the judge wouldn't allow it.
HELEN: His argument was that it was fraudulent...
LEE: ...because he thought they were trying to represent that they were married.

HELEN: The only legal ground in Ohio for not being allowed to change one's name is fraud.

LEE: So we went to court not knowing what was going to happen. Our lawyer said it was better to represent ourselves. Otherwise, we'd draw attention to our name-change petition. But she did sit in the gallery.

HELEN: She said, "I'll be there as a supporter, unless you need me as a lawyer."

LEE: I was the one between the two of us who went to court first. The judge had already done all of these other cases, because they're brought in as a package. And he was going through the papers, and then you could just see him stop at ours. "Oh crap" seemed to flash through his thoughts.

But in the end, the judge came up with a good reason – in his mind – why he could let us go forward. "Well, in the Cincinnati case, there are children involved. Do you have any kids? 'No.' Okay, it can go forward."

Other interviewees volunteered harrowing experiences with changing names. Miriam and Naomi, both age forty and together for eighteen years, reported what happened to them in Georgia:

NAOMI: When changing our names here, we went into the judge's chambers. He was probably in his sixties. An African American gentleman.

Our lawyer said, "Your Honor, this is Miriam and Naomi. They'd like to change their name."

He looked at us and said, "Is that what you do?"

Q: Seriously?

MIRIAM: Yes. "Is that what you do?"

NAOMI: As in, "Is that what *you people* do?"

And I said, "Some of us." [She laughs.] I'm surprised I came up with that retort so quickly, since his remark flabbergasted me.

What is more, after Issue 1 passed in Ohio, court personnel there developed a ritual of public hazing for partnered gay people choosing to alter their names (cf. Selten 2012). For example, Amanda, age thirty-five, and Joyce, forty, were having children together and saw the merit in unifying their family with one surname:

JOYCE: Getting my name changed was such a hassle. In the courtroom, both the clerk and judge kept reminding me publicly – over, and over, and over again – that my partner and I would have no legal rights as a married couple with a common last name.

At the same time, there was a man changing his name to that of his fiancée, before they got married. He decided to take her last name, instead of vice versa, and he had to petition to do so. But court personnel never asked *him* a question about fraudulent intent.

Even when I was taking the oath and swearing that I wasn't getting my name changed for an illegal reason, they asked me whether I was acting deceitfully. But when he took his oath, they never posed that question. It was very frustrating. I sat there the longest time before answering, saying that I did understand the issue. But I wanted to shout, "Look. This guy just took his fiancée's name, and you didn't worry about *his* honesty. So why am I being treated differently as a lesbian?"

AMANDA: And I was advised not to go to the hearing. Because if we got a judge who wasn't gay friendly, my presence in court might bother him, and the petition could be denied. So I couldn't even be there when Joyce changed her name.

We had to run newspaper ads that she was changing her name. Then we had to wait a specified time. Then we had to pay court fees. But they could still deny it.

JOYCE: People getting married don't have to do any of that. And it's another thing that cost us money. The expense for my name change was like $300 altogether.

Stewart, age thirty-seven, and William, forty, together for a decade, reported another humiliating occurrence of the name-change hazing rite:

WILLIAM: A significant reason for changing our surnames was to match our [adopted] daughter's last name.

STEWART: When I was doing the name change, I went to the courthouse here and was asked, in front of all these other people, "You're not trying to deceive anyone into thinking that this is a real marriage, correct?" I was mortified.

They asked me explicitly, "And you're willing to testify that you're not changing your name to mislead anyone to think that this is a lawful marriage?" "No. I'm changing my name because I want it to match my daughter's name and my partner's name. We all want to have the same last name, so that we can be a family. I'm not attempting to deceive anyone."

And I was the only person in a large group who got that particular question, although there were others who had different inquiries put to them.

I came home and said to William, "You're not going to believe what they asked me." I wasn't angry about it. But who would I defraud? I was trying to think of an angle where I might try to hoodwink someone by changing my last name.

WILLIAM: I think that some people switch names to escape debt.

STEWART: But the clerk's statements and questions were specific to marriage. They weren't about my dodging creditors. They were directed at our relationship.

TAX PENALTIES

Richard and Tim were introduced earlier in the health care section. Their story also touches on how Issue 1 affected the administration of some state taxes. Four years before the couple met, Tim purchased a home in a Columbus suburb. When the two decided to live together, Richard moved into Tim's house. The couple painstakingly split all expenses 50–50 and, over the next twelve years, worked hard and paid off the mortgage.

In the process of estate planning in 1996, a lawyer advised the pair that adding Richard's name to the deed would result in a gift tax on one-half of the fair market value of the property. So they decided not to change the deed.

If the two were married under state law when Tim died in 2006, or even if they had a civil union or domestic partnership, Richard's taking title of the home under Tim's will would not have been taxed pursuant to state inheritance laws. But Issue 1 required that the couple be treated as legal strangers to one another. As a result, the full market value of the property was included as part of Tim's estate, and Richard was forced to write a check to the Treasurer of Franklin County for $34,000. Richard explained the situation:

Since 1990, we painted every wall and every ceiling in the home, and covered every floor, ourselves. We put our life's blood in this house for nearly seventeen years together. Although I didn't make the down payment, I did pay half of well over 75 percent of the mortgage. And I can prove it, because we kept careful records. Even without such proof, though, there would've been no tax penalty if I were Tim's wife or his legally recognized domestic partner. I also would've received his state pension.

But the pension died with him, and I still had to "inherit" my own home from Tim, like a cousin or nephew who never paid a penny on the mortgage or never sweated to improve and maintain the property.

Tim and I had all our documents in order. But paperwork can only go so far. It couldn't say, "You two are married, and don't have to go through this inheritance process because you're spouses." That legal impediment couldn't be avoided, no matter what we did.

When people run to the polls and vote against gay men and lesbians, there's a direct toll on couples like Tim and me. We're the guys living next door, who mow our lawn and keep our property up. And in the suburbs, we pay huge property taxes so that the children of opposite-sex couples can get educated. Not our children. Tim and I had none.

In the end, Issue 1 prevented Tim and me from formalizing our relationship, as we always wanted, before he died. We were never able to say "I do" in the same way everyone else does. George W. Bush won the 2004 election with the blood of my dying partner on his hands.

Dorothy and Lisa, introduced in Chapter 1, pointed out another significant tax penalty on same-sex pairs:

Q: What did the passage of Georgia's Question 1 mean to you in the broadest sense of the word?

DOROTHY: It meant that both of us had better live to ripe old ages until the law changes, because we run in to all kinds of inheritance and taxation problems.

LISA: If we had federal marital rights at the time of my death, Dorothy would get all of our jointly held property tax free. But under current law, she'd have to pay inheritance taxes on it. So if I were to die now, the kids would lose a parent – and their house. Such a disaster doesn't happen to married heterosexual couples, where that tragic family event is uniquely protected. But it's not true for us.

And what frustrates me is that so many people, including lawyers I talk to, don't understand our tax reality. They say, "Can't you just go to an attorney and get that stuff written up?" And I respond, "How many lawyers can write partnership agreements to give couples federal tax benefits? If you know of one, I want that attorney's name." They just don't get it.

When we sit down with straight friends and talk about our taxation problems, and we've done that, it's like an epiphany for them. They instantly become pro-marriage equality. Because people don't truly understand all the benefits and rights denied us as a result of the inability to have our relationship legally recognized.

ALIENATION FROM FAMILY, FRIENDS, AND ASSOCIATES

Although the passage of Super-DOMAs did not alter gay and lesbian couples' marital status as a legal matter, the public campaigns and popular votes on constitutional amendments did force the issue front and center in their consciousness. Sue Doerfer described the awakening in the Buckeye State:

Prior to Issue 1, same-sex marriage really wasn't on the LGBT radar here in Ohio. People lived lives without really thinking much about how they were treated by government. Some had their own personal issues with employers, of course. No doubt about that.

But what happened in 2004 brought the notion of our right to marry to the surface, and in fact, slammed the matter so much in our faces that there was no way not to see it. Now, marriage equality is a household idea. Everybody talks about it.

As a result, discussions arose, in 2004 and thereafter, between same-sex pairs and their friends, relatives, and co-workers that might not have otherwise occurred. Sometimes the conversations were acrimonious with enduring effects. The clearest instance of Amendment 1's deep impact on intimate familial bonds in North Carolina came up with Maria, age fifty-six, and Margaret, fifty, who were briefly introduced in Chapter 1. They live in Charlotte, where Maria owns and operates a business with her brother.

MARIA: I'm a native North Carolinian, and Margaret and I have been together here for twenty-six years.

My sister and brother-in-law love Margaret and treat her just like my spouse. There's no issue they've ever had with us.

So what made Amendment 1 so frustrating is that even my family voted for it.

MARGARET: We think they did.

MARIA: We're sure they did. That's what's devastating. And my sister won't talk about it.

We're friends on Facebook. So all my Facebook posting was about being against Amendment 1. And I had a lot of family support from cousins on Facebook...

MARGARET: ...across different states.

MARIA: ...as well as here. But my sister and brother-in-law never said a word. And I'm not even sure how my brother – who I work with on a daily basis – voted.

So I sent an email to my brother, sister, and brother-in-law that said, "You're aware that Margaret and I fought hard against Amendment 1. And I want you to know your silence spoke volumes to me and my family. And we're very disappointed."

I came right out and said it in an email, after listing all of the family members who'd written me in support. "But my own sister, my own brother, and my brother-in-law, who love me the most, who know Margaret and me the best, and love us the most, stood in silence."

Q: Did they respond to the email?

MARIA: Only my sister. And guess what she said. "You know that we love you and Margaret and your dear children very much, Maria, and that will never change."

MARGARET: That's it.

Q: "Even though we voted to take away all of your rights."

BOTH: *Yes!*

Q: How do you think that knowledge will affect, if at all, your ongoing relationship with them?

MARIA: At first, I was really worried about it. But you know? She's my sister, after all.

MARGARET: People make decisions. They can opt to let disappointment drive a wedge between them, or they can choose to try to put the letdown in the back of one's mind. Because Maria is very close to her family, and so far, she's chosen...

MARIA: ...not to hold a grudge and let it hurt me.

But I will say that we're not quite as close now. I don't call her as often and don't talk to her nearly as much as before.

MARGARET: [to Maria:] And can't you feel it being around her? It's kind of like...

MARIA: ...there's an unspoken separation between us.

I'll always love her, just as she said she would always love me. But I know that she won't support us in terms of our civil rights.

MARGARET: When someone who's that close to you in your family can't be supportive of something so important to your relationship, how can that knowledge not affect how you really feel about the person in your relationship with them?

Q: And this alienation wouldn't have happened in the same way but for Amendment 1?

MARIA: Absolutely not. Amendment 1 brought it to the forefront.

MARGARET: There'd have been no other reason to have the discussion. Because they loved us. They've never excluded us from anything.

However, they've never wished us a happy anniversary or anything like that. But they celebrate my birthday just as though I were their sister-in-law. You'd never know that this family would have any issue with us being a couple, or being married, or anything.

MARIA: Except they've *never* said, "Happy anniversary." They've never asked, "How long have y'all been together?" Never.

Q: Whereas, you acknowledge *their* anniversaries?

MARIA: I quit acknowledging their anniversaries.

Q: Really?

MARIA: Yup. I know that's a terrible attitude. But nope, they don't acknowledge mine. There's nothing wrong with tit-for-tat.

MARGARET: One really bad problem with this whole thing is that it gives us a really bad taste for marriage itself. You know? We've come to resent, really, the traditional things that married people enjoy, and married people have going for them.

It's like, when a wedding shower comes up... [She throws her hands as in a scoff:] Whew! That's not anything we can have, and we have a better relationship than they'll probably ever have. You know? The heck with that.

It's not the way it should be, and it doesn't feel good. But you tend to think, "If marriage is good for you, but not for us, then what the hell is it?"

MARIA: Even the passion in our voices right now is revealing. Any time we talk about Amendment 1, we just get mad all over again.

We're not really angry people. But you wouldn't have believed the passion in North Carolina during the Amendment 1 battle.

MARGARET: It was amazing.

MARIA: The reason I have no confidence in my family now is because of Amendment 1. Before all that public animosity, I think I probably would've said, "Oh sure. My family respects our relationship. They'd let Margaret call the shots if something happened to me."

But now, I don't know.

MARGARET: I have no idea either, nor trust in them.

MARIA: I bet there are so many other people now in North Carolina who are in exactly the same situation as us.

Rachel, age forty-six, and Veronica, forty-eight, a Cleveland couple together for six years, reported on how the passage of Ohio's Super-DOMA affected their friendships:

VERONICA: Every month, we get together with three heterosexual couples. These friendships are interesting, because one couple is very, very religious. But to them, we're Veronica and Rachel. They love us.

But they voted for Issue 1, and it's a conundrum. We know that we test their beliefs. But they're so open and loving with us. I've never quite gotten the disconnect.

RACHEL: We're very close with the woman in that relationship. Years ago, I'd never have thought to have an evangelical Christian woman as a best friend. Yet we don't talk much about our being gay. But my hope is that, the more she knows and learns about Veronica and me, the harder she struggles with the inaccuracies her religion teaches her.

I asked her to be part of our commitment ceremony here, but she couldn't, even though she thought about it for a long time. I don't know how such people separate their love for us and what their religion tells them to feel about us.

Q: How did the two of you deal with the knowledge that your friends voted for Issue 1?

VERONICA: With disbelief. I couldn't understand why, and was so hurt by it.

So I think Rachel and I have to do all of the things – like meeting with you – that let people know we're okay.

I argued a lot with the friends and relatives I found out voted for Issue 1. I wanted them to explain why they thought this was correct. How could they have done that to us?

RACHEL: Our friends try to separate it. They try to step back from the personal. They say, "I just believe that marriage should be between a man and a woman. Not you guys, in general."

And I reply, "No. It *is* us, it *is* me, that you're denying civil rights to."

VERONICA: I have a very religious aunt who says, "You're asking for special rights. But you don't need special rights. You had your commitment ceremony. We were all there. We supported you. Why do you have to keep being out there, pounding your chest saying you're gay?" That's the pushback we get.

Another friend asked, "Why does there have to be a pride festival? What's there to be proud about being gay? Heterosexuals aren't proud to be straight." And I said, "I'm not going to be ashamed of who I am. Which is what you're asking me to do when you take away my rights."

People don't believe how many rights we're denied by not being able to marry. So they say, "You have the exact same rights as us. You have a job. You have a home. We aren't denying you anything. So you can do all those things. Just do them quietly."

Daniel A. Bloom, a politically active Atlanta family-law attorney, described how the adoption of Georgia's Super-DOMA touched his business relationships:

One lingering Question-1 effect is that it forced people to stake out their territory. So now, I still have to work with lawmakers who remain in the state legislature and also with people who've moved on to other careers. And I'm aware of how they voted on the referendum. You know?

So continuing to work with them on other issues is really a challenge, cognizant as I am that they voted against my ability to have equal rights. It's difficult talking to people while my mind is replaying what they said in speeches from the well of the House in 2004.

Or take David Adelman, who was just [January 2010] nominated as ambassador to Singapore. He represented Decatur in the State Senate, one of the gayest districts in Georgia, if not the country, and he didn't even speak up against the referendum because of political posturing.

So those events forever taint the way I look at some people.

There's a judge in Fulton County right now, who's a nice guy. In 2004, he was in the legislature representing Roswell, which isn't far from my home. I took him to lunch during the marriage-amendment debate. He said, "I was able to vote against Georgia keeping the Confederate flag. The party leadership let me get away with that. But they won't tolerate my opposing the marriage amendment. So I'm not going to change my vote. But I'm happy to suggest who I think you should talk to." Now I see this former legislator turned judge around the courthouse all the time. We shake hands and play the political game.

But I know what he did! Now, his vote wouldn't have made a hill of beans of difference for the outcome. But it's really hard to get over knowing what he did.

FEAR, INSECURITY, AND EMOTIONAL LOSS

Even though most couples could not recount concrete deprivations they had suffered from Super-DOMAs, the acute awareness of their outsider status wrought by the passage of the constitutional amendments nonetheless bred an abiding fear in many same-sex pairs that financial, legal, medical, or social calamity might easily be just around the corner. Helen provided context for this frequently described psychological state in Ohio:

Whether we have good days or bad days, there's always a basic cognizance of not being full citizens of the country, and not being entirely safe. Most LGBT Ohioans are aware that the state and its voters have designated us – who we are to one another, and to ourselves individually – as unworthy of full participation in civic and social life. And making that so clear at a constitutional level communicates to people who want to disparage us that their stance is an acceptable one to take.

Therefore, there's a relentless insecurity that comes with having discrimination, with all its underlying tendrils, sanctioned at the state level. So even though there aren't distinct, tangible losses that some lesbian and gay couples here can point to, a central malaise and disconcertion permeate all of our lives.

Beverly, age twenty-eight, lives with her partner Kelly, thirty-one, in Winston-Salem, North Carolina. She told me,

Since Kelly's a police officer, I worry every night she goes to work, "Will they automatically think to call me if something happens to her?" Everyone at the precinct knows who I am, and Kelly has a support bracelet indicating I'm her immediate contact.

But I still wonder whether they would necessarily notify me. I don't know that they would. So it worries me.

And I wouldn't have the same fear if we were legally married. They'd know then to contact an injured or fallen officer's spouse. But I don't have that protection now.

Gay and lesbian couples without a lawyer in the family typically paid attorneys to draft and execute documents such as wills, living wills, and durable powers of attorney (both for health care concerns and financial matters). Those pairs with the most rudimentary paperwork reported costs starting in the hundreds of dollars, whereas two Columbus lesbians with complicated health and immigration issues that required the creation of a legal trust paid $5,000 in attorney's fees. In most instances, these couples were trying to fill the relationship-recognition void that Super-DOMAs generated. And in virtually all circumstances, their efforts were only partially successful, because no amount of legal documentation could bind all relevant third parties during a pair's time together.

Helen and Lee explained how they incurred legal costs, as well as how Issue 1 placed an explicit limitation on their efforts:

LEE: There are financial responsibilities we've had to take on by hiring lawyers, trying to protect our family as much as we can through legal documents. People whose marriages are recognized in the state don't have to bother about such things. They don't even think about them.

HELEN: They don't even know that they don't have to think about them.

Starting with our name change, our lawyer recommended – and this was before any DOMAs were on the horizon in Ohio – not to hide what we were doing. So with that advice in mind, which reinforced our own inclination, we had a series of papers drawn up, a health care power of attorney, a durable financial power of attorney, and so forth.

Lo and behold, when Issue 1 came down, the way the Super-DOMA was worded made anything lesbian and gay couples did that attempted to approximate marriage illegal. Consequently, all the documents we had put in place to protect ourselves were now suspect, because the way that they were written made it very clear we were attempting to approximate marriage. Our papers themselves reveal exactly what our intention was. We made no bones about it. And we would have to work very hard to pretend that we weren't trying to approximate marriage in Ohio, since we're married in Canada and have a civil union in Vermont. So Issue 1 screwed up our paperwork royally and injected a sense of danger in our relationship.

LEE: If people wanted to step in, say, if one of us were ill or incapacitated, they could bring our papers into court and claim we were trying to approximate marriage. So there's all of this uncertainty around what goes on in our lives.

Even if we were to incur the substantial expense of having all our documents rewritten in a way that would seek to obscure our intention to approximate marriage, there aren't any guarantees we'd be successful at the end of the day.

Again, if we're just going to work, or to the grocery store, or we're paying the bills, or otherwise doing the countless mundane tasks of life – it doesn't really matter that we're married or not. But when potentially life-altering issues arise, our marital status may be crucially important to securing a favorable outcome. So we face imponderables and unknowns. And for some of them, we have no protections, no matter what we do.

Deborah, age sixty, and Gladys, sixty-seven, have been together for about twenty years, are in their sixties, and live in a small town in northern Ohio. A principal way in which Issue 1 affected them was inducing fear for their physical safety:

DEBORAH: Issue 1 emboldens individuals who disagree with same-sex relationships to be more aggressive and hostile, reducing our sense of safety. If we're walking down the street as a couple and someone realizes we're more than just friends or acquaintances, I feel less safe because the law doesn't protect us. Issue 1 gives people license to be more hostile toward us.

GLADYS: And this is very subtle. I don't usually allow myself to think about it, and our college town seems fairly receptive to us. But because Issue 1 made us part of an illegal class, basically, the amendment's targeting us legitimates anybody's hostility and ill intent.

DEBORAH: We're baseball fans. If you're in a public place like a baseball game, where people are drinking.... I remember that some of the insults Cleveland Indians fans throw at the opposite team deal with sexual orientation. So we're sitting there in the stadium thinking, "We're a same-sex couple, and these guys all around us are drunk. If they turn on us with all of that venom and anger, what would happen?" So the perception of vulnerability that Issue 1 highlighted is inhibiting. It makes us aware we have to be on guard all the time.

GLADYS: Homophobia exists anyway. So once something like Issue 1 countenances it, who knows what might happen.

Although Deborah and Gladys worried about being too conspicuous at times, Christine, age forty-one, struggled with the opposite issue:

CHRISTINE: Issue 1 made me feel really discounted, almost nonexistent. I can be a woman in Ohio. I can be a mom here. And I can be an ex-wife here too. You know? But my relationship with Marian doesn't count. If anything were to happen to either of us, our families would take over. Decisions would be made on our behalf that we might not agree with. So the constitutional amendment erased some of our personal rights and identity.

We're both excited about getting married [next month in Massachusetts]. We've picked out wonderful rings to wear. I so hope that tying the knot legally somewhere will make our relationship more genuine to others. Some of Marian's family members are truly happy for us.

And it will make me feel more seen and solid, instead of every day just being introduced as Christine in a crowd. You know? Where George is Marian's *brother*. And Patricia is George's *wife*. So once I have a similar designation, I anticipate feeling finally like I'm going to be seen and heard at last. A true member of the family.

MARIAN: The closer we get to making this legal, the more my parents keep holding a fear over my head. "You're going to be hurt because it's not legal in Ohio." They say that to me over and over. They think that's a convincing reason to stop us from getting married. Because it's not legal in Ohio, it's going to cause us trouble. I can't get them to be any more specific.

But they can hold the fact that it's not legal in Ohio as a reason to say, "I'm afraid to acknowledge that Christine is your partner, because I love you and don't want to see you hurt. So I'm protecting you."

Frank, age forty-four, and Jeff, thirty-nine, live in Madison, had a ceremonial wedding in 2010 among friends and family in western Wisconsin; they spoke to me about the emotional and psychological damage inflicted by Referendum 1:

FRANK: The popular vote did affect us emotionally. There's a toll taken living in a state that's not only not seen or acknowledged our commitment to one another but has now also taken an active role in disparaging our relationship, declaring that our intimacy mustn't be viewed as equal to that among opposite-sex married couples in the state. And that belittling of same-sex relationships is nothing short of oppression.

Growing up, both Jeff and I experienced harassment in school. Since getting out of high school, however, I haven't lived with any such mistreatment.

But Referendum 1 was a big, systematic, statewide effort to persecute gay people. And it takes an emotional toll.

JEFF: The 2006 vote here in Wisconsin made me much more aware of how and when other states address the issue of same-sex marriage. I follow the debate nationally now and celebrate successes when they happen, like in New York earlier this year [2011].

FRANK: I watched the last couple of legislative debates and votes in New York via the Internet. And I wasn't expecting to get as emotionally involved as I did in what happened there. But I got *very* emotional. Because this wasn't just the sixth state to legalize gay nuptials. It was New York.

Jeff was out of town at the time. During the New York proceedings, I was posting on Facebook, and didn't appreciate how important getting the legal status had become for me. Seeing it unfold right before my eyes, I realized, "Wow. This is something I really want."

Nothing will ever take the place of our 2010 wedding among family and friends, even if legal status does come to Wisconsin.

But I still sent Jeff a text right after the last vote in New York and said, "I didn't understand how much I want the legal status. And I can't wait to get this with you."

So the fact that I wasn't fully aware of my own feelings and desires tells me I was living under an oppression, that I wasn't allowing myself even to contemplate what I wanted.

The psychological effect of the constitutional amendments' denial of marital rights to same-sex couples was especially poignant to people who had experience from a prior marriage to someone of the opposite sex. Janice, age forty-one, was married to a man and had two children with him before they divorced. When I met her in Charlotte, North Carolina, in July 2012, Janice had lived with Judy, age forty-six, for almost four years.

JANICE: My husband and I moved to North Carolina two months after getting married in West Virginia, and I've lived here ever since. He and I had an immediately recognized societal relationship. We bought a house, took jobs, and had babies.

There are just so many givens with a legally recognized partnership. For better or worse, through that cycle of my life, I just came to take certain things for granted. When somebody asked the question at a coffee house, or in an emergency room, "Is that your wife?" "Why, yes it is." There's just something about being somebody's universally recognized spouse.

Let me put the idea clearly in terms of the straight world. When a female goes from being a boy's girlfriend to becoming his fiancée, there's something among his people, and among yours, that shifts. When you go from being engaged to living together, there's another increase in social status. But, when you go from living together to being legally wed, all of the earlier little hops are suddenly insignificant. Because marriage is a huge leap up. At that point, there's no confusion in anyone's mind about who you are to each other in the world. You're one family, and actually take another person's name and make it yours. You become kin with their kin.

I have an ex-mother-in-law whom I love dearly. And she was my mother-*in-law*. The words themselves tell you about what the quality of the relationship affords you.

So suddenly to be told I'm no longer allowed to have those rights and privileges is jarring. It's a lot different to stand now on the other side, as opposed to enjoying rights while claiming, "Hey, let her have some, too. I have a nice piece of cake here. Someone get her a piece, because I'm not giving her mine." Now, somebody took my piece of cake. It's just gone, and I wondered, "When did I stop being a respectable person, one who now doesn't deserve the same rights I've always had?"

My husband and I made flesh-and-blood people from a place that nobody questioned. Nobody wondered, "Where did those kids come from?"

Because Judy and I get that now. People don't know who I was before I was with her, and lots of people often think we've been together longer than we have been. And so they wonder where the kids came from. "Were they adopted?" "Did they do in vitro?" So they speculate about things like that.

Thus, Amendment 1 made me homeless. The place I'm grounded, where I built my family life, suddenly didn't want me here. And for no reason I could discern. Because it had nothing to do with me as an individual. I'm the same person, the same mom, the same everything that I ever was. I still work. I still pay taxes. I do all the same things I ever did. So I don't understand, and it's deeply, personally hurtful.

So Judy and I are trapped in an eternal engagement.

JUDY: Even when a marriage isn't healthy, the legal status still confers respect upon the couple.

JANICE: And even after a long marital relationship that wasn't entirely healthy, being a divorced mother of two afforded me compassion and respect from the community.

JUDY: So being divorced gives more status than what we have now under Amendment 1.

JANICE: When I became part of a live-in same-sex partnership, everyone from whom I'd received compassion and respect, or even casual relationships at school or at the grocery store, suddenly it was, "Oh. You're one of *those* people."

So now, I'm a different kind of mother than what I'd been before. Somehow, I became less legitimate, and from society's standpoint, I've done nothing but decrease in value steadily over the last four years.

JUDY: But the people who know Janice well would say her development and improvement have gone up over that time. But from the social perspective, the value and legitimacy of her relationships have gone down. So the two don't match up at all.

Issue 1 had significant impact on closeted LGBT people in Ohio. Deborah, who served on a local City Council for several years, elaborated:

DEBORAH: I can tell you there are people who work for the city who aren't out, because a lawyer representing them came to me privately when I sat on the City Council. We have people working for the city who have partners without health care, and because of the social stigma of being gay, are afraid to come out. Nobody at work knows they have a partner, and they're afraid even to ask for benefits for their partner, now that they're branded even more harshly. So those people are hidden in the system.

Q: And that's all as a result of Issue 1?

DEBORAH: Yes, Issue 1. The lawyer I talked to said, "If it were legal, my client would ask." In other words, if it were legal for the city to provide benefits to the same-sex partners of its employees, it would. So it's not worth it for the gay employees to come out. If the city were in a legal position to be able to offer such benefits, and in effect say, "Gee, we think you're fine, and don't have any problem with your being same-sex partners. We don't think there's anything wrong with that. And we're willing to give you benefits." Then the employees would feel more comfortable about being out and asking for benefits.

These are people who've been born and raised in Ohio. So they haven't lived somewhere else, like on the East Coast, where it's more gay friendly. So there's now nothing to be gained for them. There's no one giving them affirmation. Quite the contrary. And they're certainly not going to ask for anything if nothing's to be gained by it.

LITTLE THINGS

Finally, among all of the multifarious impacts of the state constitutional amendments on committed same-sex couples were the small daily annoyances. For example, Terri Phoenix, the director of the LGBTQ Center at UNC-Chapel Hill, said she knew of a state judge who announced that he would no longer issue domestic-violence protective orders against abusive partners in same-sex relationships because of Amendment 1. Even though one way to qualify for statutory domestic-violence coverage in North Carolina is to co-reside and have a romantic relationship, the judge said he did not want to become a test case under the referendum. So he would not sign any so-called 50b orders involving lesbian or gay pairs coming before him.

Lorie L. Burch, the Dallas attorney we met earlier, described an experience that served as another cyclical reminder of her constitutionally mandated marital status:

Shortly after my partner and I got married in California, I was summoned for jury duty, which legal notice comes from a state entity. The juror questionnaire asked whether I was married or single. Well, I take being a lawyer very seriously, and know the law. To the State of Texas and its agencies, I'm not married.

So I was very discouraged to have to check the "single" box. Because in my heart, and across multiple jurisdictions throughout the world, I *am* married. But I knew I had to check the "single" box.

Proposition 2 brought many broad-based deprivations when it comes to rights and taxes. But those losses also occur at a small, emotional level. And they really affect the sense of who we are, and what our relationships mean to other people, in terms of how we're identified and exist as families.

Georgia's Dorothy and Lisa pointed out their periodic reminders of nonmarital status:

LISA: We travel together occasionally and have to rent cars on trips. For legally married couples, there's no additional charge for a spouse as the second driver. But not for me. I have to pay ten dollars a day to drive rental cars. It's a pain in the neck.

DOROTHY: Also, even though we were legally married in Canada and have three children, we can't join the YMCA on a family plan.

Barbara and Jane, the Columbus couple raising two boys, summarized their continuous frustrations with Issue 1:

BARBARA: The constitutional amendment prompts the worst kind of discrimination, because people in authority feel perfectly comfortable dismissing us as a couple.

This week, I was at the hospital to have blood drawn. The nurse was going over the paperwork: "Barbara Wilson, single." "No, I'm not."

Ohio State University pays for my health insurance as a result of Jane's employment there. But they list each of us as "single." Because we're not married in Ohio, or divorced, or widowed. Their forms should be updated to include "partnered."

Yet these kinds of discrimination are subtle...

JANE: ...but everywhere.

BARBARA: We run into it all the time. I'd say something happens at least once each month that informs us we're not legally married. Whether it's with a doctor, or a school event, or some other form. These aren't big things. None of it denies us anything. It's surely not as overt as having to sit at the back of the bus.

But we're reminded like clockwork that we can't be married to each other in Ohio.

A Wisconsin interviewee recounted a galling episode of gross insensitivity that probably was not uncommon in Super-DOMA jurisdictions.

I remember being in a gay bar, and a bunch of young women from a bachelorette party were there, too. Because, you know, gays are fun. Right?

And I was like, "What in the hell are you doing here? You have a lot of nerve flaunting the fact that you can get married with a bunch of people who can't."

WISCONSIN'S DOMESTIC-PARTNER REGISTRY AS A RIGHTS TOUCHSTONE

The domestic-partner registry passed by the Wisconsin Legislature in 2009 provides a useful gauge regarding what basic rights were thought necessary for same-sex couples to possess in order to look after one another. By implication, Super-DOMAs in other states denied these fundamental coverages to gay and lesbian pairs.

Badger State law supplied forty-three rights and protections to same-sex couples as registered domestic partners. Many of these benefits concerned the administration and transfer of a deceased partner's estate, including the ability of a surviving partner to inherit property (such as real estate, vehicles, and personal items titled in the decedent's name) in the absence of a will. The benefits also exempted certain property transferred to a surviving partner from creditors' claims and allowed family support during the administration of a deceased partner's estate.

Other conferred rights related to the presumption of a joint tenancy in real estate owned by a couple, powers of attorney for property and finances, family leave for a sick or dying partner, hospital visitation, the ability to admit an incapacitated partner to a nursing facility, and access to a deceased or incapacitated partner's medical records. Also included were the rights to sue for wrongful death, to get death benefits if a deceased partner was killed in a workplace accident, to receive crime-victim compensation, to consent to an autopsy for a deceased partner, and to make anatomical donations in the event of a partner's death. Finally, the law granted immunity from testifying against a partner.

Legally married couples typically have hundreds of notable relationship rights, including parental responsibilities and protections touching children within families. Yet this list of rights was a decent beginning for lesbian and gay pairs who otherwise had no such protections under state law.

In July 2011, Katie Belanger, the executive director of Fair Wisconsin, elaborated on events in the Badger State:

BELANGER: We've seen an expansion in domestic-partner health care benefits, including the State of Wisconsin in 2009 providing health-insurance benefits to both the same- and opposite-sex domestic partners of state employees. Other local units of state government, like LaCrosse County, now provide those things as well. And the Milwaukee County Board just last week announced their ordinance for benefits.

Plus, private employers have continued to add them into their employee-benefits packages. This spring, Marquette University, a Catholic Jesuit school in Milwaukee, decided that, beginning in January 2012, they would provide those benefits.

So health care improvements are still moving forward. We're not seeing denials or any backtracking in the domestic-partner-benefits realm.

Q: Do you think couples who do legal planning, who get all the paperwork they feel is appropriate, can be confident that their documents will be honored when needed in Wisconsin?

BELANGER: Part of the reason we wanted to put the domestic-partner registry in place was because there's nothing quite as strong as state law.

Anything lesbian and gay couples can get from private attorneys isn't as powerful as having state law behind you. In addition, private arrangements don't necessarily bind third parties if the law itself doesn't do so.

As a result, I think there's much more confidence with the registry than what had been the case before its creation.

Q: Do you know whether people are taking advantage of the registry?

BELANGER: We've had almost 1,800 same-sex couples statewide who've signed up for it in the two years since the registry's inception.

In fact, the domestic-partner registry produced dramatic improvements for some Badger State gay and lesbian pairs. Probably the most striking instance involved Heather, age forty-four, and Teresa, forty-three, who live in Appleton.

Q: Did the 2006 passage of Referendum 1 have some direct, concrete impact upon the two of you?

HEATHER: Most definitely. I had a series of crucial health challenges. And going through these health crises, we realized quickly that part of our commitment as a couple was to take care of each other.

Yet, when my health started tanking, I didn't have the comfort to feel, "Okay. If I can't work, I know Teresa can take care of me in a way that's not going to burn us." Because after Referendum 1, we weren't protected with health insurance or taxation. All the matters that heterosexual couples take for granted weren't available for us.

And my health problems came up immediately after the marriage vote. Probably within weeks after Referendum 1 passed, I was diagnosed with an aneurysm, and eventually MS and cancer.

So it was very clear that I couldn't feel safe and comfortable. "What's going to happen?" was constantly in mind. I'm in a relationship, and we're in love. Yet I felt very much like the government was telling me I was only an individual, that I was by myself.

The irony is that I talked about going on Social Security disability. So instead of my loving partner being able to provide protection for me, through health insurance and other benefits, I'd have to go on the government dole. It just didn't make sense, or seem fair.

So that's how the referendum immediately impacted me.

TERESA: I now work for a company that provides domestic-partner benefits. But we still get taxed on their value by the federal government. So there's a blanket inability of being able to take care of each other without being penalized financially.

HEATHER: Early in 2009, I had to have some testing involving a needle biopsy, not surgery.

I have some trauma issues around my throat. So I didn't want to go through the procedure alone. I called ahead and asked if my partner Teresa could be in the room during the procedure. And I was assured that she could be.

We got to the hospital, and a nurse came, saying that I needed to change clothes. She said Teresa would be fine waiting in the reception area while I undressed.

After changing, I asked the nurse to get my partner. Then the nurse said, "Your friend is going to be much more comfortable out there. Let's leave her be."

Well, I already had trauma issues going on, and now my partner wasn't with me. And I really needed Teresa to be there. And I'd been told that it wouldn't be a problem, that procedures were done with partners present all the time.

So my stress level went up. "She's not just my friend. She's my partner. Can you please go get her?"

This nurse refused to do so for three times.

I started to hyperventilate and get freaked out. I finally said, "I'm not going to have the procedure done now. Because I need her with me."

At the same time, I was afraid I might have cancer, and needed to have the test performed. Yet I was trying to advocate for myself while in a hospital gown, naked underneath, in a vulnerable position.

Then the doctor walked in and said, "What's going on?" The nurse gave her side of the story, and I gave mine. He finally said, "Just go get her partner." So then Teresa came in, not even knowing what had happened.

And I was a wreck. Being tested was already anxiety inducing enough, and I ended up having cancer.

So after this episode, I wrote to [Democratic Wisconsin] Governor [Jim] Doyle, when he was considering domestic-partner protections. Then Fair Wisconsin saw the letter and asked me to speak to the joint finance committee of the legislature.

As a result, we were invested in this early on. Because of the MS, the aneurysm, and pulmonary embolism, we've had numerous hospital situations, whether it was surgery or testing or just visitation.

So the issue was life and death for us. That may sound melodramatic, but I really think that, in a health crisis, when you're so stressed out, and don't have loved ones by your side, you can't battle disease as well as with that support system in place.

So for us it was really, "I need her by my side, life or death." And we testified before the legislature with a very strong conviction.

We were elated when the registry passed. Although we weren't fully equal, the new law provided the basic right for Teresa to be with me in the hospital.

Also, having my end-of-life wishes honored was important since my father is an independent Baptist minister. The stories of what happens when someone goes into a coma, and the religious right comes in...and I could see my family doing that. The whole Terri Schiavo conversation went very differently for them and me. I was very worried about what would happen if I were unable to speak, because my own preferences would've been very different from my family's wishes. But Teresa knows what I want to happen.

So we have those matters protected now with the domestic-partner registry, which was of the utmost importance for us. It was about having her by my side in the hospital.

Before the registry was in effect, I had two throat surgeries and went through radioactive iodine treatment. So we carried around the wills and other documents in our car's glove compartment. Because before the registry, Teresa wasn't technically my spouse or domestic partner, and health care providers could challenge us.

To this day, we still travel with the domestic-partner-registry certificate.

TERESA: We went to Michigan, and Heather had a really serious scare with an asthma attack. She had some of the same symptoms as her pulmonary embolism. So we didn't know what was happening at the time.

I immediately panicked, because our domestic-partnership certificate wasn't valid in Michigan. We had to stop at a hospital in the Upper Peninsula, and I didn't know whether they would let me see her there.

HEATHER: And I was freaking out, too. I kept saying, "Just bring in my partner."

Filling out the paperwork, I felt like I was going to pass out. "I need her now."

TERESA: Having been through this before, we didn't know what to expect.

HEATHER: We felt like linking arms and not letting them take one of us away from the other.

Fortunately, the hospital staff turned out to be fine with us.

TERESA: But you never know.

Q: Michigan is another Super-DOMA state.

HEATHER: And that's the piece most people don't get. We're already in a vulnerable situation. Teresa was scared for my health. And I was having symptoms that only get exacerbated by stress and hyperventilating.

Plus, I have a fear of dying alone, like the lesbian in that Miami hospital room. Gay people have scenes like that play out in their heads. And one of mine is dying alone.

So I feel like the registry guarantees Teresa will be by my side no matter what. It doesn't give us much else. But it protects that. So when I die, I have hope to rest assured that the registry will be honored.

TERESA: With that law in place, the stray people who have problems with us as a couple don't have a legal leg to stand on denying us access. That's what we gained by the registry.

HEATHER: Yes, the random bigots can't say, "Your partner can't come in," because we keep the partnership certificate in our car.

TERESA: Just like married heterosexuals get asked for their marriage certificates. [She laughs.]

HEATHER: Yeah, just like that. I'm sure they all travel with their marriage certificates close at hand.

Another example of the domestic-partner registry's positive impact concerned Gloria, age forty-seven, who works at one of the campuses of the University of Wisconsin.

Q: Can you identify some concrete, tangible way in which Referendum 1 impacted you?

GLORIA: My former employer was a private institution in Ohio, and I had partnership benefits there. But when we moved to Wisconsin, those benefits ended, and my partner Evelyn didn't have health insurance any longer. So that was a really big impact.

When we lived in Ohio, Evelyn had a blood clot that moved to her lung, and she almost died. So she has to be on Coumadin for the rest of her life. And COBRA is outrageously expensive. So from a financial perspective, Referendum 1 really hit us hard. My partner almost died in Ohio, and not being able to add her to my health insurance here was a huge issue.

When I came to the University of Wisconsin, the only thing I could put Evelyn on was secondary dental coverage. That was it. There was nothing else. But if my partner had been a man, he would've gotten all kinds of benefits from my employment.

Two years ago, when the legislature passed the domestic-partner registry, Evelyn was able to get back onto my health insurance. So that helped immensely. Of course, now we have to pay taxes on that benefit.

Q: Can you estimate the dollar amount of how much you're saving because of the registry?

A: At least $5,000 a year, just on health insurance alone.

The minister of a Milwaukee church catering principally to LGBT congregants told me another story of the registry's effect:

I performed a holy union last week for a couple in our congregation.

Herman moved here from Illinois to live with Gary, in his condominium. They were hassled by the condominium management over Herman's parking in the garage and some other petty stuff. The superintendent said, "He's just visiting," claiming that Herman was a renter and not a resident.

So Gary and Herman registered as domestic partners. By doing that, Herman became a resident. The registry resolved their problem with the condominium management.

A final story about the registry, this from a Madison couple, offers a fourth variant of its impact:

We had a vehicle that was originally purchased under our own names. Later, we decided to use it for our business. I submitted the form to the Department of Transportation to transfer the vehicle's title from us to the business.

If you're married, there are some spousal transfers that are allowed free of charge. But if you're not spouses, you have to pay sales tax on the title transfer. So if we were legal spouses, and both owned the business, we wouldn't have to pay the sales tax.

I got a phone call from the person processing our paperwork at the DOT, saying we needed to pay the sales tax. I said, "Look, we're registered domestic partners." She said, "Send me a copy of your registry certificate."

We shouldn't have had to pay that fee. It was somewhat trivial. But I wanted to stand my ground. And as it turned out, the domestic-partner registry allowed us to transfer the vehicle free of charge.

It's an interesting legal benefit. But most people don't realize how marriage unfolds in their lives. Little things like that.

Thus, the forty-three rights and protections supplied to the Badger State's registered domestic partners played out in ways large and small. Yet my Wisconsin interviewees most frequently reported the consequential registry benefits having to do with the provision of health care. As with Heather and Teresa, and Gloria and Evelyn, the 2009 legislation transformed the lives of many same-sex pairs and substantially alleviated Referendum 1's adverse effects.

INABILITY TO DIVORCE OR OTHERWISE ACCESS LEGAL REMEDIES

The chapter's catalog of harmful Super-DOMA impacts has dealt, so far, just with same-sex pairs in healthy and committed relationships. But the legal and other problems prompted by the constitutional amendments were not limited to happy couples. Indeed, different challenges arose when their personal bonds soured and partners became exes.

An interview I conducted in Madison, Wisconsin, revealed a pattern of relationship evolution and dissolution that is not unique to lesbian and gay pairs. Gregory, age forty, became Josh's partner in 1998, when they were university students. Three years later, the two had a large church wedding in front of family and friends, an event that, of course, was not legally recognized. Although Gregory had a master's degree in education, he abandoned his own career plans to follow Josh around the country as his work opportunities unfolded. After three earlier relocations for the couple, a final career move for Josh landed them in Madison in 2009. With each such change of residence based on Josh's evolving professional life, Gregory found jobs as best he could in the new locations. Yet when I interviewed him in July 2011, the economy was still recovering from the 2008–9 Great Recession, and Gregory was unemployed.

Because Josh was the only person in the couple with a 2009 résumé indicating a steady career path, the credit union affiliated with his work demanded that only Josh's name appear on the title and mortgage to their Madison home. As a result, Gregory had no legal property rights when Josh said he wanted to end their relationship. Gregory explained the predicament further:

GREGORY: When Josh instigated our break-up, I had nothing. I didn't have a job. Josh had always promised to help me get back on track. Because during all the years we followed his trajectory, Josh said he'd support my career after his was settled.

So that's how we negotiated the situation we're in now. I live on one side of the house, and he lives on the other. There are two bathrooms, and the arrangement works out, more or less.

Right now, Josh gives me a small cash stipend, a kind of quasi-alimony. But I also help keep the house maintained as part of our deal. I have a credit card to use for conventional things, like shopping and gas.

Needless to say, everything was very tense for the first year.

Q: If you'd been legally married, you could've gone through a divorce proceeding after your relationship dissolved. And the law would've worked out your respective rights and responsibilities.

GREGORY: That's correct. After marriage, straight couples are in the position to have their shared experiences examined, and a court decides what's fair when they separate.

When Josh and I were breaking up, most people we knew were hands-off with regard to me. They made no ethical judgments or observations. Rather, they were completely at arm's length.

But for married straight couples, everyone recognizes that certain choices have to be made when people go different ways. There has to be a balancing out of their prior life together.

But nothing like that is in effect for gay couples. I was terrified at one point, because I felt I had no legal status whatsoever. I was just some stranger in the house. Josh could've kicked me out. Even with the few documents we'd signed, I didn't feel they'd offer any genuine protection. Because wills and such don't apply to any of the larger concerns involved in a break-up.

Q: Let me offer a counterfactual circumstance. Let's say you'd been married legally to Josh, and then you split up and went through a legal divorce.

How do you think your circumstance would be different in that hypothetical situation than it actually is today?

GREGORY: I could've at least argued my case to a judge that I should have a certain percentage of the house, some sort of joint ownership. We'd be able to clearly define our property, what should be his, and what mine.

In addition, since I gave up job opportunities and career advancements to support Josh's work goals, I could establish a legal case for alimony, whether permanent or temporary. In court, I could prove I deserved compensation for making those commitments.

Right now, however, Josh sets all the rules, and I'm totally dependent upon his good will. And that reality makes me nervous. Although Josh may have good intentions, I know at the same time he's struggling with a lot of other issues. So life's random and wild and unsettling.

Once again, Atlanta attorney Barbara E. Katz provided clarity about the legal thicket Gregory's story introduced:

Q: What practical, grassroots effects have you identified as a result of Question 1?

A: Let's start with the you-can-get-married-but-you-can't-get-divorced piece.

Since civil unions and marriages have been available in other jurisdictions, Georgia couples have gone there to get married or unioned. But most don't realize that, once back in Georgia, they can't get divorced.

Although no residency requirement is necessarily mandated to get married, every state demands residency to get divorced. So not only can people not get divorced here in Georgia, they can't get divorced anywhere else because they don't live there.

Now, does inability to divorce matter?[10] Same-sex marriages already aren't being recognized here. So they're not getting any state benefits.

But marriage licenses might be used by couples who're breaking up to demonstrate de facto partnership agreements. Such inferred or implied contracts might create property problems down the road.

If the federal DOMA were invalidated, and folks were getting federal rights – such as Social Security or immigration privileges – when they married, the problem would be even worse. Because then you'd have people married to others they're no longer living with who may be able to claim the federal benefits that might more properly go to more recent partners.

Since 2004, I've had clients contact me with just that question. "My relationship has broken up. I need to get a divorce." And I've had to tell them they need to establish residency somewhere else to do that. Because Georgia judges can't adjudicate any such rights. They certainly can't divorce gay and lesbian people. Even getting a quickie divorce in a place like Nevada might cause financial problems.

Another aspect about the you-can-get-married-but-not-divorced piece is that marriage is a spiritual and emotional event as well as a legal one. Hence, marriage certificates may not be worth anything legally, but they're very meaningful to people spiritually and emotionally. Thus, problems also arise in that way if people aren't divorced but still have new partners.

So folks are still running off and getting married, especially those with kids or who are considering having children. Because they want to tell their kids that they're married, that they were committed enough to each other to get married, and that they deserved to be married.

Although same-sex couples can't be legally married here, they still can plainly document the nature of their relationship in writing. But most people don't do that. The pairs who come to me do wills, health care directives, and financial powers of attorney. At least 95 percent of couples stop there. They don't do partnership agreements, even though I always raise the issue with them.

I tell them that if they own property together, or even if they don't want to do so, they should still have a partnership agreement. Because it makes clear what they're holding separately and what they consider to be joint.

Now, some property can't be titled. You can title a house or car or bank accounts. But you can't title a high-definition, 55-inch TV, where one partner put it on a credit card that month, while the other purchased another item thereafter, or paid the mortgage. So five years later, how does anyone know or even remember, "Is that ours or not ours?"

Without a partnership agreement, there's no way of making such matters clear later on, either to the couple themselves or anyone else. Really ugly

[10] See also Andersen (2009); Schwartz (2011); and Ellis (2015).

situations can arise if a partner dies without a will, and then the decedent's blood relatives swoop down, go through credit-card statements or other kinds of records, and try to take property out of the house.

In eighteen years of law practice, I've probably done fewer than ten partnership agreements, which are enforceable in Georgia. Hence, the vast majority of couples don't address whether their paperwork accurately reflects the reality of their relationships.

So gay and lesbian couples have very limited access to the courts in terms of dividing up property once they split up. The only legal theory that can get them before a judge is of a joint or equitable partition of property. But that's very costly.

At least with a divorce, if a couple were good with paperwork, they could go down to the courthouse and get all the forms and do it themselves. Especially if they don't have kids, the process isn't that difficult.

But there's no comparable self-help approach to do an equitable partition. And in my brief experience from several years ago, judges don't like such lawsuits. Because that theory typically isn't used for the purpose of divorce. Rather, it's usually invoked to divide land among business partners.

A common problem among couples is that, when they split up, one of them doesn't want to move from or sell the marital residence. But the other partner is desperate to sell because they can't afford renting another place while maintaining the home. If a divorce were possible, you'd go in and ask for a temporary hearing within thirty days. Then a judge would decide who gets possession of the marital residence and who has to leave it. And during the pendency of the action, you could ask for a sale of the real estate if one party could demonstrate the need to do so.

But all of that speedy action isn't available with an equitable partition, where the property division wouldn't occur in any way until after a full trial.

Question 1 made clear that Georgia judges can't adjudicate any marital rights with regard to same-sex couples. But I don't think the constitutional amendment would affect a partition, because that legal theory addresses rights related to a piece of land or other property.

However, I'm talking about trial judges here in Fulton and DeKalb Counties. I could see a judge in an outlying county saying, "This petition for equitable partition is really a divorce, and I'm not going to do it because Question 1 prohibits any such judicial action." I could see judges taking that posture.

CONCLUSION

In 2010, Sue Doerfer, Equality Ohio's executive director, summed up Issue 1's general impact, as well as the state's evolution toward achieving basic civil rights for LGBT Ohioans. What she said applied with equal force to most other Super-DOMAs jurisdictions in America's war on same-sex couples:

I worry about Issue 1's overall effects on our community and movement. I know of many people who were very politically active and then just dropped out after 2004. There was one gay man, for instance, who was *the* LGBT advocate in Cleveland. Every politician knew him. He personified political perseverance and hard work. But he's not been heard from since, although he still lives here in Cleveland. The constitutional amendment was so disheartening and discouraging that some people just gave up, although it lit a fire under others.

But the longevity of our community and its capacity to continue doing vital political work are in doubt. I don't think we can overestimate how Issue 1 adversely affected gay people, especially their ability to come out at work and in their neighborhoods, which actions lay the basic ground work for progress.

After six years, we haven't seen any substantial change here for the better. For two years, Equality Ohio has been working hard on House Bill 176 [the Equal Housing and Employment Act, which would protect Ohioans from losing jobs or housing because of sexual orientation or gender identity]. All signs indicate that it's not going to go through this year. So we'll have to start over again in 2011. Which means that this midterm election is huge for the LGBT community in Ohio. [In November 2010, Republicans swept to power in the state.]

Equality Ohio sponsors an annual lobby day at the capitol in Columbus, and we're seeing fewer and fewer LGBT people coming to talk with legislators. Instead, we witness more and more despair.

I keep saying, "We need a win. We need a win!" I don't want to give up on 176, and I'm not going to. But I also believe we should think about pushing bills that would be easier to pass, in order to show LGBT folks there's something we can accomplish, that there can be a victory somewhere. Otherwise, I don't know what's going to happen to this community, because people are just so, so frustrated.

And, seeing other states have their successes, or then lose and come back, we sit here in Ohio going, "Wait a minute. How does Massachusetts achieve what it does? How does California do it? And we can't even get basic employment nondiscrimination here?" Look at Iowa [where the state supreme court authorized marriage equality in 2009], for goodness sake. That just came out of nowhere.

Since 2004, we've gotten alternately depressed, angry, and incited to action. Now that motivation is waning because we're not seeing any results for all of our work and time.

Bowling Green, Ohio, passed a nondiscrimination ordinance last year. Then antigay activists organized and circulated petitions, and the matter's on the ballot in November to repeal the ordinance. And this's just nondiscrimination in employment and housing in a college town. It's not about relationship recognition. Now I think our chances are pretty good to win, to keep it. [In fact, 52 percent of Bowling Green voters approved the ordinance that year.]

But still, tens of thousands of dollars have to be spent on a campaign, with massive energy going into it, when that time and money could be used more productively doing something proactive. So again, we're defending ourselves. We're put in a crouch, constantly having to justify our own well-being.

Dayton has an historical marker about a famous lesbian, which was vandalized a few weeks ago. And I'm guarding against telling anybody about the incident, because I don't want to discourage people any more. I don't want them to know how horrible it really is.

So although I can't measure harmful impact in any social-scientific way, I certainly can feel it in the community, because of the work I do, trying to motivate people. And it feels like there's this enormous weight on top of us, crushing us down.[11]

House Bill 176 has never become law in Ohio, nor have comparable legislative measures been embraced in other Super-DOMA states. As of 2015, these 28 jurisdictions had no statewide legal protections against sexual-orientation discrimination in the workplace: Alabama, Alaska, Arizona, Arkansas, Florida, Georgia, Idaho, Indiana, Kansas, Kentucky, Louisiana, Michigan, Mississippi, Missouri, Montana, Nebraska, North Carolina, North Dakota, Ohio, Oklahoma, Pennsylvania, South Carolina, South Dakota, Tennessee, Texas, Virginia, West Virginia, and Wyoming.[12]

[11] See also Riggle and Rostosky (2007).
[12] Cf. Button, Rienzo, and Wald (2000); Taylor et al. (2012); and Scheiber (2015)

4

The Effects of Super-DOMAs on Families with Children Being Raised by Same-Sex Couples

LGBT people can become parents in sundry ways. For example, biological children from prior relationships with heterosexual partners may join a subsequently formed lesbian or gay partnership.[1] Same-sex pairs can also become parents by means of adoption, intrauterine insemination, in vitro fertilization, or surrogacy. In any event, the Williams Institute at the School of Law of the University of California-Los Angeles estimated that, as of 2013, 122,000 same-sex couples in the United States were raising 210,000 children under age eighteen, of whom 58,000 were adopted or foster children (Gates 2015). Thus, parenting had become an integral part of American LGBT communities by the early twenty-first century.

Regardless of how children came to join the homes of gay and lesbian pairs in Super-DOMA states, however, such families faced significant hurdles engendered and exacerbated by such constitutional amendments. If only because the two parties in a same-sex coupling cannot both be the biological parents of a single child, the legal parentage of kids being raised in households headed by lesbian and gay partners was always the most vexing perennial issue in states that denied any relationship recognition to such parental pairs as part of America's war on same-sex couples and their families.

At best, one partner could be the biological, and therefore legal, parent at the time of a child's birth. Or in the case of the adoption of children from their biological parent(s), legal status would first come to just one partner of a same-sex couple because Super-DOMA jurisdictions typically did not permit so-called joint adoptions by unmarried pairs. Thereafter with both biological

[1] The most interesting story I heard in this context among my 175 interviews involved Lois and Ruby, a lesbian couple in Georgia raising four teenage children. Each woman brought two biological offspring to the relationship from prior marriages to men. And each of the two ex-husbands themselves were subsequently partnered with other men.

and adoptive children, the other partner in a same-sex coupling might seek to attain legal parental status through a process known as second-parent adoption, which is equivalent in effect to traditional stepparent adoptions for married heterosexual pairs.

Many of the gay and lesbian couples I talked with across six states who were raising children, or who wanted to do so, were desperately trying to achieve full legal status for both partners as parents (e.g., Bernard 2011; Bosman 2015; Engel 2015, 297–99; cf. Sterett 2009). This chapter covers both the large and small reasons they sought out such standing, as well as why it was so elusive to them.

Among the most touching, as well as emblematic, discussions I had involving the complexities that same-sex pairs in Super-DOMA states faced as parents was one with Janice and Judy in Charlotte, North Carolina, who appeared in the last chapter. In our interview Janice compared her experiences first being married to a man and then being partnered with a woman:

JUDY: The kids have been asking why we don't get married.
JANICE: They talk about it.
JUDY: They bring it up a lot.

When Janice and I first got together, the kids were just six and eight, and didn't understand initially that the same kind of option available to Janice and their father didn't exist for us. And they really didn't grasp why not.

It would mean a lot to them for us to be married and for our family to have that public recognition.

JANICE: After Judy and I moved in together, the kids said, "So now you're in love, and you're going to get married." And we were like, "Well, we could have a ceremony. But it really wouldn't be a legal marriage."

Having to explain that to them was painful. Because they've watched, and even participated in, all kinds of weddings at our church. So they thought our ceremony would be just like those other ones. But they didn't understand the contract-law part of it.

They grew up in a home with their father and me, and he and I raised them to a certain age. Then they learned what a divorce is. So afterward, they thought, "Mom and Judy live together now. So we're going to be in the same kind of a family with them." It certainly feels the same to them. So they don't accept how our wedding would be any different.

That's a hard thing to explain to your own kids, that the law doesn't consider Judy and me to be a real couple. Friends and family respect us, sure. But the legal reality is heartbreaking to them and to us.

So the inequity of Amendment 1 is very fresh and tangible for all of us.

Q: What did the referendum's passage mean to you in the broadest sense of the word?

JUDY: So many times, I've been committed to a struggle, with political hope. My life experiences have taught me that, unfortunately, eight or nine times out of ten, the investment and fight have a bigger picture, longer term benefit. But the immediate battle is almost always lost. There are great rallies, and everybody goes to the voting booth. Then you realize other people just don't see the issues the same way you do.

It was harder for me this time around, however, because I saw the political process through our kids' eyes. They wanted to come to some of the rallies prior to the vote. And they saw so many people there agreeing with us. But that's not how the reality ultimately turned out. And they were totally crestfallen.

So Amendment 1 was like seeing such policy losses through fresh eyes. My world gets better, but it doesn't get well.

JANICE: We have kids leaving elementary school going into middle school, where it's already mean. Children that age always look for flaws in others. And here are our sweet kids with two moms. That fact will give other children the opportunity to take our kids down a peg.

I worry about the youngest child, my son, in particular. In a sense, I feel like I'm contributing to his life being made harder. He cried mightily the day Amendment 1 passed. He couldn't fathom how God would let that happen.

Q: Do the public schools recognize both of your involvements with the children, in terms of picking them up or signing papers or intervening if some health crisis comes up at school?

JANICE: I can sign as a parent, and their dad can, too. Judy can't sign, unless the matter involves something I've authorized her to do beforehand. I can list her as a person to pick up the kids. But I can list anyone to do that.

JUDY: The rest of it is really grace. But their school is fantastic, and the staff there seem to be geared to handle those kinds of situations.

But I find, as in many aspects of life, ... For instance, I worked at a company in Florida for fifteen years, and never felt an ounce of discrimination. My same-sex partners were always welcomed whenever we went on company gatherings. But when the business grew to have more than fifteen employees, and management had to write an employee manual, they put a nondiscrimination clause in that didn't include sexual orientation. And I responded like, "I'm sure you made this little oversight." But the issue actually turned out to be a very big problem, because they were only going to put in whatever federal law required. My boss kept saying, "What does it matter? We treat you well here. We've never discriminated against you. So don't you feel protected?" And I answered, "Although I've been treated well, I don't feel protected."

So it's the same thing at the schools. I feel fortunate I'm treated very well. But what I said in Florida is probably true for the school too.

It's like walking around, and everybody else has an umbrella on their hip, and they say, "Who cares? It's sunny outside." But if it starts to rain, and everybody but me has an umbrella they can whip out and put up, then I'm not really protected at all from the rain.

JANICE: And Judy could only get by if somebody decided to share their umbrella. That's what we mean by grace.

JUDY: Like Blanche DuBois, we always have to depend on the kindness of strangers. That's the reality of how it is at school.

JANICE: Because Judy has zero parental rights.

JUDY: But in terms of day-to-day functions, I'm well recognized. I go to a lot of parent-teacher meetings, and nobody has ever treated me any differently than a parent. And I'm glad for that.

JANICE: Judy is very insightful with regard to kid-related stuff.

JUDY: But without the legal recognition, it could just as easily go the other way, even at the same school with a different leadership or school counselor. That's where the legal and civil rights fight is so important.

I'm glad societal values are becoming more favorable toward LGBT people. Thank goodness for that. But until the laws catch up, I don't have an umbrella.

JANICE: Grace isn't the same thing as having your own umbrella. It's just not.

Had I gotten into a relationship with another man, and if we'd followed the same kind of path, moved in together and decided to get married, we could be at a point where, as my legal spouse, he'd have the children on his insurance as a stepparent. And should issues arise with their biological father, my new husband could even attempt adoption or something like it.

I'm not saying that would be the path we'd follow. But Judy would have so many more options if she simply were a man.

JUDY: There's a lot more work we need to do. Because if something happened to Janice, I'd have no right to the kids at all. And I don't know what would really happen to them.

If the kids were to go to their father, I'd really have to count on grace to see them again.

JANICE: Judy has always had a good relationship with my ex-husband. The three of us have attended the same church for many years. That's where Judy and I met.

But I know my ex-husband well. It would take a lot of grace for Judy to see the kids again.

JUDY: It would require extra effort on his behalf, and that's not something he's really good at. Going out of his way doesn't happen with him.

Plus, all of his family is in New Jersey. What would hold him in North Carolina if he got sole legal custody of the kids? Nothing. So it's a truly scary thought.

The six states in the study varied significantly regarding whether and how both partners in a same-sex coupling could become the legal parents of the children they were raising.[2] The interstate differences are sufficiently interesting to warrant beginning the chapter with state-specific oral histories comparing and contrasting the programmatic and practical variations, followed by subject-matter-specific commentary more generally applicable to all Super-DOMA jurisdictions.

I start with the states having the greatest restrictions on second-parent adoptions, then progress to those with fewer limitations, and end with the most bizarre situation.

---

[2] Engel (2015, 297) noted the variability and flux of the legal environment: "As of June 2014, 23 states and the District of Columbia permitted second-parent adoption as an option for same-sex couples, which marks a more than 100 percent increase in less than a decade."

MICHIGAN AND OHIO

Both the Wolverine State and the Buckeye State outright denied second-parent adoptions for same-sex couples (*In re Adoption of Jane Doe* 1998).[3]

A Cleveland interviewee with a good friend who worked for a local Ohio adoption agency shared how the organization handled lesbian and gay pairs who wanted to adopt children:

Our friend warns same-sex couples that, when it's time to go before a judge to finalize an adoption, only one of them can enter the courtroom. The nonadopting partner has to stay outside. Only the adoptive parent can go in.

And she warns people at the very beginning of the process that this is going to happen, because, psychologically, it's the hardest part of the adoption. It's this very visible and tangible moment when it's clear that only one person can be the legal parent. And that's horrific for couples who've hoped, and dreamed, and planned together for families.

NORTH CAROLINA

Before 2011, the law on second-parent adoptions in the Tar Heel State was in flux. Paula, age forty-five, and birth mother to son Keith, described her experience in Durham obtaining a second-parent adoption for her partner Diana:

When Keith was born [in 2004], we set about doing a second-parent adoption. Sharon Thompson is the lawyer in Durham who instigated second-parent adoptions in North Carolina. She worked with local judges in the Durham County court who'd agreed to grant such adoptions. She was seeing clients from all around the state. So people residing in other counties would get second-parent adoptions in Durham County.

So I knew about this and thought it was important for us to pursue it. We used an adoption agency to do the home visits and get all of our paperwork done. Then Diana used Sharon as her lawyer. I was to have a different one. They wanted to make sure each parent had a separate attorney to prevent lawsuits in the future.

So we went through the second-parent adoption process. Keith was still under a year old. We were thrilled to have it in place, even though we knew that it hadn't been tested. We still felt some degree of security, that it was a legally sanctioned adoption.

Yet the state wouldn't grant us a new birth certificate, despite the second-parent adoption. So to this day, Keith's birth certificate just lists me as his mother, and there's a blank line for where the father would be. We were advised not to put the other partner in the father line. We were told that could create confusion in the future.

So we did everything we thought we could. We went to great trouble and expense to have this done. And it's emotionally challenging to invite an adoption social worker into your home when you're an established couple and have decided to have a child together and have the child and are already co-parenting him. To invite a social worker into your home to assess whether you and your home environment are fit to adopt a child that you already have together – it's not just ironic, it's really insulting and heartbreaking.

[3] In Ohio, however, a parent could voluntarily share with a nonparent the care, custody, and control of his or her child through a valid shared-custody agreement (*In re Bonfield* 2002).

To know that straight couples can have children without even planning to have them and that they don't even want – all without any trouble whatsoever or any question about their legal entitlement and recognition – and for us to be so conscious and well prepared and desirous of being parents – and then to have all that under scrutiny was really challenging and disheartening for us.

In December 2010, the North Carolina Supreme Court ruled that second-parent adoption was not available in the state (*Boseman v. Jarrell*).

WISCONSIN

As discussed in the last chapter, starting in 2009, same-sex couples in the Badger State crucially benefited from its domestic-parent registry. But at the same time, they were denied access to second-parent adoptions as a result of the Wisconsin Supreme Court's 1994 *Angel Lace* decision, even though other jurisdictions like Massachusetts and New York permitted such adoptions at about the same time, as outlined in Chapter 2.

Yet, whenever there is great demand for an important product or service, a source of supply often emerges, as Katie Belanger, executive director of Fair Wisconsin, explained.

Q: I've heard a rumor that, despite the *Angel Lace* precedent, there's a single state judge in LaCrosse[4] who, on occasion, fits in second-parent adoptions for same-sex couples.

A: Yes. But there are only a few attorneys in the state who will present a couple to get one of those LaCrosse adoptions. Because there's a difference of opinion in the Wisconsin legal community about whether that's the right way to handle things. Some attorneys don't believe that, just because a judge will do something, it's necessarily legitimate or enduring.

Nonetheless, what this judge does is first grant a motion to terminate the rights of the biological parent. Then the judge permits a joint adoption for the couple. So some attorneys feel there's a loophole within the current adoption law for nonbiological parents. Because second-parent adoptions are basically stepparent adoptions.

Unfortunately, this technique is being challenged by some of the very same couples who obtained LaCrosse adoptions. There's a case in Washington County right now where a lesbian couple got such a joint adoption. But they have since broken up. And the biological mother has engaged a new attorney who says the joint adoption shouldn't stand.

So it's all a great big mess.

---

[4] LaCrosse is a city of about 50,000 on the Mississippi River, which forms Wisconsin's boarder with Minnesota.

Denise, age forty-six, exemplified a dilemma faced by many partners in same-sex relationships in Super-DOMA states. She and Tammy, forty, have lived together for three years in Madison. Tammy has custody of her nine-year-old biological son Patrick.

DENISE: Referendum 1 affects us directly every day with regard to raising Patrick. A recent example is that he fractured his toe. My work schedule is much more flexible than Tammy's. But I couldn't take Patrick to the doctor because I have no legal relationship with him. Rather, Tammy had to take off work to do so, and lose a day's pay. So those practical everyday events are huge for us.

And Patrick's identifying who we are to other people is challenging for him.

TAMMY: Married people take these simple daily things for granted. "That's our kid, and each of us can take him to the doctor."

Q: If your local public school required a parent to sign an authorization form for Patrick, would they accept Denise's signature?

DENISE: In that circumstance, I just sign Tammy's name. Because I don't know what would happen if I signed my own.

The far more difficult hurdle for me is that my inability to be Patrick's legal parent complicates my relationship with him. Because we tell him, and he tells other people, that he has two moms.

But I never really know where I fit in. When it comes down to it, if Tammy and I broke up, it would be "See yah."

Tammy has said that wouldn't happen. But I don't have any rights to Patrick. So it's a little scary to commit now with a child, knowing I don't have any legal status with him at all.

I've already dedicated my heart 100 percent. But there's always this nagging fear in the back of my mind saying, "This could go away. Don't give 110 percent."

A second Badger State couple addressed different concerns about starting a family. Irene, age thirty-two, and Marilyn, thirty-three, have been together seven years. Marilyn works for the city of Milwaukee.

IRENE: We plan to have children. I have health insurance through Marilyn's employment, because the city of Milwaukee provides domestic-partner benefits. They cover me, but not anyone I would birth.

I've written letters to the mayor and our alderman in the hope of changing the policy. The insurance for employees of the Milwaukee Public Schools was just amended to cover the children of domestic partners. And I pointed out that, if you're married, stepchildren are covered.

But in Marilyn's division of the city, my children wouldn't be. So this local policy needs to be changed before we can make any decisions.

I don't want to bring someone into the world when they won't have health care.

MARILYN: The irony is that the costs of the pregnancy itself would be covered. But once the child pops forth from the womb, it would be on its own.

IRENE: There's the possibility that, if Marilyn becomes the child's guardian, the baby might be able to be covered. But there'd still be a lapse in insurance after birth. Moreover, there's no guarantee of any ultimate coverage. So that's why we aren't sure right now about having children.

Q: Let's talk about other same-sex couples you know here in Wisconsin. Can you identify people who've been directly and concretely impacted by Referendum 1, other than what you've said about yourselves?

MARILYN: The whole two-parent adoption thing is a big issue. People are standing on their heads and spinning, trying to figure out legal ways to cover things. The options range from guardianship paperwork to folks who go to LaCrosse, where supposedly there's a judge, during a certain phase of the moon, if you go down the proper hallway, to an unmarked door on the left, and knock three times – and with a very expensive lawyer – you can get a two-parent adoption.

IRENE: It costs $15,000 if everything works out right. That's like a half-year of college at some universities. It's part of the tax on being gay in the state.

I met Ben, age thirty-four, and Ted, thirty-three, in Ohio, where one of them had just begun a teaching career after graduating the year before our interview from the University of Wisconsin. They were raising Brandon, their infant son whom they adopted in the Badger State.

TED: Second-parent adoptions have been going on in LaCrosse for about six years. At first, the state's vital statistics bureau refused to issue birth certificates with the names of both same-sex parents on them. But now they do.

So we have adoption orders and a revised birth certificate with both of our names on it as Brandon's parents.

Q: So it's official then?

BEN: Yes. But we initially didn't plan to proceed with the LaCrosse option because it's legally sketchy. With only one judge in all of Wisconsin doing it, the process is obviously heterodox.

We weren't going to go that route because we always assumed we'd relocate after graduation to a state where we'd be able to do a second-parent adoption above board.

But then, when we figured out we were moving to Ohio instead of somewhere like California, we seized on the LaCrosse alternative, knowing that Ohio would have to recognize an adoption order and birth certificate from Wisconsin under full faith and credit. It was our last chance for the foreseeable future.

TED: And cost us another $5,000.

A last Wisconsin-related interview echoed the experience of Ben and Ted and also touched on another alternative for second parents. Esther and Sheila, both in their mid-thirties, had each been the birth mother to one of their two daughters. Esther described how they approached parenthood:

I had mixed feelings about the gay community trying so hard to get the legal rights of marriage. Of all the things they could've pushed for, why marriage as opposed to anything else? But I get it.

Now, being the mother of two children, I understand even more. The state supreme court ruled there aren't any second-parent adoptions in Wisconsin. As a result, I'm the guardian of my older daughter. And Sheila will become the guardian of our younger daughter.

So I appreciate more that marriage is all about rights having very practical purposes.

Our lawyer was really against the LaCrosse option. Plus, it would cost us between $6,000 and $10,000. We had friends who did it but only because they moved to Michigan, where the circumstances were worse. So our attorney thought guardianship was the better choice.

Yet the biggest potential problem is that either Sheila or I could unilaterally dissolve the guardianship for the child we bore if we wanted to. Thus, there's no guaranteed permanency to the situation.

TEXAS

The second most populous state in the nation offered slightly more choices to gay and lesbian parents than Wisconsin. "Texas [wa]s one of nineteen states where the potential for joint adoption by same-sex couples [wa]s 'unclear,' meaning that it c[ould] vary from county to county and [wa]s at the discretion of the judge" (Engel 2015, 297).

Carl, a forty-eight-year-old journalist, and Henry, a fifty-year-old college professor, have been together for twenty-nine years, live in Dallas, and are raising two adopted sons, ages six and eleven. They provided a wide-ranging perspective on gay parenthood in the Lone Star State five years after the Texas Super-DOMA passed:

Q: Has Proposition 2 had some direct impact upon the two of you?

HENRY: It definitely impacted how we looked at bringing children into our family. Because we considered all the alternatives. Prop 2 definitely caused us to take a more conservative approach with that.

CARL: Our consideration even involved the structure of adoption for us. We had to do it twice. We first had to adopt the kids and then do second-parent adoptions.

So that complexity forces you to look at and understand what's behind it. And the marriage element is a big part of that.

HENRY: At first, we were really leaning toward adopting in California, where we both could adopt as a couple at once. But we decided to go with a local adoption for a different reason.

Representatives from the Texas Child Protective Services contacted us to participate in their program. They seek out as parents gay couples in long-term relationships. So the State of Texas actively recruits lesbian and gay parents.

CARL: Because we're more open to taking kids with special needs.

HENRY: The program has been in place for several years. We have friends who participated in it about a decade ago. So we were familiar with the project and the people who run it.

They've been expanding the program since they've found that gay and lesbian couples in long-term relationships are more open to adopting sibling groups and children with special needs.

Q: Where did the second-parent adoptions take place?

CARL: That's a good question.
HENRY: Ours took place in San Antonio [which is more than 250 miles from Dallas].
CARL: And there's a good reason for that, too.
HENRY: The San Antonio court system allows attorneys, when filing cases, to request specific judges. Here in Dallas, judges are assigned randomly.
CARL: So if we got a judge unwilling to sign second-parent adoptions for same-sex couples, we couldn't have proceeded.
HENRY: It's a lot more problematic here.
    There are quite a few supportive judges in Austin, which was our second alternative.
    But San Antonio is the quickest and safest way to do it.
CARL: The goal of Child Protective Services is to get children placed. And they have kids with special needs in their program who might age out of the system. So they look at every avenue they can. They've found that gays and lesbians are a perfect option for placing children with special needs.

Q: And this is an agency of a state with a Super-DOMA in its constitution?

CARL: Right.

Q: And they're the ones who told you to go to San Antonio?

HENRY: Yes. That's where they recommended we go.

Q: What ages were your sons when you adopted them?

CARL: Four and nine.
HENRY: We had them as foster children first, because the program is foster-to-adopt.
    And that's another reason why gay and lesbian couples are more open to it, since there's a chance in the process the children will be placed back with their biological parents.
    Yet by the time children get into this program, there's an 80 percent probability they'll be adopted. In our case, for instance, the mother had voluntarily relinquished her rights already, and the biological fathers weren't involved with the boys at all.
    But we had to go through the process of finding the fathers and having them sign off their rights.
    Also, once the fathers are identified, there's the potential that grandparents or aunts and uncles or other biological relatives could get involved. There's always that possibility.
    So a lot of straight couples don't want to participate in a program with that amount of risk.
CARL: But Texas is still a conservative state. At any point, the legislature could even make changes to these programs.

HENRY: It's a policy at the state level. And there have been some discussions about changing it.

But the agency's representatives have testified to the legislature that it's a problem for them to place all of the kids in their custody, and if the legislature changed the policy, the problem would be exacerbated. So the agency has vigorously defended the program.

Q: So there've been actual state legislative hearings?

HENRY: Yes. But nothing has changed so far. The hearings took place before our participation in the program.

Q: Was the legislative consideration before or after Prop 2 passed?

HENRY: A year or two after.

The legislature was looking at prohibiting gay and lesbian couples from adopting, which appeared to be one of the next steps after Prop 2.

Q: So the Texas legislature was considering another referendum?

CARL: Absolutely.

HENRY: After Florida and Arkansas acted to ban gay adoptions, they considered that policy here. But the bill never got out of committee.

Q: What about after you adopted the children? Did you have any legal problems as two dads?

HENRY: The biggest issue is with their medical situation. Our eleven-year-old was born with a seizure disorder because of brain damage. So he has some medical issues.

The children have Carl's last name. So my surname is different from theirs. During the foster period, there wasn't a problem, because every document had my name and Carl's name as the foster parents of these children. And the children had a different last name at the time.

But as soon as the adoptions happened, their names changed. And then it became a question of who I was to the children.

Q: Did you ever investigate the option of moving to one family name?

HENRY: We did. A hyphenated last name was the one we talked about the most.

But in the end, we decided against it, because we didn't want to complicate writing their names for the children.

CARL: That was a major issue. More than anything, it was the element that cinched the matter for us. How would the kids cope with it?

HENRY: They had difficulty dealing with the name situation to begin with. It was confusing to them.

Carolyn, age thirty-four, and Stephanie, thirty-six, have been together for eight years, live in a Dallas suburb, and are raising two-year-old son Donald, for whom Stephanie is the birth mother.

STEPHANIE: Going to San Antonio to get Carolyn a second-parent adoption would cost $5,000. For Donald. And Carolyn wants to have her own child. So that would be $10,000 just for us to stay in Texas.

If we moved to another state where we could be legally married, or even get a civil union, we'd pay $30 for a license to achieve stepparent status.

So the costs of living here continue to add up.

CAROLYN: And not just the financial ones.

STEPHANIE: Yeah, the financial is only a part of what we're thinking about.

CAROLYN: The anxiety costs are high. I'm a stay-at-home mom for a child I'm not legally tied to.

When Stephanie gave birth, she had a Caesarean section and really needed to recover and sleep.

This woman came up from the records department, because in Texas, if there's no father present for the birth, you have to sign an "absent-parent" form.

STEPHANIE: They don't say "absent father." They say "absent parent."

CAROLYN: But you know where the mom is.

STEPHANIE: This clerk was very clear who we were...

CAROLYN: ...in the situation. But you have to sign this form, basically saying the father has been informed of the birth and has had the opportunity to have a relationship, and that kind of stuff.

So the first time this woman came up, we said, "Your form doesn't apply to our circumstance, because this was an anonymous sperm donation. The other parent is right here."

STEPHANIE: And we were in the city of Dallas. And in pockets of Texas, Dallas being one of them, it's fine. We didn't experience any prejudice.

CAROLYN: There was no problem. But this woman needed to get her form done. So she said, "I'm sorry," and left.

Then she came back and said, "My supervisor says you must do it anyway." That Stephanie would have to sign it.

At this point, Stephanie was asleep. And I was like, "I'm not waking her up for this." So I just signed her name.

But there's an emotional and spiritual cost to that. *I signed a form saying I didn't exist.*

Q: What would've happened if you'd refused to sign?

STEPHANIE: She said the hospital couldn't release Donald's birth certificate until this form was signed.

GEORGIA

Among the six states in this study, Georgia without doubt provided the most complicated – indeed, simply mind-boggling and Kafkaesque – setting for lesbian and gay couples raising minor children or wanting to do so. The Peach State offered the worst-case scenario of inimical public policy regarding same-sex parenting in the era of Super-DOMAs, because Georgia added an additional major hurdle to all of the other challenges confronting lesbian and gay parents.

Unlike Texas, Wisconsin, and other states where same-sex couples could apply for second-parent adoptions in counties other than their own, the Peach State demanded bona fide residence within the counties where such adoptions were sought. Would-be adoptive parents had to deal with the judges in their own counties and nowhere else. Legal localism ruled the day in Georgia.

Jeff Graham, the executive director of Georgia Equality, supplied the political context for the Georgia case:

Q: Has Question 1 had any effect on the children of same-sex couples?

A: The most direct impact upon children is that we're very hesitant to move forward with statewide legislation to authorize second-parent adoptions here in Georgia.

Right now, the status of the law is silent on the topic. A trial-court judge, in his or her discretion, determines what's in the best interest of the child. So we have judges in the metropolitan Atlanta area who fairly routinely grant second-parent adoptions. Thus, on a case-by-case basis, second-parent adoptions are granted throughout the state.

One of our big political concerns over the last couple of years has been the legislature's enacting language that would ban second-parent adoptions or LGBT foster parents, either through legislation or yet another constitutional amendment. We believe if we lost that fight, the result could be really devastating to families that live right now in the gray areas of the law, which isn't an ideal position for them.

But we don't think we have the political strength yet to ensure a victory against such hostile actions. A proposal we currently [January 2010] have before DeKalb County, which does offer domestic-partner benefits, is that the county revisit its ordinance to ensure that nonbiological children would also be covered.

So we're making some progress, but also being very strategic about it in jurisdictions where we don't think it will be controversial or otherwise set off red flags.

Jason A. Cecil, an activist with Atlanta Stonewall Democrats, elaborated on the Peach State's political setting for families headed by same-sex couples:

One of the LGBT community's fears every year with regard to the state legislature is, "Are they going to pull the trigger and take our kids away?"

A couple of factors have prevented that kind of action so far. One is that some of our female suburban Republican legislators feel that going after children in the families of gay couples would just be cruel when there's no large-scale "problem" of judges approving lots of gay adoptions. Our hope is that their belief will remain the same.

Another reason for legislative inaction on the matter is that the Division of Family and Children Services of the Georgia Department of Human Services has lobbied to keep the issue at bay. The state's child welfare agency knows full well that lesbian and gay pairs make good candidates for kids with special needs. Many children requiring foster placements would otherwise remain institutionalized but for the LGBT community.

Yet if there were ever a good political storm where Republicans thought they had to gin up their base, I could see such an amendment coming out of the legislature.

And all hell would break loose if they ever went after the children of gay couples. It would be pandemonium.

As in the last chapter regarding Super-DOMA effects on same-sex couples themselves, Atlanta attorney Barbara E. Katz offered a comprehensive and accessible overview of how Georgia law affected gay and lesbian pairs and their children:

KATZ: I think it's profoundly true that children benefit more from having two legal parents compared to just one. Dual legal parentage amounts to a back-up plan. With co-parenting, helpmates, or whatever you want to call it, children are in more stable environments having two legal parents than just one. So it doesn't benefit children to deny marriage to their parents. Nonetheless, Georgia doesn't recognize same-sex marriages or civil unions from other states.

Under Georgia law, if a person has a baby out of wedlock, there's only one legal parent. Any same-sex partner is a legal stranger to the child. If the mother dies in childbirth or sometime before the child reaches majority, he or she has just one legal parent.

An enormous number of my clients have or want children. Clients form families in many different ways. Most women, if they're younger, are having children biologically.

Now if a straight woman were legally married to a husband who was sterile and she needed to be artificially inseminated to have a child, when she gave birth to the baby, it would have two legal parents. That's Georgia law. As long as the husband consents to the artificial insemination, he's a legal parent even though he's not the genetic father.

For the same exact facts with gay couples, the baby has just one legal parent. In order to make both parents legal, they need to do a second-parent adoption. And part of my practice is doing second-parent adoptions. The procedure costs about $2,000. A judge might require a home study, which would add $500, and fingerprinting, which is $50. Filing fees are $85. So it's a costly process. And if couples have more than one child, they pay the same outlay over again.

But that circumstance applies only if they're lucky enough to be able to do a second-parent adoption, which occurs if they live in either Fulton County or DeKalb County or Athens-Clark County.[5] Plus there may be a judge in Savannah doing it and one elsewhere. But that's it. And Georgia has 159 counties.

I did a first adoption for parents you interviewed. But I can't do a second-parent adoption for them in Cobb County. It's not going to happen because judges are randomly assigned to cases, and once an assignment is made, you're stuck with that judge for as long as she or he remains on the bench. There are a good number of judges in Cobb who won't grant second-parent adoptions. And those clients ran afoul of that reality in their first adoption, because their home study made a bare mention of the

---

[5] DeKalb County covers roughly the eastern half of Atlanta, while Fulton County extends over the western half. The University of Georgia is located in Athens-Clark County.

fact that they wanted to do a second-parent adoption. They were going to do all the paperwork that was necessary for a guardianship by the second parent if something happened to the first. And they indicated they wanted to do a second-parent adoption. And the judge went ballistic. She wasn't going to sign it. She referred it out to a senior judge. And I already knew that that judge wouldn't sign it. So we had to postpone the case and wait for a different senior judge. And the second senior judge required a meeting with me and the adoption agency's director. It was just absurd. Because the senior judge wanted to know what would happen to the fifteen-year-old in the event the judge didn't sign off on the adoption. The adoption agency told the judge that the fifteen-year-old would have to go back into residential treatment. That's where he would end up.

So there are a whole lot of people having kids in the state who can't do a second-parent adoption because they don't live in a county that grants them. I did a first adoption for a gay-male couple in Henry County, which is also in the metropolitan Atlanta area. After we finished, I asked my clients to leave because I wanted to talk to the judge about whether he would be amenable to a second-parent adoption. And he said, "I don't know anything about that." He was a very nice judge. So I asked if I could give him a case to look at that offered some precedent, although it wasn't explicitly involving a same-sex couple. The case allowed a nonstepparent to do a stepparent adoption in the best interest of the child. And I made a pitch to the judge about why the best interests of the child would be served in this case and why therefore he should grant it.

The judge went home to read the case and called me the next day. He told me he put out a question on the judges' Listserv. I didn't even know that judges had their own Listserv. He asked the Listserv whether there were any judges doing second-parent adoptions for same-sex couples. He asked for people to let him know because he was interested in the question. He did not get back one answer. So he said to me, "No one is doing them. I'm not going to be the first. I'm in a conservative county."[6]

Now I personally knew at the time that more than 90 percent of the judges in DeKalb County permitted second-parent adoptions for gay and lesbian pairs, and more than half the judges in Fulton County did them. But they didn't respond to this judge. So clearly there weren't any judges willing to acknowledge they were doing second-parent adoptions for same-sex couples. This matter occurred before *Wheeler v. Wheeler* (2007), the case that became public about second-parent adoptions and went up to our supreme court and made it known that second-parent adoptions were being done in this type of factual circumstance. This Henry County experience probably occurred between 2004 and 2006, because *Wheeler* came up in 2006.

So children living in households headed by same-sex couples in outlying counties have just one legal parent. And typically these are people who can't change their residence to different counties. If they could move, they would. And these are people who have children under school age. Once kids are in school, it's even harder for families to relocate. So I have folks who, say, have a ten-year-old kid in school, and then they decide to have a second child. They can't change counties because of the older child.

---

[6] The vast majority of Georgia judges are initially appointed to the bench and then compete in contested elections to retain their seats.

Yet some couples do move. The Henry County couple rented a house in DeKalb County and moved into it, creating a de facto living situation there, although they didn't sell their Henry County home. They became residents of DeKalb solely to be able to file their second-parent adoption there. And the strategy succeeded.

But the residence has to be real. I had one judge in Fulton County tell me that another attorney had clients who didn't have a real de facto residence in Fulton. It was just some address they picked up somewhere. Then when the couple broke up, the first parent made a motion to set aside the second-parent adoption because there was no appropriate venue in Fulton. So from that point on, that judge factually confirms a Fulton County residence. If she's familiar with the neighborhood, she'll ask you where the local Kroger supermarket is to make sure you really live there.

Thus, judges have to worry about residence, because they don't want their cases overturned later on. And they don't like having frauds perpetrated on them.

So there are all of these gay Georgians who can't move. And those who are able to do so have to spend enormous amounts of money on it, possibly maintaining two separate residences.

I do have clients who really just move. They have a child and know they can't do a second-parent adoption where they currently live. And they know they want to live in a neighborhood that will be accepting and have families like their own. So they just decide to move then.

But with the economy the way it's been in the last year, some people can't sell their homes easily. So the legal setting for these couples is a nightmare. It's incredibly burdensome.

Q: What's your estimate of the percentage of clients seeking second-parent adoptions, regardless of the strategy they use, who are successful doing so?

KATZ: If we get to the point of filing a petition for second-parent adoption, it's granted. But I'm not going to file it if they haven't established residency.

The only time I've ever had a second-parent adoption go awry was once when the clients themselves backed out. They were splitting up and needed to think more about it. Another one occurred with a venue issue, where the judge asked a few questions indicating that, although my clients were in the process of moving, they weren't there yet. She wouldn't grant it until they had in fact established a de facto residence. But eventually we were able to do it.

Other than those two instances, when I file a petition in Fulton or DeKalb, I've never had a judge not grant one. I even had a client once where there was some domestic violence between them years before, which came up when we did the fingerprint check. The judge was all right with it, but wanted a letter from the aggressor's therapist saying she was under treatment for anger management and medication for it. Then the judge was fine.

Because most judges approach these cases under a theory that they're like stepparent adoptions. As long as everything else looks right, and there are no huge red flags, and if the legal parent wants it, a judge is going to grant it.

There's just one judge in DeKalb who won't authorize second-parent adoptions, and a spattering in Fulton, where attorneys have a little flexibility in selecting judges. In DeKalb, however, it's totally random assignment. It's the luck of the draw. But I've never pulled the adverse judge.

Other lawyers I know have done so on at least two occasions. In that circumstance, your option is to dismiss the petition and then have the couple move to Fulton. I think there's one judge in Cobb County who would grant them, but it's also a random-assignment system. There's one judge in Clayton County, which is just south of our airport, who I believe would grant them. As well, I think that same Henry County judge would approve them today. But they're all random assignments. So I have to say to clients, "You're going to have to pay me, and it might not get done."

Q: Let me rephrase the question. Of those clients who come to you, how many petitions for second-parent adoptions end up not being filed?

KATZ: I'd say between 10 and 20 percent.

Right now, I have people who are waiting in Cobb County, and another couple in Paulding County. There's a third pair, in Fayette County, who are about to do the first adoption, hopefully followed by a second-parent adoption.

So I have a list of people who circle the metropolitan Atlanta area. I spoke to a couple recently who are in Forsyth County and live a block from the Fulton County line. I said they should pick up their house and move it that block.

But many couples can't move, for one reason or another. They just can't afford to do a full relocation.

One pair of clients went the furthest I've ever seen anybody go to move. They worked in Augusta. The nonparent's job had her travel around in a geographic area including South Carolina. They moved into DeKalb [more than 125 miles from Augusta]. During the week, the nonparent lived in hotels doing her sales thing, instead of being able to come home to Augusta. They were in DeKalb for at least four months, before returning to Augusta.

Judges want a home study in 75 percent of the cases, with a social worker coming to the house. So residency has to be real.

Q: Can you speak to the practical effects of failing to achieve a second-parent adoption?

KATZ: Let me address what happens to clients when they separate and don't have a marriage license and children don't legally belong to both partners.

I've had folks with kids in school, and the couple splits up. The legal parent goes to the school and says, "Don't let my former partner visit my child. Don't let her take the child out of school." The school may have thought that both people in the partnership were parents, even though only one was legal. But the other had always been involved in the child's education. So suddenly, the legal parent says no.

For the person who's left out, we're talking about a kid he or she considers their own. And when people fight, they'll do the most horrendous things to each other. So I've seen people totally lose their kids, and more than once.

The *Wheeler* case, although not mine, was a perfect example. A lesbian had a biological child. When they split up, she tried to have the second-parent adoption overturned. And if there had never been a second-parent adoption, that would've been that.

In Georgia, the nonparent has no legal right to the child, either with regard to custody or visitation. I have a case right now with a lesbian couple that I'm mediating. One of them is the biological mother. They never did a second-parent adoption.

When they split up, the nonparent filed a petition to establish custody. It's very hard to be successful with that kind of lawsuit when you're a nonparent going up against a parent. Because you have to prove a very high level of unfitness of the biological mother. So the judge wasn't going to be able to grant a custodial relationship between the two former partners. So they settled out of court whereby the nonparent got visitation on alternating weekends. The child is now seven years old. And they're trying to do a second-parent adoption. We're attempting to negotiate whether the custodial parenting plan will change, now that they both will be legal parents.

Q: So the level of hostility between the women has diminished, and the biological mother's willing to participate in this further proceeding?

KATZ: Absolutely. But it's very tense. We talked about joint legal custody, and the biological mother stopped short. We talked about leaving the current parenting plan the same, but adding a little bit over chosen holidays, and she froze up again.

If this were a straight couple, and a child had two weeks off between the Christmas and New Year holidays, the parents would split that time up evenly. But this biological mother was saying, "That's mine. You can have your weekends, as long as Christmas doesn't fall on a weekend."

That's not what parentland looks like. So nonparents have no legal rights around making decisions about health, education, welfare, and religious upbringing. And they have no obligation to pay child support, even though it's a child's right to be supported. They don't have that right over someone who often times is very willing to pay it.

Carol, age forty-two, and Donna, forty-six, a lesbian pair in Decatur, described their second-parent-adoption experience:

CAROL: We had to move to a different county to get a second-parent adoption for our son.

We live in DeKalb County, and not all DeKalb judges recognize second-parent adoptions for same-sex couples. DeKalb County's process is that you get assigned a judge, and no matter what, that assigned judge follows you forever. There's no way to change a judge once selected.

We got assigned the one judge out of nine not granting second-parent adoptions to lesbian and gay pairs. And there was nothing we could do at that point. We couldn't say, "Forget it. We'll do it again next month."

So we had to move to Fulton County and establish a temporary residence there.

DONNA: Our lawyer said we had to have a residence in Fulton County to apply for the second-parent adoption there.

CAROL: The way judges in Fulton County are selected for cases is different than what happens in DeKalb. There's a docket in Fulton indicating which judges are coming up. So an attorney knows on what day to present a petition. Thus, court procedures vary by county.

Jerry, age thirty-five, and Walter, forty, are the clients of Barbara Katz whom she mentioned were my interview subjects. They have lived in Cobb County for nine years. In 2007, Walter adopted then nine-year-old Dennis and was assigned a judge who did not grant second-parent adoptions. So the boy has

Walter's last name, which is different from Jerry's. Walter works full time, while Jerry is a stay-at-home dad, with the principal responsibility of raising Dennis. As a matter of Peach State law, however, not only was Jerry a legal stranger to his life partner Walter but Jerry also could never be Dennis's permanent legal guardian.

In 2009, Jerry took eleven-year-old Dennis to Houston to visit Jerry's parents. (Recall that Texas is another Super-DOMA state.) On the return trip to Georgia, airline personnel at the Houston airport noted the difference in last names between Jerry and Dennis, summoned the police, and suggested to the authorities that Jerry had kidnapped Dennis. The officers escorted Jerry and Dennis off their plane and questioned Jerry "in front of God and everybody on that Texas concourse." Jerry was obliged to explain his sexual orientation to an officer and had to telephone Walter in Georgia. Fortunately, on the advice of Barbara Katz, Jerry always carried notarized temporary guardianship papers whenever he traveled with Dennis. So the police ultimately let them proceed home. But in our interview, Jerry, in tears, described the public accusation of abducting his own son (this charge was made in front of the child) as the most horrifying experience of his life.

Thus, Jerry and Walter painfully knew firsthand about the challenges that same-sex couples faced when both were not the legal parents of their children:

WALTER: We could resolve the second-parent-adoption problem for our son by moving temporarily to a county with a more liberal judiciary.
JERRY: We'd have to sell this house and buy another in a different county, live there long enough to establish residency, do the second-parent adoption, sell that house, and then move back to where we actually want to live. So we'd be constantly in flux.
    We know three or four other same-sex couples who've moved to different counties to have second-parent adoptions. And they're dead broke after doing it.
    But I'm not willing to do that.
WALTER: Yes, it's expensive.
JERRY: It's like they're taking second mortgages out on their houses, and it's not fair at all.

In March 2010, an associate vice president of administration at Emory University in Atlanta published an article describing two gay and lesbian adoptive parents he knew among Emory employees who "admitted that they relocated to a different county where gay adoption was more likely to be granted." One mother said that "it was important to 'get the right judge' and on 'the right docket' and know which lawyers to hire so she would not have to 'hide her gayness'" (Hanson 2010b).

Before June 2015, while the war against same-sex couples and their families was being waged in much of the United States, one of the most invaluable services to help lesbians and gay men across the country survive the onslaught would have been the immediate receipt, after coming out of the closet, of an LGBT instruction manual or user's guide with a major chapter titled "The

Importance of Geography." Its principal message would have changed over time. But starting with the manual's year 2000 edition, the chapter might have said something like this:

If you anticipate ever being in a committed and enduring relationship with someone of the same sex, make sure you end up living soon in Vermont, because you can get a civil union there that will provide you and your partner with over 300 legally recognized relationship rights and privileges.

The message in the 2004 edition would have switched the residency recommendation to Massachusetts, where same-sex couples could be legally married for the first time. And so forth with each passing year.

At the same time, the manual's geography chapter could have been even more personalized, with the content changing according to the state or region in which the gay man or lesbian came out. Based on the information here, the instruction in the Georgia version could have been something like this:

If you, as a lesbian woman or gay male, had the misfortune to be born in the Peach State, or get a job there, and aren't able to move to a place like Massachusetts or Vermont to be married or have a civil union, then by all means be sure to live in Fulton County. Because, although your committed relationship won't be recognized anywhere in Georgia, at least in Fulton County, you and your partner can both be the legal parents of any children joining your loving family.

And if Fulton isn't within your grasp, then note the next best choice is DeKalb County. There, you have an 89 percent probability of both partners becoming legal parents.

If both Fulton and DeKalb aren't viable residence options, then be fully aware you and your kids may well be in serious legal jeopardy anywhere else in Georgia.

THE VALUE OF HAVING TWO LEGAL PARENTS RAISING CHILDREN IN HOUSEHOLDS HEADED BY SAME-SEX COUPLES

Consequential research has documented the importance of having two-parent households to children's well-being regardless of the sexual orientation of the parents.[7] Moreover, the fifty-five interviews I conducted with gay and lesbian pairs bringing up kids in Super-DOMA jurisdictions confirmed that having two legal parents in a household is a far better environment than having just one.

Bringing Children to Families

Let us begin with birth and see how these restrictive laws affected the arrival of newborns. I start with oral histories from Ohio, one of the states with the most absolute approach against second-parent adoptions.

---

[7] For summaries of these studies, see *DeBoer* v. *Snyder* (2014), 973 F. Supp. 2d at 761–65; *Baskin* v. *Bogan* (2014), 766 F. 3d at 663–64; Movement Advancement Project (2011); Bernard (2012); and Leonhardt (2015).

Amanda and Joyce, a suburban Columbus couple, told the story in the last chapter of how humiliated Joyce was when changing her surname to Amanda's. During our interview, Amanda was pregnant with twin girls and was scheduled to deliver them imminently.

JOYCE: Every time there's some medical event concerning the pregnancy, we have to exert so much more effort because we're not allowed to be married in the state.

AMANDA: Just being carried on Joyce's insurance has been an experience, because every time we go to the hospital or deal with anything regarding the pregnancy, we have to go through this whole explanation of who I am and who she is to me. Every time I call the hospital, they get it wrong. So I have to correct their errors because their system doesn't recognize same-sex couples.

Her insurance says Joyce Johnson, and I'm a dependent under the name Amanda Johnson. So they ask, "Who's this Joyce to you? Is she your mother?" So I have to explain it all again to them. When I say that we're partners or wives, they ask, "What do you mean? That doesn't make sense." "We're life partners. We're a lesbian couple." I have to take these people step-by-step....

One woman said, "I presume you don't know her Social Security number." "Well, yes, I do. I know her birth date. I know everything about her. She's my wife." It's happened throughout the whole pregnancy. Because I'm working with a high-risk unit at our hospital, we go there a lot. Every time we go in, we have to correct their information.

Since we've started a family, there's so much more to think about now than the two of us. Our children's safety has become of the utmost importance. That's why we've gone through the mountains of contracts and other paperwork, revised our wills, and all of that.

I just had conversations with my entire family about the birth of the girls. Until they're born, and have Social Security numbers, they would be wards of the state if I were to pass during childbirth. So just yesterday, I said to all my family members, "I have to say it. If something happens to me, the girls are Joyce's children, too."

But we don't have anything legal proving it. Although my family would never dispute our relationship, because they all love Joyce, it's still scary. The twins would automatically go to my parents, and then they would have to turn the girls over to Joyce. That's so alarming.

JOYCE: For me, it really is. That's the last thing I would need if something were to happen to Amanda, to have to fight the state for my children. It's so idiotic to me that I have to secure all of this stuff. In the midst of something that's so joyful, I have to worry about all of this other nonsense...

AMANDA: ...simply because we can't get married. With heterosexual couples, it's not even an issue if something were to happen to the woman in childbirth. The dad would be there.

JOYCE: Even with unmarried couples, the biological connection gives them rights. Since I can't be biologically involved in this, it's like I'm a stranger.

AMANDA: We've seen it before, where family members have said they would never challenge the partner of the biological mother...

JOYCE: ...and then they do. I love Amanda's family, and her family loves me. And they have no disagreement that they're our children. But I still want to do everything to secure my rights.

I worry about having to prove my relationship with Amanda if people refuse to honor it. So that's the reason we've been thinking about going to another state to get legally married. I want everything that's available to demonstrate she chose me to be her next of kin, and that we decided to have children together. So we make sure that my name's on every document, like all the paperwork at the insemination clinic. Yet that's all we have, a paper trail to show these were decisions we made together.

AMANDA: We do everything we can in the hope that we won't have to face worst-case scenarios. But it's always a fear – having to prove we're a family when people won't recognize us as one. It's really overwhelming at times...

JOYCE: ...having to answer the same questions over and over again, just because we can't say, "We're married."

AMANDA: And if we do say we're married, the next question is always, "Is that legal?" That's always the next question.

Angela, the minister in a rural area outside of Cleveland who provided in the last chapter a benign reading for the motives of those citizens who voted for Issue 1, offered a different take on the circumstances surrounding the birth of her son Tucker:

ANGELA: How has the 2004 constitutional amendment directly affected us? I'll start with today, and move backward. Because I went to get Tucker's birth certificate today. And only my name is on it, which made me look like a hussy. The two older women behind the office counter, once they printed the document, looked at it, and treated me differently than before they saw the birth certificate [without a father's name on it].

So there's the reality that Jessica's not recognized by the state as Tucker's legal parent. And that's frightening in many, many ways. We've done our best to shield ourselves. So a big chunk of our reality is the protections our son isn't going to have with only one legal parent. And the recognition he won't get.

JESSICA: As a physician, I have more leeway and power than many. I can say yes to some jobs, and no to others. Right now, both Angela and Tucker are on my health insurance. But getting Tucker on it was difficult. The people in our benefits office didn't really know what to do. They said, "Well, we need his birth certificate with your name on it." And I had to reply, "I'm not going to be on his birth certificate." "Well, who's going to be on his birth certificate?" "My wife, my partner." And since Angela was already on my health insurance, Tucker could be too.

But they didn't really know what to do. They weren't mean about it. Just uninformed. So I thought to myself, "Well, if he's not going to be on my insurance, I'm going to look for a new job." I was ready to quit or to sue them. Luckily, it didn't go that far.

ANGELA: Many of our challenges have come to a head since Tucker was born. Our precarious legal status was one thing when it involved just us. But the dilemma substantially increased when we became responsible for a child. For instance, Tucker can't get Social Security if something were to happen to Jessica. Things like that scare me.

One of my major concerns going into the hospital was.... Once again, we're very lucky, because Jessica sees newborns on the labor and delivery floor at the hospital. All the staff there know her. And so they were looking forward to delivering Dr. Jones's baby.

JESSICA: We got special treatment.

ANGELA: We're very aware of the privilege we had there. But I was still frightened that if something happened to me during labor, Jessica's first phone call, after calling her mother, would have been to a lawyer. Because she would've had no rights to our child in order to make medical decisions for him if something happened to me.

I was *terrified* of that throughout the pregnancy. That really wasn't where I needed to be spending my time and energy, worrying about what would happen if I died in childbirth and Jessica not being in a position to be able to take care of her son. She would have to be contacting lawyers in the midst of what would be a nightmare. So that was big for me. It helped immensely that we had the same last name as a family.

JESSICA: That was smart of us.

ANGELA: I was adamant about changing our names, because I knew that if we all had the same surname, Jessica would've been much less likely to get stopped at an airport or anywhere else. There would be fewer questions about our relationship.

We still get people who think we're sisters. In that case, one of us was clearly adopted [since the two women don't look alike at all]. It's really funny, when I was pregnant with Tucker .... Most of our neighbors are retired. They think of us as "the girls." You know, "Those nice girls. We take them baked goods." That kind of thing. One of them stopped me in the park, and said, "Hey. I heard the news [about Angela's pregnancy]." I said, "Yeah, we're really excited." "Well, *how* did this happen?" And he just kept going. It was actually really, really funny. I said, "We've been wanting kids for a long time." "You're happy about this?" "Yes." "Is *Jessica* happy about this?" "Yes."

JESSICA: I think he thought it was a kind of truck-stop affair. Angela's fling.

ANGELA: That *would* have made headlines: "Read all about it! Methodist minister gets knocked up at truckstop!" But this was the guy who, when our lawnmower broke, came over and mowed our lawn. We weren't even home. He just showed up.

JESSICA: We brought food [as a gesture of gratitude] to a different neighbor, because we didn't even realize it was him.

ANGELA: He didn't fess up. So what we need to emphasize here is that, from our neighbors' perspective, in Small Town, Ohio, we're that really, really nice couple of girls who care about their neighbors and the community ...

JESSICA: ... who just had a baby ...

ANGELA: ... and isn't it nice to see young families in Small Town again. So we've changed the face of what they think lesbian families look like.

JESSICA: It makes them think about it, because they never would've had any reason to do that otherwise.

I have two medical partners, a woman and a man. When Tucker was about six weeks old, the woman came up to me and said, "I was thinking last night, are you going to be on his birth certificate?" "No, the government won't let me." "Oh, my God." She was floored. She was like, "*What* are you going to do?" "There's nothing I can do." She's known me for four years. She's known us for four years.

ANGELA: And that's what we encounter most often, people just being blown out of the water. Jessica's medical partner was born and raised in this town. She lives next door to her mother and brother. She and her husband went to the same high school together. And they were all like, "You're kidding, right?" And probably some of them voted for Issue 1 in 2004, just because they didn't know what it meant. Maybe we're being too generous with people. But I don't think anyone really understood what they were voting for.

In our day-to-day lives, Issue 1 doesn't affect us much. We're mostly concerned about whether Tucker is sleeping, and how many times he's nursed. So that's our day-to-day. And I think at some level, people recognize that.

A straight woman down the street is expecting her third child any second. It's funny that we suddenly have something in common. She and her husband are great.

JESSICA: They gave us some lettuce and chives recently.

ANGELA: So there's the day-to-day reality of what life is, where people realize that lesbians are like everyone else. They play Scrabble and worry about whether their kid's asleep. That's much more relevant to who we are and what's important to us.

But that's also undergirded by anxiety and fear, from the messages we get from things like Issue 1 that constantly say, "You're not *really* a family. You don't count. We don't want you."

So on the one hand, "It's great. Our neighbors share vegetables with us." While on the other hand, when push comes to shove, are we going to be protected as a family? Do we constantly have to explain who and what we are?

Schools

Sue Doerfer, who was first executive director of the LGBT Community Center of Greater Cleveland and then held the same position at Equality Ohio, described how Issue 1 affected the manner in which Ohio schools dealt with same-sex couples and their children:

With regard to public schools, it varies greatly from school district to school district, and even from school to school, depending on who the principal or teacher is. Because there's no legal or other mandate that says schools must interact with families headed by gay or lesbian parents in the same way as they treat other families.

So schools have the option not to recognize the second parent – the nonbiological or otherwise nonlegal one. That choice leaves it open to the belief system of the principal or the teacher or the teacher's aide or the guidance counselor – or whoever else on a given day decides how they're going to treat the LGBT family.

Thus, kids and their parents get inconsistent messaging during their time in school. And they're always on guard, ready to be treated poorly and to put up defense mechanisms. The children, in particular, have to be prepared all the time for questioning from a host of people in whose care they find themselves. And this dynamic puts a whole different level of stress on family systems at times when their attention should be on raising kids and making sure they get good educations.

I know of children who've been harassed at school, and then the school system refuses to do anything against the instigators and instead blames the kids. I know of school systems that refuse to permit the second parent to pick up their kids from school or to sign paperwork for them. And we're often talking about the stay-at-home mom or dad here, with their nonrecognition creating logistical nightmares for families.

I know of a principal of a school here in the Cleveland system who's a lesbian. She was pretty closeted at work, because she was fearful of what would happen being out. Bear in mind that Ohio has no legal protection against sexual-orientation discrimination in employment. So gay people can be fired from jobs.

What transpired was that LGBT kids gravitated toward the lesbian principal. "Gaydar" occurred. So she started offering guidance to them, and tried to mentor and protect them. And those kindnesses fueled suspicion about her being a lesbian. This was at a high school, and students there even harassed and threatened her. Then she was up for a promotion, which was denied. So she wondered whether the suspicion of her being a lesbian doomed any hope for career advancement.

I know about her personal battles with what she believes politically, that the more LGBT people are out, the better they do. She has children of her own. So she also worried about protecting her livelihood. In short, she struggled continuously over where to draw the line, which was enormously stressful.

And Issue 1 facilitated these kinds of dilemmas in schools and elsewhere. Issue 1 legitimized heterosexual favoritism. The amendment said to Ohioans that, yes, it's okay and legal to discriminate against LGBT people. The state now officially sanctions its citizens to believe that gay men and lesbians and their families are not the same as everyone else and are unworthy of the rights afforded to heterosexuals. There's no other way to look at it. That was the message.

LeeAnn Massucci, a Columbus attorney who specializes in representing LGBT families, offered a perspective giving somewhat more benefit of the doubt regarding how Ohio schools handled families headed by same-sex parents:

I think that, initially, schools heard about DOMA – either the statutory law or Issue 1 – and took a step back to say, "We don't want to touch this. So when we have to deal with same-sex couples, we need to be very careful about what we're allowed to do."

Once the biological or adoptive parent of a child signs off in school, putting her or his partner down as "co-parent" – and that's what they're writing, "co-parent" or "guardian," or they cross out "father" and put down "second mother" – the schools are fine with it because the legal parent has made the designation. As a legal matter, then, the schools believe they're protected by such parental choices.

Yet, if the schools really thought about it carefully, saying "co-parent" or "second mother" could be challenged under the Super-DOMA.

More difficult issues arise when LGBT families split up in Ohio. In that instance, schools are usually very careful. They say to nonbiological or nonadoptive parents, "If you have a shared-custody agreement with the legal parent, we need that document to be on file. If you don't have a shared-custody agreement, you may not have contact with the child until you can give us a court order permitting it."

When couples break up, the first thing that the legal parents usually challenge is the second parents' ability to pick up the children, and so the schools take them off the list. Even though schools may have known the other parents for many years, have conversed with them often, and even though the second parents may have been the ones picking up and dropping off the children every day – the schools aren't going there after gay or lesbian pairs separate.

Now, when heterosexual couples break up, do you think the schools challenge dad if he comes in, or mom? You can bet that they don't.

So, in addition to the many other security issues that are highlighted for children today, I think Issue 1 has made schools be far more cautious. Combined with the HIPAA laws [involving federal privacy rights], the Super-DOMA has also made doctors and pediatricians far more careful.

I can't say that I blame the schools and doctors for crossing those "t"s and dotting those "i"s. Because they have to, or otherwise be exposed to lawsuits.[8]

Andrea, age thirty-four, and Louise, thirty-six, are bringing up eleven-year-old daughter Bonnie from Louise's prior marriage to a man. The women, who share Louise's maiden name, Garcia, explained challenges they faced in a suburban Atlanta school system.

LOUISE: The paperwork I fill out for Bonnie's school every year asks for the student's mother's name and the father's name. So I'm forever crossing out "Father" and writing in Andrea's name.

ANDREA: It took a while for them to recognize me as the other parent. A couple of years or so ago, if I had to pick up Bonnie and take her to the doctor ...

LOUISE: ...the nurse at the school would call me at my job ...

ANDREA: ...after I'd pointed out my name as parent on the forms that Louise had filled out and signed.

LOUISE: Finally, I just said to the woman, "If you do this to me one more time, I'll call the school board to complain and sue. This is ridiculous. You're keeping my child from getting help because you're trying to find me, when there's another parent right there."

Q: For how long did those incidents occur?

ANDREA: They happened several times over about a year or a year and a half.

At first, we just wanted to be low-key about it. Our approach isn't to start at a militant level. We didn't want to put people off, because maybe they hadn't been exposed before to our kind of family around here. But that nice, slow, let's-take-it-easy strategy didn't work in this situation.

LOUISE: So I had to make some noise.

Q: Did the situation change?

LOUISE: Oh, yes. But I had to literally threaten them. "If you do this again, I'll make your life difficult. You're discriminating against my family, and you're preventing my child from accessing medical care in a timely fashion."

Q: What if there were a medical emergency with Bonnie at school?

ANDREA: I have a piece of paper signed by Louise and notarized, saying I'm allowed to take Bonnie to the doctor and make non-life-threatening medical decisions for her.

LOUISE: We're all on the same insurance card. It has all of our names on it. So I keep my fingers crossed that will help.

ANDREA: For me, it's more of the wondering and the emotional aspect, of getting to the school and their looking at me like I have three heads. It hurts my feelings because it invalidates my relationship in our family.

Q: Does Bonnie have Garcia as a last name?

LOUISE: No, she has her father's name. We haven't changed her name to Garcia.

---

[8] See also Biegel (2010).

ANDREA: She doesn't want to change her name.

LOUISE: There are too many nuances involved. We'd have to get her dad's permission, first of all.

In any event, her last name is different from ours. So I don't know what would happen in an emergency.

Also, at the introduction to the school year, when parents were invited to attend an assembly, I asked what their policy was about bullying. And they just talked about race. I could've pushed it, but didn't.

Lois and Ruby, both age forty-seven, live in another Atlanta suburb, raising four teenage children. Each woman is the birth mother for two of the kids. Lois recounted another incident where the inability for both partners to be legal parents affected their children's education:

LOIS: Ruby and I are both band parents at our son Peter's school. We do geeky things like lug instruments around. He's in percussion, so there were things to be toted. We're both very involved with the band.

In the fall of 2006 or 2007, the band took a trip to Hawaii. So it was a pretty big deal. We signed Peter up for the trip, and indicated we'd go and be happy to chaperone. We'd done lots of chaperoning for the band in the past.

Then a memo came out from school, saying the only people who could officially go on the trip and be chaperones would be parents, which meant being a full parent. No grandparents, no aunts or uncles, no cousins. Stepparents could go, but they had to be married to parents.

So there was this dilemma, because we both planned to go. We wanted to support Peter.

I wrote the band director and said, "We're in a quandary. If I could be married to Ruby, I'd be married to her. But I'm not. But we're both band parents and have done all these things before. We volunteer and want to go to support Peter."

He wrote back and said, "No, no. The decision stands. We have to draw the line somewhere. We don't want people to go who're just living together. Because that's not enough of the commitment we're looking for. We can't control what somebody's boyfriend or girlfriend does, because there's no legal connection there."

I wrote back again and said, "Here are some of the legal connections we have. We share a bank account and a mortgage. We're registered domestic partners." And I listed all the things that would make us legitimate.

But he wrote back to say that still wouldn't do, because we couldn't be legally married.

So I wrote back a third time, because I'd consulted Lambda Legal and asked what they thought my next step should be. They said for me to document everything and to keep all the papers together. Then request a meeting with the school principal and the band director, and indicate we'd bring legal representation with us. So I did that. I said, "I know to you this seems like a small thing. But to us, it's a big deal."

The Hawaii trip could set a precedent, because we had another child coming up who might've been in the band. So I sent an email requesting such a meeting with those parties and indicated we'd have legal representation.

At that point, the school administration reversed the decision. So the ploy worked.

THE ADDED COSTS OF RAISING CHILDREN IN LGBT FAMILIES

Children are expensive to rear in any setting. Yet Super-DOMAs forced lesbian and gay pairs to incur costs obtaining and bringing up children that heterosexual parents are not burdened with.

Adam, age forty-three, and Sam, forty, live in the Morningside area of Atlanta and have three-year-old twins.

ADAM: Question 1 influenced our decision to have children via surrogate, as opposed to adoption.[9] Both before and after the marriage amendment passed, there was conversation in Georgia about outlawing gay people from adopting. Some legislators even proposed the ban be retroactive, which is insanity. But there was discussion about it.[10]

So we were very concerned that at least one of us be biologically related to the children because of the political climate in Georgia. That way, if something outrageous happened, taking a biological child away would be much more difficult than an adopted one.

So we worried about getting to the bottom of the ninth with an adoption, and then have a ban go through or something along those lines.

Q: How much more expensive was it to go the surrogate route rather than adoption?

ADAM: It was far, far more costly to go the surrogate route. It's a fortune. Nobody gets away for less than six figures, unless you're using family members who don't charge. Whereas, an adoption would be $25,000 to $30,000.

SAM: A couple we know had fertility issues and adopted a girl from China, and it was $25,000. But they knew they'd get a child.

ADAM: Couples can spend a few hundred thousand dollars on surrogacy and still not come up with a baby.

Q: So the reason prompting you to take the surrogacy route meant there was substantial more cost.

ADAM: Yes, but far less political risk. And we may have been hypersensitive to it, because we were so involved in the politics of LGBT families at the time. And I'm on a bunch of committees that deal with the adoption issue in the Georgia legislature, because the issue crops up every year.

In any event, Georgia is a state where the potential for antigay legislation is relatively high. And with children, it's important to have every piece of paper possible to show our commitment and that we're a couple, in case something comes about questioning our ability to parent the children together.

---

[9] See Bellafante (2005).

[10] "While we expect the constitutional status of same-sex marriage to wane as a focal issue in state politics, our data also suggest that political entrepreneurs may tap public apprehensions about same-sex couples in other ways. One way involves restrictions on adoption.... In particular, we would first expect to see this issue appear as proposed constitutional amendments in DCI [direct constitutional initiative] states and in southern states" (Lupia et al. 2010, 1233).

Question 1 means that, as a legal matter, anything we want between us and for our kids isn't protected. So we have to have every written scrap, every contract we can think of to ensure our wishes are carried out, if, God forbid, we get to that place.

Surrogacy was also used in Texas to overcome the dilemma of trying to secure second-parent adoptions, as Andrew, a thirty-nine-year-old Dallas suburbanite, elaborated: "Our surrogacy was purposely not done in Texas. Instead, our daughter was born in Maryland, which is one of very few places allowing the names of both same-sex parents to be on birth certificates. That option's not available here."

Kimberly, age thirty-four, and Shirley, thirty-five, living in Atlanta, have adopted three children; Shirley shared how the inability to have their relationship legally recognized potentially increased their parenting costs.

An obvious way that Question 1 impacted us is with the adoptions. We experienced discrimination because we couldn't adopt our kids together.

Our older children are considered special needs and thus get Medicaid. Plus, we receive a stipend from the state for them, called Adoption Assistance. It's combined federal and state funds. So we get money for them every month until they turn eighteen.

Since Kimberly adopted them first, she's the one who receives the checks. And we worry about what would happen if something happened to her. We're not confident the state would feel obliged to turn that money over to me.

Such an outcome would cause significant financial hardship on us, losing both Kimberly's salary and the Adoption Assistance all at once. The result would be very unfair and an economic disaster.

THE MESSAGE TO CHILDREN

The greatest tragedy among the many befalling same-sex couples and their children from Super-DOMAs may well be what happened psychologically to those kids, as Sue Doerfer explained:

For the children who were mature enough at the time to understand what happened in 2004, they got a clear message that their household wasn't an important or real family. The kids who weren't old enough in 2004 to comprehend what occurred then have since grown up to know that their parents cannot marry, or have to go to another state or country and then come back. That reality also communicates to children that their families aren't as legitimate as those led by heterosexuals.

Bertie, age fifty, a middle-school counselor, emphasized the psychological impact on children:

Public education is a bastion of morality where many expectations about life play out. The Ohio Revised Code addresses sex education in schools and has really strict parameters around what can be said. Sex education can only be taught if, as part of the classroom discussion, kids are told that children should be born into marriage.

So the underlying, legally mandated message to all kids is, "Children raised by same-sex couples (or single parents), as well as lesbian and gay kids themselves, aren't included or welcome here." Consequently, Issue 1 directly affects the educational process in the classrooms of our public schools.[11]

Super-DOMAs also incurred psychological costs on some gay and lesbian children of heterosexual parents, as a professor in an Ohio social work master's program commented:

An immediate concern for me is that Issue 1 gives license to people to be more despicable, and to feel righteous about it, toward gay and lesbian loved ones in their own families. And I'm particularly concerned about kids, adolescents who're coming out.

I remember a student we had in our program, a young African American woman who was a lesbian. She had absolutely no support within her family. And this was a woman in her mid-twenties. So she wasn't even a minor.

Every time the student went home, she heard the same grief from her parents about being lesbian. And I suspect, eventually, was truly at risk for harming herself or someone else. She was already beginning to have trouble with alcohol.

So not only does Issue 1 facilitate violence, it gives license for disenfranchising our own children. And too often, the price for that abuse is their lives.

A final cost of the constitutional amendments was, ironically, their derogation of the place of marriage in American culture, as Angela, the minister and Tucker's birth mother, noted:

The odds are that Jessica and I are going to raise a straight guy. In fact, lots of gay people in Ohio are bringing up future heterosexuals. And the message our kids get from Issue 1 is "marriage isn't important." So Tucker, as well as the other children reared by same-sex pairs, might easily think as adults, "My family was great, and my moms never got married."

Therefore, if our leaders want to foster marriage as an institution, and if they believe that not allowing same-sex unions is the way to go, they should be aware their approach forces a goodly number of kids to reach adulthood without the formal protections or the economic safeguards of having two legal parents. And those same children will grow up like, "Marriage? Why would I bother?"

MARRYING OUT OF STATE TO SOLIDIFY AND CLARIFY INTRAFAMILY RELATIONSHIPS

Numerous interviewees who were raising children went elsewhere to marry, which often benefited their children, even though such out-of-state weddings carried no legal weight when the families returned home.

Andrea, Louise, and their daughter Bonnie were introduced earlier. In 2009, the family of three traveled from their Atlanta suburb to Connecticut for the women's wedding.

---

[11] Cf. Janofsky (2005).

Q: Why was going somewhere else to get legally married important to you?

LOUISE: The wedding secured our relationship, making our commitment that much more strong.

Surprisingly, the marriage also really helped our daughter Bonnie, which is something I didn't expect, because she and Andrea have always had a great relationship. But since the wedding, it's been different. You can see a change in her attitude.

Bonnie told me the wedding made her feel more secure, convincing her that we're really a family.

She had a nickname for Andrea that, before the trip to Connecticut, she used only sporadically. Now she uses it much more consistently.

And Bonnie said that if anything happens to me, she wants to continue living with Andrea.

ANDREA: Bonnie calls me "Andremom," combining Andrea and mom. She used to call me that only on occasion. But now it's primarily what she uses, because I'm officially her stepmom.

LOUISE: Our marriage gave her a greater sense of security...

ANDREA: ...in large measure because it clarified who I was to her, a stepparent.

Dorothy and Lisa, a suburban Atlanta couple who appear in Chapters 1 and 3, explained why marrying out of state was important to their three children:

Q: Were you married [in Vancouver, British Columbia, in 2008] to achieve some concrete, tangible benefit?

DOROTHY: No. We'd wanted to marry ever since California first opened up, and also because of the children, especially our son. He kept asking why we didn't get married.

LISA: We hoped to show the kids that marriage means something. Other than the personal commitment it represented to us, we intended the kids to know that, for long-term, devoted relationships, marriage is a wonderful step to take. It's different from just living together. Even if we announced our mutual love daily, marriage just meant something more. And that was a crucial message we weren't able to send until our trip with them to Canada.

WHEN PARENTS WERE SEPARATED

Daniel A. Bloom, an Atlanta family-law attorney introduced in the last chapter, characterized some of the legal predicaments faced by same-sex couples with children in Georgia when they split up:

BLOOM: When gay and lesbian families with kids break up, Question 1 explicitly prevents state courts from addressing the separation and its related legal issues in any way that would equate it to a divorce of a married heterosexual couple. For instance, if a same-sex pair live in a county with a family court, and there's a custody dispute between the partners, that legal quarrel would go to the Family Court. And with heterosexual couples, so would all their financial disputes.

But in the situation where lesbian and gay pairs split up, the custody has to be decided in one court, and if there's an issue over home equity, that has to be addressed in another tribunal. Because the Family Court doesn't want to run afoul of the marriage amendment by treating gay people in the same way it handles heterosexuals. Many judges are interpreting the constitutional amendment that way.

There was a case that I volunteered on with Debbie Seagraves of the ACLU of Georgia, where a judge denied an adoption to a lesbian because she had a partner. Even though Georgia law allows any single person, regardless of sexual orientation, to adopt a child, because this woman had a partner, the judge thought her attempt to adopt as a single person was a subterfuge by the pair trying to adopt the kid as a couple. He believed that, if he allowed her to adopt at all, he'd be treating the lesbian couple as he'd handle married heterosexuals whom he'd permit to adopt as couples. So he denied the adoption to the single woman. And it was just insanity from an obviously antigay judge. We had to work on the case [*In re Hadaway* (2008)] forever.

So there are tangible results to couples affected by Georgia's marriage amendment, having nothing to do with whether they want to marry. Rather, it's because a court can't address their needs in the same way that it deals with other people. Even though everyone is taxed the same in the state, some taxpayers can't avail themselves of court services because of Question 1.

So when I work on such cases, I advise clients that they have to settle. Because if they can't resolve their disputes, they're going to be litigating in two or three different courts.

Q: Do they settle?

BLOOM: The majority do. And the judges we work with generally will sign an agreement addressing all of the issues.

But they won't have trials where they deal with child custody and equity in a house and how to divide joint savings or stock accounts. Because that would be something beyond custody, treating a gay couple as if they were married, which they're forbidden from doing under part B of the amendment.

One of the most emotionally charged interviews I conducted was with Lillian, a forty-seven-year-old lesbian in North Carolina. The Tar Heel State had been home for most of Lillian's adult life. In 2003, however, she got a job transfer to Virginia (another Super-DOMA jurisdiction), where she met Robin. They began cohabiting and decided to have a child together. Lillian shared her experience:

LILLIAN: I was nearly forty at the time, and hadn't ever wanted to have children. It took a lot of soul-searching for me to go there, as many people do who contemplate kids. But it was a serious commitment.

Robin was going to carry the child, with sperm from an anonymous donor, because she was younger than me. Plus there were other good reasons why she should be the birth mother.

Around this time, we heard about Virginia House Bill 751, which defined marriage as only between one man and one woman. But it went further. Contracts between same-sex couples wouldn't be allowed if they afforded the same rights as marriage.[12]

The Virginia gay community was freaked out. We knew many people who owned property and were in long-term relationships. They worried their possessions might be taken away. No one thought any contract between same-sex partners would be valid under the new law. So there was widespread fear.

In fact, we knew people who thought the only solution was just to leave Virginia, because they were told by lawyers that, no matter what they signed, it wasn't going to be valid anyway. Due to the new law, several people sold everything they had and departed the state. They went to Maryland and DC and other places where they felt safer. They divested themselves of all Virginia possessions. In particular, there were two guys who ran a business renting properties they bought together. They sold everything, all of the real estate, and moved to Maryland. This was in 2004 or 2005.

In any event, as Robin and I started the process of trying to have a baby, friends suggested we look into protecting ourselves legally. But what could we do? As far as anyone knew, we couldn't enter into a contract under the new law, and we didn't see any other legal recourse. So we never bothered to go down that road. Instead, we thought we'd always be together, and had too much else going on right then. There we were, getting pregnant. Life got in the way.

Our daughter Crystal was conceived at the beginning of 2005. And Robin's pregnancy came with medical issues that overwhelmed our lives. She had to be on bed rest. So we didn't really have time to stop and do anything else. I took care of her, and she tried to keep her own job on a part-time basis, working from her bed. I went out and got her a laptop and a printer, and helped convince her employer to keep her on their health plan.

I begged my company to get domestic-partner benefits, and they refused. They'd never offered such perks, so they weren't going to. Thus, I couldn't put Robin on my insurance, and we had to keep her on her own.

There was just this whole nightmare of stuff going on, because her pregnancy was so high risk. We couldn't take the time to pursue anything legal. We'd been together for almost two and half years at that point. Everything seemed to be fine. We were doing well together. So we just focused on getting a healthy baby and keeping Robin on her own insurance.

We couldn't get married in Virginia, of course. I didn't feel like we could have a contract, and was told by several people that we couldn't get a second-parent adoption. So at that moment in time, life was right there, with a risky pregnancy happening, and work. It was very stressful, trying to take care of Robin and get the house ready for a baby.

Speaking of which, we were renovating at the same time, because there was no room for a nursery. So when Robin went on bed rest, the home improvements became my responsibility as well. Accordingly, I had no time to contemplate sitting down with an attorney or anything like that. I was running full bore, thinking that everything would work out.

---

[12] Going into effect on July 1, 2004, H.B. 751 prohibited any "civil union, partnership contract or other arrangement between persons of the same sex purporting to bestow the privileges or obligations of marriage."

Q: When was Crystal born?

LILLIAN: In November 2005. She went full term.

The hospital recognized me as Robin's partner. All the paperwork we filled out had me written down as partner. Everyone knew us as a couple. Crystal knew us as her parents. I was mama, and Robin was mommy.

Q: How much longer were you and Robin together?

LILLIAN: For almost three years. We broke up in July 2008.

Q: And you were a custodial parent for that length of time?

LILLIAN: Absolutely. In every possible way. Financially. Emotionally. Physically. Every day. Just like any parent. We both had to work. Who was going to pick Crystal up? The whole nine yards.

Robin owned the home we lived in, having been there when I met her. Although I didn't have any title to the house, I put tons of money in the property. I renovated it for the child's nursery. I bought a refrigerator and carpeted the floors. I put a shed in the back yard. I paved in the driveway. I did all that stuff as a couple, because we needed it. So I supported Robin and the child in every way I could.

She would've preferred to be a stay-at-home mom. But I couldn't find a job that would put her on domestic-partner benefits. So I couldn't do that. I would have if I could.

Robin was resentful that she was away from the child so much. And I think that got transferred to being bitter about each and every time I was with Crystal and she wasn't. Then it just morphed into her hating my presence altogether.

So all of a sudden, I was kicked out. "I'm done with you." With all the money I spent on her, and all the time and effort I put into raising Crystal, Robin didn't care. It was like, "You're gone."

When the relationship ended, I had no legal rights to Crystal. In fact, Robin was trying to convince people that I wasn't anything more than a roommate.

I've got eight four-inch binders full of emails and cards from Robin, saying she loved me, and not only during the first year, but all the way to the very end. So there's plenty of evidence to overcome Robin's assertion that I was just a roommate.

Q: When did you last see Crystal?

LILLIAN: Robin allowed me to visit for a period of time after the break up. In the beginning, it was like once a month. Then it became less and less.

In about December 2009, Robin started changing and saying I couldn't continue calling myself mama anymore. I said, "Why? That's how Crystal's always known me. She's called me that for more than two years. It's hard enough for Crystal to understand where I went, and now you're not going to allow her to call me mama, and I can't call myself that?" "No, it's confusing her." "The only thing that's confusing her is you're not telling her and reinforcing who I am and always will be." That's when I realized Robin was trying to eliminate my role.

The last time I was allowed to see Crystal was in September 2010. [Lillian's interview occurred in July 2012.]

Q: What are you looking for now?

LILLIAN: I merely hope to be able to see my daughter and for her to know me. I want to spend some holidays with Crystal. I'm not really asking for much. I just want to be in her life and help.

Robin is fighting me tooth and nail, *using the law against me*.

We asked for a guardian ad litem[13] and a psychologist assigned by the court. Unfortunately, they said they couldn't prove that Crystal would be harmed by my absence, which is another unfortunate part of Virginia law. To get custody or visitation, you have to prove the nonbiological parent is so valuable that the child would be harmed by their absence in life. And I said, "How do I show something like that?" "Well, it's never really established very frequently."

The law is absurd. Nobody even really knows what it means. How do I demonstrate Crystal will be harmed if I'm not there? The standard doesn't involve whether the prospective parent might be good or bad as such. And this applies to other family members, like grandparents or stepparents who've been out of the loop.

In Virginia, there are cases where a father kills a mother and goes to jail, and when he's released, is able to get custody of children from grandparents because of the father's biological link to the kids. So biology rules in Virginia. And it's absolutely ridiculous.

Super-DOMAs result in children losing parents because only one has any legal connection with them. But how can both partners be connected to them if their relationship isn't recognized and they can't adopt kids by other means?

Come what may, people are still going to have children. Marriage isn't a ceremony or a party. It's a contract, a protection thing. People don't trust if their house burns down that someone will show up and pay them for it. No, you get a contract with an insurance company and agent, to say they'll pay for these things. That's what a marriage license does.

Q: Is there anything more you want to add?

LILLIAN: I just want people to know there are real effects from these harsh laws against gay couples. They provide opportunities for families to be torn apart. People should think about whether they would want children they know to lose a parent.

Some Americans may not be concerned about gay people as adults, because they're perceived as expendable. But most people seem to care about kids. So think about that for a minute. You're going to take away a child's parent just because you don't like the choice of who they were with, no matter what that does to the kid? And every study I've seen says that two parents are much better than one for raising children. So why purposely make second parents disposable? The child always loses something, financially, emotionally, physically.

I know Crystal is going to have a hell of a time with Robin, because she has mental problems, based on how she's been acting. I know Crystal won't have a great upbringing with Robin as the only parent.

In fact, at the end, Robin told me she was starting to date guys and that's why I had to disappear. Robin didn't want to have to explain who I was to these men. She

---

[13] A lawyer appointed by a court to represent the interests of minor children involved in legal proceedings.

clearly didn't want to tell prospective dates she'd been with a woman before. But I can't imagine any guy putting up with her either. Because she's so controlling.

It's horrible to think I may have lost Crystal forever. [She weeps.] And Robin has taken full advantage of Virginia law. She's used it as a club against me as Crystal's parent.

So my story is what the future might look like for lesbian and gay parents in other Super-DOMA states.

Lillian later reported she spent more than $30,000 in legal fees fighting Robin over visitation with Crystal. But to no avail.

The situations of couples bringing children into their lives and then splitting up did not always end in lamentable stories of one parent's absolute loss of the kids and the children's loss of a parent. Just as with heterosexual divorces, negotiated, even amicable, separations produce arrangements minimizing the heartache involved. Paula, forty-five, shared her experience:

PAULA: I was with my ex-partner, Diana, for fourteen years. We lived together and made a home. Then we had a child together. Our son, Keith, was born in 2004. I was the birth mother, and we used an anonymous donor through artificial insemination. Keith's eight years old now.

Diana and I have been apart for two-and-a-half years, and we're co-parenting Keith.

Q: Can you more specifically describe how the co-parenting works?

PAULA: We basically operate with an informal understanding, a verbal agreement.

Both Diana and I work full time, and break up the week. So I pick Keith up after school on Mondays and Wednesdays. Diana picks him up on Tuesdays and Thursdays. And we talk weekend by weekend to split those up.

We still do things together as a family. Keith is really involved in sports and in school activities. We attend all those events together. We also do holidays together.

I know some people have a different way of seeing this and philosophy about it. For me, I've always been clear that, even if we weren't able to be partners, we're still a family. After all, Diana and I were together for fourteen years. Our lives and families are all intertwined. Our histories are jointly woven. And we have a child together.

So it's been important for me to try to navigate these murky, unchartered waters of being family and loving each other and doing things together as a family and as parents, even though we're not partners anymore. Sometimes it's harder than I expected. Even though it's murky, I try to keep all the boundaries in place.

Q: You say Keith is now eight. So there are another ten years or so that he'll be a minor. How likely is it that you and Diana will be able to continue with this consensual arrangement? There will be a lot of choices about Keith's education and other aspects of his life that will have to be made over those ten years. There may be changes in your individual circumstances.

What do you think the probability is that you can to continue with that kind of mutually agreed-upon arrangement?

PAULA: It's tricky. As the biological parent, I'm in the ultimate position of being able to decide, because the law doesn't recognize Diana as a legal parent. To the court, she's a stranger to Keith. So it's up to me.

My worldview about relationships, and this one in particular, is that it's in Keith's best interests to have two loving parents and a whole community of families surrounding him, lifting him up.

So my intention is to maintain a relationship with Diana, because I consider her family, and also because I believe the arrangement is advantageous to Keith. Of course, if she were to do something I considered not to be in Keith's best interests . . . .

There was a time, after we broke up, that I did have concerns about her stability and some of the choices she was making and who she was dating and needing to know who this person was and where Keith would be and who he would be with. Because it's absolutely my concern what adults he's with and what's happening with them and the environment he's in.

So I made it clear I needed to know these people, that I required to see it myself. And that was really hard to negotiate. Sometimes she didn't want me to be able to do that.

But I'm the only legal parent and have the right to decide whether she continues to have a relationship with Keith. And there was a short period of time when I said I didn't want him to go with her until I felt sure there was more stability there, and what was happening would be smooth for Keith.

And you know, it's difficult. I really shouldn't have that right. Diana is his other parent. We had Keith together. So it's an awkward place to be in. But it's the position I'm in.

It's possible something could happen that would cause me to feel like it wasn't in Keith's best interest to be with Diana. But as long as I feel like what she's doing with him is good for him, then this circumstance should continue.

I have a huge desire to be partnered, to have a nuclear family. I want all those things. But it's challenging to have this relationship with Diana. Not everybody understands it, although the boundaries are really clearly in place. We haven't had any sexual contact since we ended our relationship. But she's a co-parent and family member, and we're involved in each other's lives. There aren't many models for that circumstance. And not everyone accepts our structure.

Q: From what you say, I don't see how you have a serious option to relocate for the purpose of partnering and being in a legal environment that will be welcoming to a new relationship.

PAULA: No. I don't see that as an option for me while Keith is growing up.

Q: So you may in fact have to deal with Amendment 1 indefinitely?

PAULA: Yes, I'll have to cope with the constitutional amendment. I'll not have the option to marry in North Carolina when I meet someone I might want to wed.

OTHER CHALLENGES FOR SAME-SEX COUPLES
RAISING CHILDREN

Consider a child-rearing task as mundane as getting a teenager her learner's permit to drive. Lois and Ruby, both forty-seven, have been together for ten years and co-own a retail store in Atlanta; Ruby works there on a full-time basis. Phyllis, fifteen, is Ruby's biological daughter and leaves for school at 6:00 every morning and returns home around 3:00 every afternoon. Ruby's busiest time at the retail store is from 3:00 to 6:00.

Phyllis wanted a permit to get a driver's license. Since Ruby is always at work when Phyllis gets home from school, Lois took Phyllis to the Georgia Department of Driver Services (DDS) to apply for the permit. They brought Phyllis's birth certificate, her Social Security card, and a document from school saying she was a full-time student there.

The DDS clerk noted that Lois's name didn't match Phyllis's birth certificate and asked Lois whether she was Phyllis's parent.

LOIS: Yes, I'm her stepparent.

CLERK: Are you married to Phyllis's dad?

LOIS: No, I'm a registered domestic partner with Phyllis's mom, whom you can call on the telephone. She can't be here because she works every afternoon. I've co-raised Phyllis since she was six, and her dad lives in Texas.

"All hell then broke loose," according to Lois. "Supervisors were called, as was the DDS headquarters." Ultimately, DDS staff told Lois that either her name had to match the birth certificate or she had to be a permanent legal guardian. But Georgia law allows more than two legal guardians for a child only when the third person is married to a parent.

LOIS: So Phyllis didn't get her permit that day.

When we got into the car after leaving DDS, I said to her, "You have no idea what just happened. Because to you, it was all about your not getting a permit. But to me, this is the reason.... When you hear about [Proposition 8 in] California on TV, and see other states saying that we should have certain rights, this is what we're talking about."

Among our four kids, Phyllis is the most uncomfortable with having a two-mom family. She has the hardest time with it. So she didn't even want to talk about what I told her that day. But I still said to her, "I want you to mark this as a moment. We won't talk about it again. But I want you to remember that there was a time I wanted to do something as your parent, and I couldn't." [She weeps.] That's some of what people are fighting for.

[After composing herself:] Now we live in a traditional neighborhood, north of Atlanta, in a suburb. Our four kids go to regular public schools. They're as mainstream as could be. We've experienced very little discrimination as a two-mom family. But we act like it's no big deal. We just kind of proceed through life as normal. We've learned that, if we don't act like we're weird, people won't treat us that way.

In 2001, when I first told my best friend in the neighborhood that Ruby was moving in with me, her reaction was, "Oh my God. You're going to have to move. You're going to have to leave." And I said, "I'm not leaving. You're my friends. This is my neighborhood. Ruby's moving in here. You know me. You know Ruby. We're not going to move. We're going to make it work. Here."

And we really haven't experienced any discrimination, other than the initial fear of what would happen. I worried about people writing on our garage, or doing other things to the house. But we don't have a rainbow flag in our yard. We're not out there all the time making a statement.

But regarding the DDS incident, I was trying to say, in a small way, to Phyllis, "This is the cost of not making a statement, of not standing up and saying, 'This is who we are. And this is why we want the same rights everybody else has.'"

But she's not quite ready to hear that now. I hope someday she will be.

Asked whether, in hindsight, she would have done anything differently at the DDS, Lois replied,

I could've said "yes" to the clerk's question about being married to Phyllis's dad. That fib would've resulted in less discussion, and we probably could've worked through it.

But I never lie, and as a parent, I don't want to provide examples for Phyllis to think that dishonesty's an acceptable path in life.

Ben and Ted are in their thirties and live in a town of some 25,000 people about halfway between Cleveland and Columbus. They are raising their adopted infant Brandon. The couple moved to the state a year before, when Ben took a job teaching at a local college. Ben had employment opportunities in large cities elsewhere in the nation, but the pair chose to live in small-town Ohio because of the low cost of living, which allowed Ted to be a stay-at-home dad. Their perspective as parents is a useful counterpoint to that of the many urban and suburban dwellers in the study:

TED: Living here, we feel like pioneers, in the sense of being openly gay and having a child distinguished as perceptibly different. Brandon is biracial African American and Latino. [Both Ben and Ted are white.]

For example, when the three of us go to Lowe's to buy hardware supplies to build raised beds, we're visibly marked. So not only would people assume we're gay, by our mannerisms or interactions, ... And people have these popular-culture reference points now, like the sitcom *Modern Family*, with gay couples adopting children of another race.

We haven't yet had any overtly hostile encounters. But it's just the sense we could at any moment. When might that happen? I wake up at night upon hearing sounds outside, anxious about whether the day has come when some teenagers down the street realize that this is where the fags live and they want to spray paint our house.

So it's a tricky dance we engage in, of not being too paranoid but also being realistic about the animosity out there.

BEN: It's also the case that, because this is a town where there aren't many gay people, otherwise progressive, well-intentioned folks don't have issues that concern us on their radar at all. So they'll talk about sending their kids to the local Catholic school as though that would be an option for us, when clearly it wouldn't be. Or they'll discuss the Boy Scouts as if it's not an organization defining itself precisely through the exclusion of people like us.

Thus, because there's not a social history of openly gay people here, we arrive and then are newly on the radar. It's not ideal to be the individuals who first raise issues.

TED: More pointedly, we aren't aware of any other same-sex parents in town. When we've asked around, nobody has ever known of any other openly gay parents. So that helps further explain our feeling about being pioneers.

In addition, I face my own personal struggle. Being a stay-at-home dad can be hard. I sometimes get the notion from acquaintances, other than our few friends, that, because Ben and I aren't recognized as a married couple, I'm just this guy who happens to be here, not really doing anything. After all, I'm not gainfully employed outside the home, although I have the skills to do so.

Among many gay couples, mostly those without kids, both partners tend to be career focused. So the fact that my relationship with Ben isn't considered valid as a marriage in Ohio is, in a separate way, demeaning to me. Both Ben and I think the job I'm doing raising Brandon is so important. But I'm not respected for it when folks here don't view our family as 100-percent legitimate. And that's hurtful and scary.

Miriam, a forty-year-old Atlanta lesbian introduced in the last chapter, reported on concerns she and her partner Naomi had regarding their two children:

I worry about what might occur if, God forbid, something happened to both Naomi and me. Would people read our legal documents and honor them, or would our kids end up in some foster home?

Oh yeah, I'm really afraid of that outcome, because there's no obvious line of family succession about where the kids would go. Of course, we can't carry on our lives worried about worst-case scenarios.

But do I think it could happen? Yeah, weird events go down here. I've had enough contact with the foster-care system that it scares the heck out of me. And scary things happen when chaos occurs.

Coming up with alternate custodial arrangements for children in the event of the loss of their parents is something every couple with kids struggles with. And for us, there's the added extra stress of trying to make sure that the family our kids were brought into would be honored.

We have the inclination to transmit our experience of standing as a couple in a society that wants us to disappear. It's not that our biological family members wouldn't agree with us. But it's just that they don't have the day-in-and-day-out experience of needing always to legitimize oneself.

Regardless of what I did before our kids came along, if I have a child standing right next to me, I'm going to be all out there. Because I'm now committed to my children's understanding that ours is a legitimate family, even though there's a local law against it. Law doesn't authenticate family. Relationships and love legitimize it.

So Question 1 is a big burden.

Super-DOMAs hit home especially hard on closeted gay people and their families, as Beverly and Kelly, who were introduced in the last chapter, related:

Q: What about other same-sex couples you know in North Carolina? Beyond what you've said about yourselves, are there ways that Amendment 1 will impact them?

BEVERLY: We have two friends, Connie and Tracy, who live in Greenville.[14] Connie got pregnant in vitro and gave birth to Tiffany. So she's the only one with any claim to the baby. If something happened to Connie, Tracy wouldn't have any legal right to the child.

KELLY: Where they live right now, even the babysitter doesn't know that Tiffany has two moms.

So they're very closeted. They have to be careful, because Connie teaches at a school where she isn't allowed to be out. And since North Carolina is a right-to-work state, Tracy isn't out at her job either. So it's very hard for them to have a family but not be allowed to tell people about each other or their daughter.

BEVERLY: Tiffany is in day care right now and building vocabulary. One of the first words she learned was "DaDa." Connie told us she was both irritated and sad that Tiffany was being taught to say "daddy," because there's no one fitting that description in her family.

It's hard for them, because Tiffany is too young to understand what daddy means.

KELLY: The work environments of both Connie and Tracy are forcing them right now to be closeted. I don't think they'd choose to be in the closet if they felt they had another viable option. Instead, they feel they have to put their family first.

BEVERLY: I'm sure that people who were thinking about coming out have been shoved back into the closet by Amendment 1. They'd think, "I'm not coming out in this climate. Are you kidding me? Most of the people in my state would hate me."

CONCLUSION

Bringing children into families and nurturing them to adulthood both enhance and complicate their parents' lives. The enrichment side of the formulation is no less true for same-sex couples than for their heterosexual counterparts. But the complexity of the family dynamic in Super-DOMA states was inevitably much greater for lesbian and gay parents than for mother-father households. Not only did same-sex couples have to cope with the challenges the constitutional amendments created for their own personal relationships, as elaborated in the last chapter, but they also had to finesse the hurdles that parenthood brought in America's war on their families. In particular, the widespread inability of both partners within gay and lesbian couplings to secure legal kinship with the kids they raised engendered untold obstacles to the well-being of both parents and children. Furthermore, unlike families headed by married spouses, LGBT partners lacked any legal safety nets when the ties binding couples together dissolved.

Social-scientific research has demonstrated that no significant differences appear in studies comparing children raised by same-sex couples with those

---

[14] Greenville is the tenth largest city in North Carolina, with a population of about 90,000.

of heterosexual parents (Stacey and Biblarz 2001; Biblarz and Stacey 2010; Goldberg, Gartrell, and Gates 2014; adams and Light 2015). Gay and lesbian pairs who brought up families in the era of Super-DOMAs own such empirical findings as hallmarks of their courage, love, and parental skill.[15]

---

[15] Richman (2009) argues that U.S. family law had the flexibility required to respond favorably to the needs of queer parents. Gash (2015, 89–131) offers an excellent expanded analysis of the movement for same-sex parenting rights in the United States. Bowe (2006) explores family life when lesbian couples asked gay men they knew to become sperm donors, whereas Dominus (2004) provides an intriguing firsthand account of young adults raised by lesbian mothers.

5

Super-DOMAs and LGBT Migration

Fight or Flight?

> Was it a braver thing to stay, or was it a braver thing to go?
> – Isabel Wilkerson, *The Warmth of Other Suns: The Epic*
> *Story of America's Great Migration* (2010, 12)

Q: Someone said the following to me: "After Issue 1, if an Ohio lesbian or gay couple wants to obtain any rights of marriage, they now have to move to states like Massachusetts, Vermont, or Iowa." Do you think that's an accurate statement?

PHIL BURRESS (president of Citizens for Community Values): Yeah, if they want to be married. They can go there and get married, but when they come back here, their marriage won't apply in Ohio.

Q: So they would have to relocate then?

BURRESS: Yeah. If they want to be married, they would have to relocate. There's five states that now [June 2010] allow same-sex marriage. So if they want to be married in the eyes of the law, then they're going to have to move to those states.

In the introductory story of Chapter 1, Jennifer's tragic experience after her partner Elizabeth's untimely death at the hands of a drunk driver made starkly evident to their friends Linda and Patricia that Michigan was especially inhospitable to same-sex relationships. Indeed, Linda and Patricia then felt so seriously threatened by remaining in the Wolverine State that they quickly moved elsewhere, willing to endure even the brutal winters of Winnipeg, Manitoba, just to live in a place that valued and honored their personal commitment to one another.

Their case raises profound questions. In the decade leading up to 2014, when the federal courts en masse began to invalidate state bans on civil marriage for same-sex pairs, how many gay and lesbian couples left Super-DOMA jurisdictions for more friendly legal and political environments? In light of the myriad impediments posed by Super-DOMAs to healthy and prosperous family life cataloged in the preceding chapters, did it make sense for same-sex pairs to continue to put up with such harsh challenges, when they could settle in other locations that were far more welcoming to their families? After all, the remedy for a complete lack of state familial rights was sometimes as simple as moving across a border, such as going from Virginia to Maryland, Nebraska to Iowa, Kentucky to Illinois, or Idaho to Washington State.

For example, in January 2014, the *New York Times* reported on Alvin Berg, age fifty-four, and Vincent Nelson, fifty, a couple who owned two gay bars, one in Superior, Wisconsin, and the other in Duluth, Minnesota. The cities are about five miles apart, separated by the St. Louis River. Berg and Nelson were together for nearly thirty years and built their dream home in Superior. Nonetheless, after Minnesota began authorizing same-sex marriages the preceding August, the couple decided to move to Duluth, because being able to wed legally and have their state of residence recognize their marriage was so important to them (Davey 2014; cf. Chaffee 2007).

How many other lesbian and gay pairs in Super-DOMA states responded in ways similar to Berg and Nelson? In other words, did America's war on same-sex couples and their families generate refugees?

AN ESTIMATE OF LGBT EMIGRANTS FROM SUPER-DOMA STATES

Measuring any LGBT migration in the United States is a tricky business under the best of circumstances. The 1990 U.S. Census was the first ever to make an attempt to count same-sex households in the country. Before that, no reliable national database enumerating potential gay or lesbian families existed. Moreover, in their path-breaking study, *The Gay & Lesbian Atlas*, Gates and Ost (2004) spent five pages discussing the problems encountered in relying on data from the 2000 census to determine the number of same-sex unmarried partners in the nation and its subdivisions. What is more, census data, regardless of dependability, at best ascertain only those LGBT people who live together. Queer folk who dwell alone or within extended family settings are invisible because the Census Bureau asks no questions about respondents' sexual orientation or gender identity. Thus, absent comprehensive and periodic datasets, researchers may only speculate about LGBT migration patterns.

In addition, even if demographers reliably knew from census tracts that, say, X number of same-sex couples moved from Ohio to Massachusetts between 2004 and 2014, population scientists would still not have any information as to why those families relocated. Doubtless, some of the migrants made the trek primarily to escape the deleterious effects of Issue 1 in the Buckeye State and to reap the benefits of marriage in the Bay State. But others may have changed residence principally because someone landed an ideal job in Boston and they left Cleveland or Columbus only reluctantly. Still others may have returned to care for ailing parents in Worcester or Springfield or Lowell. Then there were those who wanted to spend their retirement years near the ocean on Cape Cod. And so forth.

Accordingly, in my interviews with 175 same-sex couples, as well as in conversations with an additional six officials from LGBT state organizations, I consistently asked questions like these: "Do you know of any couples who have in fact left Ohio because of Issue 1?" and "Do you know of any couples who are thinking of leaving Ohio because of Issue 1?" In short, I attempted to build my own database of LGBT migration prompted by the adoption of Super-DOMAs.

These efforts met with limited success. Consider my discussion with Sue Doerfer, the executive director of Equality Ohio in 2010, and the executive director of the LGBT Community Center of Greater Cleveland for the five years before her statewide position.

Q: On several occasions so far, you've said you know of people who left Ohio because of the passage of Issue 1. Can you quantify that in any way, in terms of approximate numbers of people or couples you personally know who did that?

A: That I know personally, I would say probably thirty to fifty people.

Q: That you know personally?

A: Yes. Now I know a lot of people, because of the work I do. And people would tell me that kind of thing.

According to an analysis of 2010 census data by the Williams Institute of the School of Law at the University of California at Los Angeles, about 19,000 same-sex couples lived in Ohio during the time period of which Doerfer spoke (Gates and Cooke 2011a). Hence, one of the people most knowledgeable about the LGBT community in the Buckeye State could identify at most 50 individuals who left Ohio because of Issue 1, in a relevant population of at least 38,000. That amounts to 0.13 percent of lesbian and gay couples leaving Ohio because of Issue 1. And among *all* the people I interviewed for this study, Sue Doerfer knew of the most individuals who had relocated from a state because of its Super-DOMA.

A second well-informed Ohioan had long participated in a Cleveland LGBT parents group that was about ninety families strong, with some members coming and others going from year to year. She estimated that about five or six families in the group left Ohio in the six years after Issue 1 passed.

Indeed, if I were to add on to Doerfer's estimate those people whom other interviewees in Ohio mentioned to me as likely candidates to have left the Buckeye State because of Issue 1 – and presuming there was not any overlap among them – the total Ohio estimate of emigrants would be fewer than 100 individuals (or less than 0.26 percent of the relevant population).

Of course, my sample of interviewees included just thirty-seven people in Ohio's two largest metropolitan areas. If I had met with ten times that amount and had included Cincinnati, Toledo, Akron, and Dayton, the number of emigrants coming to my attention would surely have been higher. Yet I have no good reason to believe from my sample that the cumulative migrant set would have been more than 1 or 2 percent of Ohio's LGBT population.

Moreover, I could relate similar accounts from Georgia, Michigan, North Carolina, Texas, and Wisconsin. For instance, Jeff Graham, the executive director of Georgia Equality, said to me, "I wouldn't be surprised if people left Georgia because of the passage of Question 1, but I personally know of no one who did." Katie Belanger, the executive director of Fair Wisconsin, was able to think of just one individual who departed the Badger State because of its 2006 referendum.

In a nutshell, my research indicates that very few same-sex couples left Super-DOMA states primarily because of the adoption of these constitutional amendments. Rather, most queer folk preferred to stay rather than vote with their feet.

So why did not more same-sex pairs choose the exit option? Scholarly inquiries into migrations by other oppressed groups help answer the query.

OTHER RELEVANT MIGRATIONS

The question about the comparative bravery of staying or going that introduced this chapter comes from Isabel Wilkerson's magisterial study of how, between 1915 and 1975, some six million African Americans left unrestrained subjugation in the South for the hope of better lives in the cities of the North and West. Later in her book, she links her investigation into America's Great Migration to another historical episode that might have produced, but ultimately did not, a similar mass exodus.

Not unlike European Jews who watched the world close in on them slowly, perhaps barely perceptibly, at the start of Nazism, colored people in the South would first react in denial and disbelief to the rising hysteria, then, helpless to stop it, attempt a belated resistance, not knowing and not able to imagine how far the supremacists would go. The outcomes for both groups were widely divergent, one suffering unspeakable loss and genocide, the other enduring nearly a century of apartheid, pogroms, and mob executions. But the hatreds and fears that fed both assaults were not dissimilar and relied on arousing the passions of the indifferent to mount so complete an attack. (Wilkerson 2010, 38)

Marion A. Kaplan, in her award-winning book *Between Dignity and Despair: Jewish Life in Nazi Germany* (1998), documents how, after Adolf Hitler's selection as chancellor in January 1933, Jews in Germany faced and grappled with an increasingly hostile legal and political environment. She inquires into the numerous reasons why about three-quarters of Jews stayed in Germany during the five-and-a-half crucial years after Hitler's ascension. Right at the volume's beginning, in fact, Kaplan asks, "Why did German Jews not leave sooner?" (1998, 3). Four pages later, she elaborates on a goal of her book: "I want to offer a balanced rejoinder to the oft-repeated accusation that German Jews should have known better, should have left Germany sooner" (1998, 7).

Of course, analogies between American same-sex couples in the early twenty-first century and either Jews in 1930s Germany or blacks in the Jim Crow South are inexact at best. Merely moving from one region of their country to another was not a remedy for the plight of German Jews, nor were Super-DOMAs even close to being as draconian as Hitler's "Final Solution to the Jewish Question." Moreover, lesbians and gay men never directly confronted extreme and ongoing sanctions such as enforced segregation or mass lynchings.

Nonetheless, Kaplan's explanations for Jews' reluctance to leave Germany before the Kristallnacht pogrom are remarkably similar to the reasons that many of the same-sex couples I interviewed in six Super-DOMA states gave for their decisions to continue living under constitutional frameworks so hostile to their relationships and families. In addition, both German Jews and lesbian and gay pairs had roughly the same temporal range in which to act. Depending on the state, the number of years in which Super-DOMAs were in effect varied between two and ten. In contrast Wilkerson charts the African American migration over six decades.

Relying both on my own interview database and on the analyses of Kaplan and Wilkerson, I lay out here a systematic model for the factors influencing prospective migrants' decisions to stay or go. I offer first a series of reasons that Kaplan suggests to explain why Jews did not emigrate, followed by examples of what lesbian and gay pairs told me of a similar nature. My interview protocol for same-sex couples[1] included a group of questions addressing migration, the first of which is a follows: "Have you ever thought about leaving [the relevant state] for another place that would be more legally welcoming of your relationship?" The juxtaposition of both Kaplan's and my findings makes abundantly clear how similar the motivations were between the two groups for not relocating in the face of significant official governmental discrimination. Later, when reporting my discussions with same-sex couples who in fact did leave Super-DOMA jurisdictions for greener pastures elsewhere, I invoke Wilkerson's analysis regarding how and why African Americans fled the South.

KNOWLEDGE AND APPRECIATION OF THE THREAT
TO WELL-BEING

In the conclusion to her study, Kaplan observes,

Dealing with the confusion of daily life in Nazi Germany and seeking to survive from day to day – that is, simply living one's life – distracted some Jews from making the

---

[1] See Appendix B.

painful decision to flee or deceived them into thinking they could hold out until they were trapped. In the pursuit of pragmatic solutions, even in extraordinary times, contemporaries may have missed or misread the danger signals in their daily lives. (Kaplan 1998, 230)

For Linda and Patricia, Jennifer's tragic experience demonstrated, beyond their capacity to ignore, the serious legal jeopardy that total governmental denial of same-sex relationships could generate for gay and lesbian couples. No matter how many legal documents Elizabeth and Jennifer might have had between themselves – from wills, to powers of attorney, even to living trusts – their private arrangements did not bind a coroner to authorize notification of death to a surviving partner or allow her the disposition of bodily remains, or the decedent's employer to distribute pension benefits to the surviving partner, or a court to grant her standing for a wrongful-death lawsuit. All such third parties could not be coerced or persuaded to bestow a legal attribute of marriage onto a lesbian or gay partner, no matter what legal hoops the couple might have jumped through beforehand. Rather, the denial of state recognition was an absolute sanction. And that stark knowledge triggered Linda and Patricia's departure from the Wolverine State.

But rarely does such an up-close-and-personal demonstration of legal disability occur. Instead, the happenstance of Linda and Patricia's knowing Elizabeth and Jennifer facilitated the former pair's witnessing the latter couple's tragedy. And that serendipitous lesson cinched their migration from Michigan.

Most same-sex couples in Super-DOMA states probably had little idea about how fragile their legal circumstances were in those jurisdictions. My interview protocol had questions about what would happen if one partner were incapacitated, or worse, after an accident. Most of the pairs I spoke with who had wills and powers of attorney thought their legal documents would cover all contingencies, even though they sometimes worried about whether such paperwork would always be honored when needed.

But Jennifer's experience in Michigan patently revealed that such was not the case in the most catastrophic of events. And Linda and Patricia – the latter of whom had a chronic illness – took the warning to heart.

What is more, as discussed in Chapter 1, many voters who approved of Super-DOMAs probably thought they were merely reaffirming a familiar definition of marriage and did not appreciate that those constitutional amendments also denied same-sex couples all opportunities for civil-union or domestic-partner rights. There is no reason to believe that many lesbian and gay pairs were not equally misinformed. Indeed, I discovered far too often that some of the couples I interviewed did not understand the sweeping nature of their states' constitutional provisions until I explained it to them by reading aloud the relevant language and then offering examples of how those words might affect them. Some people were visibly shocked about how Super-DOMAs could influence their lives.

Thus, ignorance of the real threat to well-being from Issue 1, or Proposal 2, or Question 1, or whatever the provision's local iteration might have been helps explain how many same-sex couples never reached the knowledge threshold so essential for focused contemplation of migration options.

LOYALTY TO COUNTRY OR STATE

The first half of Kaplan's book deals with the time period before the November 1938 Pogrom, Kristallnacht (or Crystal Night), which marked the beginning of organized violence against German Jews and before which "few dreamed that developments would end in anything like Auschwitz" (1998, 6). She carefully analyzes what happened in Germany during the five-and-a-half years after Hitler's rise to power and provides a series of compelling reasons to explain why only one-quarter of the Jewish population emigrated from Germany before 1939.

Prior to the November 1938 pogrom – when Nazis inflicted widespread destruction on Jewish businesses, homes, and synagogues, thereby making it abundantly clear that Jews faced physical danger if they remained in Germany – "the majority of Jews attempted to adjust to the new circumstances" (Kaplan 1998, 5). Most of the German Jewish population was ambivalent about emigrating to other countries, and Kaplan explains the numerous reasons limiting Jewish flight from the Nazis then:

At home in Germany for many generations, [Jews] were aware of antisemitism but distinguished between its varieties and thought they understood its nuances. Even if their dreams of complete acceptance had never been fully realized, they were patriots who had entered German culture. They had achieved amazing success amid antisemitism and in spite of it....

"We were so German," "we were so assimilated," "we were so middle class" – these are the refrains we read over and over again in the words of German Jews who try to explain to us (and to themselves) what their lives were like before Nazi savagery overpowered them. They stress how normal and varied their lives were...and how "German" their habits and attitudes. (Kaplan 1998, 5–6)

Thus, one reason German Jews did not emigrate before 1939 was because many of them felt they were as much a part of the life and culture of their own country as anyone else. Unrelenting antisemitism was not a sufficient motivation for them to leave.

Some couples I spoke with expressed a similar stoicism in the face of persistent homophobia: "We lived through the era in Georgia when gay men were openly harassed in bars and elsewhere. So we can survive anything less than that now." Or this: "We feel like the first African American couple who moved into the neighborhood. 'We're not leaving. We're staying. So get used to it. No matter what you do, we're not going anywhere.'"

Innumerable pairs expressed a sense of entitlement to stay in their home states, echoing their own versions of Jews' opinions that they were "as German as Hitler." For instance, a native Michigander said, "I'm not going to let these bigoted people who plotted Proposition 2 drive me from Michigan. It's *my* state as much as it's their state. Moving away would be a victory for them that I don't want them to have."

A Columbus gay man directly invoked – remarkably, and without prompting – the German precedent:

I grew up here. It's my state. It belongs to me just as much as anyone else. I'm not going to let them push me out. It's worth fighting to stay.

It would take the gay equivalent of Kristallnacht in downtown Columbus to force me to leave Ohio.

Of course, if American states had ever visited such brutality on their LGBT communities, the exit option would likely have been foreclosed by then, as Jews and other despised minorities in the Europe dominated by the Third Reich bitterly learned.

THE BUBBLE EFFECT

Kaplan explains how German Jews found solace from the Nazi threat through congregating in their own urban communities: "[Experiences with the Nazi regime] differed according to where Jews lived – insults and isolation were not always immediate and not total, especially in big cities.... [A] vital and intense Jewish life continued, even in Nazi Germany" (1998, 230–31).

So too with same-sex couples. Time and again, they characterized the cities they lived in as "bubbles" of refuge from the hostility against them elsewhere in their states (cf. Miller and Leonhardt 2015).

Betty, age forty-one, and Sandra, forty-three, a lesbian couple affiliated with the University of Michigan, for instance, did not think about leaving the Wolverine State. Betty said, "Despite the fact that the constitutional amendment makes us feel far less secure, we still experience more protection here than we would anywhere else. That's because we've lived in southeastern Michigan for so long, and because Ann Arbor is such a welcoming town."

Carol and Donna, introduced in the last chapter, expressed a similar sentiment:

We have a community here and don't want to abandon our friends and support system. We're not just going to up and leave and move to Boston because the rest of Georgia is so stupid.

We've figured out ways to get around the denial of relationship recognition here and get what we need to protect us. We're in a community that's very diverse and open. We've found where we need to be in Georgia.

So there's no need to move just for marriage.

Michelle and Sharon, a lesbian pair from Milwaukee whom we met in Chapter 3, explained their position similarly:

SHARON: We really love it here. It's our home.

We haven't seriously considered moving to Iowa or New York or Massachusetts, because we want to stay here and help make it a better place. We like our jobs a lot. This neighborhood is the best place I've ever lived, in terms of community.

MICHELLE: It's like a little town within the city.

SHARON: Everybody knows each other.

MICHELLE: I don't ever want to move again.

SHARON: We actually made a pact that we'd done our last move.

MICHELLE: We both just really love this house. All of our possessions are combined here.

Laura, age forty-four, from Durham, North Carolina, added:

All of our chosen family is here. And our home is here. Our life is here.

To try to start again somewhere else would be incredibly difficult and painful. We would lose so much of the social support network we have. There are people I met in other places as long ago as 1979 and 1980 who chose to move here to live near me. We couldn't replace that anywhere else.

The region I visited with the clearest sense of geographic limit was Atlanta, where interviewees repeatedly referenced what living either inside or outside "the Perimeter" – the beltway formed by Interstate Highway 285 around the city – meant to LGBT residents.[2] In January 2010, attorney and native Georgian Douglas L. Brooks offered one perspective on the meaning of local geography:

Question 1 was a slap in the face, a very public rebuke, which was mean and hurtful for the Atlanta LGBT community.

But really, life goes on here. And I'm telling you, we live in just the biggest disconnect in the world. I think you will find from the 2000 census that DeKalb County [covering roughly the eastern half of the Perimeter area, while Fulton County extends over the western half] had the fourth largest concentration of gay couples in this country.[3] And I believe that. We are everywhere.

In the recent [2009] mayor's race, there were three main candidates. Two of them were fully in support of marriage equality, and the third one [Kasim Reed] favored civil unions. And Reed ended up getting in a runoff and winning in a very close election. And the political activist gay community was wholesale opposed to Reed, even though, in 2004, he voted against Question 1 in the state senate, as we wanted him to do then. He just couldn't get to the point of backing marriage equality last year. But still, he was falling all over himself to look like a friend to the gay community. He did so very publicly. This is what politics in the city of Atlanta are like.

---

[2] See also Severson (2011).

[3] Gates and Ost (2004) indicated that, among all American metropolitan statistical areas with populations in excess of 500,000 people in 2000, Atlanta had the ninth highest proportion of gay and lesbian couples. Among all U.S. counties, DeKalb and Fulton ranked seventh and ninth, respectively, for the highest concentrations of gay male pairs.

And if you go right outside the Perimeter, you'll find the total opposite. And the difference between the city and the rest of the state is as old as Georgia itself.

Debbie Seagraves, the executive director of the ACLU of Georgia, elaborated:

In Georgia, people talk about "the Perimeter." Within it is a much more cosmopolitan, freethinking, live-and-let-live approach. Outside the Perimeter, outside the area of metropolitan Atlanta, which really goes beyond the Perimeter, you have folks who aren't very much interested about what's going on in Atlanta. They're very local in the way they look at things and very community bound.

Within those smaller communities, you have judges and local legislators who don't necessarily care about what decisions are being made inside the Perimeter or in other states. They'll make rulings or laws based on what they think their community standards are.

For instance, there was such a judge in a recent case [*In re Hadaway* (2008)], who knew that Question 1 passed and interpreted it to mean that same-sex couples may not adopt children. That was his interpretation of the marriage amendment, even though its language says nothing about children. And not only did the judge say they couldn't adopt, he held one of the women in the lesbian pair of disputing litigants in contempt of court for not returning the child to its birth mother. He threatened to jail the partner. He had a marshal physically come and take the child away from her.

Miriam and Naomi, both age forty, moved to Georgia from Massachusetts in 1992 so Miriam could enter graduate school. They demonstrated the degree to which some same-sex couples regulated their lives geographically within the Peach State:

NAOMI: Working for a Jewish nonprofit organization, I often talk with Jewish young adults. I find out about how much antisemitism there still is here in the South, or at least outside of the Atlanta Perimeter area. And we compare it to the experience of people who witness homophobia and what the similarities between the two forms of intolerance are, how we've been denied rights because of our religion or our sexual orientation.

Miriam and I lived in downtown Atlanta most of the time we've been in Georgia. When our youngest son was three months old, we moved just inside the Perimeter, in the north end, just a few miles south of I-285. And we're one of the very few same-sex couples we know of in our area, and the only ones who have a rainbow flag outside their home. It's the most colorful house on the block.

MIRIAM: The flag annoys at least one of our neighbors.

NAOMI: He's never said anything directly to us, just to other neighbors. Fortunately, we've never had anyone except that disgruntled neighbor say anything

But we purposely did not go outside the Perimeter to live. So it is figuratively a bubble that we've consciously stayed within, and in work and jobs that are more open-minded. We go to a synagogue that is open-minded. We choose friends who will respect us and maybe even reflect us.

Q: So you've planned your lives as absolutely carefully as you could?

MIRIAM: Yes.

NAOMI: And we haven't been naïve. So we didn't think, "We could get this great big house and have a pool and blah blah blah. We just need to live further north, in Gwinnett County." We could've had a more physically comfortable life, but with a whole lot of loneliness and potentially other stuff we couldn't even imagine. Like people asking, "Who really stays at home? Who's the daddy here?"

If we'd chosen to live outside the Perimeter, we'd have been asking for trouble. If we moved out of our comfort zone, we'd have increased the potential of having something that wasn't necessarily outright violent, but nonetheless being left out in some way. Or having some sort of prejudice or discrimination against our children.

So yes, we've carefully planned our lives, geographically and otherwise, in ways to minimize the potential for such problems.

Some Georgia couples were more discerning about where they lived even within the Perimeter, as described by Carol, who was introduced in the last chapter.

Lesbian and gay pairs make very careful choices about where to live when kids are involved. The city of Decatur has the highest taxes in the state. But we opted to be here before we had our son, knowing the school system was so good. And it's a very open community. So we chose to pay the higher taxes, cognizant that we wanted to have a child in this public school system.[4]

Nor do I think it's merely a coincidence that all the gay men we know live in the Morningside area of Atlanta. A huge number of male couples are there, and they all have kids. I can't imagine they just ended up in Morningside by chance.

Sometimes, however, limited employment opportunities necessitated leaving the Perimeter, which then demanded significant self-censorship, as another Atlanta lesbian described:

I enter a whole different world crossing Interstate 285, and it's scary. But I have to go out there because that's where my job is.

Only my co-workers know I'm gay. None of my patients do. I don't talk about my relationship at all with them. I have my own "Don't Ask Don't Tell" policy. I never use the word "husband," only "spouse," and no pronouns. I make sure I run my sentences just right.

I worry about being threatened in rural Georgia. It's a different mindset about life in general out there.

Venturing outside bubbles and being jolted by the sobering realities encountered elsewhere were not unique to the South, as an Ohio interviewee recounted about a 2013 incident:

Part of my job involves doing workshops occasionally in other parts of the state, and in May, I had to run an event down in Cincinnati. As I was driving back home, some people road-rage harassed me on the highway. But I was in my lane only. I didn't cut

---

[4] Gates and Ost (2004, 85) ranked Decatur among Georgia communities as having the highest proportion of gay and lesbian couples living there.

anyone off. I wasn't going too slowly. So I couldn't understand what caused their hostile reactions.

I finally determined that my pro-LGBT stickers prompted the ill will. I've got one saying, "When do I get to vote on your marriage?" Plus I have the HRC [Human Rights Campaign] equality symbol. Then I have my own parody of the minivan family stickers, with two dads and three pets.

Those stickers had to be the explanation for the road rage, because my driving was perfectly legal and respectful of other motorists. So I concluded, "Oh, I'm in southern Ohio. It's different down here than in Cleveland."[5]

FAMILY TIES

Kaplan notes that kinship connections in Germany were a powerful force keeping individual Jews from fleeing to other countries where they lacked such deep personal roots. The same linchpin held gay and lesbian couples in Super-DOMA states.

Underlying family ties was a commonly felt sense of obligation. For instance, Veronica, a Cleveland woman first encountered with her partner Rachel in Chapter 3, observed,

Right now, family ties are keeping us here. Rachel's parents are elderly and not in the best of health. And Rachel's the only family member in Ohio who can take care of them now.

My mom is in her seventies here as well.

Rachel and I talked about moving to California, because we thought that was one of the states that would support us, and also because Rachel's brother and nephew live there.

So I'd hate to say that we're stuck in Ohio, but that's kind of how it feels.

There were also responsibilities that tied parents to place. Olive, from a Columbus suburb and also encountered in Chapter 3, exemplified a common parental concern:

Have we talked about leaving Ohio? Yes.

Logistically, though, it would be tough right now. Our daughter Zoey is fourteen and just starting high school. She doesn't want to leave the area because she wants to go to high school with her friends.

When Zoey gets out of high school, then we'll broach going to some other place. But we wouldn't move at this point in her education.

And sometimes, tending to children's educational needs did not end with high school, as a Texas university professor explained with regard to his twin daughters:

---

5 Cf. Stolberg (2015).

Q: If you were to quantify the probability of relocation to some other state more welcoming of your relationship in the next five years, what percentage would you come up with?

A: 75 percent, all things being equal.

Yet we made the commitment to stay put in Dallas for the girls, until they finished high school. And now, both daughters have been accepted at my university, which means they can attend college tuition-free. So my continuing to teach at the school is critical to them, for financial reasons.

Then there is the grandparent connection between the parents of couples and the children of those same couples, as exemplified by Shirley, age thirty-five, in Atlanta:

Kimberly and I have been able largely to work around the system. We've played it to our advantage.

We don't think that anything would ever happen that would strip us of our parental rights for the existing three adoptions.

Plus, I'm a native of Atlanta, and there are significant emotional ties here for me with an extended family. I'd struggle taking our children away from my parents. Our three kids are my mother's only grandchildren.

Dorothy, age fifty-seven, and Lisa, fifty-four, a lesbian pair who lived in the Peach State for fourteen years and had adopted three special-needs children, talked about the impact of having elderly parents and other extended family in Georgia:

LISA: It would be very refreshing to live someplace else where we weren't such pariahs. But my parents live across the street, and Dorothy's parents live in Tennessee, just two hours away. I have a sister who lives here who's a very good friend of ours. I see her all the time. We talk six times a day.

If we were to move, she would hunt us down like dogs.

DOROTHY: She would. Yeah. [They laugh.]

LISA: So we have family ties keeping us here. Without all of that clan nearby, however, you wouldn't be talking to us in Georgia.

David, age forty-six and a native Michigander, and his partner Harold, forty-four, elaborated on the impact of family:

HAROLD: We've thought about leaving Michigan for a more hospitable state. That would be wonderful. But I have a young son who lives with his mother. He's our anchor here.

DAVID: Besides, I'm twenty years in the automotive industry, and my parents live twenty minutes away from us. They're in their seventies now, and I'm the oldest of three children. So there's a sense of responsibility to them. Plus they're my best friends.

Although I lived six years abroad, I do feel deeply rooted here. In the end, all of this overcame any angst about the legal situation in Michigan.

HAROLD: I have a child here I can't move away from. I'm not pleased with the way he's being raised by his mother, and I'm a big positive influence in his life. I would go through anything for him.

So we'll stay here and fight.

AN EXPECTATION OF LEGAL OR POLITICAL REDEMPTION

German Jews also were hopeful that Nazism was a political aberration that would be short-lived once their country's more moderate and reasonable mainstream ultimately rejected Hitler and his extremism:

[R]andom kindnesses, the most obvious "mixed signals," gave hope to some Jews. One woman wrote that every Jewish person "knew a decent German" and recalled that many Jews thought "the radical Nazi laws would never be carried out because [of] the moderate character of the German people." (Kaplan 1998, 67)

Same-sex couples were often also optimistic and had similar positive opinions about the people of their own states. For example, Frank, age forty-four, and Jeff, thirty-nine, who are both native Wisconsinites, shared their confidence in their state:

Q: What if the two of you were in [rural] western Wisconsin visiting Jeff's family and had an accident? Or if you came down ill? How do you think the hospitals there would react to treating a patient with a same-sex partner?

JEFF: I think fondly of my people in Wisconsin. We're reasonable folks. I truly believe that.

There may be hospital staff in Wisconsin who're going to have problems with gay or lesbian pairs. But there are more people working in those institutions who're going to do a reality check on discrimination and say, "That's not right." I honestly accept that as true.

We wouldn't find a majority of hospital staff barring me from seeing Frank. There might be one person. But I expect there are enough reasonable people in a professional setting anywhere in Wisconsin, even if you went to the most northern, conservative part of the state.

I just have this confidence in Wisconsin. I'd be more apprehensive about places in the Bible Belt. But I have good feelings about folks in the Badger State.

Another illustration of faith in the likelihood of political or social moderation came from David, the Michigan native:

I still believe in my heart that people are fundamentally good, and that our state's Super-DOMA will be reversed – maybe at the federal level – in the next five or six years. Perhaps I'm just clinging to straws, but I live in hope there will be federal action wiping out all of these state constitutional impediments.

Indeed, trust in the federal judicial system was a common theme among interviewees. Consider an interchange with Christopher, age fifty-five, and Juan, fifty-seven, from Dallas.

Q: Can you imagine anything happening here in Texas, either politically or legally, that would seriously prompt you to think about moving?

CHRISTOPHER: I don't believe it could get much worse here, to be honest with you.
JUAN: I agree. The state is very polarized.

I think that if Texas tried to pass an even more restrictive law against gay people, it would be thrown out in federal court.

Q: So you have great faith in the federal judiciary?

CHRISTOPHER: I think it's our best chance to get anything changed here.
JUAN: I bank on the federal system, up to the current Supreme Court.

ECONOMIC ISSUES

A last major hindrance to Jewish emigration from Germany was economics. Too often, German Jews faced the specter of substantial financial loss by leaving established careers and moving to countries where they had no reliable job opportunities or other economic prospects.

Only when they could no longer make a living were some men willing to leave. To emigrate before they had lost their positions or before their businesses or professional practices had collapsed would have required men to tear themselves away from their lifework, their clients, and colleagues. (Kaplan 1998, 64)

Many of the American states that, before 2014, had authorized either marriage, civil unions, or domestic partnerships for same-sex couples had comparatively high costs of living; for example, California, Connecticut, Maryland, Massachusetts, New Jersey, New York, Oregon, Vermont, and Washington. In contrast, most of the twenty Super-DOMA states – Alabama, Arkansas, Georgia, Idaho, Kansas, Kentucky, Nebraska, North Dakota, Oklahoma, South Dakota, Texas, Utah, and Wisconsin – had relatively low costs of living.

As a result, gay and lesbian couples who otherwise were fully prepared to flee these harsh legal environments for more welcoming ones were unable to do so because of financial limitations. Over and over, same-sex pairs in Georgia, Michigan, North Carolina, Ohio, Texas, and Wisconsin told me they simply could not afford to move to California, or Massachusetts, or New York, or somewhere else that would recognize their relationships.

One of the most wrenching interviews of the 175 I had with couples involved a lesbian pair in Cleveland who had been together for a decade. Agnes, age sixty-four and a university administrator, and Rosemary, fifty-six and a social worker, tied the knot just a few months before I met them. They described the wedding experience to me:

ROSEMARY: Getting married in Northampton, Massachusetts, was almost overwhelming, because we were in an area where nobody really cared that we were a same-sex couple. When people found out that we were there to be married, my gosh, all of them were so congratulatory and grateful that we'd come there to do it. Plus they were visibly shocked when told of the constitutional amendment in Ohio. They'd say, "How could somebody do that to their own people?"

It was really tough coming home to Ohio. It was so difficult. If our work situations were different, we could very easily pick up and decide to go somewhere else. But Agnes's job isn't portable.

AGNES: At the point that I leave my position full-time, relocating would be a real conversation for us to have.

My family is in Ohio. I have a brother and sister here. And I have two adult children and grandchildren here.

But the idea [and here she broke into tears] of living out the rest of my life in Ohio makes me *absolutely sick*. I *loathe* the thought of it. I *hated* coming back here from Northampton. I detest dealing with this crap all the time.

Q: It looks like the probability of your leaving Ohio is increasing as we speak.

ROSEMARY: As I said, it's job related.
AGNES: At sixty-four, I'm not interested in looking for another faculty position somewhere else. It's just not feasible.

The story of one Ohio gay male pair sums up many of Kaplan's themes. One of the men, Joseph, age forty-nine, has a small business he built from scratch. The other man, Charles, forty-seven, is a partner at a large law firm, who could practice law in another state, if he needed to.

Q: What would it take to prompt you to pull up stakes and say, "We're getting out of here"?

JOSEPH: To say that, OK, I'm going to leave a business that I've built for thirty years, plus family and lots of wonderful friends here as well...[his voice trails off].

I certainly can understand why some people have left, especially those who have children, which was a huge motivator for them to say, "Enough is enough," and decide that they had to leave.

But for me, you put up with things that you have to put up with.
CHARLES: Our lives are here. Our friends are here. We cherish those friendships, because they're deep and long lasting.

We've been together over twenty years, and most of our friends have been together almost as long.

Joseph grew up here. His family is here. Some of my family is now here.

So our lives are very much rooted here. We're very active in the community, both of us. So those are the ties that keep us here.
JOSEPH: I'd like to believe that the darkest days for us are done in Ohio.

After the U.S. Supreme Court invalidated the federal DOMA in 2013 and thereby opened up the opportunity for same-sex pairs to receive all federal marriage benefits (such as the ability to file federal tax returns jointly and to receive Social Security survivor benefits), I contacted again the gay and lesbian couples interviewed in previous years to see whether this important new legal development might prompt them to think more seriously about relocation. A Dallas physician emailed a remarkable response:

Farmers Branch, a Dallas suburb, has been involved in lawsuits for several years, spending millions of dollars, because they passed an ordinance requiring every apartment complex to verify that its residents weren't illegal immigrants. The whole purpose was to get rid of Hispanics in the suburb.

The new law created a mini-Gestapo state, with Latinos being randomly stopped on the street. It was crazy stupid.

And there are people who make it their life's work to guarantee that Texas never allows same-sex marriage. What happened in Farmers Branch evidenced the level of intolerance here.

My office staff, most of whom are Hispanic, often got stopped going into the local Walmart. They were asked to show IDs proving they were legal.

No one has stopped me. But then, they aren't searching for gay people just yet.

So that's the local context, Dan, when you ask whether we'd move somewhere else.

But I still don't see that happening. We both are too heavily invested in our businesses.

For me as a physician, it just isn't possible to drop everything and move to another state. Just getting the license to practice medicine can take upward of a year. Then it takes months to get established with the insurance companies and Medicare and Medicaid in the new location. Then you have to build the practice. So I just wouldn't consider it at this stage in my life.

Quite frankly, though, it really pisses me off that I pay taxes here and provide employment to fifteen straight people, as well as health care to several thousand more, while all the time being a second-class citizen.

I want to see the change happen here. We have the right to have the same benefits as everyone else. We work just as hard and provide so much to our community that it's plain wrong not to have equal rights. And leaving Texas would make me feel I was just letting the ignorant bigots win.

So no, I don't see us moving anytime in the future.

Without sounding too paranoid, I do sometimes wonder if the Jews of Germany made the same argument before the Holocaust. Thoughts like that make others believe you're crazy. But there are a lot of really awful people out there who want to "take back" their country. And history teaches what such individuals are capable of.

THE IMPACT OF TRADITIONALLY GENDERED
RELATIONSHIP ROLES

Kaplan observes that gender had an important impact on the emigration patterns of Germany Jews in the period before Kristallnacht:

[G]ender made a difference in deciding between fight and flight. In the early years, Jewish women were more sensitive to discrimination, more eager to leave Germany, more willing to face uncertainty abroad than discrimination and ostracism at home. Women, whose identity was more family-oriented than men's, struggled to preserve what was central to them by fleeing with those they loved. (1998, 8)

Women were less involved than men in the economy.... Jewish men had a great deal more to lose. Only when they could no longer make a living were some men willing to leave.... [T]he family could be moved more easily than a business or profession. In light of men's close identification with their occupation, they often felt trapped into staying. (1998, 64)

Men's role and status as breadwinners made them hesitant to emigrate and gave them the authority to say no. (1998, 68)

Even though all of the pairs interviewed for this book were of the same gender, I still noticed striking similarities between some of them and the couples whom Kaplan examined from afar in her study. If one were to substitute the words "partners in the role of breadwinner" for "men," and "partners in the role of homemaker" for "women," in Kaplain's findings, her summary could easily be used to describe the circumstances I discovered in several gay and lesbian families across the six Super-DOMA states of the investigation.

I spoke with couples where one person was adamantly opposed to moving away, while the other was eager to leave. More often than not, the individual against emigration had the higher, or only, income in the household, while the one ready to pack up and go had more responsibility for looking after the family unit, especially in homes with minor children.

Kathleen, age thirty-seven, and Pamela, forty-two, have been together eleven years and have two adopted girls, ages three and six. Kathleen is a social worker, and Pamela is in business administration. I suspect that Pamela earns substantially more money than Kathleen, although I do not know that for a fact because I did not ask couples how much they made at their jobs.[6] The family lives in the Atlanta metropolitan area, outside of the Perimeter.

Q: What did the passage of Question 1 in 2004 mean to you in the broadest sense of that word?

PAMELA: It was frightening to me. This isn't an accepting place for our relationship. At the same time, though, it's my home.

Question 1 meant to Kathleen that we needed to move. She's always thinking, "Let's leave. Let's just go somewhere else." I don't think we need to do that necessarily.

Q: So the two of you have had conversations about relocating?

KATHLEEN: At least for a good year afterward, I said, "We need to move."

If 76 percent of the state thought we weren't the same as them, looking straight couples in the eye doesn't feel equal, if your head has to be down.

Our oldest daughter has social anxiety fears. And I wonder how much of her psychological state I create because of the worries I carry around, about myself and our relationship, and knowing the people I'm surrounded by.

---

[6] I worried about wearing out my welcome if I inquired into how much money people made. After all, an interviewer can ask only so many intrusive questions before being shown the door.

Q: What would have to happen here in Georgia that would indeed prompt you to leave the state?

PAMELA: If I were denied decision making for, or access to, Kathleen if something happened with regard to health .... If the right were given to her family to make decisions rather than to me.

KATHLEEN: [to Pamela:] But don't you prefer to live in a social milieu where you know people want you to be treated in the same way they are, instead of a climate where neighbors don't think we should be equal? Even though they're nice to us, they don't see our relationship as comparable to theirs.

PAMELA: [to Kathleen:] Where is that?

KATHLEEN: I'd like to believe it occurs in Vermont.

PAMELA: But there are plenty of people in Vermont who don't accept you and me. The whole state of Vermont isn't gay friendly. It's simply more so than Georgia, because I know of their voting record there.

Q: Same-sex marriage is now legally recognized in Vermont.

KATHLEEN: [continuing to address Pamela:] So if the top people in the state do recognize it as legal, then that generosity of spirit has to trickle down to other people's mindsets.

PAMELA: Certainly. But you act like there's some utopia out there. And I don't know that's necessarily true.

I feel that, if Decatur [a very progressive town inside the Perimeter] could vote by itself, Decatur would approve of gay marriage. So why not move to Decatur and be surrounded by those people?

I may be ignorant, but until something drastic happens, I don't have a strong desire to move.

Q: Both of you are very similar in a sense. You're both native Georgians. You both have biological family nearby, more or less. I presume you have pretty much comparable roots in the community.

Yet one of you is much more prepared to relocate, and the other isn't. I wonder if there's any way to understand that difference in light of the similar foundations.

PAMELA: I think Kathleen is smarter than me. That's the key. [She laughs.]

You make a good point. If something serious happened, I'd be like, "Hello!" But then it would be too late. What sense does that make?

I think part of the difference comes from my parents and Kathleen's. Our childhoods were very dissimilar.

Kathleen is a lot more driven and demanding and has higher expectations of others than I have. Whereas, I say, "Well gosh, these people aren't running me out of town. They're letting me live here." You know what I mean? "It's not *that* bad."

I went from being totally ashamed of who I was, just all that humiliation and stuff, to being excited to find one other person who was like me.

While Kathleen has greater expectations and demands more, which I appreciate, and it makes me think more carefully. So probably, I'll be where she is at some point.

But that's the root of it. I don't have the same outlook. I have very low expectations for my parents and other family. If they ask me about my day or my life, great. And then Kathleen responds to me, "How do you do that?"

So there are fundamental personality differences. I'm a lot more laid-back and accepting. And part of it is fear of the unknown.

INTERNALIZED HOMOPHOBIC SOCIAL STIGMA

Pamela's concluding comments suggest that another force, different from traditionally gendered relationship roles, was also prompting her reluctance to relocate: an internalization of the social stigmatization of being homosexual in America.

I would be hard-pressed to characterize the bulk of my sample of interviewees as feeling stigmatized because of their being lesbian or gay. Indeed, quite the contrary, most interviewees had well-developed political and social identities as LGBT citizens. They firmly believed that the legal impediments to civil marriage where they lived were ethically, morally, and socially mistaken, as well as hurtful. To be sure, the overwhelming number of people I spoke with were prepared to stand up proudly and with confidence against the repressive laws around them, rather than cower in fear generated from internalized homophobia.

As discussed in Chapter 1, the sample's distribution is skewed by having a larger proportion of highly educated and financially better off people than in the larger LGBT community. Thus, Pamela may well have represented a more commonly occurring phenomenon among the same-sex couples who were not significantly drawn into my sampling net.

The clearest examples of the kind of LGBT people who typically did *not* meet with me are Debra, age fifty-six, and Martha, fifty, who have been together for nearly a decade and who live in a suburb of the Dallas-Fort Worth metroplex. Martha was three years away from retirement in a civilian training department of the U.S. Defense Department.

Debra and Martha never felt any need for a ceremony to celebrate their relationship nor had they ever talked about getting married. Neither of them was familiar with the passage of Prop 2 in Texas five years earlier. Moreover, the terms "civil union" and "domestic partnership" as applied to same-sex couples were unknown to them. Also consider these comments:

MARTHA: Debra isn't that, ah .... She doesn't need to have the world know [that she's gay].
   And for me, too. It doesn't have to be written on the walls.
   We're kind of old-fashioned.
DEBRA: Today, I was in the car with friends from high school. So that shows how long I've known these people. My best friend, that I lived with for a long time, that I've known since junior high ....
   Nobody else is aware that I live with Martha. And I don't feel comfortable .... I don't know how to explain it.

They all have husbands and kids and grandkids and such. And they talk a lot about their families. And on the way home this evening, it kind of came up....

I'm sick of this. One girl who was driving knows that I live with Martha. But the other one kind of really didn't. And it brought up....

And I'm exhausted with this. One of the main reasons I retired is because I had to live a lie at my school. I was a counselor at an elementary school for thirty years. And today, in the State of Texas, I could possibly lose my job if they knew I was living with a woman. Because some of the parents would be like, "I don't want my child talking to this lady if she lives with another woman. It might rub off and harm my child."

Q: So now, since you recently retired, you no longer have that as a worry?

DEBRA: Pretty much. Except that I've chosen to go back and tutor children. But I'll probably stop doing that after the end of this school year.

Because you have to play this game. There are people in the school system who would change their opinion of me if they knew I'd been living with Martha for ten years.

Q: Well now that you'll soon be permanently retired, and that psychic limitation shouldn't be there any longer, do you think you'll change your behavior with people like your high school friends?

DEBRA: No. [Shaking her head.] Because I've lived this way for so long.

I dated guys most of my life.

Every so often, I might be with friends at somebody's lake house. Just me, without Martha.

MARTHA: I've never met *any* of Debra's friends.

DEBRA: Because I'm still playing this game. And I think it's taken a toll on me. I'm tired of it. Because I feel like I've lost all of my friends.

But then I go back to playing this person that I was in high school with them. It's kind of crazy. But I do this to myself. I was dating guys with these friends. They still contact me to get together for reunions or whatever. And I just never speak up. Because that's who I was then, and that's how they knew me.

I don't blame it on the State of Texas, because I do it to myself. I grew up in such a conservative family and then went on to work at such a conservative job in such a conservative state. Homosexuality is such a taboo here that I could never have become a counselor if they'd known I was gay.

Texas was the fourth of the six states I visited to conduct interviews for this study. So by the time I met Debra and Martha, I had already spoken with many lesbian and gay pairs. Yet the women's interview proved difficult to carry out because assumptions I had come to take for granted about couples – primarily that they were unambiguously out of the closet – did not apply to this lesbian pair. Thus, many questions, prepared with a presumption of openness about sexual orientation, simply were not relevant to them. And any notion of relocating from their homes for the purpose of obtaining civil marriage was virtually alien to their experience.[7] In fact, even after the U.S. Supreme Court invalidated all Super-DOMAs in June 2015 and thereby made civil marriage available to same-sex couples in Texas, Debra and Martha informed me they did not intend to wed.

Mark, age forty-seven, and Paul, forty-two, each lived in Atlanta for a decade or longer and, in 2007, left Georgia together to live in Massachusetts, where they were married the next year. According to the couple's own estimate, the

---

[7] Readers should appreciate that, although I note how closeted gay people decreased LGBT emigration from Super-DOMA states, I seek *not* to demean hiding as an appropriate coping mechanism. Rather, closets were safe havens for good reason, as evidenced by the comments of a lesbian in the clinical pastor-education residency program at the Carolinas Medical Center (CMC) in Charlotte:

I won't be getting unemployment benefits after my residency ends in a month or two. So the need to get a job will be fairly intense soon. As I look for positions, and read about employers' policies, no hospital environments south of the Mason-Dixon line include sexual orientation in their equal-opportunity employment guidelines. So I struggle with whether I should tell people I'm a lesbian in job interviews. Do I say, "Will I be safe here working as a lesbian?"

I worry about how to protect myself in a position where there's nothing in writing that prohibits sexual-orientation discrimination. My supervisor believes I overthink the issue – even though one of my current colleagues lost a job because she's gay.

This woman was the chaplain in a nursing home for nine years. When she got the position, she was married to a man. Then her husband died, and she fell in love with a woman. The two had a commitment ceremony, and when the nursing home learned about the event, they fired the chaplain.

This discrimination happened just a year and half ago in North Carolina. Yet our "ally" boss is too dense to see it, because of his lack of understanding of the kind of risks we face as gay people.

The staff members in the hospital department that's supposed to teach chaplains about diversity aren't even aware of their own heterosexism. They literally didn't appreciate the fact that I could be fired in this state because I'm gay. A chaplain colleague said, "You've got to be kidding me. This is 2012."

Their inability to see any of the difficulties confronting gay people is remarkable. They fully understand all of the employment and other economic and social problems facing people of color. I've been told by supervisors, "Well, you can hide being gay. You don't really comprehend oppression, because you can pass as straight." And this from an individual who's an ally.

So if I respond to them with, "As a gay person, I can be kicked out by my family and my house of worship. Churches can tell me I'm an abomination before God," all of that just goes right over their heads.

The Carolinas Medical Center considers itself an inclusive and diverse place, and has a standing committee on that very topic. Yet, when the CMC had a whole, big, long educational-workshop day on diversity in hospital environments, there was *nothing* included about LGBT issues.

There's a huge amount of heterosexism going on in the workplace they don't get. For example, they don't realize that when a chaplain knocks on the door of a gay person and says, "I'm the chaplain. Would you like a visit?" the gay person is the one who says, "No, thank you," because most – and especially those of us in the South – have learned to expect only antigay prejudice from the clergy.

So the CMC doesn't know how, or cares, to identify lesbian and gay patients in order to accommodate their needs in the same way the hospital does for all other users.

Peach State's Super-DOMA accounted for only about 20 percent of the reasons for their departure. Nevertheless, their commentary about the lesbian and gay couples they knew in Georgia reinforced my experience with Debra and Martha:

Q: Are you aware of any other same-sex couples who left Georgia and for whom Question 1 was an important factor?

BOTH: No.

MARK: It's a funny situation. We certainly know other gay and lesbian pairs in Atlanta, and couples who've been together for a long time.

People have such roots there that they would never leave. There's no reason for them to do so. They wouldn't resettle just to get married.

Bertram and Leonard are friends of ours. They're older and have been together for thirty years. I'm not even sure what they think about us being married. We received congratulations from them. But it's odd. They know that they're not going to move. So I think Bertram in particular just kind of sets marriage aside. He doesn't really even want to talk about it that much.

PAUL: Bertram's not even been out of the closet with his family. Even though he's lived with Leonard for thirty years, he's still the "roommate."

MARK: Larry and Alan would probably get married if they had the opportunity. But I think they're practical in the sense that they know they wouldn't want to move from the South. In fact, I think their plan is to relocate to Florida. They wouldn't put getting married as tremendously high on a to-do list.

PAUL: No, they wouldn't.

MARK: Certainly not high enough to take action on it.

Q: So what are the factors distinguishing you as a couple from them?

PAUL: For them, even though they're gay and in a long-term, committed relationship, they're somewhat closeted. Larry, in particular, is extremely southern. It's about his persona. Even at work, I don't think a lot of people know he's gay. It would be an image thing for him. He tries to pretend like he's straight in many situations.

MARK: That's true, except of course in our circle of friends.

Another thing is that, continuing to use them as an example, Alan was married to a woman and has children. So I wonder how gay men who've been married in a heterosexual relationship view this question. I really don't know.

I think Paul is on to something. I wouldn't consider myself to be a political activist in any way. But this is one question where I'm very clearly in a position to make a public statement. I'd never work in a place where I'd have to hide being gay. We're in a different place from our friends now.

PAUL: Our activism is just being ourselves and not being ashamed to say, "I'm married to Mark Williams," with co-workers, with clients, with whomever. It's not something that I'm hesitant to do.

But a lot of our friends in Georgia aren't at that point.

MARK: I think it's really hard in Atlanta, and probably in other cities as well, to sustain a same-sex relationship. I have it in my head, and maybe I'm biased, but I feel like it's so much harder in Atlanta for a gay couple, for a lot of reasons, many of which are related to how society views same-sex pairs. There's no encouragement for them there. And when there's no approval, what do you do?

Paul and I were lucky enough to find each other and know that we're all the incentive we needed. Our friends Larry and Alan are a very strong couple as well. But in some ways, Paul and I had more freedom than they did, because I'm anything but southern.

So in terms of being tied to the region, we weren't as closely linked. Paul has an interest in life and where he wants to live and everything that goes beyond regionalism.

I'm not being critical of the area. I love the South. But Paul is more adventurous and able to be bold in terms of family ties and other such social parameters than a lot of our friends.

Thus, our life circumstances allowed more of an opportunity to relocate than many people I can think of down there.

Q: How many of the people you mentioned are either native Georgians or otherwise native southerners?

MARK: Almost all.

PAUL: Yup.

MARK: Bertram moved to Atlanta probably forty years ago. I'd say that at least three-quarters, and maybe more, of our circle of friends is native to the South.

Q: So your backgrounds would've provided greater flexibility than theirs?

MARK: I would say so.

PAUL: And jobwise.

MARK: We've just been used to ranging farther.

PAUL: The gay people in Georgia just don't have exposure to a better life. How to live more fully as LGBT citizens still isn't on their radar screens. Doing what they've always done, they don't have any exposure to the full opportunity of a truly open and self-affirming lifestyle.

Here in Massachusetts, our being gay isn't even a big deal. We live in a small town and haven't encountered even a single instance of negativity. Diversity with regard to sexual orientation is just normal here.

Whereas, most gay people in Georgia don't have it in their paradigm that being gay could ever be normal.

MARK: It's almost as if Question 1 took normalization off the table. It's alarming to contemplate.

I wasn't raised to believe I'd ever be married. So I understand how new possibilities coming up can be scary.

Gay Georgians might think, "How do I feel about saying I'm married to a man?" That thought would dismay many in our community down there.

An Atlanta friend once asked me, "What's it like in Massachusetts when you go here or there or when you visit the doctor or something like that?" And it's been a learning experience for us that people don't really care.

I remember after we got married and went to the Social Security office so Paul could start processing a change of name. I didn't say this to him, but I thought, "Oh my gosh. Who are we going to see on the other side of that glass, or what are they going to say when two guys walk up there?" And the clerk was like, "Oh, you just got married? Congratulations! Let me get the paperwork." And I thought, "How disappointing! Hey, wait a minute!" [They laugh.]

We have some friends in Georgia who'd love to be married someday. But I feel like they almost set the opportunity aside, because it's either too painful or too foreign or too much not a possibility to consider. It's like they've been beaten down. And I'm not sure what it would take to motivate people to action in a state where something like Question 1 has already happened.

PAUL: I don't see people in Georgia doing a grassroots effort to try to overturn the constitutional amendment.

As D'Emilio (2000, 48) observed, "[T]he defining feature of gay experience [is] the fact that almost all gay men and lesbians are neither raised in nor socialized at an early age into a gay community." Sherrill (1996, 469) elaborated on the idea:

Gay people, by virtue of being born into a diaspora, are not highly concentrated geographically. More important, identity is not transmitted within the family. Unlike almost all other demographic groups, gay people are unique by virtue of being minorities within their own families and by virtue of going through childhood socialization experiences designed to make them the opposite of what they are. That is, almost all gay people are born into heterosexual homes, are imbued with heterosexual norms – including the belief that heterosexuality is superior to homosexuality and, perhaps, the beliefs that homosexuality is deviant and morally inferior behavior – and are expected to act as if they were heterosexual.... [T]hese socialization experiences must contribute to the reluctance or inability to classify themselves as lesbian, gay, or bisexual.

Completing the analysis, Wald (2000, 13) concluded,

Psychologically, this isolation and stigmatization [of gay people] may produce a crippling level of self-hatred. Politically..., these experiences undermine the formation of a common political identity and discourage people from mobilizing to achieve common goals.

Hence, the probability is high that this investigation significantly undersampled closeted same-sex couples, for whom the prospect of relocating for the purpose of marrying one another would not have been on the horizon. And this sampling limitation further helps explain the minuscule gay-and-lesbian emigration rate for Super-DOMA states detected here.

THE ABILITY TO PASS AS MEMBERS OF THE MAJORITY OR OTHERWISE PLAY THE SYSTEM

The penultimate chapter of *Between Dignity and Despair* is titled "Life Underground," where Kaplan discusses how some German Jews hid from the Nazis: "'Hiding' could mean ducking out of sight for the duration of the war or removing the yellow star and assuming an 'Aryan' identity, with or without papers" (1998, 201). Likewise, Wilkerson noted the "passing" phenomenon among African Americans (2010, 202–3, 218). I discovered that lesbian and gay couples developed similar coping mechanisms.

Of course, "hiding in the closet" has always been available to homosexuals everywhere, because virtually every society presumes all people are heterosexual without substantial evidence to the contrary. So passing as heterosexual is an ancient self-protective strategy for queer folk.

Yet the hiding or passing at issue in this section is not the same phenomenon as being closeted, although the effect may be similar. Rather, what I refer to here concerns how same-sex pairs with well-developed LGBT identities learned, in both systematic and impromptu ways, to grapple with the adverse legal conditions they faced in Super-DOMA jurisdictions – and this ability to play the system diminished their perceived need to emigrate.

Consider, for instance, that sometimes the added costs of medical care for children being reared by gay and lesbian couples involved more than dollars and cents. Bertie and Olive, who were introduced in Chapter 3, live in suburban Columbus with their daughter Zoey and shared this experience:

OLIVE: Once, when I took Zoey to urgent care, the woman at the admissions desk was confused about who I was. So finally, I just told her that I was Bertie [Zoey's birth mother]. I impersonated Bertie. And Zoey got it. She's quick, and she understands.
BERTIE: Our kids have learned. [To Olive:] Haven't they?
OLIVE: Yes, they appreciate the need to navigate sometimes. So Zoey went right with me on this one, "Oh, Mommy! I feel so sick." Then the woman behind the counter said to me, "Just sign here."
   I wonder whether that clerk might still have been suspicious, but didn't want to get involved with challenging me. But initially, the nature of my relationship with Zoey appeared to be a problem for her admission.

Q: How did you feel about having to pose as Bertie?

OLIVE: I hated it. Why should I have to lie for my daughter to get medical care? It's ridiculous. I shouldn't have to pretend to be somebody else.
BERTIE: The fact that my name is Bertie has even allowed me to perform sleights of hand a few times when I needed to. So I'll pretend to be Olive, the wife, with strangers. "And your husband, ma'am?" Well, he's somewhere else, away.
   But again, who wants to have to do that?
OLIVE: And we don't typically resort to that. Most people know, and we're fairly open about it. We don't want to have to hide.
   But when it concerns your daughter's health care, that's one of those times where you go, "Yep. Okay. Gotta lie here." Even though we'd prefer not to.

Thus, Olive's ability to impersonate Bertie saved the day, and playing the system to their advantage reduced the need to think about relocation.

A Cleveland couple, Doris, age forty-three, and Ruth, forty, provided another example of improvisation:

RUTH: We have lesbian friends with two children. One of the women had a really nice job. The other is a preschool teacher without many benefits from her work. The one who made more money had domestic-partner benefits for the entire family. And then her job got outsourced. Although she landed a position elsewhere, her new employer doesn't provide partner benefits.

DORIS: So the preschool teacher – who's the children's birth mother – and the two kids aren't covered by employment-sponsored health insurance any more.

RUTH: If the couple were legally married in Ohio, that wouldn't be the case, because the partner would be a spouse. Now the preschool teacher and the children are on Medicaid. That's what they have to use.

When taxpayers get mad because others are using the system, you know what? Fix it. Because the new employer would cover the whole family if it had the legal responsibility to do so. Same-sex couples shouldn't be forced to use the system like that. But working people like our friends don't have the kind of money to pay for health insurance out of pocket. So Issue 1 has greatly affected them.

Another federal opportunity that allowed same-sex couples to game the system involved the adoption of children. Ben and Ted and their son Brandon were introduced in the last chapter.

Q: What was the combined expense for your adoption of Brandon?

TED: All of the costs were probably $27,000 or $28,000.

BEN: The upside is that some gay couples end up with a significant benefit, because often each partner gets to claim the adoption tax credit on the same child. So if we lived in a state where we were able to adopt Brandon at the same time, we'd have just one tax-credit claim. With us, however, Ted claimed it once, and I'm in the process of doing so again now.

TED: That's because there were separate adoption proceedings to establish the parentage of each of us.

BEN: In the end, we'll be able to recoup about $20,000 over the course of five years.

Federal expedients like the adoption tax credit and Medicaid were not the only stopgaps employed by resourceful couples to make up for some of all the rights and privileges automatically awarded to married people. George, age fifty, and Kenneth, forty-seven, together for twelve years, illustrated how state systems were played as well:

Q: Did the passage of Wisconsin's marriage amendment directly affect the two of you in some concrete, tangible way you can identify?

GEORGE: Same-sex marriage was already illegal in Wisconsin. And that status wasn't going to change any time soon in the legislature.

There's a domestic-partner registry now that would provide us more rights than what we currently have.

Yet it's hard for us, because I don't have a corporate job providing me health care benefits. And I don't get them through Kenneth's employment, since we haven't registered as domestic partners. Because we're married, dammit. Why should we have to register as domestic partners?

Q: So, George, do you have any health insurance?

GEORGE: I do. And this goes back to Wisconsin's progressive tradition.

Farmers are typically very poor, and qualify for free health care from the state. So I get that, being a destitute farmer.

KENNETH: Oddly enough, it's a reverse benefit. Since George is a farmer and makes almost no money, he qualifies for the state's excellent Badger Care health insurance supplied to low-income working people. But if we were married in the eyes of the government of Wisconsin, they'd take my income into account, and George would lose the coverage.

So he has excellent health insurance.

I also have superb coverage through my job with state government. But he's not recognized as a person who could be on a family policy. If we were married, George could be on that. In addition, if we were to sign the domestic-partner registry, George would be entitled to my benefits. But then I'd have to pay income tax on its value as imputed income.

So we're better off financially to consider him as a poor farmer.

GEORGE: I get a Cadillac health care insurance package with no deductible. And I also get food stamps.

Isn't that wild? So we're totally playing the system.

KENNETH: If the state of Wisconsin refuses to acknowledge that I could provide for George, then he can take advantage of the opportunities the state offers its citizens who don't have legal spouses making money.

GEORGE: The Badger Care is probably worth $550 per month to me.

Thus, this gay pair found a coping mechanism allowing them to hide in plain sight while saving at least $6,000 annually in health-insurance costs. Otherwise George's having to pay for expensive insurance might have prompted a calculus to contemplate relocation.

Then there is what Christopher and Juan, who were introduced earlier in the chapter and who own a small accounting business together, did to work the system:

Q: I have a question that falls under the heading of "playing the system." Let me give you some examples of what I mean .... Is there anything like that in your experience?

CHRISTOPHER: This house [in Dallas] is in Juan's name, with a homestead property-tax exemption. Our Abilene house is in both of our names, and I could get a homestead exemption there. But the property taxes are already very low in Abilene.

Before we bought this house, I lost everything in a restaurant that went belly up. So I had a terrible credit score. Juan was able to purchase this property on his credit alone. If we were married, he'd have been responsible for my losses.

JUAN: Christopher is an employee of our accounting firm. Pretty much every time we go out to eat at a restaurant, especially if it's just the two of us, the cost of our meal is run through the company. If we were legally married, the IRS would have strict rules against that.

CHRISTOPHER: Since we're not married, our meals together are a business expense. In a small business, we're always talking about business.

So we do game the system. And it's a perfectly fair trade-off.

A final example of turning outsider status to economic advantage comes from Maria and Margaret, a North Carolina couple who have appeared in earlier chapters:

MARGARET: Yes, we play the system.

MARIA: We game it every chance we get. Absolutely. If the government won't give us equal rights,...

MARGARET: we'll take what we can get.

Our daughter's college financial aid is an example. Maria is Jean's only legal parent.

MARIA: And the economy has been really bad the last five years. So our company isn't.... We've made it, and we're still alive. But my brother and I don't take big salaries.

Jean is my adoptive daughter...

MARGARET:. and if we were married and added our incomes together, Jean wouldn't get any financial aid. But instead, she qualifies for Pell grants and student loans. Plus she has a work-study at school.

And it's entirely legal. I read word for word everything we signed. "Name all of the relatives by blood or marriage in your household."

So by golly, we take advantage of every opportunity that comes our way. You darn right.

Accordingly, some same-sex couples could, and did, use their outsider, unmarried status for economic and other gain, thereby offsetting the losses visited on them by Super-DOMAs and helping tamp down impulses to head for greener pastures.

SAME-SEX COUPLES WHO LEFT SUPER-DOMA STATES PARTIALLY OR TEMPORARILY

Some gay and lesbian pairs worked out partial migration solutions to escape Super-DOMA effects. For instance, a librarian at the University of Michigan told me of a professor there whose partner and adopted son lived in Vermont. After Proposal 2 passed, the family was not comfortable having the partner and child remain in Michigan. So the U of M faculty member commuted, spending weekends, holidays, and vacations in Vermont and the work week in Ann Arbor when classes were in session.

I met other couples during my interview trips who had resettled in more LGBT-friendly jurisdictions for several years in order to marry or adopt children and then were forced to return to their Super-DOMA home states because of economic necessity. For instance, Amy, age forty-one, and Brenda, thirty-nine, met in Georgia, became a couple in 1997, and wanted to have children. They shared their experience:

BRENDA: We tried to be foster parents in Georgia, and had been certified and ready for two years, but never had a child placed with us.

Q: For two years? I'd have thought there'd be a big demand for foster parents.

AMY: So did we.

BRENDA: We'd offered to take a sibling group of up to three kids. But we still didn't get anyone placed with us. And then we were in line to foster to adopt.

AMY: We wanted to make them part of our family.

BRENDA: I'm a pediatric physical therapist, with professional experience dealing with children. But nothing ever panned out for us.

So we saw the writing on the wall that things weren't really going to happen here, and moved to New York in 2005. There, we chose to work with the state because its recruitment brochure displayed same-sex couples as foster parents. We registered with the agency in July, and they matched us with a family in August. It took about a month.

AMY: It was very fast.

BRENDA: We were in New York for less than a year and had three foster children placed with us. Then we were chosen to adopt a baby and got our son Thomas. Plus we were able to do it with just one court proceeding and not have to worry about a second-parent adoption, as we would have had to do here. In New York, lesbian and gay couples adopt jointly.

We've always wondered whether we were discriminated against in Georgia, because our attempts to foster happened while Question 1 was in the works. After all, there was such a huge need in the Atlanta metro area for people to adopt sibling groups. How could we not get one? We weren't even asking for a baby, and I have a pediatric background. So it seemed mighty suspicious to us. Whereas in New York, we were open to a host of situations almost immediately.

Q: What did the passage of Georgia's Question 1 of 2004 mean to you in the broadest sense of that term?

BRENDA: I told my friends right then that we weren't going to stay in Georgia. I wouldn't remain someplace where people made an unusual effort to discriminate against me. It's one thing not to give me rights. It's quite another event to go out of your way with such a far-reaching amendment.

We were really worried that it would affect our ability to adopt. And the legislature introduced bills banning gay people as foster parents. That's what drove us to New York, with private adoptions failing in Georgia. We felt we were running out of time because Georgia might pass a law like Florida's, and we'd never get to have a family.

So we fled to a blue state. If our house had sold here, we wouldn't have come back to Georgia.

AMY: We'd probably be in Massachusetts. But the housing market tanked in Georgia. So we sold the home in New York, and still have the one here.

BRENDA: We moved back to regroup, because we couldn't get rid of our Georgia property. That's why we came back.

We'd decided we weren't going to adopt any more children because it had taken so long the first time. We have Anna because we got a phone call from Thomas's birth parents. Our children are biologically related.

So that's our story. We had to move out of state to achieve a family.

Q: How long were you in New York altogether?

AMY: Almost two years.

BRENDA: We returned to Atlanta in 2007. We don't plan to stay in Georgia. We'll definitely target a state where we can get married.

Q: How much were you giving up in 2005, in terms of your friends and positions here, to go to New York?

BRENDA: I had just gotten a promotion. So I pretty much gave up my career path.
   I took a job in New York that just paid the bills. I wasn't interested in it at all. But it got us out of Georgia.
AMY: I didn't get a job in New York for a while. In Georgia, I was writing technical documents for companies. I was under the illusion it wouldn't be difficult to find a similar position, when actually it was very challenging.
   So we ended up giving up a fair amount of income. Plus we had two mortgages then.
BRENDA: We pretty much lost our savings to do that.

Q: So relocation really inflicted a substantial financial sacrifice?

BRENDA: Yes. And at the time, I was doing pediatric sports medicine, which is a specialty that's only offered in a limited number of places. It's not a common job. I can be a physical therapist anywhere. But the line of work I like to do has very few openings. It took me over ten years to secure my position in Atlanta. So when we fled Georgia, I left my career behind. I gave all of that up.

Q: I've spoken with lots of same-sex pairs since I've been in Atlanta. This is my twenty-eighth interview. Not all of them have been with couples. But most were. And I've heard repeatedly that they live in a circumstance of disconnect, where the law is one thing, and their daily lives are another. And there's little commonality between them.
   How do you respond to that? In other words, quite a few couples really don't appear especially concerned or upset by what happened with Question 1. They say they didn't have anything before 2004, and they don't have anything now. So nothing really changed. "But Atlanta is so tolerant," they say.
   Clearly your disappointment with the foster-care experience in 2005 was consequential. But from what I can tell, you gave up a tremendous amount in order to leave Georgia for New York.

BOTH: Yes.
BRENDA: And we'd do it again.

Q: So my question is this: How are you so different from all of these other couples I'm seeing?

AMY: I don't know. Had we known we were going to be so devastated financially, I think relocation would have been a more challenging decision. We thought we were going to come out on the good end of everything. We also expected to get jobs equal to the ones we had. We anticipated it was going to be so much better in New York because it was on the cusp of passing marriage equality.

BRENDA: I also knew we had savings and that we'd be okay. Now the savings are gone.

AMY: I think we'd have done the same thing. But I understand now why other people were more hesitant than us. They were far more cautious.

Q: Is there anything else that distinguishes you from them?

AMY: I grew up in Massachusetts, and Brenda in New York. So the Northeast was already a familiar place. If we'd moved to a location unknown to us, like say Wisconsin, it would've been much more challenging. We already knew people and had family in New York.

　　But if all of what you know and are comfortable with is here, I think it's a far more difficult decision.

Q: And you have no family in Georgia?

BRENDA: No. I also think part of it's that I really believe I deserve equality. It's not okay for me not to have it. And I'm willing to sacrifice to get it. Fairness and equality are really essential to me. They're more important than having an affordable cost of living or lots of possessions or an easy life. I never pondered why.

AMY: I haven't thought of us being all that different from other people. So it's really odd for you to ask that question.

Q: Well, maybe I'm wrong.

BRENDA: But maybe we *are* different. We were at a party during the Virginia Highlands Festival, talking about Question 1 passing and how we weren't going to stay. And I said to the other people we knew there, "What are you guys going to do?"

AMY: And they were like, "What do you mean?"

BRENDA: And that's when I realized how different we were.

AMY: Because we were fired up.

BRENDA: I was beside myself. How could you stay where they treat you like that?

Q: I've asked all the other couples I've met the same question. "Do you know people who have left?" And I've been able to identify very few who did in fact move out of Georgia because of Question 1.

BRENDA: I can definitely say we got out because of Question 1, and the adoption thing. We were hoping to get kids and then leave.

AMY: That's true.

BRENDA: Because by 2004, we were already so entangled in the process. But we were committed to abandon Georgia no matter what.

AMY: We had put the wheels into motion to find a place to live that was going to be more fair, and closer to our families.

BRENDA: People are too complacent here about the equality issue.

Amy and Brenda exemplify many migration determinants introduced earlier, such as their total lack of nativist loyalty to or family ties within Georgia. Yet exceptional fealty to notions of equality and fairness distinguishes them from other couples with similar migrational attributes. Brenda and Amy were prepared to forgo significant creature comforts in a quest for ideals they felt were indispensable to their core identity. Few others I came in contact with in

Super-DOMA states were willing to travel the same kind of path, leading to what more timid souls might have concluded would be a pyrrhic victory.

Migration certainly is a complex function with many casual factors, some of which are Janus-faced. Despite what distant observers might think, relocating one's home is rarely a simple or easy task, even in the face of harsh political persecution.

Kaplan reports that, although about one-quarter of Jews fled Germany before November 1938, virtually all of those who remained sought to leave after the violence escalated then. As the reference to Kristallnacht by the Columbus gay man suggests, many same-sex couples in Super-DOMA states would leave only under the most extreme circumstances. When asked what events would indeed prompt them to change residence, lesbian and gay pairs typically offered examples of physical violence or imminent and serious threats to the well being of their children. They acknowledged that, in terms of black-letter law, their status could not likely get worse. But that alone was not sufficient to propel them to leave.

Thus, whether with regard to Jews facing Nazi oppression before the 1938 pogrom, or lesbian and gay couples in Super-DOMA states during the first decade and a half of the twenty-first century, the ties binding them to home, work, family, and community were profound and immobilizing. Only the harshest forms of government mistreatment motivate most discrimination victims to break those links and relocate to more welcoming locales.

SAME-SEX COUPLES WHO DID EMIGRATE PERMANENTLY

During the course of our conversations, whenever interviewees mentioned they knew of queer folk who left a state due to its adoption of a Super-DOMA, I always asked whether they could put me in touch with those migrants. Then, I followed up such in-person requests with emails to interviewees, reminding them of my interest to speak to people whom they knew had moved away.

Unfortunately, most attempts to identify and track down refugees from America's war on same-sex couples were unsuccessful. Either my interviewees did not feel comfortable giving me their particulars or had lost touch with them and did not have current contact information. In some instances, interviewees did in fact reach out to former friends or acquaintances, who in turn declined to speak with me.

In the end, I was able to secure either telephone or in-person interviews with seven such couples. In addition, I learned that another eight pairs I originally talked with in Super-DOMA states subsequently relocated to jurisdictions without constitutional marriage amendments. I had follow-up telephone discussions or email correspondence about their moves. Finally, in a twist of pure serendipity, I discovered that an acquaintance at my own New York City college had moved from Michigan with her partner many years before, and I talked with them about the prospect of returning to live in the Wolverine State.

Accordingly, I offer here notable excerpts from such conversations with emigrants as an index of the considerations and conditions that prompted their exits from Super-DOMA states.

Michael Falk

If there were an archetypical refugee among all the people identified as having relocated from the six states in this study, it would be Michael Falk,[8] as the highlights of his interview make clear.

MICHAEL: Matthew and I met in 1999, and have been together ever since. We moved to Ann Arbor in 2000, when I started teaching in the field of materials science at the University of Michigan.

    Matthew and I got married – not legally, but with all of our family – in 2002 in Ann Arbor, where we lived for approximately eight years.

Q: What was the occasion for your leaving Michigan?

MICHAEL: There were multiple reasons, but the primary trigger was the passage of the antigay marriage amendment in 2004, followed by court rulings indicating Prop 2 would have a direct impact on domestic-partner benefits.

    At the time, we didn't face any immediate loss of benefits. But we saw that such an outcome was likely.

    When the 2004 amendment passed, Matt was working for a small business that didn't offer health insurance. So he was using domestic-partner benefits available through my position at the university.

    In 2005, Matt contacted the university's office that helps place spouses of faculty in jobs. They found a position for him at the Arboretum in Ann Arbor. So he worked at the Arboretum from 2006 on. Accordingly, he had his own health care through the university because of his own employment status there.

    But we had relied upon my health benefits in the past, and we were concerned that such an arrangement might occur again.

    And we were just very disappointed to be in a state where we felt we could be targeted politically that way. So it made us think: did we really want to settle and put down deep roots and remain in Michigan for the long haul? Or was it time to look around while we remained fairly mobile and think about moving somewhere else?

    So that was the trigger. But there were other things also. Neither of us is from Michigan originally. So we didn't have a big investment in staying there. We have family and friends back East. We were interested potentially in moving closer to my parents and to Matt's brother, who lives in the Washington, DC, area. And we were tired of Michigan's cold winters.

    So with all these issues taken together, it didn't make sense not to test the waters.

[8] I do not use pseudonyms here because, subsequent to my telephone conversation with Professor Falk in February 2009, he agreed to participate in a media story about his and his partner Matthew's relocation (Cosentino 2011). Moreover, one would be hard pressed to recalibrate the particulars of this narrative for the purpose of concealing his identity because Falk's tale is so fact specific.

Soon after I started looking around in early 2007, which was shortly after the appeals court ruling came down [expanding the marriage amendment's adverse impact on same-sex couples], one of the first places I contacted was Johns Hopkins University [in Baltimore, Maryland], which had a search going on. They said they'd be happy to interview me.

So everything happened and fell into place rather quickly.

Q: Let me ask a counterfactual question. If Proposal 2 had not been adopted in Michigan, do you think that you and Matt would otherwise have left?

MICHAEL: I think most likely we would have stayed.

At the time, my parents were retiring. Part of the retirement process required them to move. In 2004, Matt and I were encouraging them to relocate to Ann Arbor. So it was our intention then that we'd be there for the long term.

Even after the passage of the ballot initiative, which of course disappointed us, we were hopeful that at least there'd be some guidelines in place, where the courts would find that Prop 2 was an isolated thing. Because we didn't really believe the citizens of the State of Michigan intended to take away health care from people like us. Rather, we expected that the voters just wanted to codify a religious definition of marriage.

So we were hopeful the courts were going to rule that the constitutional amendment didn't affect things like domestic-partner health-insurance benefits. Thus, although Prop 2 was disappointing, it wouldn't affect us in a material way. And the trial court did rule in that direction. So the initial judicial result was somewhat reassuring.

It was really after the appeals court said, "No, we're going to interpret this amendment in the most draconian way possible," that the legal reality of our situation truly hit us. Furthermore, the Michigan Supreme Court was pretty conservative, and we didn't think it would go against what the appeals court did.

So nobody in the state was willing to stand up and say, "This is wrong. This isn't what the voters intended," and provide any protection for the kinds of rights that were important to us.

Q: After you felt secure about the new position at Johns Hopkins, did you share with your Michigan colleagues the reason for the decision to move?

MICHAEL: Oh yes, definitely. They all knew what the motivating factor was.

Actually, when I mentioned it to one colleague, she said, "I was wondering, after the appeals-court decision came down, whether we were going to lose you over this." She was a senior colleague of mine.

Moreover, when a faculty member announces a departure, and the university values you, the department chair will usually try to retain you and ask, "What would it take to keep you here?" So I had that conversation with the chair of my department as soon as he found out about the Hopkins job offer. I told him the only thing I could imagine changing my mind was if somehow he could alter the Michigan constitution, which wasn't likely.

So I didn't see the benefit of dickering over dollars and cents and office size and lab space. Because they weren't the issue.

Then the dean of the College of Engineering asked me to come and meet with him. I said basically the same thing to him.

Q: So the University of Michigan administrators obviously really appreciated you.

MICHAEL: Yeah, I think so. I'd just gotten tenure and was as productive as I've ever been. So I felt very valued there. They'd always been forthcoming with lab space and support for students and other things that were required. I enjoyed working with colleagues at the University of Michigan. They're very nice people. And they appreciated having me there as someone who was dedicated to teaching and who had an active research program. I tend not to make a lot of drama at faculty meetings. I'm not a disagreeable colleague to have. I'm collegial. And a number of people told me they were sad to see me go.

Q: Did any Michigan graduate students come with you to Hopkins?

MICHAEL: One moved from Michigan to Baltimore. So he's still officially a Michigan student and is funded by a grant from the University of Michigan. His paycheck still comes from the University of Michigan, although he's now sitting at Hopkins.

There's another student who didn't move to Baltimore but who's still sitting in Ann Arbor who's finishing up his Ph.D. He's also funded through the University of Michigan.

Then there's one postdoc who's working with me at Hopkins. There's another student who came over with independent financing from the Chinese government.

Q: In other words, the loss to the University of Michigan when you left was not just you alone, but some students as well.

MICHAEL: You have to figure that my arrival at the U of M in 2000 represented quite a substantial investment on their part. They gave me start-up monies of approximately $350,000 to buy computer equipment, to hire students, to get my research program started.

The university invested a lot of money in me. They pay good salaries, you know. The hope for them is they're bringing someone in as an assistant professor, who's untested, who doesn't have a big reputation. And they're going to give him or her some money and time to build up a reputation that in turn will increase the university's prestige.

So when an associate professor who just got tenure, who made his way from being an untenured assistant professor, decides to leave, that means the school has two options if they want to maintain their competitive position. Either they can take in another junior person and go through the whole investment again, maybe at this point of $500,000 and six years. Or they can try to bring someone in who's a tenured associate professor elsewhere. But then they're talking about a larger investment of money and bringing someone in at a higher salary.

So my loss to Michigan certainly wasn't beneficial to the university, either financially or in terms of its reputation.

Q: When you decided to put yourself on the market to leave Ann Arbor, and the position at Hopkins was a possibility, did you investigate the comparative legal environment of that potential destination?

MICHAEL: Yes. Both Matthew and I went online and read a lot about what the current situation was in Maryland. And we were heartened by what we learned.

Maryland certainly wasn't in the same position as, say, Massachusetts or Connecticut. But it had a couple of things going for it. While we were in the process of moving, there was a case wending its way to the Maryland state supreme court, seeking marriage rights for same-sex couples. And that litigation hadn't been decided by the time we moved. It has since been resolved, with the high court ruling that the state didn't have any obligation to provide marriage rights to LGBT citizens, although they simultaneously said there was nothing to prevent the legislature from granting them.

Our understanding of the state constitution here is that Maryland was spared the wisdom of the Progressive movement. So the only way to amend the Maryland constitution is to go through the legislature. You just can't do it through petition, as happened in Michigan, which is the most ridiculous thing.

Q: So as far as you could tell at the time you put yourself on the market, the Maryland circumstance was a substantial improvement over what then existed in Michigan.

MICHAEL: Right. There was hope for forward progress, with little risk of backsliding.

In addition, I was moving from a public institution that was subject to state intervention, to a private institution, which has considerably more latitude to write contracts in the way the institution itself sees fit. Even if a similar constitutional amendment passed in Maryland, that event wouldn't necessarily affect benefits at Hopkins.

Q: From what you say, it seems the net result is that you have no substantial regrets about the move.

MICHAEL: That's right. When I look at the big picture, not just the professional one, it's a net positive. I'm very happy that we moved. If I were to take the Johns Hopkins and Michigan situations in isolation, and strip out everything else about the weather and such, I would say that the positives balance out the negatives.

Q: But it's still clear to you that, but for Proposal 2 passing in 2004, you and Matthew would most likely be in Ann Arbor today?

MICHAEL: I think that's true.

Q: Is there anything else about your departure from Ann Arbor and relocation to Baltimore we haven't discussed that you'd like to add?

MICHAEL: The conversation I had with the dean of engineering at the time of my departure was a little strange. I'd hoped that, as a higher administration person, he'd have a better understanding of the situation. Again, he asked me to come to his office.

After we talked for a while, the dean basically said, "Yes, we're all very unhappy that this law passed. This isn't a good thing, and the university is committed to guaranteeing domestic-partner benefits. I'm not a big fan of George Bush. I don't like a lot of his domestic policies. But I'm not going to leave Michigan for Canada."

Q: So he didn't really appreciate how intimate an attack this was on your relationship?

MICHAEL: Right. The dean didn't understand that the comparable scenario would be George Bush's coming to take *his wife's* health benefits away. In short, there was no material risk whatsoever for the dean and *his* family to stay in George Bush's America.

But the dean was willing to make a false comparison to appeal to my Michigan patriotism, which he didn't realize was essentially nonexistent.

So that meeting put a bizarre twist on my departure from Ann Arbor.

Note these important attributes of Professor Falk's migration story:

- He fully understood and appreciated the threat to well-being posed by Michigan's Super-DOMA and subsequent state-court interpretations of the amendment. No one needed to demonstrate in unequivocal or graphic terms the problems that Prop 2 caused his family.
- As a non-native of Michigan, who had been living there less than a decade, he had no allegiance to the state as such. The idea that Michigan was *his* state didn't cross Falk's mind.
- Ann Arbor was not a bubble for him. Although Falk and his partner liked living there (but for the harsh winters), the city did not guarantee the kinds of protections that he perceived his family most needed.
- He and his partner had no blood relatives in Michigan. Nor did they have children in school there.
- He had no hope for redemption from Prop 2's effects. On the contrary, Falk clearly saw the state-judicial writing on the wall and did not bet on federal judges serving as knights rescuing gay damsels in distress.
- Perhaps most importantly, he had highly marketable skills that greatly facilitated his securing a comparable work position in a more welcoming state. Indeed, Falk's reading of the Maryland tea leaves was spot-on. In November 2012, voters in the Old Line State approved of the legislature's grant of civil marriage to same-sex couples.
- He was not closeted and did not suffer from internalized homophobia, nor were hiding and playing the system viable options for his family and personal goals.
- Finally, he was young enough (thirty-eight) at the time of migration to believe both that he and his partner could establish significant personal and professional roots somewhere else and that they were not sacrificing a considerable home-state history by emigrating.[9]

Rebecca and Virginia

Among the seven interviews with couples who left Super-DOMA jurisdictions before my visits to their former home states, two such conversations – with

---

[9] Professor Falk was also distinctive for being an out gay academic in the sciences (Suri 2015). Cahn (2013) and Jones (2013) reported how LGBT faculty left public universities in Oklahoma and Virginia for higher education institutions in marriage-equality jurisdictions.

Linda and Patricia (first reported in Chapter 1) and with Professor Falk – revealed the clearest instances of departures prompted primarily by the state constitutional amendments. Among the other five couples, motivations for relocation were more complicated, with other factors (such as new work opportunities opening up elsewhere) being significant. Although I return later to these other aspects and to those five interviews in this category, I continue my focus on couples whose principal reason for moving was a Super-DOMA, in order to tease out further the refugee phenomenon and why the choice to depart was so exceptional. To do so, I draw on two conversations among the eight couples whom I originally talked with during field trips and who subsequently left their homes to escape Super-DOMA effects.

Rebecca, age fifty-five, and Virginia, fifty, were the pair whose departure from Wisconsin (where we spoke first in July 2011) surprised me the most, if only for the following exchange from our initial conversation:

Q: Did the passage of Referendum 1 affect the two of you in some tangible, concrete way?

VIRGINIA: We're criminals now. Because in 2008, we left Wisconsin to get married in California.

Q: Violating Wisconsin's criminal marriage-evasion statute.

VIRGINIA: Referendum 1 truly changed our retirement plans. We'll probably move to northern California much earlier than we would've otherwise, because we'd have lived in this house as long as we were physically able to.

But we'll probably go sooner, because we need the marriage protections that the constitutional amendment denies us.

Q: Can you envision a departure sooner than retirement if political or legal events here in Wisconsin got worse somehow?

VIRGINIA: Sure.

REBECCA: We've got a fairly aggressive and conservative governor, legislature, and state supreme court. So I wouldn't rule out the possibility that they'd take advantage of the constitutional amendment to support legislation that would be even more restrictive. Coming into an election year, if they saw it would be helpful to galvanize their base, to show how strong they are against gay marriage, I could imagine a world where something's introduced that would be more draconian than what we have now. For example, if they took away the domestic-partner registry or invalidated our ability to have legal agreements together.

With an impediment like that, staying here would be too dangerous for us. For some couples, the problem is not being able to afford the legal documents. For us, it's not being able to afford not having them. We've got investments. We've got retirement savings. We've got this house.

If the state took away our ability to form the contractual arrangements we have together, we'd have too much at stake to able to stay here. So that would be one event prompting us to leave earlier than retirement.

Another would be if the social or political atmosphere deteriorated so much that it was no longer physically safe for us to be here.

VIRGINIA: Yet we do have a wonderful church community. So we'd have a safe harbor here.

REBECCA: My examples are far-fetched. I don't really see either of them happening. There's only a remote chance for things to go appreciably backward for us in Wisconsin.

Q: What probability would you give for relocating on retirement? What percentage would you supply in terms of the likelihood of your going somewhere else then?

BOTH: 90 to 95 percent.

VIRGINIA: That amendment just set our mind as to when we were going.

Q: And your attitude is based exclusively upon Referendum 1?

BOTH: Yeah.

VIRGINIA: We came here from California twenty years ago. So we think it'd be really great to return there to live again. We don't believe it's tenable to stay here past retirement. It'd take too much nerve when we got old. Rather, early retirement, while we're still active, would probably be fine.

But at the end of life, we don't want to be in a place where it's not fully expected that Rebecca would wheel me around to the beauty parlor.

Q: Let's say as a counterfactual example that, in 2006, Referendum 1 had not passed here in Wisconsin. Would that 90 percent probability of relocation after retirement have changed?

REBECCA: Yes. It'd be like a 50–50 chance then.

VIRGINIA: We'd be trying to figure out what to do now, like "So should we keep this house and just travel?"

If we thought we could finesse our end of life in Wisconsin, we'd probably keep the property here.

Q: So the amendment really was decisive to your relocation plans?

BOTH: Yes.

Across all six states I visited, and regardless of what legal documents couples put together for themselves, resettlement after retirement was the most commonly articulated strategy for countering the adverse effects of Super-DOMAs. Thus, the plans Rebecca and Virginia explained were in no way exceptional. What was truly surprising, however, was the email I received from Rebecca and Virginia two years later when I recontacted interviewees after the Supreme Court's *Windsor* decision: it read, "We're in the process of moving to…Delaware!" In fact, my August 2013 follow-up telephone conversation with them occurred as they were during there on the interstate in Illinois:

Q: So you're literally on the road to a new adventure.

VIRGINIA: We certainly are.

Q: Well, I want to hear all about it.

VIRGINIA: We're on our way to Wilmington, Delaware. We closed on the sale of our Wisconsin house yesterday afternoon. We're driving with a small trailer, and our possessions are in a moving van on its way heading east.

I have about twelve years until retirement, and Rebecca has about six. We still plan to go to northern California then.

But since we spoke last, Dan, I got a new job that I absolutely adore. I love the company where I've been for about eighteen months. And it's based in Philadelphia. I'm on the road quite a bit with the new position and often have to go into the corporate headquarters.

So the idea of moving east was, "I wonder whether there's a gay-marriage state we could move to where I'd be closer to Philadelphia." Looking at a map, we discovered that Delaware [which recognized same-sex marriages starting in July 2013] was a short commute away.

REBECCA: Just to back up a bit: It was the Supreme Court arguments last April, when the pundits said there really was no way the Court couldn't overturn the federal DOMA, that started us thinking. Because if DOMA were overturned, it didn't make any sense to live in a state without marriage equality.

If we'd waited, in three years I'd be sixty, and it'd be time for us to think seriously about retirement and next-stage-of-life planning. So to live in a state where we'd lose not only sleep but also federal benefits just didn't seem like a smart thing to do.

VIRGINIA: If there'd been marriage equality in Wisconsin, we'd have had no thought of moving away. Because I was working at my job just fine.

And since we're not moving because the corporation required it, the change is a huge financial investment for us.

But we needed to be in a place with marriage equality.

We're significantly uprooting ourselves. We've got friends. We've got family. We've got a church we're extremely involved in. And we're leaving all of that behind. Which is just huge.

Not to be overly dramatic, but our future financial security calls for it.

Q: When I spoke with you two years ago, you talked so fondly about your religious community in Wisconsin. You also had Rebecca's family there, three of whom were actually visiting the house when I was in the living room.

REBECCA: It's a long way to go to get rights that straight couples take for granted.

VIRGINIA: We think it's worth it. But we're still in Illinois right now. [They laugh.]

REBECCA: I was watching the *Rachel Maddow Show* last week. She was interviewing people from states like Mississippi and Arkansas. Part of the conversation was, "Will you move to a state that has gay marriage?" "No, we want to stay and fight for it here."

I'm grateful that people believe in and do that. But at our stage of life, and given the politics of Wisconsin, we don't have long enough to wait for marriage rights there.

Q: Rebecca, you don't have any problem with your job in terms of being in Wisconsin or Delaware, right?

REBECCA: I had to win my supervisors over, and there's still some skepticism about whether I can do the job remotely. So there's a little bit of a risk. But I'm convinced I can make it work. And I'll assure them that I can do it. So I'm not having to give up a job in order to go.

Q: And you explained the reason why, correct?

REBECCA: Yes.

Q: They were sympathetic to that?

REBECCA: Totally. They just wished I'd come out to California.

VIRGINIA: We know that we're fortunate. Most people can't move out of state and have the same job. So we recognize we're just lucky our jobs are portable.

REBECCA: Among the expenses of the moving company and the real estate commissions and buying a new home, it's probably costing us between $20,000 and $25,000 to make this decision. Not everybody can do that.

Q: So it really becomes a question of how much equality you can afford, right?

REBECCA: Exactly.

Q: Are there any other regrets about leaving Wisconsin, other than what you've already said?

REBECCA: Last year, I was on a backpacking trip with the Sierra Club. One night around the campfire, the question we were all supposed to talk about was, "If you could go anywhere in the world, what would be your ideal place to live?"

I said I really couldn't think of any other place I'd prefer to be. I loved our house. I loved our yard. I loved our community. I loved our church. I'm close to my family. I said I was totally happy where we were. I couldn't say there was any other place I'd rather live.

Except for the fact that – and I told them then, last September – I knew we would have to leave it one day, as we got older and closer to retirement, in order to move to a state with marriage equality.

VIRGINIA: One other thing we haven't mentioned is that we both have strong affiliations with our national and regional professional associations, although we're in completely different careers.

Rebecca was elected for this term to be the Wisconsin state president of her organization. So she's having to abdicate that position.

I've been extremely involved in my professional society. I'm a past president of its central chapter.

So we're both leaving regional commitments.

Q: You're giving up everything that's personal to you?

VIRGINIA: We are.

But we're not giving up our quality of life. We have means. So the new house will be as lovely as our last home.

But other than that quality of life, we're giving up everything.

REBECCA: With that being said, we got our new insurance policy. And it listed us as "married." That was amazing.

VIRGINIA: It was addressed to Mr. and Mrs. Smith. And I just choked up. I never felt in my life that I wanted to be called "Mrs." But it was so awesome for them to do it. I won't refer to myself that way. But I get to claim it now. And it's tremendous.

Because I think of myself as married, and love to be considered as such. We're buying a house as a married couple. We'll file federal income-tax returns as a married couple. It's just great. It's huge.

Q: Rebecca, what did the other people around the campfire that night say to your commentary?

REBECCA: They were affirming to a person. "That's just not right." There were no other gays or lesbians on the trip. It was all straight couples.

They swore they'd recommit to supporting marriage equality in the states they lived in. It reminded them about how important it is.

VIRGINIA: What I've found is that people who weren't immersed in the discussion didn't really understand its details.

For example, my boss said, "If the Supreme Court overturns DOMA, you can stay in Wisconsin." And several people in our church said, "With DOMA reversed, you can stay in Wisconsin."

So that wasn't an awareness they walked around with.

As with Michael Falk, one can list the most salient properties of Rebecca and Virginia's emigration tale:

- They were fully cognizant of Referendum 1's threat to their well-being.
- As transplants from California, they had no significant allegiance to Wisconsin as a state.
- Whatever bubble might exist there was not strong enough to guarantee the end-of-life protections they sought.
- Although Rebecca did have blood relatives in Wisconsin, those family connections did not tie her sufficiently to the Badger State. And they had no children in school.
- They had no hope the Super-DOMA effects would abate in time to meet their needs.
- They both had jobs that were portable to other states.

Carolyn and Stephanie

Unlike Rebecca and Virginia's move from Wisconsin, the relocation by a second couple whom I initially interviewed in a Super-DOMA state did not take me by surprise. Carolyn, age thirty-four, and Stephanie, thirty-six, were together for eight years and have a son Donald, for whom Stephanie was the birth mother. In 2005, the pair moved from Chicago to a Dallas suburb so that Carolyn could attend a two-year pastoral internship in a ministry career path. Stephanie became a vocational counselor with an insurance company. In our January 2011 conversation, they talked about migration issues:

CAROLYN: You'll meet a lot of folks in Texas who say, "We never meant to stay here. And with the low cost of living, now we can't afford to get out." Dallas is a city full of people who will tell you that fact.

And hearing it the first time, I thought, "Well, not us. We're leaving." But the cost of living meant that, on Stephanie's salary, supplemented with my part-time work, I could be a stay-at-home mom. And that was great.

STEPHANIE: But we're reaching the end of the window, which is still open for a couple of more years. Donald is two-and-a-half. As he gets older, marriage as a family-protection issue rises to the forefront.

Our conversations about what's next are almost weekly now. So something's likely to happen in the next two to four years.

CAROLYN: Our relocation calculus has to include the cost of second-parent adoption.

STEPHANIE: There's one judge in Texas...

CAROLYN: There may be another one.

STEPHANIE: Okay. So there are one or two judges here who'll do second-parent adoptions for same-sex couples. It's not an exaggeration.

CAROLYN: Right. The guy most people are aware of is in San Antonio.

STEPHANIE: But it would cost $5,000 for Donald. And Carolyn wants to have her own child. So that would be $10,000 just for us to stay here. Compare that to if we moved to another state and got legally married, paying $30 for a marriage license. Thus, the costs of remaining in Texas continue to mount up.

Q: Let's talk more about the idea of relocation. What do you see during the next three to five years?

CAROLYN: We've already given birth to a Texan! My God, that was *not* the plan.

STEPHANIE: A snapshot picture for me involves Carolyn's securing the ministry certification she needs. And there's some additional training required before her credentials are established.

Once that's done, I'm already at a point in my career where I can start to consider working remotely with the same company. Or if that's not an option, I'll still choose family over this particular organization, though I love it.

Since our move here, I've not wanted to stay in Texas permanently because of how conservative it is. We're in a bubble, in a little blue spot. But the state culture isn't within our value system.

So I've been trying to get out as quickly as we got here. But I like the job situation, and there's a tension there.

CAROLYN: When we think about where we want to live, the legal climate of those places weighs heavily, although not exclusively.

STEPHANIE: Minnesota pops up a lot...

CAROLYN: ...even though gay marriage isn't legal there yet.

But we have family in Minnesota, both biological and spiritual. There are centers of value there where our son could be raised. So weighing that, and the cost of living, and career opportunities....

Another place we have a large quantity of family is out in Massachusetts.

STEPHANIE: Then the high cost of living there becomes an issue. So we're taking into account levels of friendliness.

CAROLYN: I considered a residency program in Iowa City. And we never would've looked at it except for the gay-marriage issue. [The Iowa Supreme Court legalized civil marriage for same-sex couples in 2009.]

We're both Midwesterners, originally from Ohio. We have continuous conversations with both of our mothers explaining that we're not moving back home [to another Super-DOMA state].

STEPHANIE: If money were no object, we'd move to Massachusetts tomorrow. Because we know the marriage situation is secure there. If Carolyn had her credentials, I'd move there in a heartbeat.

CAROLYN: The issue boils down to: what's the cost for protecting our family?

You hear us talking about our careers. Plus we're concerned about how to put family first. There's always that tension.

After all, I'm going to be a minister. I'm really far more of an institutionalist and traditionalist, and in some ways, a conservative person. Where I choose to place my values and spend my money....

When I listen to Christian radio, there's this huge part about living your values with conviction, and they're speaking my language. Then it just breaks my heart that we can't find common ground.

So those are the important things for us. That's certainly what we're looking at when we think about where to go.

STEPHANIE: I can see compromise and common ground in different areas. I just don't know whether the compromise will be with career or with family. Because what kind of a family are we going to have? Or what kind of a career are we going to have?

I'm a vocational counselor. I understand all of the identity one has with a job and career. But if you're in a hospital and incapacitated, all of that goes out the window.

So first things first. That's where I go back to. Take care of the big stuff. I'm employable and marketable and can work in another state. So we have choices.

We don't believe that we're victims and trapped in Texas.

CAROLYN: We're college educated. I moved to go to school. Then after school, I moved to Chicago. I came here for this internship.

So I'm already of a class and professional mindset that expects to have to move. I wonder about the economic impact of bright, educated, engaged people making decisions about where they want to live.

STEPHANIE: And then add in kids. I feel it's a moral obligation to provide everything you possibly can for them. So protection first, and then choices second.

Even though I want to leave, I really still like Texas. We bought this house. I like my job and my company. We've made friends. We've got a network here now.

It's not that we're running away, but more heading for a better option. But we do like Texas, mostly.

Q: So if Texas didn't have a Super-DOMA and instead were entirely neutral on same-sex marriage...

STEPHANIE: Maybe our window of opportunity would be longer. But I still think there'd be a window.

CAROLYN: It would be entirely neutral, but with no hope.

Q: So hope makes a difference?

CAROLYN: Hope makes a big difference.

STEPHANIE: Which is why we consider Minneapolis. Hope is there. And there are good reasons to believe it's not a futile hope. [After Minnesota voters rejected a constitutional amendment to ban same-sex marriage in November 2012, the state legislature passed, and the governor signed, a gay-marriage bill the next year.]

CAROLYN: With Texas, our expectation is...

STEPHANIE: ...that the people and politicians would fight it.

CAROLYN: Texas would be among the last to fall in line.

STEPHANIE: Texas, Mississippi, and South Carolina.

CAROLYN: The religious person in me says that I should be where the fight is. Then I look at my son, and say, "Maybe not."

STEPHANIE: There are certain things that I feel deserve our energy.

CAROLYN: But it doesn't feel worth it here.

STEPHANIE: The Super-DOMA has done so much damage that I'd rather go and be publicly out and set an example for our son in a place that acknowledges our rights. Or be in a friendly environment to do what I do and be who I am, where I feel like the fight means something. And here, it doesn't feel like it means anything.

If we didn't have Donald, it wouldn't be as big of an issue. It would still weigh on us, because that's who we are. But once you add in children, it's not about us anymore.

Accordingly, I was not surprised to learn of Carolyn and Stephanie's relocation back to Chicago, after they legally tied the knot in New York State in 2012. In a July 2013 telephone interview, they explained the particulars:

STEPHANIE: Thankfully, the housing market changed in Texas, turning a corner this spring. There was no inventory, and the market became a seller's advantage.

So we got lucky. We put our home up for sale in May, and it closed within two months. Had the market not turned, I think we'd still be stuck there.

CAROLYN: Particularly if I were to stay at home for a while, taking care of a growing family. We couldn't have afforded that if we'd not sold the house. We'd still be there.

But by the time we left Texas two weeks ago, we had a really good community of folks, and we loved our neighborhood.

There were a couple of factors influencing our decision to depart. One was the legal climate. That absolutely was a reason to go.

Plus we were homesick. When I hear families say, "This is our home. We won't leave," I get it. Because part of our need was to come home. Not only is Chicago a place where we have lots of friends and community that we've been in touch with the whole time we were in Texas, but the majority of our biological family is also in Minnesota, Ohio, Indiana, and Michigan – the Great Lakes region.

So we were definitely the outliers in Texas.

Q: Tell me what happened with your employment.

STEPHANIE: I was willing to leave the company I loved and seek positions elsewhere to be able to move north. I have the choice and the privilege to do that, which others typically do not.

But in the end, I didn't have to resign, because for about two years, I've been cultivating the ability to work 100 percent remotely. I'd developed a virtual team of eighteen people across the country. So there wasn't a convincing argument to remain in Texas anymore, especially to the detriment of my family. I was able to keep the position with my current employer.

We watched very closely the Illinois state-senate proceedings online. We were up late once or twice, waiting to see whether the Land of Lincoln was going to pass gay marriage. Because our hope was that the federal DOMA would fail in the Supreme Court. And it did.

CAROLYN: Yay!

STEPHANIE: Then we hoped that Illinois would go from civil unions to everything. That hasn't happened yet. [The Illinois same-sex marriage law took effect in 2014.]

But we were also looking at the climate in Texas, a Super-DOMA state, and our son of five.

CAROLYN: And the fact that the fight in Texas could get ugly. We really didn't want him to be there for that. He's already conscious of the issue.

STEPHANIE: Then everybody in Texas kept saying, "It's going to happen. It's going to happen in five or ten years." And that's five or ten years of a childhood.

CAROLYN: It's a long time for him.

STEPHANIE: That wasn't something we were willing to gamble on or compromise with. So we knew that Illinois was closer, although not quite there.

CAROLYN: And I'm nineteen weeks pregnant.

STEPHANIE: We wanted the next baby to be born on free soil.

CAROLYN: That's what we kept joking about. "The next baby on free soil!"

STEPHANIE: We pay state income taxes here. [Texas does not collect a personal income tax.] But we feel our whole family is being recognized in Illinois.

And we're able to change our names with the New York marriage license.

CAROLYN: Getting wed in New York, we filled out the marriage-license application so that our marriage certificate would use our hyphenated last names together, because we intended to formally change our family surname to Brown-Davis.

Then we went home to Texas, which was hard.

STEPHANIE: But the certificate was really cool when it came in the mail, addressed to Brown-Davis. So we thought we could change our name through the Social Security Administration. But the federal level defers to the state Department of Motor Vehicles to start the process.

CAROLYN: And we couldn't get it done at the Dallas DMV, because Texas law expressly forbids it. They wouldn't recognize a same-sex marriage certificate from another state, even for name-change purposes. And it was like, "Wow, even for that. Really?"

That hurt. It felt like they really went out of their way on that one.

STEPHANIE: The prohibition was on their website, appearing both in bold and in red.

Using the New York marriage certificate would've been the only way we could've done a name change in Texas without having to spend $1,500.

CAROLYN: So we've been in Chicago for two weeks, and went to the Illinois DMV.

We initially joked that it was the American dream. We got treated as poorly at the DMV as everybody else. [They laugh.]

But then we were doing a lot of paperwork, changing address, state, names. And they needed to make sure all the ducks were lined up.

So on the first day, we showed this clerk our papers to see if we had all of the stuff right. And she said to me, "Oh yeah, your wife can sign just above the residence address."

And I started to cry.

STEPHANIE: The clerk said it so matter of factly and nonchalantly, as though it was no big deal.

We had never heard a government official legally recognize either of us as a wife. Ever. In the seven years since 2005, when we had what we consider our religious wedding.

And the event was so mundane. At the DMV, with a two-hour wait. And the room was packed with every ethnicity you can imagine. Most people would walk in and think, "This is inner-city," because it's the busiest and most diverse DMV in Chicago.

CAROLYN: And we were a part of that.

STEPHANIE: It was a very unique, magical moment, since we'd never gotten the full recognition before.

And we still don't, because only civil unions are recognized here for same-sex couples. But city and state officials don't treat it that way when it comes to regular stuff.

Q: And Illinois probably recognizes out-of-state marriages as well.

BOTH: Yes.

CAROLYN: They will recognize our marriage certificate on the level of a civil union.

I've been working professionally using the name Brown-Davis for years.

STEPHANIE: Under the radar.

CAROLYN: But that practice never lined up with my legal name.

STEPHANIE: I couldn't do the same thing because my corporation required all of the legal paper trail.

CAROLYN: Churches are a lot more forgiving about taking a political stance on how you view yourself. At the hospital where I worked as a chaplain, they wouldn't do anything officially with my badge. But my department felt I could call myself whatever I wanted to.

STEPHANIE: I couldn't do that in Texas. But now I can. It took less than four hours for my name to be changed legally in my company's system using my Illinois drivers license. That's all it took. They didn't ask for a marriage certificate. They needed one form of identification.

So that's been our biggest triumph so far.

CAROLYN: That's why I cried when the clerk referred to Stephanie as my wife. And then I cried a little bit more when I filled out the paperwork and put "wife" on the document – and they didn't change it.

And then I was able to legally sign something as Brown-Davis. I'd always had the tension of signing legal documents versus when I was writing as myself. So those two events came back together here in Illinois.

STEPHANIE: We're excited about the possibility of taking Donald to a state rally for same-sex marriage down in Springfield. We're willing to fight for this state.

CAROLYN: Illinois is worth the wait for gay marriage.

STEPHANIE: The wait here doesn't feel like it will rob Donald's childhood, with the kinds of ugly fights and robocalls that would've occurred in Texas.

The most important patterns emerging in Michael Falk's and Rebecca and Virginia's migration stories also appear in Carolyn and Stephanie's narrative: (1) understanding and appreciation of the Super-DOMA threat to well being; (2) no appreciable state loyalty; (3) insufficient "bubble" protections; (4) no consequential blood-family ties and no children in school; (5) no expectation of relief from Super-DOMA effects; and (6) job portability. And among ten other same-sex pairs I know of who moved permanently from Super-DOMA states to jurisdictions without such constitutional provisions, virtually all of them had the same or similar attributes.

Yet two consequential personal characteristics are not sufficiently revealed in these lengthy narratives: age and education. Only five couples, or one-third of the relevant refugees, were age forty or older, whereas ten pairs were all under forty years old. And among these younger couples, most changed residence in large measure because they reached turning points in their educational or career paths that greatly facilitated relocation, such as finding jobs elsewhere after completing college or graduate degrees. In other words, emigration from Super-DOMA states to greener legal pastures was in substantial measure a phenomenon of younger and well-educated people. Similarly, Wilkerson found that the African Americans who left the Jim Crow South were better educated than those they left behind (2010, 528).

This was especially evident among interviewees I met in Super-DOMA states who had moved there from other places specifically to attend graduate or professional schools or to participate in internship or residency programs. Anthony, age twenty-seven, and Ronald, twenty-six, came from Maryland together so that Anthony could pursue a degree in molecular genetics at a North Carolina medical school. They shared their odyssey with me:

Q: What did the passage of Amendment 1 mean to you in the broadest sense of the word?

ANTHONY: It means we're getting out of North Carolina as soon as we can. I still have another two years or so in my Ph.D. program.

We figured anyway that, after I graduated, we'd be moving again. But if Amendment 1 hadn't passed, we might have stayed in the area. I'd at least have looked for jobs around here.

But now, we're not even going to bother. As soon as I'm done with the degree, we're leaving the state.

RONALD: I really love this area. It's a great place to live.

My parents are looking to move someplace cheaper than Maryland. So they were talking about investigating North Carolina. But after Amendment 1 passed, it was like, "Don't bother. We're not going to be here."

Q: So that's certain? There's no doubt about it in your mind?

ANTHONY: Not unless there's some miracle with the Supreme Court, and they invalidate Amendment 1.

Otherwise, there's no chance we're sticking around. We'll be gone in a couple of years. There's no point in starting a family in some area where we can't protect our kids. That's just playing with fire. I don't want to do that.

Q: So you'll definitely limit yourselves to states where the protection of your family won't be an issue?

ANTHONY: Yes. We want to adopt kids and get legal recognition of our union. We don't want to do that someplace where we can't protect each other and our children.

RONALD: Second-parent adoptions aren't available here.

Q: How representative do you think the two of you are of gay and lesbian couples of your generation with regard to this issue? In other words, are there other people in North Carolina like yourselves, who have a desire at some point to have a family, who are as prepared to relocate as you are?

ANTHONY: I think the desire to have a family is definitely growing in our generation. And a lot of people our age take it as a given that, even though they're gay, they'll grow up and have a family. I can't speak to how willing they'd be to relocate.

RONALD: It's different for us in our circumstance. We have a support system elsewhere. Whereas, for people who've grown up here, it could be hard to move away from everything they've ever known, from family and friends.

ANTHONY: We have no ties in North Carolina to speak of. We met in Maryland and only came here because I got into the graduate medical program.

RONALD: I've sectioned myself off, little by little, from even trying to make or encourage friendships, especially after Amendment 1, since I know I won't be staying here.

ANTHONY: Ronald used to do a lot of theater work. There's a good community theater program in this area, and I kept saying to him, "They've got tryouts coming up. You should go do them. Or try volunteering there, because I'm sure you'd really enjoy it." And Ronald's response was, "Why bother? We're going to have to leave here anyway. And that will make it all the harder."

So we've been avoiding making any ties here, because we know we're going to have to move away.

RONALD: Originally, before Amendment 1 was on the horizon, we made more of an effort. We tried to engage other people.

But especially within the last couple of months, after the constitutional amendment passed, we've become far more reluctant to be outgoing with others.

Thus, one of Carolyn's statements is particularly telling: "I'm already of a class and professional mindset that expects to have to move. I wonder about the economic impact of bright, educated, engaged people making decisions about where they want to live."[10] And with that thought in mind, I turn to the flip side of the emigration coin.

SUPER-DOMA EFFECTS ON IMMIGRATION INTO
SUPER-DOMA STATES

This chapter has been concerned so far with the factors influencing same-sex couples' decisions to leave Georgia, Michigan, North Carolina, Ohio, Texas, and Wisconsin (as exemplars of the nation's twenty Super-DOMA states) for environments more welcoming of queer folk. Yet an equally legitimate inquiry into LGBT migration involves whether gay people relocated *into* states after they adopted Super-DOMAs.

As a first attempt to investigate the issue, I asked interviewees whether they knew of queer folk who had the opportunity to move into their states but who ultimately decided not to do so because of the constitutional amendments. Although most people I spoke with said they did not know of anyone who fit that bill, enough interviewees did provide sufficient information to construct some telling glimpses into the nonimmigration phenomenon.

A number of people who worked in higher education, for example, knew of national searches conducted at their institutions that concluded with offers of employment being extended to lesbian or gay candidates, who eventually declined the opportunities to relocate there. I heard from at least three sources that, in 2005, the top candidate for the deanship of the College of Arts and Sciences at Oakland University (a public institution just north of Detroit) was a gay man who had to pass up the school's offer because his partner refused to relocate to Michigan after Proposal 2 passed and there was no guarantee that domestic-partner benefits like health insurance would be available through the position. The following year, the best candidate for a tenure-track faculty position in the Oakland University Library turned down an offer, also because of concern over availability of benefits for her partner.[11]

---

[10] Some interviewees were very politically astute about residence choices. In January 2011, for instance, I met a Dallas couple, Jason, age forty-six, and Kevin, fifty-three, with more than $1 million in assets to spend on a home and business. Since New Hampshire began authorizing same-sex marriages in January 2010, the men settled on purchasing two insurance agencies and a house in Manchester, the Granite State's largest city. However, once Republicans took control of New Hampshire government in November 2010 and announced that one of their top priorities was to repeal the gay-marriage legislation, Jason and Kevin quickly turned to Vermont as a safer bet for their economic and personal investments.

[11] In January 2010, the *Chronicle of Higher Education*, which describes itself as "the No. 1 source of news, information, and jobs for college and university faculty members and administrators," published an article with a list of strategies for the recruitment and retention of top gay and lesbian job candidates (Hanson 2010a). The enumerated categories included health benefits, housing policies, partner policies, and state law. Thus, LGBT faculty and administrators did not have far to look for advice about securing positions in fully welcoming employment environments.

Higher education institutions and their employees figure prominently throughout this book, if only because so many interviewees were affiliated with colleges and universities. Yet even with that sampling bias, it is no surprise that higher education? campuses came up conspicuously in narratives about fundamental legal, political, and social change in the United States. One need only think back to how important colleges and universities were to the enormous transformations in the America of the 1960s and '70s.

Another higher education report emphasizes how significantly public colleges and universities in Super-DOMA states were affected by same-sex-marriage debates, even beyond the vital issue of availability of health insurance and other benefits for the partners of state employees. Two sources at the University of North Carolina told me this story:

In addition to the absence of domestic-partner benefits for the same-sex partners of UNC faculty and staff, we've had another problem in Chapel Hill. In the university's central campus, there's a section called the Pit, where there's a big eating hall, the undergraduate library, and a free-speech area. A lot of students gather to meet and socialize in the Pit.

There's been a guy who seems to be a preacher, as well as a few other people, who come there and *do nothing but publicly condemn homosexuals*. There was a time when they preached their hatred in the Pit every day.

UNC's LGBT faculty and staff complained to administration officials about these public tirades, but the free-speech issue always won out. But similar race-based attacks, or even the same gender-based remarks, or antisemitic blasts, would never have been put up with on campus. But the antigay vitriol was tolerated.

So UNC has a serious problem it doesn't want and doesn't know how to deal with. There's a blind spot here between where free speech ends and hate speech begins with regard to the dignity and rights of LGBT citizens.

And how do departments successfully recruit and retain bright and talented faculty and staff when such conspicuous odium is a fundamental part of a public university's culture?

Sue Doerfer, the executive director of Equality Ohio who was a good data source for other chapters, also provided information about gay and lesbian immigration into her state:

Q: What about the flip side of the migration coin? People who had the opportunity to come to Ohio from somewhere else, because of a job opportunity or what have you, but who chose not to because of its legal environment. Are you aware of any circumstances like that?

A: Yes. The event that sticks out the most in my mind concerns Cleveland's Great Lakes Science Center, which is a huge nonprofit organization, with an annual budget of several millions of dollars. They hired an executive director, probably in 2004 before the Issue 1 election.

As was typical in such circumstances, the newly retained executive director wanted to bring in some of her own people. She was a straight woman, recruited out of San Francisco, who attempted to hire either the associate executive director or the director of development. I forget now which position exactly, but it was a significant job at the science center.

She made an offer to a gay man in California. He researched Ohio, and said no, he wouldn't come here because of the lack of legal protections and the political environment.

The science center's executive director has told that story many times publicly, testifying before legislatures considering nondiscrimination ordinances. The instance sticks out in my mind clearly because it was so soon after the 2004 election, and she was so public about how frustrated she was. The episode demonstrated to her, as a straight woman, how Issue 1 impeded her ability to run an organization where she hoped to bring in the best talent.

Super-DOMAs also reduced states' attractiveness as retirement oases, as Alice, age seventy-two, and Julie, fifty-three, explained:

Q: Did the passage of Amendment 1 prompt any thoughts in your minds about moving to a place that would be more legally welcoming of your relationship?

ALICE: No.
But we have friends in Oklahoma who want to do that. They've had it there. Both are attorneys in Oklahoma City, and are close friends of ours. One works with the state supreme court, and the other teaches law.
And not only do our friends want to leave Oklahoma, but they also don't want to move back to North Carolina. For years, they talked about coming to live in the mountains here. And we've looked forward to their being closer.
JULIE: As a result of Amendment 1, they probably won't retire here, or at least that's what they say now. And we expected them to settle in North Carolina, because they have long-standing ties here.
ALICE: One grew up in Monroe, which is just down the road.
JULIE: The other also has family in North Carolina. So we expected they'd relocate here, and that we'd spend significant time with them after they retired.
So we were hurt and a little bit surprised to hear that they were no longer considering North Carolina as an option.

Q: So what will they do now that North Carolina isn't on their list?

JULIE: They're more likely to retire in Massachusetts or someplace like that, rather than come here, even though I believe they'd prefer to live in North Carolina.
I think Amendment 1 has caused them not to want to pay North Carolina taxes and not be supportive of North Carolina economically.
So if you asked our friends about their reasons, they'd tell you the constitutional amendment had a significant impact. Because they've talked about retiring here for a long while.
ALICE: Julie and I are both activists, and want to stay and fight, and be part of the attempt to reverse this setback someday.
But we fully understand our friends' reasoning, too.

My January 2010 interview with John F. Szabo, who was then the director of the Atlanta-Fulton Public Library System in Georgia,[12] also serves well as a transitional conversation for the chapter:

Q: Are you aware of any effects that Georgia's Question 1 of 2004 has had on your library system?

A: It has to have had an effect. Measuring it is the tough issue.

Knowing my profession and line of work well, my instinct is that the amendment has to have affected our location and geography as an attractive place for talented people within the library profession, which is made up of fairly forward-thinking, progressive folks who have a genuine respect for opposing points of view, and where tolerance is a theme professionally. So professional librarians look for employment in those kinds of environments.

There are attributes within the Atlanta area that are attractive in that regard. We have an enormous LGBT population and culture in the metropolitan area.

But what happens when Des Moines is leaps and bounds more progressive than Atlanta with regard to same-sex relationship rights? And what's going to happen when other cities and states around the country are more progressive, and everyone wakes up and realizes that something like Question 1 is an employment issue?

That's happened I think to a great extent in the business community. Many of our large corporate entities here in Atlanta are progressive and thoughtful when it comes to LGBT issues. Why? Because they have to be to be competitive.[13]

And that's going to come home here when cities like Des Moines are more attractive to people as a legal matter. Hopefully, we won't be last in Atlanta.

Given the size of our metropolitan area, with over five million people, there are a lot of libraries here. There's a large employment base. On average, we pay better than a lot of our counterparts. So we're able to attract talent locally.

But I'm going to be hiring a deputy director this year [2010] in a national search. There may be people coming from other places like the Boston Public Library, where there isn't something like a Super-DOMA. And I may never hear from them because of our situation in Georgia. I may never learn that Question 1's a barrier to their seeking employment here, *since they never would apply in the first place.*

---

[12] Mr. Szabo subsequently became the City Librarian of the Los Angeles Public Library, in charge of the public library for the largest city in the nation's most populous state.

[13] See also Davey (2015).

Q: The Michigan Supreme Court has interpreted Michigan's Super-DOMA to mean that the same-sex partners of public employees in the Wolverine State may not receive domestic-partner benefits like health insurance.

What would the impact be here if the Georgia Supreme Court followed the Michigan example?

A: We could certainly lose employees. And if not geographically, then to the private sector. Because there are other employers of librarians.

I think our library would have a number of things going for it to ebb that tide, particularly salary issues.

Yet it would still be devastating for the morale of our staff and its attitude toward their employer. And frankly, not just for those who take advantage of our domestic-partner benefit. That is, those who are eligible for the benefit but choose not to take advantage of it.

People have a need to like where they work and have an employer they believe is fair. I know that I'm proud of our having domestic-partner benefits available to employees. Coming from the Tampa Bay area, I felt good about Fulton County and its offering those benefits.

So a change to the Michigan example would concern me greatly.

Q: Is there anything more you'd like to add that we haven't covered?

A: An issue like this pits the state of Georgia against the Atlanta metropolitan area. Yet it's incredibly important for a library system like ours.

We love our colleagues in every corner of Georgia. But our peers in how we look competitively and by whom we benchmark ourselves, with regard to issues ranging from turnover rates of library materials, to use of virtual resources – all of the things that big libraries do – we compare ourselves with other large urban library systems, not other library systems in the rest of Georgia.

Having an environment, legal and otherwise, that's attractive to employees is incredibly important. So Georgia's Super-DOMA absolutely puts us at a disadvantage compared to large library systems in other parts of the country. And frankly, in all of North America. I can think of Toronto or Montreal as other examples.

I'm on the executive board of the Urban Libraries Council, and we talk about the issues that are important to large urban public libraries, which are very different from suburban or rural libraries. And I've been a director of a rural library. And their issues are unique, separate, and important as well.

Libraries deal with all of the issues in the social fabric of the community. We address them head on.

We also discuss matters that affect recruitment. Both Calgary and Toronto are members of the Urban Libraries Council, and the environment in Canada is extremely attractive, as it is in Massachusetts. And all of that matters when you have talented librarians and senior public library administrators and library directors looking for positions.

As Mr. Szabo suggested, measuring Super-DOMA effects that biased gay people *against* relocating to Super-DOMA states from other places is exceptionally difficult to accomplish, because doing so necessarily involves researchers' observing *non*events, such as the decision not to apply for the deputy directorship of the Atlanta-Fulton Public Library System. In other words, how does a distant observer in effect read people's minds when they opt not to do something?

I came up with an admittedly imperfect approach. In addition to eliciting *specific and perceptible* instances of people declining to accept offers of employment in a state, my question about whether interviewees were familiar with failures to immigrate also prompted stories about *likely and invisible* missed opportunities.

Take, for example, what Janet and Marie told me. Together for more than twenty years, the couple was living in a suburb of Columbus, Ohio, and both women were fifty-six years old at the time of our conversation. Janet is an attorney, and Marie is a family doctor.

MARIE: The people who are twenty or thirty years younger than us are getting the hell out of Ohio. If they're professional or otherwise have options, they're not even looking here.

Every year, we go to the national conference of Women in Medicine, which is a lesbian physicians network. People there ask us, "Why do you live in Ohio?"

There's absolutely no interest among the women we meet at these conferences to live anywhere other than Massachusetts or California or Vermont or Canada or other places that recognize their relationships.

Q: You anticipated my next line of questioning, Marie. Are you aware of any gays or lesbians who left Ohio after the passage of Issue 1 and because of it?

JANET: Oh, yeah.
MARIE: Absolutely. We know of one gay male couple who moved to New Jersey.
JANET: We do know such people.

And from this conference standpoint, there are any number of physicians in the group – primarily young people who are just finishing medical school and looking for placements – and they're surely not considering Ohio. So there are people who avoid coming here.

Q: So what about that flip side of the coin? Do you know of someone who's been offered a job in Ohio but who chose not to come from somewhere else because of Issue 1?

JANET: With the people we know, it's not gone that far. For the queer folk we're familiar with, they're not even looking for jobs in Ohio in the first place.

I also spoke with a physician who was a former director of family medicine at the University of Michigan's Medical School in Ann Arbor and who shared with me some experiences in recruitment the medical school had because of Proposal 2's passage.

The one recruitment activity I had the most experience with was talking to young physicians about coming to train in family medicine at the U of M. Proposal 2 affected our process for at least two or three years that I'm aware of. After 2004, there was an applicant or two annually who commented that they were aware the same-sex marriage ban was an issue in the state, that they assumed the university would be a sympathetic employer, and that the Ann Arbor environment would be supportive of them.

But they wondered how the amendment affected the state as far as attitudes, and their implied, if not explicit, question was always whether the assumptions they made about a supportive situation here were in fact true, given that a substantial majority of Michigan voters passed the initiative.

And I'm talking here about candidates who were prepared to come to Ann Arbor for an interview with us, and were willing to ask these questions. In the end, I don't know how Prop 2 ultimately affected their decision making. But I do know the matter was clearly on their minds.

I also don't know how many young physicians weren't willing to make the trip in the first instance. Because it was plain to me that even people outside the state knew this was an issue in Michigan.

Separate from residency-program recruitment, the other more cogent experience was hiring someone to take my position as director of our program when I stepped down from that job. We had a two-stage process. First, there was an open, public posting for the position. Second, there were targeted invitations for highly qualified people to consider an early interview for the post. We identified several people around the country whom we thought would be exceptionally well qualified, extended them early interviews, and had a good response from a number of people.

However, one of the folks, who was already the director at another program, specifically declined even to accept an early interview in our process. She told me that, because of Proposal 2, she and her partner wouldn't be comfortable coming to a state and supporting a program they knew would be subject to such a law. Even though this person lived in New England, she was fully aware of Michigan's constitutional amendment, and was simply not willing to interview for a position where it might potentially negatively affect her and her family. Plus, I think that Prop 2 served as a moral compass for her, in the sense of "I don't want to be there, because I don't know what's going to happen next." So the amendment caused our department to lose the opportunity of even considering her candidacy.

The *New York Times* reported that the nation's top law firms, fearing that their participation on behalf of federal or state laws prohibiting same-sex marriage would inhibit the elite bar's ability to attract and maintain both clients and lawyers, declined to take part in such defenses (Shear and Schwartz 2011; Liptak 2015; cf. Fausset 2015).

Consider the experience of someone in another profession: the clergy. Angela is a minister who was introduced with her partner Jessica in Chapter 3.

ANGELA: I graduated from college in 2000, and graduate school in 2006, both from institutions in the Northeast. When Jessica and I were talking about coming back to Ohio, our friends were appalled. "Why would you go there? Why would you return? Why would you want to live in Ohio?" They couldn't imagine why anyone would want to go to that state, largely around the reelection of Bush and Issue 1.

I know a lot of people in the Episcopal Church who wouldn't take a call to Ohio because of the laws here.

Q: So they wouldn't even apply for ministerial positions?

ANGELA: They wouldn't even consider them.

The gay and lesbian clergy that have come to Ohio don't have kids. There are some with kids who were married to an opposite-sex partner in Ohio. But I can't think of a single gay or lesbian family with children that's moved into the state in the priesthood of the Episcopal Church.

And I have parishioners who would love for their gay or lesbian children who live elsewhere to move home. But those adult children have their own kids. So they're not going to come back.

Meanwhile, here's this grandmother who desperately wishes that her grandchildren were closer, and is aware that it's the state's fault they aren't. It's explicit. So we do know some folks whose kids have left and will not come back.

Real-estate brokers and agents have their fingers on the pulse of housing markets, which in turn provide some indication of migration patterns. I therefore interviewed realtors who supply services to the LGBT community in two Super-DOMA states.

Patrick Tester has lived in Texas for thirty-four years and has been in the Dallas real-estate industry for four of those years. He estimated that between 50 and 60 percent of his clients were lesbian and gay couples and individuals, most of whom came to him from realty websites catering to the LGBT market.

Q: Did the passage of Proposition 2 in Texas have any impact on your business?

A: There have been some practical implications. In the last six months, for example, I've lost two clients who were going to relocate to the Dallas area. One couple was from Connecticut, the other from Massachusetts. They really talked to me a lot about Texas and its attitudes toward gays and lesbians.

I know that the couple from Massachusetts was legally married. They ended up going to Iowa instead, for about the same kind of money. The other couple stayed where they were, in Connecticut.

Q: Did they tell you the reasons for the choice against Texas?

A: They weren't specific about it. They said they were more comfortable in Iowa. The other ones really didn't want to move.

Q: So each couple had a job opportunity in Dallas?

A: Yes. They came here and interviewed, and I showed them houses. I spent two days with each of them. They both got job offers.

One of them decided to stay where they were. They didn't want to uproot because they had children, and that was understandable.

The other said, "We've got this job offer in Iowa and just feel more comfortable there."

And I've had some clients who did move to Dallas, and they're moving back to California. They just don't feel comfortable here. And I've asked them what the reasons are. "Is it the gay and lesbian issue in Texas?" And they kind of hedge the matter. They won't tell me precisely what their motivation is. "We're more comfortable and more free to be ourselves in California." I don't know exactly what that means.

Another indication of a possible Prop-2 impact is that, for people living outside the state, usually the first question when they contact me is, "What's the climate like there to be lesbian or gay?" It's almost always the first question. They're alert to the issue.

Q: What do you tell them, if anything, with regard to Proposition 2 and the marriage issue?

A: I say that, constitutionally, we're not allowed to get married here. And if they're married in other states, it's not recognized here.

I do think Prop 2 is an issue. And somewhere down the line, it's going to become an economic matter. Some of the largest employers in the state, like American Airlines, are so pro-gay-and-lesbian, and so many firms offer partnership benefits, that a lot of companies may make a decision that the constitutional provision doesn't foster a good business climate. That's my feeling on it. There'll be an eventual economic backlash.

Q: Among the people from out of state who think about relocating to Dallas whom you have contact with, can you quantify, in terms of a percentage, the number who are seriously troubled by the marriage prohibition?

A: I don't know about seriously troubled. But the fact remains that, in every single first contact I have with people, the question comes up. So I could almost say it's 100 percent for whom it's a question. Is it a serious issue? Not for a lot of people. So maybe 50 percent are seriously troubled.

Q: Half of the people?

A: Are seriously troubled by the gay-marriage ban here.

Q: Half is a substantial number.

A: Yeah. That's what I see in my experience.

Q: In a given year, how many out-of-state clients contact you?

A: Eight to ten. And I'll do business with probably half of them. And that may be for a variety of reasons.

Q: What about issues involving clients with children? Has Prop 2 come up in any way there?

A: Yes. In the last three months, I dealt with a couple from Maine. I don't know what their status is yet, because their company's still in transition.

    They have two kids. Their first concern was for good schools. Their second worry was, "Will our kids face problems having two gay parents?" And if clients have children, they always ask that question.

    And sometimes schools here are a problem for the kids of same-sex parents. In that circumstance, I rely on my experience as a former public-school teacher, since I know the school districts here and which ones operate in certain ways.... So I can help point clients in the direction of more welcoming schools.

    Generally, I can tell the parents where the good schools are and those places where it won't be a problem that they're a lesbian or gay couple.

Q: What percentage of the couples coming from out of state have children?

A: It's small. I probably work with two pairs a year who have children.

Patrick Tester told me that, among roughly 8,000 real estate agents in the Dallas-Fort Worth metroplex, he estimated that at least one thousand were themselves gay or lesbian. "I work for a large national realty firm, and among our forty agents, can count on the fingers of one hand those who aren't gay or lesbian." Thus, one could multiply his numbers by a factor of one thousand to estimate the complete picture of LGBT migration in the Dallas area.

I met with realtor Jaye J. Kreller in Chapel Hill, North Carolina, two months after the Tar Heel Super-DOMA passed with 60 percent of the popular vote.

Q: What about the flip side of the migration issue? In the sense that people outside of North Carolina may have occasion to move here because of job offers or what have you, and they wonder, "Do I really want to go to a state with a constitutional provision like Amendment 1?" And then they decide not to do so.

A: I can tell you that's already happened. Absolutely.

    Every year, one of the larger moving companies does demographics about the states where people are moving from and where people are moving to. It's not a strictly scientific study, but this large moving company's internal information about where they're carrying people. They label the states either blue or gold. Gold are exit states, where people are leaving. Blue are states that people are coming to from other parts of the country.

    North Carolina has been a blue state for as long as I've been in real estate, which is nine years. So every year this company produces the statistics, and you look at North Carolina, and more people are coming in than are leaving.

In this area, we have a huge employer with the University of North Carolina, and another one with the Research Triangle Park, where there are multiple businesses. And both large employers recruit people from all over the country, from states like California and New York.

People have come down here and love what they see. Five years ago, if you came from California, the ticket prices on the houses were so much less, and you could get so much more house for the money. If you were coming from New York, a walk-in closet here was a guest room there. So people loved the quality of life here.

This area thus had this great era of being a wonderful place to live in and relocate to. And by and large, gays and lesbians were being recruited, because they're more mobile.

So far this year, I've had more conversations with people who were thinking about coming here to hook up with a company, but now are worried. They're anxious about entering a state with a law like Amendment 1.

Many people thought that North Carolina would be different, given the companies coming here. And now, all of a sudden, I'm seeing these kinds of reactions.

My statistics aren't scientific by any measure, but I've shown three same-sex couples around so far this year who voiced that issue as a concern. And to date, none of those three has actually moved here. All of them considered relocating from other states, and none of the three did. And in each case, we had that conversation.

Two of the couples have children. And I can't help but think that dynamic was definitely a factor.

Q: Who brought up the topic?

A: They did. Because Amendment 1 has been very public all year. So as people were visiting in January and February, they'd say, "What about Amendment 1? Is it going to pass?" "Yeah, it's going to pass. This is North Carolina. We're in a very blue pocket of a bright red state."

Q: How representative do you think your sample is of the general population in that regard?

A: I don't know that, because there's no way to get that kind of data. But my experience in prior years, and having the same conversation with people now....

Because people are worried about coming to North Carolina. It's still North Carolina, the land of Jesse Helms. But prior to Amendment 1 and all the hoopla around it, I'd explain to them, "Living in the Research Triangle, you'd never know you were in North Carolina. You would *never* know it. Because it just doesn't feel like it here. But if you drive in the rural parts of the state, you'll feel self-conscious. That's going to happen."

But I never before had anyone who was thinking about moving here, and who was being recruited by a local company, not do so, among those who in fact did get jobs here. And three in a row? That's never happened before.

And I can't help but feel like, "You know what? We're shooting the business community here in the foot." Because we're talking about talent and revenue, about gifted people who are choosing not to come to North Carolina.

Q: Do you think this phenomenon will continue?

A: I think it's a blip. I don't think it will continue, because it happened when Amendment 1 was so public. Everybody had the "No on One" stickers on their car. So of course, it was what everyone was asking about.

And then the referendum passed with a 20 percent majority, which caused everybody on the outside to think "Oh my God!" They weren't aware that, when the amendment was first proposed last year, there was a 40 percent margin of approval in the polls. So a 50 percent reduction within just seven or eight months is pretty significant.

Q: Let me ask a question that may be difficult, and I apologize if it is.

Let's say that you continue doing the same kind of real-estate work in North Carolina for years to come. Same-sex couples contact you from out of state and show interest in housing here. And they don't initiate conversations about Amendment 1.

Would you feel any obligation to do so?

A: Probably. Yeah. I'm very much in the full-disclosure camp. So I'd say, "This is where we are."

But a lot of it is spin too. When you try to sell an area, you're selling *your* area. I'm not selling North Carolina. I'm selling the Triangle.

So I can tell people that the Triangle voted overwhelmingly against Amendment 1. Once again, our area's a very blue pocket in a bright red state. And I've no problem saying that to clients.

In a lot of ways, my answer makes them feel comfortable, because this is where they're going to spend at least 90 percent of their time. And *I* certainly feel comfortable here.

You can drive around right now in neighborhoods in Durham and Chapel Hill, and still see the "No on One" signs. You don't see any "Yes on One" signs still up.

So yes, I'd bring the issue up. Absolutely.

How 'Ya Gonna Keep 'Em down on the Farm?
(after They've Seen Paree)

I did not interview any same-sex couples outside of the six states in my study who had no prior connections with those jurisdictions but who nonetheless were thinking about moving into one of them, but then decided not to do so because of its Super-DOMA. As intimated earlier, I do not know of any research method to identify such people because there would be no overt gestures for me to observe at a distance by which to recognize them.

However, I did speak with three gay or lesbian pairs who had moved away from one of the six states for reasons other than their constitutional amendments. These are people with consequential, preexisting ties to their former home states who had good reasons to return there to live. Moreover, all three couples are well educated with successful careers, the kinds of productive citizens whom any state would eagerly welcome into its workforce. I spoke with each pair about their inclinations to go home.

Edward, age twenty-seven, and Steven, twenty-eight, live in New York City. Edward recently graduated from the Harvard Business School and works as a banker in a private-equity firm. Steven is a fundraiser for a major New York philanthropic organization. When I interviewed them at their Manhattan apartment in July 2012, Edward and Steven had been away from North Carolina for six years.

Q: Tell me about your ties to North Carolina.

STEVEN: I was born and raised in North Carolina. My family has lived there for a very long time. I grew up in Charlotte and went to school at UNC, where Edward and I met.

EDWARD: I was born in Chapel Hill and raised there until age five or six, and then went to the DC area. I returned to Chapel Hill for college. My mother has always lived in Chapel Hill.

STEVEN: North Carolina is home for both of us.

EDWARD: My family that was in DC retired back to North Carolina.

Q: What did the recent passage of North Carolina's Amendment 1 mean to you in the broadest sense of the word?

EDWARD: You have to put Amendment 1 in the context of North Carolina being the last state in the Southeast to have kept such a provision out of its constitution. And so we were all very proud of that. For years, both legally and socially, we'd very effectively kept that dialogue out of our state.

And then for it to spring up, almost out of nowhere.... The legislative vote came and went very quickly. So it was especially disappointing.

We've lived up here for a while, and obviously have very strong connections to North Carolina family and friends. I've always wondered about what the likelihood would be we'd ever move back. And for me, the passage of Amendment 1 resulted in a distancing from the state. Steven feels more strongly that he'd like to relocate to North Carolina at some point.

But if I were to ponder what our lives would be like, both with regard to legal protection and socially, what environment you're living in and raising kids in, I think some place where that could happen is very disappointing and less attractive. And especially relative to New York, where we do have same-sex marriage, Amendment 1 makes it harder to build a case for North Carolina.

We have enough resources that we probably could live anywhere we wanted to. So why would we choose to put ourselves in a place like that?

STEVEN: Look, I don't want to live under a rock because so many states have passed these marriage amendments. If someone wants to give me trouble, then I can give them trouble right back. It's just that simple.

Being in New York doesn't mean I have some sort of immunity from homophobia and bigotry. I think that, whether we're vacationing in the Outer Banks or in the Adirondacks, we could have trouble. And I'm perfectly prepared to deal with it. I'm going to do what I want, not what I necessarily think is the safest.

Q: You've told me you intend to have a family. How does that commentary play when there might be children involved?

STEVEN: Amendment 1 changes things. It does. It'd be a lot harder to move back to North Carolina with small children in tow. If we were to have children in New York, I don't see how we could justify moving back to North Carolina with the status quo. It would put the kids in jeopardy, creating a risk in a way I wouldn't feel comfortable doing. They shouldn't have to live through my fight. It wouldn't be fair.

But if we do have children, we'd still make visits to North Carolina. That's where our family is. Similarly, if we wanted to take our kids to the Grand Canyon, I wouldn't say, "Arizona doesn't recognize our marriage. So we can't go there." If something, God forbid, happens on a trip like that, then I'll do whatever I have to to defend my rights and those of my family.

Having kids would keep us from living again in North Carolina. If we have children, then there's zero percent likelihood we'd move back to North Carolina. Which makes me very sad.

EDWARD: [to Steven:] And that percentage was higher before Amendment 1, and now it's zero?

STEVEN: Sure.

EDWARD: Interesting.

Q: You anticipated my next question. How much difference?

EDWARD: [to Steven:] Your original comment was, "I'm going to live the life I want. If I need to deal with it, then I will." And now it's zero percent.

STEVEN: [to Edward:] What you're saying doesn't follow directly from my first comment.

I'm going to live the life I want, and if that means having kids, then it's no longer just my life. That's what it means to be a parent, to do first what's best for your children. However much I want to move back to North Carolina, and raise a family where I grew up, doing that is a lot riskier with Amendment 1.

EDWARD: [to Steven:] And there's no amount of resources to mitigate that risk? Say you put away $1 million. You got a house in Meadowlawn. The best legal counsel in North Carolina. Those sorts of things.

STEVEN: I think that's an arbitrary distinction. There are risks, and money isn't going to alleviate them. It's going to cover them up. You can't buy your way into civil rights.

Q: Again, hypothetically, what if Amendment 1 had never passed? Whatever the case might have been, North Carolina would have continued to be the southern exception to the state-constitutional-amendment rule. Would your percentage have increased?

STEVEN: Yes.

Q: To what percentage?

STEVEN: In the next five to ten years, if there were no Amendment 1, if and when we have children, I'd push a lot harder to raise those children in North Carolina. And that's not something we've ever discussed, because it's never come up.
EDWARD: [to Steven:] And what would the percentage change to?
STEVEN: [to Edward:] What's the percentage chance that we're going to have kids?
EDWARD: I guess it's 100 percent.
STEVEN: Then there'd have been a 100 percent chance I'd try to twist your arm to move back to North Carolina to raise those kids.

Q: Really?

STEVEN: I would have.

Q: So Amendment 1 is a big deal then. A huge deal.

STEVEN: Yes. It's a huge deal.

Q: You went from a 100 percent chance of relocating back to North Carolina to a zero percent probability. Correct me if I'm wrong.

STEVEN: No, you're not wrong.
  Amendment 1 is a really dramatic law for those people who choose to make their lives in North Carolina.

Q: So you're saying that it's life-altering for the two of you?

STEVEN: Yes.
EDWARD: That's right.
STEVEN: And we're probably not alone in that regard. Edward's mother is a real-estate agent in Chapel Hill,[14] and is currently trying to sell a house to a gay couple who lives in New York, and like us, wants to have a second home in Chapel Hill. One person in the pair went to UNC.
  But the process of purchasing the home seems to have stalled. I'd guess there's some hesitancy in their minds about whether it makes sense for them to buy a place in Chapel Hill – and they have two kids – after Amendment 1. The legal hurdles for people like us are higher there now.

Excerpts from my telephone interview with Mark and Paul appear earlier in the chapter, regarding their description of same-sex couples who were friends

---

[14] His mother is not Jaye J. Kreller, but another realtor in Chapel Hill.

living in the Atlanta area. Paul resided in Georgia for seventeen years, whereas Mark was there for nine. They moved to Massachusetts in 2007.

Q: If you were to quantify how important leaving Georgia because of Question 1 and its effects was in your relocation, what percentage would you come up with for its level of importance?

MARK: 20 percent.

PAUL: I'd agree with that. It certainly didn't help us want to remain in Georgia. If we could've gotten married in Georgia, maybe we would've considered staying there.

Q: Let's say, hypothetically, that some marvelous, terrific, absolutely wonderful job opportunity were to make itself available to the two of you back in Atlanta. After having been married and living in Massachusetts for three years, would you move back to Georgia now?

PAUL: It's funny you should ask that question. Because Mark's company has merged a couple of times since we've been married. And we talked about the possibility of what would happen if they wanted him to move back to Atlanta and assume an executive position in the organization.

And it just frightens us both. I wouldn't want to. Our quality of life here [in Massachusetts] is so much better. We both make plenty of money, and so I don't think that would be a driving factor.

MARK: I'd have to answer "No" to your question. I really can't think of a circumstance where I'd want to move back there. And at this point, the marriage question is a part of that decision.

I've joked with Paul, "If we leave Massachusetts, we can move to Iowa, or Washington, DC, or Connecticut." The places where we could be married are those that are lit up. Frankly, any state that doesn't recognize our marriage . . . It's a factor for me now. Absolutely.

Q: Let me ask you again to quantify it. You said earlier that, in leaving Georgia, Question 1 was about a 20 percent factor. What would be the percentage now with regard to relocating to a place that would not legally recognize your relationship?

MARK: For me, it's extremely high on the list. I would say 80 percent.

PAUL: Or higher.

MARK: Yes.

PAUL: In 2007, Mark secured employment at Williams College, which is located in Williamstown, in the extreme northwestern corner of Massachusetts, right near the borders with both New York and Vermont. We decided we were going to move to Williamstown or the local area. So we live just a few miles from New York and Vermont.

When we started looking at housing, it was much less expensive to live in Vermont, just two miles down the road. But the primary driver for wanting to live in Massachusetts was the ability to get married. At the time, same-sex couples couldn't wed in Vermont.

MARK: I'd actually applied for a job and was at the interview stage for a position at Brown University [in Providence, Rhode Island]. If I'd worked at Brown, we still would've lived in Massachusetts in order to get married.

Once we focused on New England and knew there were some job opportunities there, we did hone in pretty quickly on living in Massachusetts because of the marriage issue.

Q: When you were looking for a place to live in the Williamstown area, Vermont at the time did offer full civil unions to same-sex couples. In light of the cheaper cost of living in Vermont, a civil union wasn't a viable option for you?

PAUL: It was the same thing with New York. We knew we could be recognized there.

But we wanted to live in a state where we could actually get married. It held more weight for us to live in such a place.

MARK: For me, it was like, "Well, that's nice for Vermont. But I can get something better by living a few more miles down the road." To me, civil unions and marriage aren't equal. And we had the opportunity to have the full deal.

I remember thinking at the time, "Well, Vermont is Vermont. It's not going to be too far behind." I was fairly confident there'd be states other than Massachusetts to offer marriage to gay couples, and that has in fact occurred. But why would I settle for less, when I could have everything?

Catherine, age forty-four, and Frances, fifty-one, have been together for twenty-one years and live in New York City. Catherine has been employed in higher education management for fifteen years, and Frances is an attorney who works for a federal government agency.

Q: What are your ties to Michigan?

FRANCES: I was born and raised in Michigan, went to school there, and practiced law in Detroit for about ten years. All told, I've lived thirty-five years in Michigan, and most of my family is still there.

CATHERINE: I initially went to Michigan for law school and then clerked for a judge there. Frances and I returned to my home state of New York for two years. Then we went back to Michigan, and I practiced law there. I've lived a total of not quite eight years in Michigan.

FRANCES: We left to come back to New York in 1995 and have lived here ever since.

CATHERINE: But we're constantly visiting Michigan because of our family ties there. We make trips back all the time.

Q: So what did it mean to you when Proposal 2 passed in Michigan in 2004?

CATHERINE: Proposal 2 really colored my entire picture of the state.

In 2004, I was in an administrative position at a large university in New York, where I did good work. But I wanted to get back to having more direct and consistent contact with students, which is why I went into higher education in the first place.

So I looked for faculty positions that were available elsewhere, and Frances and I talked about what cities would be options for us.

FRANCES: Places to which I could easily transfer my own job in a government agency.
CATHERINE: And lo and behold, there was a full-time faculty position advertised at the University of Michigan in Ann Arbor, which I felt had my name written all over it. I applied for the job, got an interview, and was offered the position.

And since Frances is very sought after in her agency, she could have easily transferred to its Michigan office.
FRANCES: My family would have been very happy if I'd come back home.

And our standard of living would have improved. We could have sold our New York apartment and bought a much nicer place in Michigan because of the difference in the costs of living.

Q: When did you get the offer from the University of Michigan? I ask because Proposal 2 passed in November of 2004.

CATHERINE: The application and interview process began before that November. But the offer itself came in January or February of 2005.
FRANCES: Soon after the constitutional amendment passed.

Q: And was Proposal 2 a decisive factor in your response to that offer?

CATHERINE: It was *the* decisive factor. I declined the job. And turning down a full-time faculty appointment at the University of Michigan is hardly something one does lightly.

In the same way that I've taken everything I love about Michigan and sort of bottled it up into this silly ginger ale which is called Vernor's, all my discomfort about how reactionary the state has become, and how many fewer opportunities there are for me to live out a normal life there – all of that was balled up into my feelings about Proposal 2.
FRANCES: I actually take advantage of some of the domestic-partner benefits that Catherine has at her jobs, because the federal benefits I get through my position have very limited dental and optical coverage. And Catherine's working in higher education frequently gets her better dental and optical benefits.

So one of our considerations when she takes a job is ""What are their domestic-partner benefits?" The University of Michigan certainly had those benefits, and so that sounded great when she was going through the recruitment process. But then, when the constitutional amendment passed, and we didn't know how that was going to affect the U of M benefits, that's something we took into account.

Moreover, Proposal 2 indicated in the most dramatic way possible that the attitudes toward LGBT people in Michigan weren't favorable. And was that really the kind of environment we wanted to live in?
CATHERINE: I love Michigan and loved my time there, and wanted to return if at all possible. And certainly, Frances's family is my family. They're very embracing of me and us as a couple.

So Prop 2 colored everything. It meant that it took Michigan off of our list of possible places to consider moving to. Entirely.

And that greatly saddened us, for the loss of being able to be around all of our nieces and nephews as they grew older there. And of being around other family members, and of having great job opportunities there, and the like.

FRANCES: Even if we weren't saying "Let's get married right away," Prop 2 still reflects a fundamental attitude – and I think hatred – of LGBT people. And who wants to live in an environment where that exists? And especially since the amendment was so extensive.

CATHERINE: Proposal 2 completely shut down the possibility of our making what should have been a very legitimate life choice to join family members in one of our home states, and to make a career choice that would have been substantially beneficial. I love being a higher education administrator, but would have enjoyed just as much being a faculty member. So it was a very significant loss to me and us.

FRANCES: And I've maintained professional ties to Michigan. I still paid my bar dues in Michigan and dues to professional lawyers' associations there. And I'd been a contributor to a law book published in Michigan. I kept those links in the event that, if opportunities arose to go back to Michigan, I'd have much easier entree.

And to be honest, since Proposal 2 passed, although I continue to maintain my Michigan bar membership, I'm no longer a member of various sections of the bar there, nor a member of the trial lawyers' associations, like I used to be. Also, I've told the law book's editor I'm not interested in doing any more updates, and suggested that they find a local person to do them now.

CATHERINE: And Frances either wrote portions of that book or edited it for many, many years.

FRANCES: So I've definitely limited my direct professional involvement with Michigan, because I no longer think it's important to maintain professional ties in a state I don't have any interest now in going back to, not even enough concern to keep the door open to go back.

CATHERINE: That's very sad.

My conversations with Edward and Steven, Mark and Paul, and Catherine and Frances offer compelling evidence of the enormous impact that Super-DOMAs had on same-sex couples who lived elsewhere, but nonetheless had positive, binding, even enticing ties to those states. These were pairs who were predisposed to return to places they knew well and loved. Yet the Super-DOMAs – combined with a keen awareness of a better life that the couples discovered through exposure to far more LGBT-welcoming legal, political, and social environments – became absolute barriers to immigration back into the constitutional-amendment-adapting states.

Thus, it should not take a great leap of faith to acknowledge that young and well-educated gay and lesbian couples who did not have any such prior positive associations with Super-DOMA states would also be repelled by the relationship-recognition bans, as reinforced by the interviews in this section.

Same-Sex Couples Who Did Move to Super-DOMA States

Among my 175 interviews with same-sex couples across six states, I found just a handful who had in fact relocated from more LGBT-friendly places to Super-DOMA jurisdictions. Stewart and William, who told their remarkable surname-change experience in Chapter 3, stand out in this category. They are

Ohio natives who settled in New Jersey in March 2004, months before Issue 1 even qualified for the ballot and was on Ohio's political agenda. The timing of their departure from the Buckeye State accounts for why Stewart and William had little awareness of its constitutional amendment when they moved back to Ohio in 2007.[15] In New Jersey, William adopted a daughter, Diane, for whom Stewart then secured a second-parent adoption in the Garden State. So both men were Diane's legal parents when they returned to Columbus.

Q: What was the occasion for your homecoming to Ohio?

WILLIAM: It was a tough decision. We were content in New Jersey. Diane was coming into our lives.

But both of our families were predominantly back here in Ohio. We thought long and hard in terms of making a career change that would allow Diane to grow up closer to her grandparents and aunts and uncles. And that's the decision we made.

STEWART: If our families weren't here, we wouldn't have come back to Ohio.

WILLIAM: That was the deciding factor. I loved my job in New Jersey, and would go back there in a heartbeat.

STEWART: If William found a job in New England in the next two to three years, it's my opinion we would leave Ohio. But if Diane starts school here, the likelihood drops. When she gets older again, the probability goes up. But it all depends upon her and job time frames.

WILLIAM: I'm actively looking now for a new position. The Northeast would be a part of my calculus, as well as locally. I go back and forth about it.

Because there's a reason we tend to end up in Columbus. We met in Columbus, and moved away to Cincinnati. We came back to Columbus. We went to New Jersey, and came back to Columbus. So there's something we like about this city. We have a really strong and close-knit network of gay friends here. So ideally, I'd like to stay in Columbus.

But if a career opportunity opened up in New Jersey, Connecticut, or Massachusetts, I'd probably take it. That is, again, if it occurred in the next few years.

Three years after our interview, William got a new position in Michigan, and the family moved there. I regret not having the opportunity to speak with them again to understand their reason(s) for relocating to another Super-DOMA jurisdiction. I suspect it was because the best job opportunity arose in the Wolverine State.

I did not systematically ask interviewees whether they knew of queer folk who had moved from more LGBT-friendly jurisdictions into Super-DOMA states. Yet my query about whether they were familiar with people who had resisted opportunities for such immigration sometimes – but not frequently – sparked remarks about pairs who had in fact relocated, such as an exchange with Agnes and Rosemary (whose other interview excerpt appears in the chapter's "Economic Ties" section):

[15] In 2006, the New Jersey legislature passed, and the governor signed, a bill creating full civil unions for same-sex couples. The law became effective in 2007.

Q: What about the flip side of the migration coin? Do you know of anybody who had opportunity to move into Ohio from elsewhere because of a job offer or what have you, but chose not to do so because of Issue 1?

BOTH: I don't.

AGNES: I know of a lesbian couple with two children who just moved here from Massachusetts. They apparently came to Cleveland for a very lucrative deal.

I met one of the partners and said to her, "What were you thinking? Did you really look into this before you came here?" She said to me, "Maybe we can keep our children protected in Shaker Heights [an affluent suburb just east of Cleveland]." And I said, "I wish you the best."

But I don't get it. Both of these women have terminal degrees in their fields. They're both white, with two adopted, biracial children. They moved from Massachusetts, right around Smith College in the Northampton area. And they resettled in Ohio.

So you've got to be looking at substantial money there for them to have changed environments so profoundly.

ROSEMARY: There are Cleveland suburbs that are very welcoming places. Cleveland Heights has a domestic-partner registry, and folks there have worked so hard.[16]

AGNES: But a registry means nothing as a practical matter, especially when kids are involved.

I also spoke with Dallas real-estate agent Phillip D. Archer, who had an understanding distinctly different from that of Patrick Tester about Super-DOMA effects on immigration by same-sex couples into the Lone Star State.

Q: Let me ask a question while you wear the hat of real-estate agent. In 2005, Texas passed Prop 2 with 76 percent of the popular vote. The constitutional amendment not only prohibits marriage for same-sex couples but also civil unions and domestic partnerships.

Another Dallas realtor, who handles only residential properties, told me that at least half of his customers are gay and lesbian. He knew of eight to ten prospective clients every year who come from out of state and who're thinking of relocating to Texas from somewhere else.

He said the first question out of their mouths is, "What's the political climate like here for gay people?" He said that some of them, after coming here and investigating thoroughly, decide this isn't the kind of place they want to live, because of Prop 2 and other indicators of hostility toward gay people.

What's your experience been with regard to that?

A: I don't think I know of a single couple that's not relocated here because of Prop 2.

My take on the Texas political climate is different, probably because I've lived here my whole life. We're not a bunch of stupid hicks that don't know what's going on in the rest of the world. Texas used to be its own republic,

---

[16] See Biggers (2014, 124–25).

after all, and there are a lot of wealthy people here. So many of us have a good lifestyle.

There are a lot of Texans with very traditional mindsets. The mayor's chief of staff, the head of the Dallas Visitors Bureau, and I argue over whether Dallas is gay friendly. I say the city is gay tolerant, but not gay friendly. And we need to make a concerted effort to change that, because we're right on the cusp.

Let me offer my own experience as an example. When my ex-partner John and I had issues with his ex-wife at one point, a white, Republican, female judge awarded us full custody of John's son. And she knew we were a gay couple up against his ex-wife. But the judge also knew the ex-wife was crazy.

So people here aren't unfair, typically. Folks do tend to be Republican, and the Republicans in Texas fight nasty. And they do prioritize things differently. If you told them they had to choose between schools and health care for children, on the one hand, and gay people having equality, on the other, they're going to go, "Well, my gay friends don't have any problems. They live in a big house down the street. They both drive Jaguars. They're just fine. But schools and health care are serious issues."

So it's really the way things are presented that counts. And I'm certainly not saying we have a good political environment. After all, we've got Rick Perry for governor. How much worse could it be?

When I walk a boyfriend to his car in front of my house, I kiss him good night. When we're strolling through the West Village, I'll hold his hand. I don't feel uncomfortable. Nobody in this town is going to hurt me because I'm gay.

It's not unsafe. It's unjust. And there's a difference. So from a justice standpoint, we live in a state that treats us inequitably, just like Alabama and Mississippi and many other southern states. The law hasn't caught up with the consciousness of the society. So it costs gay people more money to protect our rights. And we probably should be more concerned about that. But those are things we can do.

Would I like for my domestic partnership to be acknowledged? Absolutely. But I want it to be recognized on a federal level. Who cares about Texas [where there's no state income tax]? I want to file a joint federal tax return with a partner.

So I don't think same-sex couples don't move to Texas because of Prop 2. Rather, we have to educate people who do relocate here. The first thing I do with clients is say, "You're buying a house. Do you have wills?" "No." "Here's the card of [attorney] Lorie Burch. Call her up, right now. Also, you're worth $1 million. Do you have a trust set up?" "No." "Here's Rebecca's card. Call her, too."

You can spend $1,000 on wills and $3,000 on a trust, and you're good to go. You don't have to worry about all that crap. You don't have to care about crazy relatives.

But gay people should be doing that everywhere, including Massachusetts. It's better to have everything in writing.

Lorie L. Burch, the Dallas attorney to whom Phillip Archer referred clients, also confirmed LGBT immigration into the Lone Star State.

I know of a gay male couple who moved here from San Francisco recently and who caught hell from their friends. "Why would you go there?" But the pair found they liked Texas.

And this shows how regular these couples are, because one of the big draws of this area is the cost of living. Dallas has such an undervalued market for real estate. People who sell a tiny condo in San Francisco can buy a mansion here with the California proceeds. Plus, with all the amenities you have, the arts and cultural life, this is a great place to live.

Accordingly, I did find empirical markers that some lesbian and gay pairs indeed migrated from places like California and Massachusetts to Super-DOMA states, either because of the reduced costs of living and other economic reasons, or sometimes for family (as with Stewart and William).

Some queer folk apparently believed that money could insulate them and their families from the deleterious effects of hostile legal environments. Miriam and Naomi, the Georgia couple who first appear in "The Bubble Effect" section, commented on that phenomenon:

Q: Is there anything else about Question 1 that you'd like to add that we haven't covered?

NAOMI: I want to go back to the whole financial issue. We have two very close friends, and I don't know whether they've consider the impact of Question 1 because they feel so privileged financially. I'm not sure they've done the legal maneuvers to protect their relationship.

I think that money is a huge way that some people feel secure, because it legitimizes them as a couple, at least in their belief system.

MIRIAM: I understand our friends think money will save them, and that they can buy their way out of difficulty. But I fear for them. They routinely drive to Florida, which isn't the most progressive place, to see a set of parents. They have to drive all the way through south Georgia.

I wonder what would happen to them if, God forbid, they were in an auto accident. And they're down in Thomasville, Georgia, and it's tiny. If they're lucky, they're going to be met at the hospital door by somebody who's progressive. But if they're not, are they carrying papers? Do they have a way of looking out for each other?

So does money save gay couples in Super-DOMA states? At best, only if they've used it to protect themselves.

But you can't buy your way into an intensive-care unit in a rural town, no matter how hard you try.

Steven's telling admonishment to his partner Edward is especially instructive here: "There are [legal] risks, and money isn't going to alleviate them. It's going to cover them up. You can't buy your way into civil rights." As the many harrowing experiences recounted earlier in the book indicate, there were, in truth, grave Super-DOMA-based predicaments that people could never buy their way out of.

Moreover, even putting such quandaries aside, I learned that wealth itself did not guarantee the freedom to emigrate. In May 2012, the *New York Times* profiled Bob Page, the gay founder and chairman of Replacements, Ltd., a business based in Greensboro, North Carolina, with annual revenues of $80 million (Stewart 2012). Mr. Page's history reads like an LGBT version of an Horatio Alger story, and his net assets are by far the largest of anyone I have ever interviewed. Yet mark this exchange from our conversation:

Q: You have substantial roots in North Carolina, both personally and in terms of your business. Did the passage of Amendment 1 provoke any thought of relocation to a place that would be more welcoming to you and your family?

A: If life were simpler, I'd definitely want to move my kids somewhere else.

But Replacements is here. We have 450 employees. It would be practically impossible to move the business. And we have people who've worked for us twenty-five to thirty years, with an incredible amount of knowledge that we couldn't replace overnight.

So leaving North Carolina wouldn't make any sense at all. It would probably bankrupt the company to relocate. That's not a feasible option.

Thus, just like the many, many couples I met across seven field trips who lived from paycheck to paycheck, even someone with abundant resources like Bob Page was trapped, for all intents and purposes, in his Super-DOMA state.

CONCLUSION

After initially wondering whether it was braver for African Americans to stay in the Jim Crow South or to depart it, Wilkerson concludes her study by noting that "the common denominator for leaving was the desire to be free" (2010, 536) and with the conviction that the correct inquiry to make about the folks who participated in the Great Migration involves "how they summoned the courage to leave in the first place" (2010, 538).

The same-sex couples I interviewed certainly shared a comparable desire to be treated fairly and equally. Yet, answering the question about whether staying or going is the braver act is more complicated when the level of overt oppression against the minority group here is substantially less, both in degree and duration, than was that against people of color in the Jim Crow South.

Although Super-DOMAs created serious, and sometimes severe, challenges in the daily lives of same-sex couples and their families, my research indicates that very few LGBT people – probably no more than 1 or 2 percent – left states with these harsh constitutional regimes to settle in more inviting legal and political environments. Typically, too many economic, personal, and social impediments blocked meaningful emigration opportunities, even for those LGBT citizens who fully understood and appreciated the threat to well-being posed by the relationship-recognition bans.

Any one of numerous circumstances – from jobs that were not portable to sturdy home-state loyalty, from seeking refuge in local safe havens to having children in school, from blood relatives needing care to hope for judicial salvation, and from internalized homophobia to agility in playing the system – was often enough to squelch flight. And a combination of two or more such factors was tantamount to a guarantee against relocation.

In contrast, the few pairs who did opt for greener pastures usually had a history of resettlement for career or education, had no family ties or other preexisting personal connections to their Super-DOMA state, had portable work situations or otherwise possessed highly marketable skills, did not count on legal or political redemption from Super-DOMA impacts, had hardy LGBT identities and strong expectations of fair and equal treatment, were well educated, and were often under the age of forty.

With regard to queer folk living elsewhere but with opportunities to move into Super-DOMA states, I found convincing evidence that the repellent effects of these initiatives and referenda were extensive. In particular, for the decade beginning in 2004, young, well-educated LGBT citizens looking nationwide for career opportunities rarely considered migrating to jurisdictions that were not prepared to recognize their personal relationships. Indeed, the queer share of the up-and-coming pillars of the American workforce shunned places like Georgia, Michigan, North Carolina, Ohio, Texas, and Wisconsin once those states adopted conspicuously antigay constitutional amendments.

In short, Super-DOMAs in large measure repulsed most effectively those categories of people, putting sexual orientation aside, whom governments usually want more than any others to attract and maintain as citizens and taxpayers. If nothing else, proponents of these constitutional provisions were spectacularly successful in shooting the economic vitality of their states in the foot.

6

How the Federal Courts Rescued Same-Sex Couples and Their Families

The final battle in America's war on gay and lesbian couples and their children ended decisively on June 26, 2015, when, in *Obergefell v. Hodges*, the U.S. Supreme Court declared that the Fourteenth Amendment of the federal Constitution provided same-sex pairs a right to civil marriage, thereby invalidating all remaining state prohibitions on gay nuptials. After *Obergefell*, there may have been skirmishes here or there, where a recalcitrant county clerk denied a marriage license to a same-sex couple (Katz 2015; Mura and Pérez-Peña 2015), or when a baker refused to create their wedding cake (Healy 2015), or a photographer declined to take pictures of the event (*Elane Photography, LLC v. Willock* 2013). But the same pair then went to a clerk in a different county a few miles away or another baker or photographer in a nearby town to meet their needs. So although *Obergefell* did not absolutely quell temporary insults or fleeting setbacks, it did unalterably fix, across the entire land, gay people's fundamental right to marry.[1]

And I am confident that the use of "unalterably" in the previous sentence is accurate, because there are just two ways in which *Obergefell* might be formally disturbed, with each being extremely improbable. The first option is a constitutional amendment to overturn the decision. However, as long as Democrats hold at least thirty-four seats in the United States Senate or 146 in the House, two-thirds majorities in both chambers of Congress are unavailable for such a constitutional rewrite. Indeed, the Federal Marriage Amendment (a Republican Super-DOMA-like proposal) failed by substantial margins in both houses of Congress in 2004 (Pinello 2006, 20), when public opinion in favor of marriage equality was far less robust than in 2015. What is more, even if Congress, through some severe quirk of political fate, in fact cobbled together

---

[1] See also Doan, Loehr, and Miller (2014).

such super-majorities, there are at least seventeen states (California, Connecticut, Delaware, Hawaii, Illinois, Maine, Maryland, Massachusetts, Minnesota, New Hampshire, New Jersey, New Mexico, New York, Oregon, Rhode Island, Vermont, and Washington) that would never approve the constitutional revision, thereby denying the three-quarters necessary to ratify an amendment.

The other route to overcoming *Obergefell* would be for the U.S. Supreme Court itself to overrule the precedent, which would require at least five votes among the nine justices. After the death of Antonin Scalia in February 2016, there were at most just two members of the Court who might act that way: Samuel Alito and Clarence Thomas. Even though Chief Justice John Roberts dissented in *Obergefell,* he is a sufficiently strong believer in the institutional integrity and legitimacy of the federal judiciary not to favor overturning recent precedents, no matter how convinced he may be they were decided incorrectly. In addition, Justice Alito may prove to be in the Roberts' institutionalist camp as well. Thus, at least two or three new Supreme Court appointments of conservative ideologues in the mold of Scalia or Thomas to replace members of the *Obergefell* majority would be required for an overruling. Such judicial designations would only be made by a Republican president. Hence, if a Democrat won the White House in 2016, *Obergefell* would be entrenched forever in the constitutional firmament. Furthermore, even if a Republican prevailed in 2016, there would be no guarantee that the Senate would confirm nominees perceived to be as ideologically extreme as Scalia or Thomas. Even as the Senate minority, Democrats might still mount a successful filibuster of such a judicial candidate. Moreover, securing two or three appointments of that ilk in a row would demand herculean presidential political talents and power. In any event, with a likely three-fifths or more of all Americans approving of marriage equality in 2016 and beyond, the probability of a Republican president and Senate ultimately undermining *Obergefell* is very remote as a practical political matter. And just as the nation moved the Supreme Court to embrace marriage equality in the first place, public opinion will also persuade the other federal branches not to interfere with the High Court's precedent.[2]

THE IMPACT OF LOWER FEDERAL COURTS

Despite the absolute victory for marriage equality in the Supreme Court, that tribunal's edict directly affected just thirteen of the fifty states: Alabama, Arkansas, Kentucky, Louisiana, Michigan, Mississippi, Missouri, Nebraska, North Dakota, Ohio, South Dakota, Tennessee, and Texas. But among the thirteen, only three (Mississippi, Missouri, and Tennessee) were not Super-DOMA jurisdictions. Thus, although *Obergefell* itself struck down marriage bans in merely 26 percent of the states, the ruling wiped out 50 percent of the nation's Super-DOMAs. Thus, the High Court's achievement was telling.

[2] See also Bishin et al. (2015).

But fully half of the most restrictive state constitutional amendments regarding the recognition of same-sex relationships had already been nullified by the time the Supreme Court acted in June 2015. Indeed, the number of legally married gay and lesbian pairs *tripled* – from about 130,000 nationwide to 390,000 – in the two years *prior* to *Obergefell* (Gates and Newport 2015). And many of those new weddings took place in states that formerly had Super-DOMAs in effect.

Hence, the story of how same-sex couples and their families were saved from antigay state constitutional amendments is not just one of the Supreme Court coming to their rescue. Rather, the narrative must necessarily include the consequential ways in which other federal judges also quashed charter provisions so inimical to the well being of families headed by lesbian and gay pairs.

THE LEGAL PRECEDENTS

Obergefell did not spring fresh from the brows of five justices. Instead, it emerged from a landscape of precedents that the Court's majority believed ineluctably led to the conclusion that the Fourteenth Amendment guaranteed marriage equality. Four precedents in particular were decisive to the outcome, as indicated by how frequently Justice Anthony Kennedy's majority opinion referenced them: *Loving v. Virginia* (1967), *Zablocki v. Redhail* (1978), *Lawrence v. Texas* (2003), and *United States v. Windsor* (2013). Interestingly, the factual settings of the first two decisions had nothing to do with gay people.

Of course, *Loving* is the poetically named case that struck down state prohibitions against interracial marriage. Mildred Jeter, an African American woman, and Richard Loving, a white man, wed in Washington, DC. When the Lovings settled in Virginia, the pair was prosecuted under two state statutes: one prohibited mixed-race couples from marrying out of state and then returning to Virginia (not unlike Wisconsin's criminal marriage-evasion law), whereas the other outright criminalized so-called miscegenation. Chief Justice Earl Warren's 1967 decision for a unanimous Supreme Court held that such interracial-marriage bans violated both the Due Process and Equal Protection clauses.

Zablocki is less well known than *Loving*, but no less interesting factually. While still in high school, Roger Redhail fathered a child in Milwaukee, Wisconsin, and was ordered in a paternity proceeding to pay monthly child support. But Redhail had no source of income as a student, and thus, his child-support arrearages mounted into thousands of dollars. More than two years later, Redhail sought a marriage license in Milwaukee, but ran afoul of a state law mandating that Wisconsin residents who were noncustodial parents had first to secure a court order before getting a marriage license. And to receive such an order, the noncustodial parent could not be in arrears on child support. The court also had to be convinced that the children at issue would not become wards of the state. Redhail, a man of modest means, was unable to overcome the statutory hurdles to marry and sued Thomas Zablocki, the clerk of Milwaukee County who had denied him a marriage license. Writing for a majority of five, Justice Thurgood Marshall cited *Loving* and *Griswold* v. *Connecticut* (1965) to declare that marriage was a fundamental federal constitutional right secured by the Equal Protection Clause. Three other justices concurred with the majority's judgment that Wisconsin's statutory impediments to marriage were unconstitutional. Only Justice William Rehnquist dissented.

Unlike *Loving* and *Zablocki*, *Lawrence* was not directly concerned with the issue of a federally protected right to marry. Rather, the 2003 decision overruled *Bowers* v. *Hardwick* (1986), which held that state criminal consensual-sodomy statutes enforced against same-sex couples in the privacy of their own homes did not violate the federal Constitution. Writing for a majority of five in *Lawrence*, Justice Kennedy relied on the Due Process Clause to determine that adult gay people have a protected liberty interest of consensual sexual expression conducted in private. Justice Sandra Day O'Connor concurred with the Court's judgment, but declined to overrule *Bowers* (in which hers was one of the five majority votes). Instead, she opted to invalidate the Texas sodomy law at issue in *Lawrence* because the statute applied only to same-sex couples. That singling out of gay people for the same behavior practiced by heterosexuals violated equal protection in her mind. Three justices (Rehnquist, Scalia, and Thomas) dissented in *Lawrence* in a scathing opinion by Scalia, in which he prophetically wrote:

Today's opinion dismantles the structure of constitutional law that has permitted a distinction to be made between heterosexual and homosexual unions, insofar as formal recognition in marriage is concerned. If moral disapprobation of homosexual conduct is "no legitimate state interest" [quoting from the majority opinion] for purposes of proscribing that conduct; and if, as the Court coos (casting aside all pretense of neutrality), "when sexuality finds overt expression in intimate conduct with another person, the conduct can be but one element in a personal bond that is more enduring"; what justification could there possibly be for denying the benefits of marriage to homosexual couples exercising "the liberty protected by the Constitution"? Surely not the encouragement of procreation, since the sterile and the elderly are allowed to marry. This case "does not involve" the issue of homosexual marriage only if one entertains the belief that principle and logic have nothing to do with the decisions of this Court. (539 U.S. at 604)

The last, and most important, precedent for *Obergefell* was *Windsor*, which did touch directly on same-sex marriage. In 1996, Congress passed, and President Bill Clinton signed, the Defense of Marriage Act. Section 3 of the statute limited federal marriage benefits to unions between one man and one woman. In 2007, a New York couple, Edith Windsor and Thea Spyer, wed in Canada; their out-of-state marriage became recognized the following year under evolving New York State law. Another year later, Spyer died, leaving her estate to Windsor. Married couples have a federal estate tax exemption that was denied to Windsor because of DOMA. As a result, she had to pay the federal government more than $350,000 in estate taxes that a similarly circumstanced surviving opposite-sex spouse would not have incurred. In another five-vote majority opinion, Justice Kennedy invalidated DOMA's Section 3 in an analysis that melded elements of both federalism, on the one hand, and Due Process and Equal Protection, on the other.

Consider this commentary which appears first in Kennedy's *Windsor* opinion:

[T]he Federal Government, through our history, has deferred to state law policy decisions with respect to domestic relations. In *De Sylva* v. *Ballentine* (1956), for example, the Court held that, "[t]o decide who is the widow or widower of a deceased author, or who are his executors or next of kin," under the Copyright Act "requires a reference to the law of the State which created those legal relationships" because "there is no federal law of domestic relations." In order to respect this principle, the federal courts, as a general rule, do not adjudicate issues of marital status even when there might otherwise be a basis for federal jurisdiction.... Federal courts will not hear divorce and custody cases even if they arise in diversity because of "the virtually exclusive primacy...of the States in the regulation of domestic relations."

The significance of state responsibilities for the definition and regulation of marriage dates to the Nation's beginning; for "when the Constitution was adopted the common understanding was that the domestic relations of husband and wife and parent and child were matters reserved to the States." *Ohio ex rel. Popovici* v. *Agler* (1930). Marriage laws vary in some respects from State to State. For example, the required minimum age is 16 in Vermont, but only 13 in New Hampshire. Likewise the permissible degree of consanguinity can vary (most States permit first cousins to marry, but a handful – such as Iowa and Washington – prohibit the practice). But these rules are in every event consistent within each State.

Against this background DOMA rejects the long established precept that the incidents, benefits, and obligations of marriage are uniform for all married couples within each State, though they may vary, subject to constitutional guarantees, from one State to the next. Despite these considerations, it is unnecessary to decide whether this federal intrusion on state power is a violation of the Constitution because it disrupts the federal balance. The State's power in defining the marital relation is of central relevance in this case quite apart from principles of federalism. Here the State's decision to give this class of persons the right to marry conferred upon them a dignity and status of immense import. When the State used its historic and essential authority to define the marital relation in this way, its role and its power in making the decision enhanced the recognition, dignity, and protection of the class in their own community. DOMA, because of its reach and extent, departs from this history and tradition of reliance on state law to define marriage....

The Federal Government uses this state-defined class for the opposite purpose – to impose restrictions and disabilities. That result requires this Court now to address whether the resulting injury and indignity are a deprivation of an essential part of the liberty protected by the Fifth Amendment. What the State of New York treats as alike the federal law deems unlike by a law designed to injure the same class the State seeks to protect.

In acting first to recognize and then to allow same-sex marriages, New York was responding "to the initiative of those who [sought] a voice in shaping the destiny of their own times." *Bond* v. *United States* (2011). These actions were without doubt a proper exercise of its sovereign authority within our federal system, all in the way that the Framers of the Constitution intended. The dynamics of state government in the federal system are to allow the formation of consensus respecting the way the members of a discrete community treat each other in their daily contact and constant interaction with each other.

The States' interest in defining and regulating the marital relation, subject to constitutional guarantees, stems from the understanding that marriage is more than a routine classification for purposes of certain statutory benefits.... By its recognition of the validity of same-sex marriages performed in other jurisdictions and then by authorizing same-sex unions and same-sex marriages, New York sought to give further protection and dignity to that bond. For same-sex couples who wished to be married, the State acted to give their lawful conduct a lawful status. This status is a far-reaching legal acknowledgment of the intimate relationship between two people, a relationship deemed by the State worthy of dignity in the community equal with all other marriages. It reflects both the community's considered perspective on the historical roots of the institution of marriage and its evolving understanding of the meaning of equality. (133 S. Ct. at 2691–93)

Consequently, this analysis suggests that the legal impediment with DOMA's Section 3 was that the federal statute undermined New York State's ability to define civil marriage as the Empire State itself saw fit. Thus, in light of Kennedy's federalism reasoning, Uncle Sam should have deferred to New York's definition of marriage to determine that Edith Windsor indeed deserved to receive the federal estate-tax exemption she claimed as a legally married surviving spouse under the law of her state of residence.

Yet the *Windsor* majority opinion did not stop there. Instead, Justice Kennedy went on to say more:

The power the Constitution grants it also restrains. And though Congress has great authority to design laws to fit its own conception of sound national policy, it cannot deny the liberty protected by the Due Process Clause of the Fifth Amendment.

What has been explained to this point should more than suffice to establish that the principal purpose and the necessary effect of this law are to demean those persons who are in a lawful same-sex marriage. This requires the Court to hold, as it now does, that DOMA is unconstitutional as a deprivation of the liberty of the person protected by the Fifth Amendment of the Constitution.

The liberty protected by the Fifth Amendment's Due Process Clause contains within it the prohibition against denying to any person the equal protection of the laws.... While the Fifth Amendment itself withdraws from Government the power to degrade or demean in the way this law does, the equal protection guarantee of the Fourteenth Amendment makes that Fifth Amendment right all the more specific and all the better understood and preserved.

The class to which DOMA directs its restrictions and restraints are those persons who are joined in same-sex marriages made lawful by the State. DOMA singles out a class of persons deemed by a State entitled to recognition and protection to enhance their own liberty. It imposes a disability on the class by refusing to acknowledge a status the State finds to be dignified and proper. DOMA instructs all federal officials, and indeed all persons with whom same-sex couples interact, including their own children, that their marriage is less worthy than the marriages of others. The federal statute is invalid, for no legitimate purpose overcomes the purpose and effect to disparage and to injure those whom the State, by its marriage laws, sought to protect in personhood and dignity. By seeking to displace this protection and treating those persons as living in marriages less respected than others, the federal statute is in violation of the Fifth Amendment. (133 S. Ct. at 2695–96)

This language in the *Windsor* majority opinion suggests that DOMA's constitutional impediment was not merely founded on a violation of federalism principles. Rather, the congressional statute's more important legal dilemma was its encroachment on rights accruing to same-sex couples under the Due Process and Equal Protection clauses of the Fourteenth Amendment, a flaw separate and apart from DOMA's degradation of federalism.

Chief Justice John Roberts' dissenting opinion attempted a preemptive strike against reading *Windsor* too broadly as a precedent:

The majority extensively chronicles DOMA's departure from the normal allocation of responsibility between State and Federal Governments, emphasizing that DOMA "rejects the long-established precept that the incidents, benefits, and obligations of marriage are uniform for all married couples within each State." But there is no such departure when one State adopts or keeps a definition of marriage that differs from that of its neighbor, for it is entirely expected that state definitions would "vary, subject to constitutional guarantees, from one State to the next." Thus, while "[t]he State's power in defining the marital relation is of central relevance" to the majority's decision to strike down DOMA here, that power will come into play on the other side of the board in future cases about the constitutionality of state marriage definitions....

We may in the future have to resolve challenges to state marriage definitions affecting same-sex couples. That issue, however, is not before us in this case.... I write only to highlight the limits of the majority's holding and reasoning today, lest its opinion be taken to resolve not only a question that I believe is not properly before us – DOMA's constitutionality – but also a question that all agree, and the Court explicitly acknowledges, is not at issue [i.e., the constitutionality of state bans on same-sex marriage]. (133 S. Ct. at 2697)

Justice Samuel Alito's dissenting opinion also hoped to limit *Windsor*'s value as a precedent:

Rather than fully embracing the arguments made by Windsor and the United States, the Court strikes down Section 3 of DOMA as a classification not properly supported by its objectives. The Court reaches this conclusion in part because it believes that Section 3 encroaches upon the States' sovereign prerogative to define marriage.... Indeed, the Court's ultimate conclusion is that DOMA falls afoul of the Fifth Amendment because it "singles out a class of persons deemed *by a State* entitled to recognition and protection to enhance their own liberty" and "imposes a disability on the class by refusing to acknowledge a status *the State finds* to be dignified and proper" (emphasis added).

To the extent that the Court takes the position that the question of same-sex marriage should be resolved primarily at the state level, I wholeheartedly agree. I hope that the Court will ultimately permit the people of each State to decide this question for themselves. Unless the Court is willing to allow this to occur, the whiffs of federalism in today's opinion of the Court will soon be scattered to the wind. (133 S. Ct. at 2719–20)

In characteristic fashion, Justice Antonin Scalia's *Windsor* dissent was far less circumspect:

In my opinion,...the view that *this* Court will take of state prohibition of same-sex marriage is indicated beyond mistaking by today's opinion. As I have said, the real rationale of today's opinion, whatever disappearing trail of its legalistic argle-bargle one chooses to follow, is that DOMA is motivated by "'bare...desire to harm'" couples in same-sex marriages. How easy it is, indeed how inevitable, to reach the same conclusion with regard to state laws denying same-sex couples marital status. Consider how easy (inevitable) it is to make the following substitutions in a passage from today's opinion:

This state law's [in place of "DOMA's"] principal effect is to identify a subset of *constitutionally protected sexual relationships* [in place of "state-sanctioned marriages"], see *Lawrence*, and make them unequal. The principal purpose is to impose inequality, not for other reasons like governmental efficiency. Responsibilities, as well as rights, enhance the dignity and integrity of the person. And *this state law* [in place of "DOMA"] contrives to deprive some couples *enjoying constitutionally protected sexual relationships* [in place of "married under the laws of their State"], but not other couples, of both rights and responsibilities.

Or try this passage:

This state law [in place of "DOMA"] tells those couples, and all the world, that their otherwise valid *relationships* [in place of "marriages"] are unworthy of *state* [in place of "federal"] recognition. This places same-sex couples in an unstable position of being in a second-tier *relationship* [in place of "marriage"]. The differentiation demeans the couple, whose moral and sexual choices the Constitution protects, see *Lawrence*,....

Or this – which does not even require alteration, except as to the invented number:

And it humiliates *thousands* [in place of "tens of thousands"] of children now being raised by same-sex couples. The law in question makes it even more difficult for the children to understand the integrity and closeness of their own family and its concord with other families in their community and in their daily lives.

Similarly transposable passages – deliberately transposable, I think – abound. In sum, that Court which finds it so horrific that Congress irrationally and hatefully robbed same-sex couples of the "personhood and dignity" which state legislatures conferred upon them, will of a certitude be similarly appalled by state legislatures' irrational and hateful failure to acknowledge that "personhood and dignity" in the first place. As far as this Court is concerned, no one should be fooled; it is just a matter of listening and waiting for the other shoe. (133 S. Ct. at 2709–10; emphasis in the original)

In short, Justice Scalia announced to the world that the Supreme Court was on the verge of striking down all state bans on same-sex marriage. Much like his *Lawrence* dissent, Scalia's *Windsor* pronouncement heralded the news that nationwide marriage equality was just around the corner. What is more, his *Windsor* opinion provided an explicit recipe for lower federal courts to follow in reaching that outcome. Whereas Roberts and Alito tried in measured manner to step the *Windsor* decision back from the precipice, Scalia picked up a bullhorn to shout that the Court had already fallen over the cliff.

So a fascinating question after June 2013 became, Whose voice would lower federal judges hear in the months and years to come?

THE LOWER FEDERAL COURTS' LOPSIDED INTERPRETATIONS OF WINDSOR

The Supreme Court's *Obergefell* majority opinion has a useful appendix listing both federal and state judicial decisions addressing same-sex marriage. The supplement reveals seven decisions from U.S. courts of appeals rendered after *Windsor*, forty-five from U.S. district courts, and three from state courts of last resort. In other words, *Windsor* prompted a torrent of mostly federal lawsuits brought by same-sex couples and their advocates against Super-DOMAs and other state marriage bans. Not only the sheer magnitude of so much litigation within less than two years of *Windsor* was remarkable but also the judicial outcomes themselves went overwhelmingly one way: in favor of marriage equality.[3]

However, tallying the actual results is a bit tricky because some of the decisions in the *Obergefell* appendix were more procedural than substantive, whereas others represented duplicate efforts by the same judge or panel of judges. Accordingly, as a methodological matter, I focus here only on the federal cases listed in the Supreme Court's addendum, at either the district- or circuit-court level, that decided, after *Windsor*, whether state prohibitions of marriage equality violated either the Due Process or Equal Protection clauses of the Fourteenth Amendment.

At the same time, I omit from the analysis multiple decisions by the same bench in different cases. For example, I include the Tenth Circuit's June 2014 ruling in *Kitchen* v. *Herbert*, but discard the same panel's *Bishop* v. *Smith* holding from July. Likewise at the district-court level, I use Ohio Judge Timothy S. Black December 2013 decision in *Obergefell* v. *Wymyslo*, but not his *Henry* v. *Himes* analysis from the following April. Furthermore, I exclude district-court rulings that implement binding circuit-court precedents, such as

---

[3] I limit my investigation here to federal cases and not those in the states, primarily because the nature of judicial selection and retention may be substantially different between the two sets of courts. Federal judges are appointed by the president for life tenure, whereas states judges, especially at the lower court level, are often elected to fixed terms of office. The nature of judicial selection and retention may affect judicial policy making (e.g., Pinello 1995).

Hamby v. *Parnell* in the Ninth Circuit and *Fisher-Borne* v. *Smith* in the Fourth. Such trial-court enforcement of unambiguous higher court doctrine does not represent independent judgment by the lower bench. I also do not include the district-court decision in *Latta* v. *Otter*, decided by a magistrate judge. Unlike federal district judges, these officials are not appointed by the president, and they serve for fixed terms. Finally, I leave out *Conde-Vidal* v. *Garcia-Padilla* because the case did not involve state law.

After thus winnowing the field, I end up with five relevant decisions by U.S. courts of appeals[4] and twenty-one from U.S. district courts.[5] Among the five circuits, four ruled in favor of civil marriage for same-sex couples. Among the federal trial judges in twenty-one states, fully twenty did so as well. Hence, lower federal courts across the country resoundingly interpreted *Windsor* – bolstered by other precedents such as *Loving* and *Lawrence* – to require findings that the Fourteenth Amendment dictated marriage equality.

What is even more extraordinary is that the Supreme Court itself ultimately let most of the lower court judgments go into effect *before* deciding the merits of the constitutional issue at the heart of all this litigation (Liptak 2014). Specifically, on October 6, 2014, the Supreme Court declined to hear state appeals from three federal circuits – the Fourth, Seventh, and Tenth – that had struck down gay-marriage prohibitions. And the next day, the Ninth Circuit issued a decision in line with the others. Consequently, the number of marriage-equality jurisdictions in the nation jumped from nineteen to thirty-five[6] within a very short time (Healy, Shear, and Eckholm 2014; "One Step Closer to Marriage Equality" 2014; Hesse 2015) – resulting in the tripling of legally married gay and lesbian pairs in the two years before *Obergefell*, as referenced earlier. In other words, the Supreme Court did not initiate a national transformation in 2015: it joined one already very much in progress.

Accordingly, explaining the lower federal-court tsunami in favor of marriage equality is really key to understanding what happened in June 2015. In fact, once the justices' inaction allowed the number of marriage-equality states

---

[4] *Kitchen* v. *Herbert* (CA10 6/25/2014); *Bostic* v. *Schaefer* (CA4 7/28/2014); *Baskin* v. *Bogan* (CA7 9/4/2014); *Latta* v. *Otter* (CA9 10/7/2014); and *DeBoer* v. *Snyder* (CA6 11/6/2014).

[5] *Kitchen* v. *Herbert* (Utah 12/20/2013); *Obergefell* v. *Wymyslo* (SD Ohio 12/23/2013); *Bishop* v. *United States ex rel. Holder* (ND Okla. 1/14/2014); *Bourke* v. *Beshear* (WD Ky. 2/11/2014); *Bostic* v. *Rainey* (ED Va. 2/13/2014); *De Leon* v. *Perry* (WD Tex. 2/26/2014); *Tanco* v. *Haslam* (MD Tenn. 3/14/2014); *DeBoer* v. *Snyder* (ED Mich. 3/21/2014); *Geiger* v. *Kitzhaber* (Ore. 5/19/2014); *Whitewood* v. *Wolf* (MD Pa. 5/20/2014); *Wolf* v. *Walker* (WD Wis. 6/6/2014); *Baskin* v. *Bogan* (SD Ind. 6/25/2014); *Burns* v. *Hickenlooper* (Colo., 7/23/2014); *Brenner* v. *Scott* (ND Fla. 8/21/2014); *Robicheaux* v. *Caldwell* (ED La. 9/3/2014); *Lawson* v. *Kelly* (WD Mo. 11/7/2014); *Jernigan* v. *Crane* (ED Ark. 11/25/2014); *Campaign for Southern Equality* v. *Bryant* (SD Miss. 11/25/2014); *Rosenbrahn* v. *Daugaard* (S. D. 1/12/2015); *Searcey* v. *Strange* (SD Ala. 1/23/2015); and *Waters* v. *Ricketts* (Neb. 3/2/2015).

[6] The sixteen states formally added to the marriage-equality column in late 2014 were Alaska, Arizona, Colorado, Idaho, Indiana, Kansas, Montana, Nevada, North Carolina, Oklahoma, South Carolina, Utah, Virginia, West Virginia, Wisconsin, and Wyoming.

nearly to double in October 2014, the outcome in *Obergefell* was preordained. The facts on the ground by mid-2015 meant that the justices could not have invalidated so many recent weddings among so many families in so many states. As an administrative matter alone, the task of dismantling tens of thousands of marriages would have been of herculean proportions. Moreover, the Court would have had to make a mortifying public admission amounting to "Oops! We were asleep at the switch in October 2014, when we let all of those gay weddings sneak through in sixteen states. Sorry! We simply weren't paying attention."

And if the High Court was indeed unprepared to upset the legal status quo in so many otherwise unwilling jurisdictions, but nonetheless wanted to uphold marriage bans in the thirteen states where they remained in effect as of 2015, the result would have amounted to constitutional law by geographic lottery: "If you live in the Fourth, Seventh, Ninth, or Tenth Circuits, you can legally marry; but if you reside in the Fifth, Sixth, Eighth, or Eleventh Circuits, you can't." Marriage roulette was not a solution that most rational judges would have found satisfactory. Thus, by the time of *Obergefell*, the Supreme Court had backed itself into a corner. There was just one empirically viable option left: to nationalize marriage equality.

So what happened with all of those lower federal judges after June 2013? As discussed earlier, Justice Kennedy's majority opinion in *Windsor* was ambiguous as a precedent. Was the decision merely a federalism-based holding that had nothing to do intrinsically with the issue of the constitutionality of state gay-marriage prohibitions (as both Chief Justice Roberts and Justice Alito argued in their *Windsor* dissents)? Or had the Court already fallen off into the deep end of the matter (as Justice Scalia vigorously maintained in both his *Lawrence* and *Windsor* dissents)?

THE IMPACTS OF GOOD FORTUNE AND POLITICAL PARTY

One element of a multipronged answer to the question of why lower federal courts so overwhelmingly backed marriage equality after *Windsor* is that, as a group in 2013 and 2014, same-sex couples were lucky. The federal lawsuits that they and their attorneys initiated after *Windsor*, and the intermediate appeals that were taken from those cases, ended up largely in the hands of judges who had been appointed to the bench by Democratic presidents. For instance, among five panels of three judges each that decided marriage-equality appeals in the U.S. Courts of Appeals for the Fourth, Sixth, Seventh, Ninth, and Tenth Circuits, nine of fifteen jurists – or 60 percent – were Democratic appointees. And among the twenty-one district court judges who initially handled those lawsuits, the component of jurists nominated by Democratic presidents was even higher: sixteen, or 76 percent. Why is this important?

My book *Gay Rights and American Law* provides the key. That investigation analyzed 398 state and federal appellate-court decisions adjudicating rights claims by lesbian and gay litigants between 1981 and 2000. The volume's concluding chapter made this observation:

Federal judges selected by Democratic presidents, compared with Republican appointees, positively determined an astonishing 40.5 percent of the probability "space" between complete success and utter failure of lesbian and gay rights claims in federal appellate courts. Among 45 federal cases in the study not influenced by controlling precedent, only 26.7 percent of 116 votes by judges nominated by Republican presidents were favorable to sexual minorities, while 60.2 percent of 83 votes by Democratic appointees supported homosexuals – a difference of 125 percent! Indeed, presidential party predicted case outcome far better than any other personal attribute [such as age, gender, race/ethnicity, or religious affiliation] of federal judges in the investigation. Pinello (2003, 151–52)

In fact, the (admittedly smaller) sample of federal judges in this survey had even more astonishing voting patterns based on the political party of the presidents who selected them. Among both the sixteen district-court and nine circuit-court judges who were Democratic appointees, *100 percent* of their votes – every last one – went in favor of marriage equality, representing a 66 percent improvement over the 1981–2000 Democratic-nominee voting record. With regard to the jurists chosen by Republican presidents, four of their six circuit votes, or 67 percent, went against the right of civil marriage for same-sex pairs, compared to just one of five trial-court decisions, or 20 percent. In total, six of eleven Republican appointees, or 55 percent, embraced marriage equality. Hence, although the gap established by presidential party was not as dramatic in 2013–14 – at 82 percent – as it was in the last two decades of the twentieth century (125 percent), the disparity, nonetheless, was still substantial.

The reasons why Democratic judicial appointees voted in lockstep to back a right of same-sex couples to civil marriage may be multifaceted and complicated, but a simple, if superficial, explanation is that, by 2013, the national Democratic political establishment had fully and publicly incorporated marriage equality into its belief system. On May 6, 2012, for example, Vice President Joe Biden endorsed gay marriage on the nationally televised NBC News program *Meet the Press*. Less than a week later, President Barack Obama followed Biden's lead on an ABC News show, making him the first sitting president to lend support to the marriage movement. The same pattern continued with most Democratic members of Congress. Consequently, by June 2013, the national Democratic Party was completely in the marriage-equality camp, even though that had not at all been the case as recently as the 2008 national elections. And the political and social forces – summarized by the Gallup organization's July 2013 polling data showing 54 percent of Americans backed civil marriage for lesbian and gay pairs – that prompted such an overpowering partisan transformation more than likely also influenced Democratic judicial appointees in the same way. Occam's razor suggests such an account to be the sound one.

Consider a similar shift in the attitudes of Republican appointees to the federal bench. As quoted earlier, between 1981 and 2000, just 26.7 percent of their votes were favorable to sexual minorities. By 2013–14, that proportion had more than doubled to 55 percent. Therefore, few federal jurists were wholly immune to the tide of history.

Yet, good fortune still had a vital role to play. Based on my 2003 findings regarding the importance of partisanship to federal judicial votes, one could have expected a five-to-four outcome in the Supreme Court *against* finding a constitutional right for same-sex couples to marry. Indeed, eight of the nine justices in both *Windsor* and *Obergefell* voted in the direction the party of their appointing president would have predicted. Anthony Kennedy (selected by Republican president Ronald Reagan) was the one crucial exception to the rule. For reasons unique to him, Justice Kennedy has been a consistent supporter of LGBT rights, authoring majority opinions favoring sexual minorities in *Romer v. Evans* (1996), *Lawrence*, *Windsor*, and *Obergefell*.

THE IMPORTANCE OF PRECEDENT

Another significant component of a multifaceted answer to the question of why lower federal courts so wholeheartedly sanctioned marriage equality after *Windsor* is that the precedents were there on which to build a sound doctrinal foundation for district and circuit holdings striking down state marriage bans. For instance, consider this language by Terence C. Kern, the third federal trial judge among the twenty-one in the sample to interpret (in January 2014) the meaning of *Windsor*:

Windsor supports [the State of Oklahoma]'s position [defending its Super-DOMA] because it engages in a lengthy discussion of states' authority to define and regulate marriage, which can be construed as a yellow light cautioning against *Windsor*'s extension to similar state definitions. See [Justice Kennedy's majority opinion] explaining that state marriage laws vary between states and discussing states' interest in "defining and regulating the marital relation." Again, however, the "yellow light" argument has its limitations. In discussing this traditional state authority over marriage, the Supreme Court repeatedly used the disclaimer "subject to constitutional guarantees" [and cites] *Loving v. Virginia* (holding that Virginia's prohibition of interracial marriage violated equal protection and substantive due [process] rights). *A citation to* Loving *is a disclaimer of enormous proportion.* Arguably, the "state rights" portion of the *Windsor* decision stands for the unremarkable proposition that a state has broad authority to regulate marriage, so long as it does not violate its citizens' federal constitutional rights. (*Bishop v. United States ex rel. Holder*, 962 F. Supp. 2d at 1278–79; emphasis added)

Accentuating the centrality of *Loving* to the right of same-sex couples to marry, nine district and three circuit judges also pointed in their written opinions to this language from the Supreme Court's 1978 *Zablocki* precedent: "Although *Loving* arose in the context of racial discrimination, prior and subsequent decisions of this Court confirm that the right to marry is of fundamental importance for all individuals" (434 U.S. at 384).

Of at least equal importance, references to Justice Kennedy's majority opinions in *Lawrence* and *Windsor* saturated lower federal-court rulings after June 2013. Virtually all the judicial writings in the post-*Windsor* sample of twenty-one district- and five circuit-court decisions invoked these landmark precedents as binding authority.

However, that observation does not explain exactly *how Lawrence* and *Windsor* bound lower federal courts in June 2013 with regard to their future disposition of gay and lesbian pairs' claims that Super-DOMAs and other state marriage restrictions violated the Fourteenth Amendment. As intimated earlier, Justice Kennedy's majority opinions were not paragons of doctrinal clarity.

Accordingly, I suggest that lower federal judges in substantial measure invoked other guideposts to discern the central meanings of *Lawrence* and *Windsor*.

JUSTICE SCALIA AS A DOUBLE AGENT

Dissenting opinions as such have no binding value as precedents in future disputes on related legal questions. After all, dissents represent the losing side in adjudication, and taking the time and energy to write explanations as to why vanquished constitutional and legal postures should have prevailed seems a pointless undertaking. Yet, as the four referenced *Lawrence* and *Windsor* dissents suggest, judges frequently upend such logic by publicly objecting in lengthy written form. As well, those four dissents manifest the most important aim of dissent writing: influencing future judicial action. In fact, the lower federal-court decisions that followed *Windsor* provide a natural experiment to gauge how effectively these dissenters' strategic objectives were achieved. And the findings are remarkable.

I searched the judicial opinions among the five circuit-court and twenty-one district-court decisions in the condensed sample from the *Obergefell* appendix to find out how frequently lower federal judges referenced either Justice Scalia's *Lawrence* dissent or the *Windsor* dissents of Justices Alito and Scalia and Chief Justice Roberts. I did so because dissenting opinions can help clarify what doctrinal or policy goals court majorities intended to achieve.

Among the twenty federal trial-court dispositions that found a marriage right for same-sex couples, thirteen – or 65 percent – referenced one or both of the Scalia dissents in *Lawrence* and *Windsor*. In contrast, just three decisions (or 15 percent) mentioned Chief Justice Roberts' *Windsor* dissent, whereas merely two (or 10 percent) cited Justice Alito's *Windsor* dissent. Among the five circuit-court resolutions, four of five opinions (whether for the majority or in dissent) supporting marriage equality referred to a Scalia dissent. That is 80 percent. In contrast, three (or 60 percent) of those same writings mentioned Alito's dissent, and only one (or 20 percent) the Roberts' dissent. In total, seventeen among twenty-five opinions, or *68 percent*, in favor of gay marriage found what Justice Scalia had to say to be useful, whereas just five (or 20 percent) turned to Justice Alito's words for assistance and four (or 16 percent) to the chief justice's language. In short, lower federal judges who concluded that *Lawrence* and/or *Windsor* mandated marriage equality consulted – *by a factor of three- to four-fold* – Scalia's interpretations of those majority opinions over the renditions of either Alito or Roberts.

On the flip side of the coin, with regard to the judicial outcomes against marriage equality, none of the pool of four pertinent opinions (one at the district level and the three others by circuit judges, again whether writing for the majority or in dissent) referenced Scalia, whereas two (or 50 percent) brought up Alito's *Windsor* dissent and one (or 25 percent) cited the chief justice's opinion. Thus, no lower court judge who reasoned that neither *Lawrence* nor *Windsor* demanded the recognition of a federal right of same-sex pairs to civil marriage believed that what Justice Scalia said was helpful to understanding those precedents.

Beyond these statistics, I also note what the lower court judges wrote regarding Scalia's influence on their reasoning. For example, in *Kitchen* v. *Herbert* (2013), the very first district-court ruling after *Windsor* (a mere six months later) to address the constitutionality of a state gay-marriage ban (Utah's Super-DOMA), Judge Robert J. Shelby referenced both Scalia dissents:

The Constitution's protection of the individual rights of gay and lesbian citizens is equally dispositive whether this protection requires a court to respect a state law, as in *Windsor*, or strike down a state law, as the Plaintiffs ask the court to do here. In his dissenting opinion, the Honorable Antonin Scalia recognized that this result was the logical outcome of the Court's ruling in *Windsor*:

> In my opinion, however, the view that this Court will take of state prohibition of same-sex marriage is indicated beyond mistaking by today's opinion. As I have said, the real rationale of today's opinion ... is that DOMA is motivated by "bare ... desire to harm" couples in same-sex marriages. How easy it is, indeed how inevitable, to reach the same conclusion with regard to state laws denying same-sex couples marital status.

The court agrees with Justice Scalia's interpretation of *Windsor* and finds that the important federalism concerns at issue here are nevertheless insufficient to save a state-law prohibition that denies the Plaintiffs their rights to due process and equal protection under the law. (961 F. Supp. 2d at 1194)

...

The court's holding is supported, even required, by the Supreme Court's recent opinion concerning the scope of protection that the Fourteenth Amendment provides to gay and lesbian citizens. In *Lawrence* v. *Texas*, the Court overruled its previous decision in *Bowers* v. *Hardwick* (1986), and held that the Due Process Clause protected an individual's right to have sexual relations with a partner of the same sex. The Court ruled: "The Texas [sodomy] statute furthers no legitimate state interest which can justify its intrusion into the personal and private life of the individual." While the Court stated that its opinion did not address "whether the government must give formal recognition to any relationship that homosexual persons seek to enter," the Court confirmed that "our laws and tradition afford constitutional protection to personal decisions relating to marriage, procreation, contraception, family relationships, child rearing, and education" and held that "[p]ersons in a homosexual relationship may seek autonomy for these purposes, just as heterosexual persons do." The court therefore agrees with the portion of Justice Scalia's dissenting opinion in *Lawrence* in which Justice Scalia stated that the Court's reasoning logically extends to protect an individual's right to marry a person of the same sex:

> Today's opinion dismantles the structure of constitutional law that has permitted a distinction to be made between heterosexual and homosexual unions, insofar as formal recognition in marriage is concerned. If moral disapprobation of homosexual conduct is "no legitimate state interest" for purposes of proscribing that conduct,... what justification could there possibly be for denying the benefits of marriage to homosexual couples exercising "the liberty protected by the Constitution"? (961 F. Supp. 2d at 1204)

...

The traditional view of marriage has in the past included certain views about race and gender roles that were insufficient to uphold laws based on these views. See *Lawrence* v. *Texas* (2003) ("[N]either history nor tradition could save a law prohibiting miscegenation from constitutional attack"); *Nevada Dep't of Human Res.* v. *Hibbs* (2003) (finding that government action based on stereotypes about women's greater suitability or inclination to assume primary childcare responsibility was unconstitutional). And, as Justice Scalia has noted in dissent, "'preserving the traditional institution of marriage' is just a kinder way of describing the State's moral disapproval of same-sex couples." *Lawrence* (Scalia, J., dissenting). (961 F. Supp. 2d at 1213–14)

...

In contrast to the State's speculative concerns, the harm experienced by same-sex couples in Utah as a result of their inability to marry is undisputed. To apply the Supreme Court's reasoning in *Windsor*, Amendment 3 "tells those couples, and all the world, that their otherwise valid [relationships] are unworthy of [state] recognition. This places same-sex couples in an unstable position of being in a second-tier [relationship]. The differentiation demeans the couple, whose moral and sexual choices the Constitution protects." *Windsor*; see also Scalia, J., dissenting (suggesting that the majority's reasoning could be applied to the state-law context in precisely this way). (961 F. Supp. 2d at 1214–15)

Obergefell v. *Wymyslo* (2013) was the second federal-district-court decision after *Windsor* and was rendered just three days after *Kitchen* in Utah. Derailing Ohio's Issue 1, Judge Timothy S. Black also relied on what Justice Scalia said in dissent:

This conclusion flows from the *Windsor* decision of the United States Supreme Court this past summer, which held that the federal government cannot refuse to recognize a valid same-sex marriage. And now it is just as Justice Scalia predicted – the lower courts are applying the Supreme Court's decision, as they must, and the question is presented whether a state can do what the federal government cannot – i.e., discriminate against same-sex couples ... simply because the majority of the voters don't like homosexuality (or at least didn't in 2004). Under the Constitution of the United States, the answer is no ....

In a vigorous dissent to the *Windsor* ruling, Justice Scalia predicted that the question whether states could refuse to recognize other states' same-sex marriages would come quickly, and that the majority's opinion spelled defeat for any state's refusal to recognize same-sex marriages authorized by a co-equal state. As Justice Scalia predicted: "no one should be fooled [by this decision] ... the majority arms well any challenger to a state law restricting marriage to its traditional definition ... it's just a matter of listening and waiting for the other shoe [to drop]." *Windsor* (Scalia, J., dissenting). (962 F. Supp. 2d at 973–74)

The third district-court decision after *Windsor* was *Bishop* v. *United States ex rel. Holder* (2014), submitted less than a month after *Kitchen* and *Obergefell*. Upending Oklahoma's Super-DOMA, Judge Kern also depended on the Scalia dissents in *Lawrence* and *Windsor*. What is more, he even referred to a Scalia oral-argument question:

During oral arguments [on March 26, 2013] in *Hollingsworth* [v. *Perry* (2013)], Justice Scalia asked Mr. Theodore Olson, counsel for the opponents of [California's] Proposition 8, when it became unconstitutional "to exclude homosexual couples from marriage." Mr. Olson responded with the rhetorical question of when did it become unconstitutional "to prohibit interracial marriage" or "assign children to separate schools." As demonstrated by Mr. Olson's response, the mere fact that an exclusion has occurred in the past (without constitutional problem) does not mean that such exclusion is constitutional when challenged at a particular moment in history. This Court has an obligation to consider whether an exclusion, although historical, violates the constitutional rights of Oklahoma citizens. (962 F. Supp. at 1291)

In the first appellate ruling after *Windsor*, the Tenth Circuit, in *Kitchen* v. *Herbert* (2014), continued the trend of looking to Justice Scalia in dissent for guidance:

Instead of explaining why same-sex marriage qua same-sex marriage is undesirable, each of the appellants' justifications rests fundamentally on a sleight of hand in which same-sex marriage is used as a proxy for a different characteristic shared by both same-sex and some opposite-sex couples. Same-sex marriage must be banned, appellants argue, because same-sex couples are not naturally procreative. But the state permits many other types of non-procreative couples to wed. See *Lawrence* (Scalia, J., dissenting) ("[W]hat justification could there possibly be for denying the benefits of marriage to homosexual couples ... ? Surely not the encouragement of procreation, since the sterile and the elderly are allowed to marry."). (755 F. 3d at 1220)

I could single out many more post-*Windsor* lower court references to the Scalia dissents in *Lawrence* and *Windsor*, but continuing to do so would be tedious and redundant. Suffice it that more than two-thirds of all such decisions invoked his authority.

The federal judiciary in the trenches after *Windsor* also found the dissents by Chief Justice Roberts and Justice Alito far less convincing. Indeed, the only prevailing opinion that the chief justice's federalism argument unambiguously influenced was in *Robicheaux v. Caldwell* (2014), where Judge Martin L. C. Feldman upheld Louisiana's Super-DOMA. Yet not even the majority opinion in *DeBoer v. Snyder* (2014), the one circuit-court holding to vindicate Super-DOMAs (Michigan's Proposal 2 and Ohio's Issue 1), mentioned either Roberts or Alito by name.

Accordingly, the outsized power of Antonin Scalia's dissenting opinions to persuade judges in future same-sex-marriage cases is patent – but just not in the policy direction he would have liked.

Or maybe he *did* approve of their outcomes. Because a conspiracy theorist could make a persuasive argument that, had the national leadership of the U.S. LGBT movement been able to place a mole on the Supreme Court, such a double agent would have been hard pressed to be more successful than Justice Scalia in securing marriage equality nationwide.

In August 2005, I published an essay on my personal website (www .danpinello.com) that was titled "Is Supreme Court Justice Antonin Scalia a Homophobe?" The work was an empirical analysis of the linguistic references that Justice Scalia had made to gay people in his opinions as of that date. I let readers decide for themselves what the answer to the question in the essay's title was.[7]

Yet in light of this chapter's empirical investigation, I believe the response to my earlier query is now unequivocal: Antonin Scalia was one of the best judicial friends the American gay community has ever had. Frankly, the only other Republican appointee on the high court who was a better advocate for marriage equality than Scalia was, of course, Anthony Kennedy.

But I jest. In truth, legal historians will never count Antonin Scalia among the Supreme Court's most effective strategic actors. Quite the contrary occurred in the realm of LGBT civil rights, where his egocentric, scorched-earth dissent style utterly backfired.

THE ALTERNATIVE TO JUDICIAL ACTION: THE ROBERTS-SCALIA-ALITO THESIS OF WAITING, AND WAITING, AND WAITING FOR THE DEMOCRATIC PROCESS

Justice Scalia's *Windsor* dissent ends with this language:

By formally declaring anyone opposed to same-sex marriage an enemy of human decency, the majority arms well every challenger to a state law restricting marriage to its traditional definition. Henceforth those challengers will lead with this Court's declaration that there is "no legitimate purpose" served by such a law, and will claim that

---

7 See also Posner and Segall (2015).

the traditional definition has "the purpose and effect to disparage and to injure" the "personhood and dignity" of same-sex couples. The majority's limiting assurance will be meaningless in the face of language like that, as the majority well knows. That is why the language is there. The result will be a judicial distortion of our society's debate over marriage – a debate that can seem in need of our clumsy "help" only to a member of this institution.

As to that debate: Few public controversies touch an institution so central to the lives of so many, and few inspire such attendant passion by good people on all sides. Few public controversies will ever demonstrate so vividly the beauty of what our Framers gave us, a gift the Court pawns today to buy its stolen moment in the spotlight: a system of government that permits us to rule *ourselves*. Since DOMA's passage, citizens on all sides of the question have seen victories and they have seen defeats. There have been plebiscites, legislation, persuasion, and loud voices – in other words, democracy. Victories in one place for some are offset by victories in other places for others. Even in a *single State*, the question has come out differently on different occasions.

In the majority's telling, this story is black-and-white: Hate your neighbor or come along with us. The truth is more complicated. It is hard to admit that one's political opponents are not monsters, especially in a struggle like this one, and the challenge in the end proves more than today's Court can handle. Too bad. A reminder that disagreement over something so fundamental as marriage can still be politically legitimate would have been a fit task for what in earlier times was called the judicial temperament. We might have covered ourselves with honor today, by promising all sides of this debate that it was theirs to settle and that we would respect their resolution. We might have let the People decide.

But that the majority will not do. Some will rejoice in today's decision, and some will despair at it; that is the nature of a controversy that matters so much to so many. But the Court has cheated both sides, robbing the winners of an honest victory, and the losers of the peace that comes from a fair defeat. We owed both of them better. (133 S. Ct. at 2710–11; emphasis in the original)

These are powerful words, evoking a democratic process that is messy but that ultimately sorts out civil-rights issues for minority citizens with fairness and decency. In fact, earlier in the dissent, Scalia pointed out that, seventeen years after Congress passed the 1993 "Don't Ask, Don't Tell" policy preventing gay and lesbian service members from serving openly in the military, Congress itself repealed the antigay law. Hence, same-sex couples should be patient for the same national political process to prompt a similar congressional revision regarding federal recognition of gay marriages that home states had sanctioned.

The political context that framed Justice Scalia's *Windsor* dissent is important to understand. When Barack Obama was inaugurated as president in January 2009, Democrats controlled both houses of Congress. For part of that congressional session, they even had a filibuster-proof super-majority in the Senate. So the first two years of the Obama presidency were productive, with the Congress and president working together to pass significant pieces of legislation such as the Affordable Care Act. And the congressional repeal of "Don't

Ask, Don't Tell" occurred in December 2010, at the end of a lame-duck session of the still Democrat-controlled legislature.

But in the November 2010 midterm elections, everything changed. Congressional Democrats suffered massive defeats, with net losses to Republicans of six seats in the Senate and sixty-three in the House. The GOP also gained nearly 700 seats in state legislative races, resulting in Republicans controlling twenty-six state legislatures, compared to fifteen for Democrats. What is more, the GOP took charge of governorships in twenty-nine states.

Indeed, the Democrats' losses at the state level were far greater because after the 2010 U.S. Census, Republicans handled legislative redistricting for both state and congressional offices in many more states than did Democrats. So the GOP perpetrated substantially more legislative gerrymanders than its rival. As a result, Republicans would likely maintain majorities in the U.S. House of Representatives for the twelve years between January 2011 and January 2023, when the opportunity for a less Republican-fabricated body was next available, after the 2020 Census. For example, in the first national elections after the redistricting of 2011 and 2012, Democratic candidates cumulatively won at least 50.5 percent of the popular vote versus their Republican rivals in November 2012, but obtained just 46 percent of House seats, leaving the GOP with a thirty-three-seat margin in the chamber. Thus, to secure a simple majority of seats, Democrats would have to win a countrywide popular majority in the range of at least 54 percent to overcome the built-in Republican-gerrymandered advantage. But such electoral outcomes rarely occur. In 2008, for instance, Democratic House candidates received 53 percent of the national vote. Yet that was a time of significant Democratic advantage. The country was then reeling from the Great Recession, which blighted the outgoing Republican administration of George W. Bush and catapulted Barack Obama to a 68-percent victory in the Electoral College. Such favorable national opportunities for one party happen only infrequently in American politics.

In any event, should the Supreme Court have reached the result in *Windsor* that Justice Scalia advocated, the prospect of a Republican-controlled House of Representatives subsequently voting to repeal DOMA was virtually nonexistent (cf. Innis 2015).[8] After all, the 2012 Republican Platform encapsulated the enduring GOP policy position on civil marriage for same-sex couples:

We reaffirm our support for a Constitutional amendment defining marriage as the union of one man and one woman. We applaud the citizens of the majority of States which have enshrined in their constitutions the traditional concept of marriage, and we support the campaigns underway in several other States to do so.

Hence, the first conceivable political opportunity for Congress itself to countermand DOMA would have been in 2023 – a full decade after *Windsor* – and

---

[8] Neither was the Republican-controlled House of Representatives inclined to ban sexual-orientation discrimination in the workplace (Bobic 2013).

even then there would be no guarantee of a successful repeal. So Scalia's 2013 entreaty for legally married lesbian and gay couples and their families to be compliant and uncomplaining while the national democratic process worked its way through presumed all such families had the patience of saints.

Two years later, the same blind faith in benign political processes that in the end treat minority groups fairly and equally – but this time at the state level – reemerged in the *Obergefell* dissents. Chief Justice John Roberts had this to say:

Today,...the Court takes the extraordinary step of ordering every State to license and recognize same-sex marriage. Many people will rejoice at this decision, and I begrudge none their celebration. But for those who believe in a government of laws, not of men, the majority's approach is deeply disheartening. Supporters of same-sex marriage have achieved considerable success persuading their fellow citizens – through the democratic process – to adopt their view. That ends today. Five lawyers have closed the debate and enacted their own vision of marriage as a matter of constitutional law. Stealing this issue from the people will for many cast a cloud over same-sex marriage, making a dramatic social change that much more difficult to accept.
...

Understand well what this dissent is about: It is not about whether, in my judgment, the institution of marriage should be changed to include same-sex couples. It is instead about whether, in our democratic republic, that decision should rest with the people acting through their elected representatives, or with five lawyers who happen to hold commissions authorizing them to resolve legal disputes according to law. The Constitution leaves no doubt about the answer. (192 L. Ed. 2d at 639–40)
...

Over the last few years, public opinion on marriage has shifted rapidly. In 2009, the legislatures of Vermont, New Hampshire, and the District of Columbia became the first in the Nation to enact laws that revised the definition of marriage to include same-sex couples, while also providing accommodations for religious believers. In 2011, the New York Legislature enacted a similar law. In 2012, voters in Maine did the same, reversing the result of a referendum just three years earlier in which they had upheld the traditional definition of marriage.

In all, voters and legislators in eleven States and the District of Columbia have changed their definitions of marriage to include same-sex couples. The highest courts of five States have decreed that same result under their own Constitutions. The remainder of the States retain the traditional definition of marriage. (192 L. Ed. 2d at 643)
...

Here and abroad, people are in the midst of a serious and thoughtful public debate on the issue of same-sex marriage. They see voters carefully considering same-sex marriage, casting ballots in favor or opposed, and sometimes changing their minds. They see political leaders similarly reexamining their positions, and either reversing course or explaining adherence to old convictions confirmed anew. They see governments and businesses modifying policies and practices with respect to same-sex couples, and participating actively in the civic discourse. They see countries overseas democratically accepting profound social change, or declining to do so. This deliberative process is making people take seriously questions that they may not have even regarded as questions before.

When decisions are reached through democratic means, some people will inevitably be disappointed with the results. But those whose views do not prevail at least know that they have had their say, and accordingly are – in the tradition of our political culture – reconciled to the result of a fair and honest debate. In addition, they can gear up to raise the issue later, hoping to persuade enough on the winning side to think again....

But today the Court puts a stop to all that. By deciding this question under the Constitution, the Court removes it from the realm of democratic decision. There will be consequences to shutting down the political process on an issue of such profound public significance. Closing debate tends to close minds. People denied a voice are less likely to accept the ruling of a court on an issue that does not seem to be the sort of thing courts usually decide. As a thoughtful commentator observed about another issue, "The political process was moving..., not swiftly enough for advocates of quick, complete change, but majoritarian institutions were listening and acting. Heavy-handed judicial intervention was difficult to justify and appears to have provoked, not resolved, conflict." Ginsburg, "Some Thoughts on Autonomy and Equality in Relation to *Roe v. Wade*" (1985). Indeed, however heartened the proponents of same-sex marriage might be on this day, it is worth acknowledging what they have lost, and lost forever: the opportunity to win the true acceptance that comes from persuading their fellow citizens of the justice of their cause. And they lose this just when the winds of change were freshening at their backs. (192 L. Ed. 2d at 653–54)

Justice Scalia's *Obergefell* dissent added this to the matter:

Until the courts put a stop to it, public debate over same-sex marriage displayed American democracy at its best. Individuals on both sides of the issue passionately, but respectfully, attempted to persuade their fellow citizens to accept their views. Americans considered the arguments and put the question to a vote. The electorates of 11 States, either directly or through their representatives, chose to expand the traditional definition of marriage. Many more decided not to. Win or lose, advocates for both sides continued pressing their cases, secure in the knowledge that an electoral loss can be negated by a later electoral win. That is exactly how our system of government is supposed to work.
...

We have no basis for striking down a practice that is not expressly prohibited by the Fourteenth Amendment's text, and that bears the endorsement of a long tradition of open, widespread, and unchallenged use dating back to the Amendment's ratification. Since there is no doubt whatever that the People never decided to prohibit the limitation of marriage to opposite-sex couples, the public debate over same-sex marriage must be allowed to continue. (192 L. Ed. 2d at 656–57)

Justice Samuel Alito's dissents in *Windsor* and *Obergefell* made similar democratic-process arguments. I do not quote from them here in the interest of avoiding repetition, because the excerpts from the Roberts and Scalia opinions provide sufficient indication of Alito's similar sentiments.

As a response to these let-the-democratic-political-process-play-out-in-the-states entreaties, I offer Michigan as a case study. Chapter 1 discloses that, among the six Super-DOMAs in this study, Proposal 2 in the Wolverine State, along with Wisconsin's Referendum 1, received the smallest popular statewide majorities: 59 percent. Yet the Michigan vote was in 2004, while the Badger

State referendum occurred two years later. Thus, since the *Obergefell* dissenters intimated that American public opinion was moving steadily in support of recognizing same-sex marriages, the proportion of Michiganders in favor of Proposal 2 should have shrunk by the time 59 percent of Wisconsinites passed Referendum 1 in 2006. In other words, Michigan ought to be the one state among the six in this investigation demonstrating most clearly the effects of the democratic process that Roberts, Scalia, and Alito invoked in their dissents.

There is no doubt that attitudes did shift in Michigan. According to an October 2004 poll by the Glengariff Group of Chicago that was commissioned by the *Detroit Free Press*, just 24 percent of Michiganders then supported civil marriage for same-sex couples, while 42 percent backed legal recognition of civil unions. As shown in Chapter 1, a June 2009 poll by the same organization found that 63.7 percent of Michiganders approved of civil unions for same-sex couples. Moreover, 57.5 percent of respondents in the Wolverine State backed adoption rights for gay people; 65.5 percent supported domestic-partner benefits for government employees; and 70.9 percent were in favor of inheritance rights for same-sex partners. Glengariff pollster Richard Czuba described the four-and-a-half-year shift in Michigan public opinion on gay rights issues as "seismic" and said that the opinion change "was evident in almost every demographic group, including self-identified Republicans" (Bell 2009). Presumably, this public-opinion trend so favorable to gay and lesbian couples in the Wolverine State continued to strengthen well after 2009.

According to the Roberts-Scalia-Alito theory, therefore, the Michigan democratic process should have surely reflected such dramatic changes in public opinion in how Wolverine State law treated same-sex pairs and their families. After all, Michigan is one of the four states within the Sixth Federal Circuit, from which the *Obergefell* appeals were taken to the Supreme Court. Proposal 2 was in effect for just over a decade, having been adopted in November 2004 and invalidated in June 2015. Given that public opinion in that time evolved so steadily and rapidly against the policy embodied by the constitutional amendment, what occurred in the Wolverine State during those ten years to ameliorate the Super-DOMA's deleterious effects on lesbian and gay pairs and their children? No doubt, the state legislature and governor must have heeded – as Chief Justice Roberts and Justices Scalia and Alito suggested elected representatives indubitably do – the striking change in public opinion throughout Michigan and done something to improve the circumstances of such families.

After the Michigan Supreme Court's 2008 *National Pride at Work* decision (discussed in Chapter 2), some public employers in the Wolverine State revised their employee benefit plans to introduce a status of "Other Qualified Adult." This change allowed employees to designate someone (regardless of gender) with whom they lived and shared their finances to receive benefits. Moreover, in January 2011, the Michigan Civil Service Commission extended health care benefits to certain adult co-residents of state employees. In response to these developments, the Republican-controlled Michigan legislature passed, and Republican governor Richard Snyder signed (on December 22, 2011), the

Public Employee Domestic Partner Benefit Restriction Act, which prohibited state government employers from continuing to furnish health care and other fringe benefits to their employees' domestic partners (*Bassett v. Snyder* 2014). Thus, more than two years after nearly two-thirds of Michigan poll respondents registered their approval of domestic-partner benefits for government employees, their elected representatives did not act to sanction such benefits, but instead voted to deny them.

An October 2014 statewide poll of Michigan voters by EPIC-MRA, a survey research firm in Lansing (the state capital), found that 47 percent of respondents approved of same-sex marriage, and 47 percent did not (Oosting 2014). Accordingly, in the ten years since Proposal 2 was adopted, the percentage of Michiganders supporting gay marriage improved by at least six points (from the 41 percent who opposed the 2004 initiative), while opposition to same-sex weddings decreased by twelve points (from the 59 percent who voted in favor of Prop 2). In short, the eighteen-point margin in 2004 between the two perspectives shrank to zero in a decade. A fair-minded observer can only interpret such an opinion shift as a significant boost in support for the LGBT community in the Wolverine State. Plus, recall the Glengariff poll found back in 2009 that 57.5 percent of Michigan respondents were in favor of adoption rights for gay people.

Nonetheless, in June 2015, the Michigan legislature passed, and Governor Snyder signed, laws permitting child-placement agencies to refuse state referrals for the placement of children in homes if that service conflicted with agencies' sincerely held religious beliefs as stated in written policy. The *Detroit Free Press* Editorial Board and LGBT advocates viewed the Wolverine State action as designed to prevent same-sex couples from adopting children ("Anti-Gay Adoption Bill Another Shameful Moment for Michigan" 2015; Johnson 2015a).

In short, although public attitudes toward same-sex relationships dramatically improved after the adoption of Michigan's Super-DOMA, that seismic opinion shift was never manifested on the ground in the democratic political process there. Rather, the much more hostile climate of 2004, memorialized in Proposal 2, controlled how gay and lesbian couples were treated by Wolverine State lawmakers until *Obergefell v. Hodges* forced a political sea change. Indeed, if there had been an award for the "Super-DOMA State Most Aggressively Opposed to the Civil Rights of Same-Sex Couples and Their Families," Michigan would have been a fierce competitor for the prize. All three branches of the Wolverine State government – the legislature, the governor, and the supreme court – demonstrated consistent and overt hostility to the legal and social interests of lesbian and gay Michiganders and their kids.[9]

---

[9] Governor Snyder's implacable hostility to LGBT rights was epitomized when, in April 2015, he successfully persuaded a federal district judge in Michigan not to recognize the 2013 New York marriage of an East Grand Rapids couple where one of the partners was fighting terminal brain cancer and might not have lived long enough to benefit from the Supreme Court's *Obergefell* decision, anticipated to be rendered more than two months later (Livengood 2015).

Hence, the state most likely among the six in the study to bolster the Roberts-Scalia-Alito let-the-democratic-political-process-play-out-in-the-states thesis failed to furnish a shred of evidence that same-sex couples' rejection of the litigation option would eventually have been rewarded in a fair and honest political debate producing positive outcomes for such families. Moreover, in Ohio, where the 2004 majority of 62 percent for Issue 1 was just three percentage points higher than for Proposal 2 in Michigan the same year, leading gay rights groups opposed revisiting a Buckeye State gay-marriage ballot measure in 2014 because Ohioans still remained too closely divided on the issue to guarantee a victory for marriage equality (Sanner 2014). And if such lamentable results occurred where only three-fifths of voters approved Super-DOMAs, what hope for political (as opposed to judicial) redemption could there possibly have been for gay and lesbian pairs in places like Georgia and Texas, where 76 percent voted in favor of their amendments? Or Louisiana where 78 percent backed a Super-DOMA? Or Mississippi where 86 percent approved a Mini-DOMA?[10]

In 2010, Jeff Graham, executive director of Georgia Equality and one of the most knowledgeable political advocates for the Peach State's LGBT community, shared his assessment of the probability for same-sex relationship recognition in Georgia:

I think the challenge for us going forward is: How do we build the political support so that the politics can catch up to the public opinion? So as long as we can continue to increase public-opinion support, that makes it safer for the relationships that do exist not to have a legal challenge come forward, since it would just be considered untenable then. And although I do feel we're getting near that place, we're not there yet. But I could see that easily happening within the next four or five years here in Georgia.

We had two or three legislative sessions in a row where the issue of legislation hurting LGBT folks who wish to adopt or foster children had to be killed in committee through some really good friends who didn't want to take public credit for it at all, leaning on lawmakers and saying, "We cannot do this." Then in the last legislative session, when we thought those bills would come up again, they didn't. And this session, we're not hearing anyone talking about it.

So I feel we're slowly inching our way out of the scary part of the woods. And it gives me great hope for the future. But we've still obviously got a lot of work ahead of us here in Georgia before we can really look at making challenges to the constitutional amendment or even pushing in a serious way the issue of civil unions. Now we're kind of stuck in the limbo of domestic-partner benefits here in Georgia, at least for the foreseeable future.

Jason Cecil, a perennial officer of Georgia Stonewall Democrats, had a far less sanguine prognosis:

I don't think Georgia will ever willingly repeal Question 1. Good luck in getting so many legislators to do that, let alone winning the popular vote.

---

[10] See also Lax and Phillips (2009); cf. Innis (2015).

The only way Georgia will ever recognize same-sex marriage is if it's done through the federal system. That's the only way it will ever happen here.[11]

OTHER DIFFICULTIES WITH THE ROBERTS-SCALIA-ALITO DEMOCRATIC-PROCESS THESIS

At least two other major problems are apparent with the claims by Chief Justice Roberts and Justices Scalia and Alito that the majority justices in *Windsor* and *Obergefell* wrongfully frustrated the political process in the nation and states. The first arises in this paragraph from the chief justice:

In all, voters and legislators in eleven States and the District of Columbia have changed their definitions of marriage to include same-sex couples. The highest courts of five States have decreed that same result under their own Constitutions. The remainder of the States retain the traditional definition of marriage. (192 L. Ed. 2d at 643)

The second sentence of this quotation observes matter of factly that five state courts of last resort, relying on their own state constitutions, redefined civil marriage to include lesbian and gay pairs. Roberts' paragraph is prosaic and appears to evaluate what transpired in the first two sentences on equal terms: Some state legislatures changed the definition of marriage, and so did some state courts. Nothing out of the ordinary there.

Yet in terms of political process, the judges on those five state courts of last resort acted in exactly the same way the *Obergefell* majority did. They shut down democratic debate and deliberation over same-sex marriage in their respective jurisdictions. Why did the chief justice gloss over that problem? He assailed Justice Kennedy's *Obergefell* opinion as antidemocratic, but ignored identical judicial assaults on the political process by five state supreme courts.

Indeed, if the Roberts-Scalia-Alito democratic-process thesis were honored consistently, by 2015, just eleven states had legitimately achieved welcoming same-sex couples into the institution of civil marriage: Delaware, Hawaii, Illinois, Maine, Maryland, Minnesota, New Hampshire, New York, Rhode Island, Vermont, and Washington. In contrast, the actions by courts of last resort in Connecticut, Iowa, Massachusetts, New Jersey, and New Mexico mandating statewide adoption of marriage equality did not qualify as democratically pure.

I suspect the reason why the chief justice did not point out this discrepancy is that the acknowledgment would have substantially diminished his argument's potency. After all, among the eleven "legitimate" marriage-equality jurisdictions, just Illinois and New York ranked within the nation's ten most populous states, whereas, Delaware, Maine, New Hampshire, Rhode Island, and Vermont fell in the ten smallest. In other words, twenty-two years after the Hawaii Supreme Court's 1993 *Baehr* v. *Lewin* decision triggered the national debate over same-sex marriage (Pinello 2006, 25–28), only 18 percent of the country's

---

[11] See also Severson (2011).

population lived in states where gay and lesbian pairs could marry as a result of political outcomes validly achieved through democratic processes. So with that rate of democratic change (i.e., 18 percent of the population every twenty-two years), nationwide marriage equality in the United States would likely have occurred by 2115 – a full century after *Obergefell*! As Lupia et al. (2010, 1233) convincingly argued:

> Barring an unprecedented acceleration of permissive attitude changes amongst Republicans or southern Democrats, or wholesale changes in many state-level partisan voting patterns, it is likely to be a very long time before many non-DCI states [i.e., those without direct constitutional initiatives, such as Alabama, Alaska, Georgia, Idaho, Louisiana, North Carolina, South Carolina, Tennessee, Texas, Utah, Virginia, and Wisconsin] will be capable of making their constitutions more permissive [to permit same-sex marriage].[12]

Hence, my calculation certainly would not have recommended the Roberts-Scalia-Alito approach to heedful citizens craving meaningful social change.

In my interviews with 175 same-sex couples conducted between 2009 and 2012, probably the most common unsolicited remark I received was something like the following: "I don't expect to be able to get legally married in [Georgia/Michigan/North Carolina/Ohio/Texas/Wisconsin] during my lifetime." Such comments are strewn throughout my conversations with lesbian and gay pairs in Super-DOMA states. And since the average age of my couples sample was 46.7 years, these references were to substantial lengths of time. Consequently, if a majority of the Supreme Court had in fact heeded in *Windsor* and *Obergefell* the plan of judicial inaction advocated by Chief Justice Roberts and Justices Scalia and Alito, then as the calculations in this chapter suggest, many of my interviewees' temporal predictions would have truly come to pass. They would have never been able to marry legally in their home states. Moreover, as the last chapter documents so extensively, the overwhelming majority of same-sex couples across the land were not capable of relocating to greener marriage pastures. Instead, the great bulk were stuck in place.

The other major dilemma for the democratic-process thesis is that neither Chief Justice Roberts nor Justices Scalia and Alito practiced what they preached. Indeed, all three were hypocrites. For example, Congress passed, and President Lyndon B. Johnson signed, the Voting Rights Act of 1965 (VRA). Then, the Supreme Court, by a vote of eight to one, upheld the statute's constitutionality in *South Carolina* v. *Katzenbach* (1966). In 2006, Congress reauthorized the VRA by huge majorities: 390 – 33 in the House of Representatives – or a majority of 89.7 percent of the chamber – and a unanimous vote in the Senate. Then President George W. Bush signed the bill into law. Thus, a clearer example of the democratic process playing out at the national political level would be difficult to identify.

---

[12] See also Pappas, Mendez, and Herrick (2009) and Dyck and Pearson-Merkowitz (2012).

Nonetheless, in a five-to-four decision in *Shelby County* v. *Holder* (2013), Chief Justice John Roberts authored the majority opinion striking down the crucial preclearance provision of Section 4 of the 1965 law, reauthorized in 2006. Moreover, Justices Scalia and Alito were among the four associate justices joining Roberts in the majority. *Shelby County* had the effect of severely incapacitating the long-revered statute (Liptak 2013).

Bear in mind that *Shelby County* was rendered *the day before* Justice Scalia issued his *Windsor* dissent, which began, and ended, with this moving language:

This case is about power in several respects. It is about the power of our people to govern themselves, and the power of this Court to pronounce the law. Today's opinion aggrandizes the latter, with the predictable consequence of diminishing the former. We have no power to decide this case. And even if we did, we have no power under the Constitution to invalidate this democratically adopted legislation. The Court's errors on both points spring forth from the same diseased root: an exalted conception of the role of this institution in America. (133 S. Ct. at 2697–98)

...

We [the Supreme Court] might have covered ourselves with honor today, by promising all sides of this debate that it was theirs to settle and that we would respect their resolution. We might have let the People decide.

But that the majority will not do. Some will rejoice in today's decision, and some will despair at it; that is the nature of a controversy that matters so much to so many. But the Court has cheated both sides, robbing the winners of an honest victory, and the losers of the peace that comes from a fair defeat. We owed both of them better. (133 S. Ct. at 2711)

The nearly identical poignant words of Justice Scalia could have been used by the four dissenters against the judicial heavy-handedness apparent in the action of the *Shelby County* majority of which he, Chief Justice Roberts, and Justice Alito were a part. What is more, the congressional majorities on DOMA in 1996 were 342 yea votes in the House of Representatives – or 78.6 percent of that chamber – and 85 (or 85 percent) in the Senate. Accordingly, the majorities in both the House and Senate were substantially larger for the 2006 VRA reauthorization than for DOMA a decade earlier. Nevertheless, Roberts, Scalia, and Alito in *Shelby County* had no problem whatsoever overlooking such overwhelming political support for the reauthorized VRA that was evidenced in the democratic process.

And the *Shelby County* decision was issued just two years before the chief justice wrote this in *Obergefell*:

[This dissent] is...about whether, in our democratic republic, th[e] decision [about important public policy issues] should rest with the people acting through their elected representatives, or with five lawyers who happen to hold commissions authorizing them to resolve legal disputes according to law. The Constitution leaves no doubt about the answer. (192 L. Ed. 2d at 640)

Again, the *Shelby County* dissent could have used these words to make the identical point against the Roberts majority opinion there.

A second major example of hypocrisy by Chief Justice Roberts and Justices Scalia and Alito is their participation in the five-vote majority opinion of *Citizens United* v. *Federal Election Commission* (2010), which upended the Bipartisan Campaign Reform Act of 2002 (also known as the McCain-Feingold Act). That federal statute limited expenditures by corporations and unions in campaigns for federal office. The *Citizens United* ruling not only held that such prohibitions violated the First Amendment political-speech rights of businesses but also overruled two important Supreme Court precedents on the topic to reach that result (Liptak 2010). In other words, to achieve their preferred policy outcome, Roberts, Scalia, and Alito neither deferred to the democratic political process nor honored the Court's own prior decisions. And there certainly was no beating of their chests to bemoan such upheavals of democracy by "five lawyers who happen to hold commissions authorizing them to resolve legal disputes according to law." None whatsoever.

Other instances of such dissembling are available in the voting records of Chief Justice Roberts and Justices Scalia and Alito. But itemizing them would be tiresome and repetitive.

In any event, taking the *Windsor* and *Obergefell* dissents seriously is a tall order in light of all the impediments listed here.[13]

---

[13] See also Sommer et al. (2013) and Posner and Segall (2015).

7

Conclusion

No union is more profound than marriage, for it embodies the highest ideals of love, fidelity, devotion, sacrifice, and family. In forming a marital union, two people become something greater than once they were. As some of the petitioners in these cases demonstrate, marriage embodies a love that may endure even past death. It would misunderstand these men and women to say they disrespect the idea of marriage. Their plea is that they do respect it, respect it so deeply that they seek to find its fulfillment for themselves. Their hope is not to be condemned to live in loneliness, excluded from one of civilization's oldest institutions. They ask for equal dignity in the eyes of the law. The Constitution grants them that right.

– Justice Anthony Kennedy, *Obergefell v. Hodges* (2015)

With these words, the Supreme Court brought to an end America's two-decade-long war against same-sex couples and their families. Together with numerous lower federal-court judges across the country, the five justices who voted with Anthony Kennedy's *Windsor* and *Obergefell* majority opinions freed gay and lesbian pairs and their children of the shackles imposed on them by federal and state laws. After June 2015, all American families headed by same-sex couples were constitutionally protected against further government-sponsored relationship-recognition discrimination. What a spectacular turn of events that transformation was for the millions of law-abiding, tax-paying citizens who never thought they would be able legally to marry their life partners in front of, and in celebration with, family and friends in their own home states. All the people who had attended dozens of weddings of opposite-sex pairs within their circles of family, friends, and associates could now participate in the same rite of passage that is one of life's most important benchmarks and that had been denied them for so long.

To gauge the impacts of this titanic shift in American constitutional law between July 2013 and July 2015, I contacted again the couples I had interviewed to see what changes the various court decisions had brought to their lives. As discussed in the last chapter, the legal alterations evolved from the invalidation of the federal DOMA's Section 3 in *Windsor*, to the district-by-district and circuit-by-circuit federal-court offensives on state DOMAs between December 2013 and March 2015, and then to the culminating struggle in the Supreme Court's *Obergefell* ruling. So I first surveyed interviewees in the late summer of 2013 to see what effects the prospect of federal marriage benefits might have had on them. Then, after October 2014, when the Supreme Court declined to hear state appeals from the Fourth Circuit (including North Carolina) and the Seventh (covering Wisconsin), I emailed couples in the Tar Heel and Badger states to see what their fully established right to civil marriage meant for them. Lastly, after June 2015, I did the same with folks in Georgia, Michigan, Ohio, and Texas.

I intended to include in this final chapter some striking examples of how these legal improvements actually affected families. At the same time, I realized that the most pervasive consequences of judicial rulings sweeping away the federal DOMA, state Super-DOMAs, and other marriage impediments would simply be to remove all of the numerous disabilities – cataloged at length in Chapters 3 and 4 – that those antigay laws imposed in the first place.[1] For instance, all of the same-sex partners and kids who were not formerly able to be covered by employer-sponsored family-health-insurance programs could now qualify for such benefits. And in those jurisdictions where second-parent adoptions were not available for same-sex couples, full nationwide marriage equality ought to have meant that either joint or stepparent-like adoptions would finally be accessible to them (Engel 2015; Bernard 2015; cf. Lewin 2015a). But the likelihood of narratives as attention-grabbing as those earlier in the book was low, if only because the human-interest value of pain remedies typically is not as great as for the discomfort they relieve.

Much of the post-*Windsor* reports I received from couples involved money. For example, in the fall of 2013, an Atlanta pair said their federal income taxes would be reduced by as much as $14,000 annually when they could file a joint return that claimed one of the partners (who is a stay-at-home parent) and their two children as the full dependents of the partner who works outside the home. Another Georgia informant wrote in July 2015,

One high-earning gay couple we know had some large business losses during the economic downturn. The IRS permitted them to share the losses as a married pair, saving them somewhere in the range of $100,000 in federal taxes. However, the State of Georgia didn't let them do the same. So they lost what would have been a $20,000-plus state refund. Now [after *Obergefell*], they should be able to get that back.

[1] See also Doan, Loehr, and Miller (2014).

After marriage equality reached Wisconsin in 2014, George and Kenneth (whose experience of getting Badger Care as a coping mechanism appeared in Chapter 5) said,

> If we both made about the same amount of income, we'd save very little in taxes. But because George is self-employed at a business that receives no money on paper, Kenneth makes much more than him.
>
> We just amended our state and federal income tax returns for the last four years. We're due to get an additional $12,000 in refunds from the United States and Wisconsin. We'd not have been able to revise our taxes if we'd not already been married in California in 2008. Too bad we can't go back past 2010!

Another Badger State couple reported an estimated $5,000 in annual tax savings as a result of their ability to be legally married.

A Texas woman shared this information:

> Since we talked last, my partner had to have an expensive, and uninsured, dental procedure. So I postponed retirement and took a new contract to help pay her dental costs. But because we were married in Iowa before her dental problem came up, we could deduct that money on a joint federal tax return and saved probably $10,000.

Hence, numerous families headed by lesbian and gay pairs experienced significant financial gains from marriage equality.

Yet as George and Kenneth's commentary intimated, others did not. In fact, many interviewees ran up against what is known as the "marriage penalty" in income taxation, a phenomenon long familiar to married heterosexual couples in which both husband and wife are employed. Federal income tax is progressive in the sense that people with lower salaries pay a proportionately smaller rate of taxation than those with higher earnings. As individual incomes increase, the additional amounts are taxed in brackets with higher rates of taxation. The bracket range in 2015 was from a low of 10 percent for about the first $10,000 dollars of income to the highest rate of nearly 40 percent for amounts over $400,000. Usually, married pairs would pay less in joint taxes if they could each file as single taxpayers, rather than combining their incomes and thereby increasing their joint tax liability because of the elevated rates of taxation in the higher income brackets.

In fact, the marriage penalty apparently stopped at least one of the couples in my sample from tying the knot after marriage equality reached their state. Debra and Martha, the closeted lesbian couple outside of Dallas who were introduced in Chapter 5, emailed me this note in July 2015:

> We have no exciting stories for you, Dan. Debra has had health insurance through Martha's employer, as well as her own, since 2012.
>
> There are no plans for us to get married now that it's legal to do so in Texas. Our tax CPA has advised against it.

Thus, as suggested in Chapter 5, highly closeted same-sex pairs may well have no emotional, psychological, or sentimental attachment to the idea of marriage that would prompt them to wed, even if given the opportunity.

Yet those interviewees who did value the status of marriage for whatever reason were not deterred by the marriage tax penalty. For example, an Atlanta couple responded to my July 2015 inquiry by first writing two long paragraphs about how much the marriage penalty had affected them at both the federal and state levels. Yet their next paragraph said this:

But despite the marriage penalty, there are, and will be, substantial benefits for us. The most salient one is that our three children can now say with confidence that their parents are married, and not be questioned about it (not that we've had any real problem with that).

We attach some writings our daughter did in First Grade (2013–14). So you can see this is important to her. And we don't sit around the house talking about the matter. Rather, it came up organically for her.

I wish I could reproduce here the handwritten documents I received as attachments, because they are so visually authentic, written in the script of a five- or six-year-old girl who is working to master the arts of penmanship and self-expression. Yet the best I can do is offer her words in print.

The first document is described as the daughter's "Family Writing on Back-to-School Night" of August 22, 2013.

In my family I have a dog, two brothers, a fish, two dads, and a grandma. We like to play together. Our favorite meal is Mexican. We like it because nachos and burritos are so juicy. In this picture we are all dressed up.

Attached to the daughter's note is a holiday photograph of the two beaming men in business suits surrounded by three adorable children. If there ever were a competition for a family to serve as ambassadors for marriage equality, this irresistible image would win the contest.

The daughter's second, and final, document is longer, and on the top are embossed the words, "I have a dream..."

Dr. Martin Luther King had a dream. I have a dream also. My dream is that one day gay people will be able to marry in Georgia. There are three ways I can help my dream come true. My first way is, I will write notes to the government. Next, I will tell people that don't like gay people that we shouldn't have segragation [sic]. Finally, I will gather a crew of people and we will hang up gay flags and fite [sic] for rights. Will you help my dream come true like Martin's did?

The lengthy email from the same male couple contained another interesting tale:

We're in the process of purchasing a lake house in north Georgia. The real property is technically a "lease" through the Georgia Power Company. So we'll "lease" the land but own the house, which is a typical procedure on man-made lakes with power-generating dams.

Anyway, we'll be the first gay couple whom the Georgia Power Company has allowed *both* partners to be on the lease documents. In the past, they've permitted only one member of the (few) gay pairs to be named on the lease.

And the power company actually requested a copy of our marriage certificate. In the ten years since we wed in Massachusetts, this is the first time that's happened!

Another remarkable story came to me in July 2013, from the Dallas women who earlier reported their tax savings on the uninsured dental procedure:

Yes, the Supreme Court's *Windsor* decision made a big difference to us. Within a few days of the ruling, we sent in our marriage-license application and bought airline tickets to Des Moines for us and our pastor and his wife to be in Iowa on the date of our 29th anniversary.

Our very straight and extremely supportive pastor and wife asked us repeatedly to be able to perform the ceremony. He even offered to pay their own way, which we refused. (Dude, seriously???!! We're supposed to pay *you*.)

In Chapter 3, Heather and Teresa recounted a very upsetting experience with a hospital nurse in Appleton who insisted on denying their relationship. When admitting Heather for an important procedure, the nurse would not allow Teresa – Heather's "friend" – in the room. After marriage equality arrived in the Badger State in 2014, Heather sent me this update:

I had a terrible attack of kidney stones last month that required surgery and a slow recovery.

Our first clue that things had changed happened in the emergency room one night when I was so sick from pain and in no position to sign legal documents. A hospital staffer came to my bed with a consent form to sign, and Teresa asked her to come back later because I was so overwhelmed with pain.

The staffer told Teresa that she was my wife and could sign the form for me if I was unable to do so. At the time, we didn't reflect much on the event because I was so indisposed. But the next day, we realized how different it felt to be treated as spouses, and how validating that experience was.

Then, as I was going into surgery for the kidney stones, a doctor asked if I'd brought a friend with me, and Teresa immediately said, "I'm her wife." I let them know she was also my power of attorney, because I'm so used to saying that.

From then on out, Teresa was treated like my spouse and given information by the doctors on my condition. While groggy in recovery, I heard one nurse say to another, "It's time for you to go and get her wife and bring her back." After the terrible experience we had in 2009, this very different approach brought tears to my eyes to have such acceptance.

Teresa is going to be signing onto the health insurance at my job because it's a more affordable plan, and now we won't be penalized with any taxes on the benefit. I'll also be joining her flex plan because her employer offers better options for payment than mine. The resulting benefits package will save us quite a bit of money each year.

We've had marriage equality in Wisconsin only for a couple of months, but those are the immediate benefits we've seen thus far.

In addition, when someone asked Teresa if marriage felt any different, she replied, "I feel emboldened." Because we both now have added rights and protections as spouses with the law on our side. It's supplied a sense of security and safety that we've never had before.

As you know, we've been through the mill with my health: MS, cancer, aneurysm, pulmonary embolism, etc. This last medical situation was the first time I felt a sense of safety rather than fear about our rights. That goes a long way to help aid healing for someone heading into surgery and afterward during recovery.

We now own a home together, have three grandchildren, and are married. Life is pretty good these days!

Five couples in my sample involved partnerships between a U.S. citizen and a foreign national. The *Windsor* decision and its aftermath greatly helped these binational pairs. In July 2013, the Department of Homeland Security announced that American citizens could sponsor their foreign same-sex spouses for immigration and ultimately secure their permanent-resident status within the United States (Preston 2013).

Yet not all the accounts I received after the federal-court rulings were of unsullied celebration. A Michigan man wrote this:

Yes, we're finally fully married and doing well.

I've been working more lately as a realtor, and noticing that my work and personal worlds still collide. For example, a few days ago, a prospective customer was talking to me in my yard, and seeing Todd, asked, "Is that your brother?" Even after our marriage, it's still a baffling question. The correct answer now is "husband," but I said "partner." I'm still afraid to be honest and forthright for fear of losing business. A moral dilemma for sure.

It's ironic, because whenever I meet a straight man, he blurts out "wife" within the first minute or so, as if he's won the Medal of Honor.

DID SUPER-DOMAS IN FACT DEFEND AND PROTECT MARRIAGE?

Did America's war on same-sex couples and their families result in the outcomes that Super-DOMA sponsors and defenders proclaimed were their objectives? That is, did formally excluding gay and lesbian pairs from the institution of civil marriage, and from civil unions and domestic partnerships as well, have the intended effect of fortifying marriage for heterosexuals and their children?

Consider divorce rates. Because divorce is the most conspicuous measurement of the failure of marriages, an excellent empirical indicator of the success of this American war would be that the rate of divorce among opposite-sex couples would have declined in those states that added Super-DOMAs to their state constitutions. In 2013, the American Bar Association and the Centers for Disease Control and Prevention used 2011 Census Bureau data to compile the divorce rate for each of the fifty states (Huffington Post 2013). The rates came from the number of people who identified as divorced per 1,000 residents and ranged from a low of six per 1,000 residents (in New Jersey) to a high of fourteen (for Alaska).

Using these data, I calculated that the mean value of the divorce rates for the twenty Super-DOMA states was 9.95 per 1,000 residents, whereas the median was 9.5.[2] The mean for the twenty states that never amended their constitutions to exclude same-sex couples from marriage was 8.7, and the median, 8.5. In other words, Super-DOMAs did *not* reduce divorce rates as an empirical matter. Instead, the rate at which heterosexual marriages failed in Super-DOMA jurisdictions was consistently *higher* than in states without any antigay-marriage amendments.

Next consider the rate at which children were raised in two-parent households. The sponsors and defenders of Super-DOMAs consistently argued that kids should be brought up in families with a mother and a father. In much of the federal litigation discussed in the last chapter, lawyers defending state constitutional amendments prohibiting marriage equality often pointed to this issue in their legal briefs, in addition to the argument that children born from unplanned pregnancies would be better protected if their biological parents reliably had the option to marry and thereby were encouraged to do so. Accordingly, another empirical marker for Super-DOMA success would be that the rate of two-parent households would be higher in such jurisdictions than elsewhere.

In June 2015, the *New York Times* reported on a scholarly study that charted the rate of two-parent households by state (Leonhardt 2015). Among the ten jurisdictions with the highest percentages of two-parent households were four Super-DOMA states and six without any antigay-marriage amendments. In contrast, among the ten places with the lowest proportions of two-parent households were six Super-DOMA states, three Mini-DOMA jurisdictions, and just one state with no such constitutional amendment. Again, these data do not support an hypothesis that denying same-sex couples access to civil marriage helped ensure that children would be raised by both of their biological parents. Rather, the opposite circumstance appears to have been closer to the empirical truth about parenting.

Super-DOMA defenders also claimed that regulating marriage in the manner their states did promoted a policy of reducing the number of children born out of wedlock, because the constitutional amendments encouraged men and women who were "mak[ing] babies" to marry (Associated Press 2014). Using data supplied by Martin et al. (2015) for 2013 state-level estimates of the percentage of births to unmarried mothers, I calculated that the mean value of the unwed-birth rates for the twenty Super-DOMA states was 39.6 percent of all births, and the median was 42.1 percent. The mean for the twenty states

---

[2] The median has a decimal point here because the tenth place among twenty arrayed values was nine, while the eleventh position was ten.

without constitutional gay-marriage bans was 39.4 percent, and the median, 40.2 percent. Once again, Super-DOMAs did not achieve the empirical objectives their apologists ascribed to them.

In short, there are no hard facts that demonstrate Super-DOMAs did indeed strengthen marriage for opposite-sex couples and their families in the way the constitutional amendments' sponsors had claimed would be the case.[3]

THE ECONOMIC LOSSES TO SUPER-DOMA STATES

Wars are expensive, and the battles waged against gay and lesbian couples and their children were no exception to this maxim. So not only did families headed by same-sex pairs experience multifarious losses from the presence of Super-DOMAs in their home states (as recounted in Chapters 3 and 4) but the states themselves also suffered economically from their constitutional amendments. Using my sample of in-depth interviews with the study's 175 couples, I can estimate what some of the lost revenues were in Georgia, Michigan, North Carolina, Ohio, Texas, and Wisconsin. Although most gay people did not leave Super-DOMA jurisdictions for greener pastures permanently, a significant number of them did so temporarily. And those out-of-state jaunts were costly to home jurisdictions.

For example, only about 10 couples in my distribution of 175 expressed no interest in marrying each other.[4] Rather, most pairs had some economic, emotional, legal, psychological, or sentimental reasons to wed. By the time of the interviews (conducted between 2009 and 2012), about one-third of the pairs I spoke with had traveled to Canada, Massachusetts, or somewhere else to be legally married.[5] Some of those couples had celebrations with family and friends after they returned home. So if I reduce the one-third proportion of pairs who went out of state to marry by one-half (for the purpose of excluding those couples who later had some traditional festivity in their home states), I can calculate that roughly 16 percent of all gay and lesbian pairs in my distribution married out of state without any conventional celebration of the event on their return home. Yet, as discussed in Chapter 1, my sample is biased in

---

[3] See also Langbein and Yost (2009) and Dillender (2014).

[4] Some lesbian pairs were strong feminists who objected to the patriarchal nature of the institution of marriage. Many couples indicated they were not interested in the religious aspect of marriage, but did seek its legal rights as a civil matter. So I do count them as wanting to marry.

[5] After the U.S. Supreme Court invalidated Section 3 of the federal DOMA in June 2013, I learned in subsequent email correspondence with interviewees that substantially more of the couples in my sample soon ventured elsewhere to wed once the prospect of receiving federal marriage benefits was on the horizon (see also Badgett and Mallory 2014). But my figures do not include such post-interview out-of-state marriages.

As the last chapter indicated, the number of legally married gay and lesbian pairs tripled in the two years before *Obergefell* (Gates and Newport 2015). Thus, the estimates of Super-DOMA-state financial losses in this section are particularly modest, in light of my choice to err on the side of caution.

favor of better educated and financially secure people who would have been more likely to have a celebration. As a result, I further reduce the estimate of the proportion of lesbian and gay pairs who wed out of state but who did not formally celebrate with family and friends upon their return from 16 percent to 10 percent.

Based on data from the 2010 U.S. Census, Gates and Cooke (2011b) provide approximations of the number of same-sex couples living in each of the fifty states. Relying on their numbers, I calculated that at least 127,000 gay and lesbian pairs resided in this study's six states. Hence, I concluded that, by 2012, a minimum of 12,700 (i.e., 10 percent of 127,000) of them had traveled out of state to wed, but did not spend any money at home in the process.

Now some of the couples in this group might never have paid for taking family and friends to a restaurant for a meal together, let alone buy flowers, hire DJs or photographers, or rent gowns, tuxedos, or wedding venues for more elaborate (and costly) affairs. Going to a local county clerk's office with two witnesses might have been adequate for their needs. Yet I have good reason to believe the proportion of people with such modest goals would be small. For instance, among the two-thirds of all couples in my sample who were not already legally married somewhere, more than one-third of them still had already had some public observance in their home states to celebrate their relationships, events they described as weddings or commitment ceremonies. Even among the people who eventually did go out of state to marry, some 30 percent of them had had earlier church weddings or other ceremonies to celebrate with family and friends. Hence, the desire for public recognition of their relationships was substantial. In truth, gay people are no less social creatures than their heterosexual counterparts.

Therefore, and to achieve a round number, I subtracted 2,700 couples (from the prior estimate of 12,700) to represent those pairs who would have eloped to a clerk's office without further fanfare, thus leaving 10,000 couples in Georgia, Michigan, North Carolina, Ohio, Texas, and Wisconsin who were married elsewhere, but would have paid for a traditional wedding celebration in their home states if they had had the opportunity to marry there.

To estimate how much revenue the six states lost, I presumed that an average wedding party would consist of fifty guests (i.e., a total of twenty-five family members, friends and associates for each partner). A meal, drinks, tax, and tips at a restaurant would likely cost $50 per person at a minimum. So that's already $2,500. Then there are the costs of clergy or other officiant, flowers, formal wear, photography, wedding cake, and so forth. In short, the smallest amount a couple might spend for a wedding in a home state would be $5,000 during the time frame at issue in the study.[6] And of course, a larger guest list or more elaborate celebration would mean more money spent locally. But at a minimum, I

---

[6] The Williams Institute at the School of Law of the University of California-Los Angeles estimated that, as of 2015, the mean cost of weddings for same-sex couples was $8,467 (Mallory 2015).

judged that the economies of Georgia, Michigan, North Carolina, Ohio, Texas, and Wisconsin collectively lost at least $50,000,000 (10,000 couples × $5,000 per wedding) in revenue, and possibly much more, from all the marriages of their own state residents that had to be performed elsewhere because of Super-DOMAs.

Moreover, including the other fourteen Super-DOMA states into the calculation increases the estimate by another $44,000,000, resulting in a total of at least $94,000,000 in losses to the economies of the twenty states.[7] This approximation is modest when compared with the total costs of weddings nationwide estimated by the Williams Institute to have been paid by 96,000 same-sex couples and their guests in the four months after *Obergefell* v. *Hodges* was decided: $812,832,000, of which $51,940,000 represented sales tax revenues (Mallory 2015).

A second category of economic deprivation for states with these constitutional amendments involved procreation. Four male pairs in my distribution went the route of surrogacy to obtain seven children among the four sets of families (see Bellafante 2005). To boot, each couple made sure their kids were born in states that allowed both fathers' names to be placed on the birth certificates. Thus, all of their money devoted to the surrogacy process was spent outside home jurisdictions, and the sums they incurred for the assisted reproduction technology were substantial. The minimum amounts my interviewees paid for a successful pregnancy by surrogate ranged from $75,000 to $100,000. For instance, egg donations alone could cost as much as $10,000 each (Lewin 2015b). But in surrogacy, there is no guarantee of success with the first embryo transfer with a first surrogate. Indeed, one pair reported they did not achieve pregnancy until the sixth embryo transfer with a third surrogate. Yet their earlier unsuccessful attempts still had to be paid for, and my understanding is that each such failed effort might cost as much as $25,000. Thus, I estimated that the average outlay for each successful birth by surrogacy in my sample was $100,000. That means the total amount spent out of state for the six births in

---

[7] Marriage-equality jurisdictions were more than happy to take up the slack from Super-DOMA and Mini-DOMA states. For example, after New York State legalized same-sex nuptials in 2011, New York City actively marketed itself to lesbian and gay couples as a destination to visit, get married, and take a honeymoon. The Big Apple predicted that weddings of out-of-state same-sex pairs would generate $310,000,000 over three years in incremental revenues (Wieder 2012). In fact, the number of weddings at the Manhattan Marriage Bureau increased by nearly 50 percent between 2008 and 2015, in large measure because of the legalization of same-sex marriage (Flegenheimer 2015).

Chibbaro (2013) reported that, after the Supreme Court's *Windsor* decision in June 2013, the demand by same-sex couples from Virginia and elsewhere for marriages in the District of Columbia caused the number of applications for marriage licenses filed with the DC Superior Court to more than double in both July and August of that year. The DC Marriage Bureau had to increase its staff and add two rooms to accommodate all of the lesbian and gay pairs wanting to wed there.

the four families (where two of the seven children were twins) was $600,000. Therefore, the average expense per family was $150,000 ($600,000 ÷ 4).

Among my distribution of 175 couples, 94 were lesbian pairs and 81 were gay males. Thus, the four families with children through surrogacy represented 4.9 percent of the male portion of the couples sample. As addressed in Chapter 1, however, my distribution was skewed toward better educated and more economically successful people within the LGBT community. Thus, I discounted the percentage of male pairs having children through surrogacy in my sample by a factor of three-quarters to be confident that I achieved a conservative estimate of what happened with male couples nationwide; I thereby reduced the proportion to 1.2 percent (4.9 percent × 0.25).

Gates and Cooke (2011b) determined that 49 percent of all American same-sex couples are male pairs. Hence, among the estimated 127,000 gay and lesbian pairs residing in the study's six states, 62,230 were male couples. Using my estimate that 1.2 percent of male pairs had children born out of state through surrogacy, therefore, means a total of approximately 746 families in Georgia, Michigan, North Carolina, Ohio, Texas, and Wisconsin used this approach. Because the average expense per family for surrogacy in my sample was $150,000, the total estimated costs of surrogacy for the 746 families across the six Super-DOMA states here was $111,900,000. And again for the sake of erring on the side of caution, I round that figure down to $100,000,000. Adding the other fourteen Super-DOMA states to the estimate increases it by $88,000,000, bringing the total surrogacy-related losses to $188,000,000.

Yet male couples using surrogacy were not the only category of same-sex pairs going out of state to obtain children in the study. Recall Amy and Brenda from Chapter 5. For two years, these Atlanta lesbians tried to start a family in Georgia, even to the point of offering to foster a sibling group of up to three kids. Yet their efforts in the Peach State were futile. So Amy and Brenda were forced to go to another jurisdiction to adopt and, in New York, had a child placement within a month of registering as foster parents. Of course, a significant benefit of their experience was the Empire State's policy of placing both names of same-sex partners on adoption decrees. So when economic circumstances forced a return to Atlanta, both Amy and Brenda – not just one of them – were legal parents in their family.

In my interview protocol, I did not systematically ask couples with children who were adopted where those adoptions occurred. I presumed the vast majority took place in home states, if only because that approach is more affordable. Additionally, the Medicaid and adoption assistance programs that Kimberly and Shirley described in Chapter 4 greatly facilitated placements of children with special needs. Nonetheless, the strong and widespread motivation I observed among interviewees to have both partners' names placed on birth certificates or adoption decrees must have prompted some gay and lesbian pairs to go to places like New York to adopt, just as it incentivized out-of-state surrogacy. I include both female and male couples in this category because adoption generally is much less expensive than surrogacy. The challenge is to estimate the size of the out-of-state adoption population among same-sex pairs with children.

Gates (2015) found that "[n]early 27,000 same-sex couples are raising an estimated 58,000 adopted and foster children in the United States" and that "[t]he portion of same-sex couples raising children under age 18 does not vary much across regions." Moreover, Gates claimed that 17 percent of all same-sex couples had adopted children, and 2 percent had kids in foster care. So the ratio between formally adopted children and those being fostered was 17 to 2, meaning about 89 percent of the combined number of 58,000 adopted and foster children should have been in the former category. Hence, approximately 51,500 adopted kids nationwide were being raised in families headed by same-sex pairs. Relying on the Gates finding that such families were fairly evenly distributed around the country, I estimated that, since 43 percent of the American population resides in formerly Super-DOMA jurisdictions, about 22,000 adopted children were being raised by lesbian and gay couples in those twenty states in 2013 (the year of the Gates data).

This is the important question: how many of these 22,000 kids were adopted out of state for the purpose of securing both parents' names on birth certificates or adoption decrees? Recall that my judgment on the proportion of male couples who were willing to spend a rock-bottom minimum of $75,000 for out-of-state surrogacy to get both of their names on birth certificates was 1.2 percent. Thus, the extent of people with the dual-legal-parentage goal who could not afford to pay as much for that outcome must have been higher, and substantially so. As such, I estimated that 3 to 5 percent of the 22,000 children in the twenty Super-DOMA states were adopted out of state – or from at least 660 to as many as 1,100.

The bare minimum cost of out-of-state adoptions was $20,000 each, according to what interviewees consistently told me. Moreover, adoption websites (such as adoption.com) indicate the expense for infant adoptions ranges from a low of $20,000 to a high of $40,000. Thus, the total money calculated to have been spent out of state by same-sex couples acquiring through adoption children whose birth certificates or adoption decrees would have both parents' names is between $13,000,000 and $22,000,000. The share attributable to the six states in my study runs from $6,900,000 to $11,700,000.

Accordingly, using my couples sample for reference, I can identify at least $156,900,000 that was lost to the economies of Georgia, Michigan, North Carolina, Ohio, Texas, and Wisconsin as a direct result of their Super-DOMAs, and the combined financial loss to all such jurisdictions was a minimum of $295,000,000.

What is more, there was a third significant category of costs to the states with either statutory or constitutional bans on same-sex marriage: the expense of defending those prohibitions in federal court. I am not just referring here to what the lawyers working on behalf of the states were paid, although their salaries and incidental costs no doubt were considerable.[8] Rather, the litigation expenses I discuss here probably are not familiar to most Americans, because the general rule of thumb in our country's court system is that each side pays its own attorney's fees and other court costs regardless of who wins and losses. Yet there is an important wrinkle in federal law that deviates from that general American principle.

In 1976, Congress passed the Civil Rights Attorney's Fees Award Act (also known as Section 1988), which provides that, in a civil rights lawsuit brought under Section 1983[9] of the Civil Rights Act of 1871, "the court, in its discretion, may allow the prevailing party, other than the United States, a reasonable attorney's fee as part of the costs." In other words, when individual plaintiffs sue in federal court for the breach of constitutionally protected civil rights and win such lawsuits, then the losing side has to pay their reasonable attorney's fees. Consequently, because *Obergefell* determined nationwide that the Fourteenth Amendment protects the right of same-sex couples to marry, all of the American states and their political subdivisions (such as counties and municipalities) that were sued by gay and lesbian pairs for marriage rights were liable for those couples' attorney's fees. And as the last chapter suggests, there were dozens of such Section 1983 lawsuits across the land.

By November 2015, such attorney's fee awards, or agreements between the parties on such fees, had been determined in seventeen states. The cumulative amount of money paid by those jurisdictions was substantial: $8,014,005.[10] Eleven of the seventeen states had Super-DOMAs, three (Michigan, Ohio, and Wisconsin) of which were in this study. The mean cost for the eleven Super-DOMA states where plaintiffs' attorney's fees were determined was $541,355 per state. Hence, using that figure for each of the twenty relevant jurisdictions results in cumulative attorney's fees of $10,827,100. Accordingly, a reasonable estimate of the total Super-DOMA-state obligation for plaintiffs' attorney's fees is well over $10,000,000.[11]

---

[8] Kentucky alone paid $260,000 for private lawyers to handle that state's participation in appeals to the U.S. Court of Appeals for the Sixth Circuit and then to the U.S. Supreme Court (Associated Press 2015a).

[9] "Every person who, under color of any statute, ordinance, regulation, custom, or usage, of any State or Territory or the District of Columbia, subjects, or causes to be subjected, any citizen of the United States or other person within the jurisdiction thereof to the deprivation of any rights, privileges, or immunities secured by the Constitution and laws, shall be liable to the party injured in an action at law, suit in equity, or other proper proceeding for redress."

[10] AR – $66,000; AZ – $200,000; CO – $95,000; ID – $397,300; KY – $70,325; MI – $1,900,000; MO – $31,610; ND – $58,000; OH – $1,300,000; OK – $298,000; OR – $132,690; PA – $1,500,000; SC – $135,276; UT – $95,000; VA – $580,000; WI – $1,055,000; WV – $99,804 (Associated Press 2015b; Biskupic 2015; Hawes 2015; Tillman 2015a, 2015b, 2015c; cf. Marusic 2015).

[11] Hood County, with a population of just over 50,000, paid more than $40,000 in attorney's fees unsuccessfully defending its clerk's post-*Obergefell* decision not to issue marriage licenses to same-sex couples (Tinsley 2015). Thus, each Texan in Hood had to pay almost one dollar for his or her public official's refusal to comply with the Supreme Court ruling.

Thus, the grand total of identifiable financial losses for the twenty American jurisdictions whose constitutions prohibited all forms of relationship recognition for same-sex couples was likely to be a bare minimum of $305,000,000. Therefore, the presence of Super-DOMAs cost every man, woman, and child in the twenty states at least $2.19. More remarkably, the price of preventing each same-sex pair in each Super-DOMA state from marrying or having any other relationship recognition was about $1,275 per couple.

What is more, I have not included in this estimate any of the costs of the political campaigns that were conducted to embed Super-DOMAs in state constitutions in the first place. For example, Phil Burress of Cincinnati's Citizens for Community Values told me that the Family Research Council provided CCV with between $1,500,000 and $2,000,000 for the expenses of placing Issue 1 on the 2004 Ohio ballot and promoting the initiative. Further, those figures do not include any of the funds raised locally in the Buckeye State on behalf of the ballot measure. A. Lynne Bowman, the founding executive director of Equality Ohio, informed me that at least $500,000 was raised and spent by the committee organized to defeat Issue 1. So in Ohio alone, well over $2,000,000 was expended by the campaigns for and against the initiative.

In Texas, the total amount of contributions surrounding the 2005 passage of Proposition 2 was $1,288,400 (Wikipedia 2015). And recall from Chapter 1 that each of North Carolina's two Catholic bishops donated $100,000 to the 2012 Amendment 1 campaign in the Tar Heel State. Thus, this limited information from interviews and elsewhere suggests that the cumulative campaign costs for all twenty Super-DOMAs could have easily amounted to $10,000,000 or higher.

Finally, states with these constitutional amendments lost lots of money in amounts that are difficult to quantify, but the financial costs were real nonetheless. Chapter 5 details how Super-DOMAs repulsed young, well-educated LGBT people like Michael Falk, who estimated the University of Michigan would have to invest $500,000 to replace him after he relocated to Johns Hopkins University from Ann Arbor.

In July 2013, another Michigan interviewee wrote about an additional financial loss for the Wolverine State in a story that is less dramatic than Falk's, but probably occurred more frequently:

Since our 2009 interview, I've finished my degree [a Ph.D. in chemistry] and postdoc at the University of Michigan and moved to California, where I got a teaching job at a state university.

In the job search, we were hoping to end up in a state with more progressive laws than Michigan. But I didn't feel, given the specialized nature of the faculty position I was looking for, that I could limit my search just to those kinds of states. So I applied for nearly every position I could identify, which ended up being five: two in California, one in Michigan, one in Illinois, and one in Iowa. Among those, only Michigan didn't provide any sort of civil union or marriage rights. Early on, I received phone interviews for the two California positions and a follow-up in-person interview at one of them, which made me an offer before the other three institutions had even begun phone interviewing. Given the perfect job fit and the laws here (which at the time were up in the air, but California at least had full statewide domestic partnerships for same-sex couples), the decision was pretty easy. I didn't even wait to hear back from the folks at the Michigan school.

When I got the job offer from the California dean, I mentioned to him that we'd need a week to decide because my partner wanted to fly out to see the area. The dean's response was to send me a link to his university's domestic-partner-benefits webpage, to make sure I knew about those benefits as I was considering their offer.

Moving wasn't easy, as we were both born and raised in Michigan, and all our family, friends, church, and social and professional networks were located there. I also felt a bit of an obligation to stay if possible since *Michigan taxpayers had spent considerable money funding my three graduate degrees, paying my stipends as a teaching assistant while a graduate student in Ann Arbor, etc. But I'm happy now to spend the capital Michigan invested in me on behalf of the students of California.*

When people talk about the economic impact of Michigan's discriminatory laws, I think they forget to factor in those sorts of costs, in addition to the tax revenue that we're now spending here rather than there. (Emphasis added)

A different category of financial loss involved Deborah and Gladys, who were first mentioned in Chapter 3, and who are also both college professors. Deborah shared this with me:

Gladys and I are both involved in professional organizations, and you know, Ohio needs economic activity.

But Issue 1 makes me much less willing to get together with other faculty members to say, "We'll sponsor a regional conference here." Such an event would bring economic income into the area. But I'm not speaking up to say, "Oh, I'll take the regional organizing for . . . ." It's just not happening.

I don't want to compromise anybody else in ways they don't need to be endangered by. Rather, our professional associates should go to states that have better guarantees for the protection of all citizens.

Thus, the kinds of people like us who are involved in professional organizations that could bring economic activity into Ohio aren't working toward those outcomes.

So yes, the war against same-sex couples and their families was a very expensive affair.

SPONSOR MOTIVATIONS FOR SUPER-DOMAS: BIGOTRY OR NOT?

Chief Justice Roberts' *Obergefell* dissent articulated a belief that was commonly held and stated over the years by the sponsors and other supporters of same-sex-marriage bans.

Perhaps the most discouraging aspect of today's decision is the extent to which the majority feels compelled to sully those on the other side of the debate. The majority offers a cursory assurance that it does not intend to disparage people who, as a matter of conscience, cannot accept same-sex marriage. That disclaimer is hard to square with the very next sentence, in which the majority explains that "the necessary consequence" of laws codifying the traditional definition of marriage is to "demea[n] or stigmatiz[e]" same-sex couples. The majority reiterates such characterizations over and over. By the majority's account, Americans who did nothing more than follow the understanding of marriage that has existed for our entire history – in particular, the tens of millions of people who voted to reaffirm their States' enduring definition of marriage – have acted to "lock...out," "disparage," "disrespect and subordinate," and inflict "[d]ignitary wounds" upon their gay and lesbian neighbors. These apparent assaults on the character of fairminded people will have an effect, in society and in court. Moreover, they are entirely gratuitous. It is one thing for the majority to conclude that the Constitution protects a right to same-sex marriage; it is something else to portray everyone who does not share the majority's "better informed understanding" as bigoted. (192 L. Ed. 2d at 654–55)

I want to address this matter head on. And just like the majority in the Michigan Supreme Court's *National Pride at Work* decision (discussed in Chapter 2), I start with dictionaries. My own favorite (*Webster's New World Dictionary of the American Language*, 2nd College Edition) is well worn, dating from 1984 and used regularly. There, the noun "bigot" has two alternate definitions: "1. a person who holds blindly and intolerantly to a particular creed, opinion, etc. 2. a narrow-minded person." The noun "bigotry" is defined as "the behavior, attitude, or beliefs of a bigot; intolerance; prejudice." For comparison, the online *The Free Dictionary* says a "bigot" is "[o]ne who is strongly partial to one's own group, religion, race, or politics and is intolerant of those who differ," and "bigotry" is "[t]he attitude, state of mind, or behavior characteristic of a bigot; intolerance." Finally, the online Dictionary.com holds that "bigot" is "a person who is utterly intolerant of any differing creed, belief, or opinion," whereas "bigotry" is "stubborn and complete intolerance of any creed, belief, or opinion that differs from one's own." Hence, the meaning of "bigoted" has been fairly uniform over time, with intolerance of other creeds, beliefs, or opinions as its core.

Two public examples of abject bigotry arose during the political campaign surrounding North Carolina's Amendment 1, the last of the twenty Super-DOMAs to be enacted. Ten days before the May 8, 2012, vote on the Tar Heel referendum, Pastor Sean Harris told his congregants at the Berean Baptist Church in Fayetteville, North Carolina the following:

Dads, the second you see your son dropping the limp wrist, you walk over there and crack that wrist. Man up, give them a good punch, OK? "You're not going to act like that. You were made by God to be a male and you're going to be a male."

And when your daughter starts acting too butch, you reign [SIC] her in. (Huffington Post 2012)

And just five days after the North Carolina vote, an independent Baptist minister, Charles Worley, told his congregation at the Providence Road Baptist Church in Maiden, North Carolina,

I figured a way out, a way to get rid of all the lesbians and queers but I couldn't get it past the Congress: build a great big large fence, fifty or a hundred miles long. Put all the lesbians in there, fly over and drop some food. Do the same thing with the queers and the homosexuals. And have that fence electrified so they can't get out.

And you know what? In a few years they will die out. You know why? They can't reproduce. If a man ever has a young'un, praise God he will be the first. (Bluemke 2012)

I hope Chief Justice Roberts would agree that these are clear instances of bigotry against gay people. After all, the first admonition promotes physical violence toward children seen as nonconforming, whereas the second sermon amounts to encouraging concentration camps for the extermination of LGBT folks, not unlike what the Nazis did to Jews during World War II.

Indeed, in *Between Dignity and Despair: Jewish Life in Nazi Germany*, Marion Kaplan made a particularly astute observation that is especially pertinent to the American marriage-equality context.

[T]he [Nazi] regime perversely attempted to make the abnormal seem normal, matter-of-fact, even sensible – for example, by labeling its cruel anti-Jewish measures with names like the "Law for the Protection of German Blood and Honor" or the "Social Compensation Tax" and, later, announcing that Jews would be "evacuated" to the East. (Kaplan 1998, 9–10)

Thus, consider how the American sponsors of measures to preclude same-sex couples from marrying named their policy instruments. Were the titles of their proposals "An Act to Prevent Same-Sex Marriage" or "The All Gay-Relationship-Recognition Denial Act"? No. Rather, Congress chose "The Defense of Marriage Act," transforming an aggressive indignity into virtuous benevolence to the eyes of uninformed observers. And all of the states followed the duplicitous congressional lead. Remember, for example, from Chapter 1 that Phil Burress explained his actions by observing, "Protecting the institution of marriage is my first line of defense.... My purpose in why I did what I did was to protect the institution of marriage. It wasn't to be anti-anything."

To be sure, if national or state legislatures had in fact been concerned about "defending" or "protecting" marriage – in the true sense of improving or guarding or championing the institution – they could have done so in several direct ways. For instance, in the 1950s, most American states had just one legal ground for divorce: adultery. Alleging and proving the sexual infidelity of a marital partner were the only mechanisms the law provided for the dissolution of marriage. Nothing short of one party being at fault for serious misconduct did the trick. Starting in the 1960s, however, states began liberalizing domestic-relations law to permit other, less onerous "no-fault" grounds for divorce, such as the amorphous "irreconcilable differences." Especially in circumstances where separations were uncontested, with no need for judges to apportion property, grant maintenance, or resolve child-custody disputes, married couples could secure a divorce easily, quickly, and inexpensively. Consequently, if legislators or interest-group activists were truly alarmed about escalating divorce rates, they could have restricted again the legal grounds for departing the institution. Yet, I am not aware of any such organized, let alone successful, legislative or interest-group efforts in the two decades starting with the 1996 passage of the federal DOMA.

Another method for "defending" or "protecting" marriage would have been to limit multiple entrances to the institution. Roman Catholic doctrine, for example, has long held that the sacramental nature of marriage cannot be broken. The Catholic Church does not believe it has authority to breach the life-long seal that God imparts on valid marriages. Hence, a second path for lawmakers and marriage advocates to "defend" and "protect" the civil institution would have been to pass legislation or amend constitutions whereby people could marry only once in their lifetime. No second or third or further attempts would be allowed. Just one. But again, I have no knowledge of any such organized efforts during the relevant time frame.

At the very end of his 2010 interview, Phil Burress brought up a third technique to improve, guard, or champion marriage.

Q: A final question: Someone said to me something like the following about Issue 1. "There was an important part left out of the constitutional amendment. It's not just that marriage should be between one man and one woman. It's that marriage should be between one man and one woman *for just one time*." How do you respond to that?

A: I would hope for that. But you can't by law lock people into being married for the rest of their lives when you have physical abuse, pornography addiction, or anything else. There's many times that even counselors, pastors that I know that are adamantly opposed to divorce, that will sign off and say you need to get a divorce, especially where there's physical abuse.

I met my wife at a meeting fighting porn. Her marriage was destroyed because of pornography. She intended to be married, as I did, for the rest of her life. Now I was never violent, but she was physically abused. The judge issued a restraining order against her husband to get him out of the house. Plus her life was being threatened. I'm not about to be part of something that says that you've got to stay in a relationship.

Now, should it be harder to get a divorce? I think yes, when there's children. *I think so. It should be harder.*

Frankly, what we're talking about is standing at the bottom of a waterfall catching water. We should be up at the top.

People should know when to get married through premarital counseling. I would probably support some sort of legislation like that. My stepdaughter just got married. She went through premarital counseling at a church here in Cincinnati. And I was absolutely thrilled at the questions they were asking. The pastor told them to bring in all their finances. Both of them had hidden stuff from each other, getting ready to get married. I was thrilled that they were going to get counseling on how to handle money. *That was a great idea.* (Emphasis added)

Put differently, a principal architect and sponsor of Super-DOMAs readily acknowledged there were meaningful, direct, and proven methods for strengthening heterosexual marriages that had *nothing* to do with denying same-sex couples access to the civil institution. Indeed, his own family's experience attested to the merit of premarital counseling as a mechanism for "defending" and "protecting" marriage. Yet, for all the time and energy that Burress and Citizens for Community Values expended embedding Issue 1 into the Ohio Constitution, as well as implementing the provision in state courts for a decade, they did not do anything even remotely comparable either to make the law harder for people to divorce or to make premarital counseling more readily available to opposite-sex pairs.

Imagine just how many premarital and marital counseling centers could have been set up around the nation with the tens of millions of dollars that instead went into promoting and defending antigay legislation and constitutional amendments, not to mention the hundred of millions that would have been infused into local economies if gay and lesbian couples had been permitted to marry there.

In addition to Phil Burress, Chapter 1 also presented Tami Fitzgerald, chairwoman of, and spokesperson for, Vote for Marriage NC, which promoted North Carolina's Amendment 1 during the nation's last Super-DOMA campaign. After the Tar Heel referendum passed, she was quoted as saying, "We are not antigay; we are pro-marriage." Two months after her remark, I asked all North Carolina interviewees what they thought about it, and I learned that Terri Phoenix, the director of the LGBTQ Center at the University of North Carolina at Chapel Hill, had publicly debated Tami Fitzgerald during the Amendment 1 campaign. Terri and her partner recounted what happened.

TERRI: Tami Fitzgerald is the person who calls Sarah my "sex partner."

SARAH: Terri and Fitzgerald were on a panel together, and I was in the audience. Fitzgerald pointed me out in the crowd and referred to me as Terri's "sex partner." And I thought to myself, "Where's your husband? Your 'sperm donor.'"

TERRI: The line about their being pro-marriage is false. If they're really honest about supporting marriage, why aren't they pushing adultery laws and their enforcement?

SARAH: The much more accurate statement from Tami Fitzgerald would be, "We're not antigay; we're pro-heterosexism." Yet that's an oxymoron, because favoring heterosexism *is* being antigay.

What upsets me the most is the bigotry and hatred there. Having sat in front of Fitzgerald, with her calling me a sanitized version of a very ugly thing, and to see the look on her face, and the ways in which the folks who supported Amendment 1 so dehumanized me, my partner, and my community – and then for them to want a get-out-of-jail-free card by saying "I'm not antigay" – when everything about their behavior, spoken and unspoken, suggests they are – whom are they trying to convince?

TERRI: And these state constitutional amendments haven't either reduced the rate of heterosexual divorce or increased the incidence of heterosexual marriage. There's no correlation between these amendments that allegedly defend and protect marriage and the actual statistics about what happens with marriage.

Perhaps the most memorable response to Tami Fitzgerald came from Albert, age seventy-three, and Harry, seventy-two, who live in Winston-Salem and have been together for forty-eight years:

HARRY: If they want to defend marriage, protect it against divorce. Pass constitutional amendments against cheating husbands and adulterous wives. Or spousal abuse, on both sides.

A loving same-sex couple doesn't hurt heterosexual marriage.

ALBERT: The motion picture *The Music Man* is relevant here. The lead character comes into town, looking for a problem, and then creates one. And guess who has the only solution for this manufactured difficulty? He does. So he sells the remedy and picks up to move.

There's a parallel between that story and what they've done here politically regarding gay marriage.

HARRY: The National Organization for Marriage[12] is funded substantially by the Catholic and Mormon churches.[13] Why don't they take that money, and instead of

---

[12] The National Organization for Marriage (NOM) describes itself as "a nonprofit organization with a mission to protect marriage and the faith communities that sustain it. Founded in 2007 in response to the growing need for an organized opposition to same-sex marriage in state legislatures, NOM serves as a national resource for marriage-related initiatives at the state and local level. For decades, pro-family organizations have educated the public about the importance of marriage and the family, but have lacked the organized, national presence needed to impact state and local politics in a coordinated and sustained fashion. NOM seeks to fill that void."

[13] The University of Notre Dame, near South Bend, Indiana, is among the more prominent Roman Catholic universities in the United States. In September 2015, the Notre Dame website stated, "The University of Notre Dame does not discriminate on the basis of race, color, national or ethnic origin, sex, disability, veteran status, genetic information, or age in the administration of any of its educational programs, admissions policies, scholarship and loan programs, athletic and other school-administered programs, or in employment."

The Mormon Church is the official sponsor of Brigham Young University (BYU) in Provo, Utah. In September 2015, the BYU website stated, "Brigham Young University is committed to providing academic and employment environments that are free from unlawful discrimination. Unlawful discrimination on the basis of race, color, sex, national origin, religion, age, veteran status, and/or disability will not be tolerated."

Thus, apparently neither institution of higher education was concerned about sexual-orientation or gender-identity discrimination on its campus. Although virtually every other variety of human diversity was welcomed at those two schools, LGBT folk would have to look elsewhere.

For decades, the Boy Scouts of America (BSA) had a nationwide policy against gay people serving as scout leaders. The organization was so enamored of its right to expel gay men from scouting that it defended the policy all the way to the U.S. Supreme Court (*Boy Scouts of America* v. *Dale* 2000). When BSA finally changed its mind in 2015 and allowed openly gay men and lesbians to serve as leaders, the Mormon Church – the largest single sponsor of BSA units in the country – threatened to sever its long-standing relationship with BSA (Eckholm 2015c).

See also Gordon and Gillespie (2012); Campbell, Green, and Monson (2014); and Goodstein (2015).

fighting loving same-sex couples, do something really radical, like feeding poor people? Or go to Africa and help the AIDS crisis there. Or go to India and help combat overpopulation.

But no, they need to spend millions and millions of dollars in this country to keep two old queens from marrying.

Daniel A. Bloom, the politically active Atlanta family-law attorney introduced in Chapter 3, summarized well some of the issues about what does, and does not, defend or protect the institution of marriage.

Q: So there was nothing in the Georgia political campaign surrounding Question 1 about the fact that the amendment also addressed civil unions and domestic partnerships?

A: In the legislative debate, amendment opponents argued that, if the ballot measure was just about marriage, why not take the civil unions part out of it. And Question 1's sponsors said, "Oh no, no, no."

Then, opponents of the amendment said, "If this is about protecting marriage, then let's have a constitutional amendment about adultery." And again, the answer was, "Oh no, no, no."

The effort was so clearly antigay, and not about protecting marriage.

After all, I'm a divorce lawyer, and know about all of the things to do to strengthen marriage and families. And prohibiting the recognition of same-sex relationships isn't among them.

I was also a family-court judge for five years. Not one family came to me and said that the reason they were getting divorced was because the gay couple next door got married. You know?

The whole thing was ludicrous. But that was their campaign: gay marriage would somehow delegitimize heterosexual marriage.

To continue my comprehensive response to Chief Justice Roberts' dismay at the *Obergefell* majority's proffer that those who energetically resisted the right of same-sex couples to marry were bigoted, I return to the interview with Phil Burress for more indication of what sponsors' motivations were for promoting Super-DOMAs so vigorously. I focus on Burress because he played such a prominent public role in those campaigns. Recall from Chapter 1 that, after the 2004 elections added anti-same-sex-marriage amendments to thirteen state constitutions, when the *New York Times* wanted an interest-group leader to symbolize the national story, the country's newspaper of record chose to profile Burress, who boasted to the *Times* that the movement against gay marriage was like "a forest fire with a 100 mile-per-hour wind behind it" (Dao 2004b).[14]

More than two-thirds of the way through the 2010 interview, while Burress was answering a question about the capacity of Ohio same-sex couples

---

[14] Other newspapers like the *Boston Globe* also focused on Burress (Greenberger 2004), as have legal and political scholarly analyses (e.g., Campbell and Robinson 2007, 147–48; Rosenberg 2008, 379; Klarman 2013, 106–7 and 184).

to execute binding legal documents under Issue 1, he spontaneously added an exceptionally revealing commentary.

My wife and I served for four years on the board of Exodus International. That's an international organization that helps people walk away from homosexuality. I know these people. I know what they go through. The same-sex attraction is real. It is real.

But the choice to act out on that same-sex attraction.... There's a choice. The vast majority, probably 90 to 95 percent, of the thousands and thousands of people I know who were engaged in homosexual behavior were usually abused as children, sexually abused, or were in a household where they were mentally abused. Like calling a boy a little sissy, dressing him up in dresses. Gender-identity disorder is real.

So I have a lot of compassion for people who are in this. I don't want to hurt them in any way. If they want to live together, that's their business. But they don't have the right to change the institution of marriage.

Founded in 1976, Exodus International was an organization designed to help people suppress homosexual desires. It claimed to offer a cure for homosexuality and was a forerunner of what in more recent times has been known as gay "conversion" or "reparative" therapy. When it ceased its activities in June 2013, Exodus International actually issued a public apology to the LGBT community for years of undue and harsh judgment (Lovett 2013). Moreover, states like California and New Jersey have since outlawed such therapies, and other jurisdictions have considered doing so (Shear 2015; see also American Psychological Association 2009).

Later in our interview, Burress said this:

Q: Does Issue 1 affect same-sex couples who have children?

A: I don't think so. I haven't heard that it does. I know that there are a lot of same-sex couples out there living together that have children. And I haven't heard about Issue 1 affecting that.

Q: I understand there are four or five lawsuits currently pending around the state, all of them involving lesbian couples, where one of them gave birth and therefore was the biological mother, and the partner helped to raise the child for a significant period of time. Then the couples split up, and the biological mothers are claiming that Issue 1 prevents any right to visitation or custody by the nonbiological mothers. That's the legal argument I believe is being made.

A: I hear what you're saying. *That's a problem being created by lesbians having children in the first place. This is the byproduct of a relationship that should never have happened in the first place.* When they start having children like that, then they have to sort through who has visitation rights and so forth. I don't know how that's going to shake down.

If I'm not mistaken, I think that David [Langdon] is involved in one or two of those cases. And how they're using Issue 1 I have no knowledge of. I just heard him briefly talking about it the other day that he's representing a lesbian. In fact, he was taking some heat from it he told me from somebody for representing a lesbian. He was chuckling about it.

I'd think that the biological mother has the right to say who the child is going to see. *Because there's no relationship there, and there shouldn't be.* (Emphasis added)

In summary, then, Phil Burress, the archetypical leader of the American Super-DOMA movement, accepted the following propositions as manifestly true:

- At a minimum, gay people need to be repaired. Ideally, queer folk, having first chosen to be homosexual,[15] should all ("thousands and thousands") be converted into heterosexuals.
- The vast majority ("probably 90 to 95 percent") of gay people were psychologically or sexually abused as kids, and such cruel and inhumane treatment in childhood explains their homosexuality.
- Same-sex relationships should never exist in the first place. They are fundamentally illegitimate, artificial, and wrong.
- There cannot, and should not, ever be meaningful bonds between (a) same-sex partners who are not the biologically related parents of children being raised by lesbian or gay couples and (b) those very same kids they help bring up.

How would fair-minded individuals describe or characterize someone like Phil Burress who genuinely believed these statements? Would it be reasonable to judge him or her as being intolerant of, or prejudiced against, gay men and lesbians? Does the profile of "one who is strongly partial to one's own group, religion, race, or politics and is intolerant of those who differ" apply here? What about "a person who holds blindly and intolerantly to a particular creed, opinion, etc."? If the answer to any one of these three questions is yes, then, *by definition*, Burress, Tami Fitzgerald, and the other people like them who were among the legislative and interest-group sponsors of Super-DOMAs were in

---

[15] See Wilcox and Wolpert (2000); Haider-Markel and Joslyn (2008, 2013); American Psychological Association (2009); Lewis (2009); and Whitehead (2010, 2014).

The best refutation from my couples sample of the Burress position that sexual orientation is mutable came from Florence, a North Carolina lesbian mentioned in Chapter 1.

Would it be easier not to be gay? Would my life be simpler if I were married to some man who was out there working so I could be a stay-at-home mom? Absolutely yes! And if that were a real choice for me, *I would do it.*

I didn't wake up one morning and go, "Hmm. I wonder how I can make my life hell. Oh, I think I'll be gay." How anybody could believe we act that way is beyond me. It's crazy. It just floors me, like we're all simply masochists, and that I opted to have life completely beat me down.

fact bigots, in spite of protestations to the contrary by Chief Justice Roberts and others.[16]

Please do not misunderstand me. I am very grateful to have been granted the opportunity to interview Phil Burress and other individuals I've talked with (such as Tim Nashif of the Oregon Family Council, quoted at length in my 2006 book) who did significantly help plant gay-marriage prohibitions in state constitutions or unsuccessfully sought to do so (like former Massachusetts Family Institute President Ronald Crews). These interviewees voluntarily invited me into their homes or places of business to answer candidly and thoroughly – as well as on the record – my many questions. Indeed, the historical value of our conversations is such that the Department of Manuscripts and Archives at Yale University's Sterling Memorial Library has agreed to preserve for posterity my videotaped interviews for this book and the 2006 volume. Thus, I have heartfelt appreciation for interviewees' gracious cooperation with my research, because they certainly were under no obligation to speak with me.

Moreover, I want to dispel any idea that these men – and all of my relevant conversations were with males – were somehow monsters or savages or otherwise worthy of universal, unalloyed scorn. Quite the contrary. In entirely different settings, I might admire, or even be fond of, them as individuals if they were, say, co-workers or cousins or known to me in other ways.

But as a researcher who evaluates empirically founded data, I can say with confidence that Phil Burress, Tami Fitzgerald, and other interest-group and legislative leaders like them who were involved in the national movement to deny all relationship recognition to same-sex couples lived up to dictionary-based definitions of the word "bigot." The oral histories documented in this book in large measure were byproducts of the ambitious assaults by these antigay-movement kingpins. For years, they devoted untold time and energy to a single-minded pursuit to delegitimize as thoroughly as possible the lives of families headed by gay and lesbian pairs. Burress, Fitzgerald, and their cohort were the five-star generals in America's war on same-sex couples and their children. The impulse that drove such warriors to wage battle so relentlessly harkens back to the motives compelling lawmakers in earlier American eras to fashion state and local policies embodied in signs like "Whites Only" or "No Catholics or Jews" or "Membership Limited to Gentlemen," where shut-out groups were viewed as so inferior and contemptible that institutionalized exclusivity became the legal, political, and social norm of the age.[17]

Meanwhile, as stated in Chapter 1, I do not view everyone who voted in favor of Super-DOMAs as bigots. Average voters had no large-scale, overweening commitment to subvert totally the legal and social interests of this segment of American citizens. Instead, polling data suggest a different posture. Since 2004, respondents have consistently supported providing civil unions for same-sex

---

[16] See also Herman (2000); Oliphant (2004); and Shorto (2005).
[17] See also Cahill (2007).

couples at rates appreciably higher than for the legalization of gay marriage itself (Pew Forum and Research Center 2009). In fact, a majority of respondents nationwide were in favor of civil unions as early as 2005, whereas fewer than 40 percent ever backed same-sex marriage outright during that decade (cf. Gelman, Lax, and Phillips 2010; Roberts 2010).

Moreover, generational differences in opinion were staggering. A March 2007 *New York Times*/CBS News poll, for example, found that, although only 18 percent of Americans sixty-five years of age or older supported legal marriage for gay and lesbian couples, 39 percent of adults under thirty did. Adding in the option of civil unions changed the proportions to 49 percent of seniors believing same-sex pairs should receive some form of legally recognized relationship recognition, and 68 percent of the youngest cohort backing either marriage or civil unions for everyone (Elder 2007).[18] Furthermore, by 2005, most Americans believed that gay people deserved equal rights in the workplace (Saad 2005).

Although the language of Super-DOMAs was broad enough to entangle civil unions within their prohibitions, the public campaigns on behalf of these constitutional amendments focused exclusively on marriage and virtually ignored the concepts of civil unions and domestic partnerships. As the excerpts from state-court opinions in Chapter 2 suggest, and as confirmed to me in countless interviews, proponents' public stances were consistently, "This is all about marriage, and nothing else." Indeed, Chapter 1 pointed out the extreme instance of the Georgia legislature's failure to include on the 2004 ballot the entire second part of Question 1. Accordingly, there is good empirical reason to believe that, although well over 50 percent of voters cast ballots in favor of Super-DOMAs, significant proportions of those majorities did not understand the breadth of the initiatives and referenda or supported banning civil unions and domestic partnerships for the LGBT community. And such is not the attitude of bigots.[19]

Nor were all Republicans steadfastly prejudiced against queer folk. Several prominent opinions from lower federal-court judges appointed to the bench by Ronald Reagan and George W. Bush attest to the fact. A notable trial-court illustration came from U.S. District Judge John E. Jones III, of the Middle District of Pennsylvania, whom notoriously antigay Pennsylvania Republican senator Rick Santorum enthusiastically recommended in a 2002 statement to fellow senators urging his confirmation (Weigel 2014). Striking down a 1996 Pennsylvania statute that prohibited same-sex marriage, Judge Jones concluded his decision in *Whitewood* v. *Wolf* (2014) with this sentence: "We are a better people than what these laws represent, and it is time to discard them into the ash heap of history" (992 F. Supp. 2d at 431).

---

[18] See also Lipka (2010); Becker and Scheufele (2011); and Saulny (2012).

[19] See also Wilcox and Wolpert (2000); Wilcox et al. (2007); Lofton and Haider-Markel (2007); and Egan, Persily, and Wallsten (2008).

A second instance of even-handed and unbiased treatment of lesbian and gay couples by Republican appointees occurred with U.S. District Judge Bernard A. Friedman, nominated to the Eastern District of Michigan by President Reagan. Judge Friedman was among the very few jurists to order a full trial (involving testimony of the parties and of expert witnesses) on the constitutionality of a state gay-marriage ban (Michigan's very own Proposal 2), rather than just resolving the controversy as a legal matter using written briefs submitted by counsel. Friedman's findings of fact and conclusions of law in *DeBoer* v. *Snyder* (2014) ended with this paragraph:

In attempting to define this case as a challenge to "the will of the people," state defendants lost sight of what this case is truly about: people. No court record of this proceeding could ever fully convey the personal sacrifice of these two plaintiffs [April DeBoer and Jayne Rowse] who seek to ensure that the state may no longer impair the rights of their [three] children and the thousands of others now being raised by same-sex couples. It is the Court's fervent hope that these children will grow up "to understand the integrity and closeness of their own family and its concord with other families in their community and in their daily lives." *Windsor*, 133 S. Ct. at 2694. Today's decision is a step in that direction, and affirms the enduring principle that regardless of whoever finds favor in the eyes of the most recent majority, the guarantee of equal protection must prevail. (973 F. Supp. 2d at 775)

Yet the most extraordinary lower federal-court opinion from a Republican appointee was written by Circuit Judge Richard A. Posner, nominated to the U.S. Court of Appeals for the Seventh Circuit by Ronald Reagan. In fact, Judge Posner's factual and legal analysis in *Baskin* v. *Bogan* (2014) was not only the death knell for Wisconsin's Referendum 1 but also set the gold standard by which to measure *all* of the twenty-six post-*Windsor* lower federal-court decisions addressed in the last chapter. One by one, Posner decimated each of the arguments given by the states in support of their same-sex-marriage bans. I offer here two examples of his rigorous and engaging analytic style:

Marriage confers respectability on a sexual relationship; to exclude a couple from marriage is thus to deny it a coveted status. Because homosexuality is not a voluntary condition and homosexuals are among the most stigmatized, misunderstood, and discriminated-against minorities in the history of the world, the disparagement of their sexual orientation, implicit in the denial of marriage rights to same-sex couples, is a source of continuing pain to the homosexual community. Not that allowing same-sex marriage will change in the short run the negative views that many Americans hold of same-sex marriage. But it will enhance the status of these marriages in the eyes of other Americans, and in the long run it may convert some of the opponents of such marriage by demonstrating that homosexual married couples are in essential respects, notably in the care of their adopted children, like other married couples. (766 F. 3d at 658)

...

At oral argument the state's lawyer was asked whether "Indiana's law is about successfully raising children," and since "you agree same-sex couples can successfully raise children, why shouldn't the ban be lifted as to them?" The lawyer answered that "the assumption is that with opposite-sex couples there is very little thought given during the sexual act, sometimes, to whether babies may be a consequence." In other words, Indiana's government thinks that straight couples tend to be sexually irresponsible, producing unwanted children by the carload, and so must be pressured (in the form of governmental encouragement of marriage through a combination of sticks and carrots) to marry, but that gay couples, unable as they are to produce children wanted or unwanted, are model parents – model citizens really – so have no need for marriage. Heterosexuals get drunk and pregnant, producing unwanted children; their reward is to be allowed to marry. Homosexual couples do not produce unwanted children; their reward is to be denied the right to marry. Go figure. (766 F. 3d at 662)

I wholeheartedly recommend all of Judge Posner's spellbinding *Baskin* opinion.[20]

JUDICIAL EFFICACY

I ended *America's Struggle for Same-Sex Marriage* with a nineteen-page discussion about "whether courts can effect significant social change in the United States or whether they are just deceptively hollow hopes that sap social reformers' resources and spirit" (Pinello 2006, 175). My analysis was prompted by the fact that "[t]he scholarly literature in political science ... reveal[ed] a conspicuous absence of consensus over whether American courts are important governing institutions with their own distinct power" (30). The last paragraph of *America's Struggle* summarized my conclusion on the topic:

These findings diminish the perception that courts are hollow hopes for significant social reform. With nearly all other state and national policy makers at odds with its goal, the Massachusetts Supreme Judicial Court [in *Goodridge v. Department of Public Health* (2003)] nonetheless achieved singular success in expanding the ambit of who receives the benefits of getting married in America, in inspiring political elites elsewhere in the country to follow suit, and in mobilizing grass-roots supporters to entrench their legal victory politically. (Pinello 2006, 193)

My analysis challenged, inter alia, the research of Gerald N. Rosenberg, the duly celebrated author of *The Hollow Hope: Can Courts Bring about Social Change?*, a landmark 1991 book that was so widely discussed and well received that, in 2003, the volume was given the Lasting Contribution Award of the Law and Courts Section of the American Political Science Association (APSA). As the website (lawcourts.org) of the APSA's section describes, this prize is given annually for scholarship "that stands the test of time, work that inspires long after" its publication and that "has made a lasting impression on the field of law and courts."

---

[20] A free edited version of the decision is available in my online *Casebook on Sexual Orientation and the Law* at www.danpinello.com.

And make no mistake. I am a huge fan of *The Hollow Hope*. For fifteen years, I taught a senior seminar on "Judicial Processes and Politics" to my college's criminal justice and political science majors, and *The Hollow Hope* was required reading every semester I offered the class, which was at least once a year and sometimes even twice annually. I thought Rosenberg's study was essential knowledge for my students to have, and invariably, they were completely engaged with his analysis.

Two years after *America's Struggle* was released, Gerald Rosenberg published a second edition of *The Hollow Hope*. The *only* significant alteration from the volume's first edition was the inclusion in the second of a fourth major subject part of an additional eighty-one pages, with an introduction and two chapters, all focusing on same-sex marriage. In other words, Rosenberg felt it absolutely crucial to encompass the impact of state-court marriage-equality adjudications in his thesis that courts are not reliably useful instruments for meaningful social change.

What is more, Rosenberg was fully aware of my analysis in *America's Struggle*, as seen in this excerpt from the second edition[21]:

Overall, then, it is clear that, in general, same-sex marriage litigation mobilized group support for same-sex marriage. Specifically, the victory in *Goodridge* mobilized some supporters of same-sex marriage who held elective office to issue marriage licenses to same-sex couples. It also mobilized many same-sex couples. Pinello writes that "*Goodridge* brought about enormous social change" and "had a profound inspirational effect for the marriage movement, among elites and the grass roots, at home and abroad" (Pinello 2006, 192). Pinello continues, writing that "the same-sex weddings in San Francisco, Portland, and elsewhere would not have occurred without the example of *Goodridge*" (Pinello 2006, 193). Indeed, he argues that "*Goodridge* radicalized and coalesced the gay community like no other event since the advent of AIDS in the 1980s" (Pinello 2006, 193). (Rosenberg 2008, 360)

Rosenberg's eighty-one-page disquisition on same-sex marriage closes (in a section titled "Conclusion: When Will They Ever Learn?") with this paragraph:

Ultimately, the use of litigation to win the right to same-sex marriage lends further support to the argument that courts are severely limited in their capacity to further the interests of the relatively disadvantaged. While I can understand the frustration felt by advocates of same-sex marriage, succumbing to the "lure of litigation" appears to have been the wrong move. While it is conceivable that few people could have foreseen the negative reaction to the Hawaii litigation (other than readers of this book!), after 1996 it was clear that any further litigation victories would produce continued backlash. To continue to litigate in the light of these events confused the rhetoric of rights with the reality of reaction. By litigating when they did, proponents of same-sex marriage moved too far and too fast ahead of the curve, leaping beyond what the American people could bear. The lesson here is a simple one: those who rely on the courts absent significant

---

[21] Rosenberg also quotes from or otherwise references *America's Struggle* on six other pages of *The Hollow Hope*'s second edition.

public and political support will fail to achieve meaningful social change, and may set their cause back. (Rosenberg 2008, 419)

In April 2015, less than a week before the *Obergefell* oral argument at the Supreme Court, the *New York Times* published an article about how opponents of same-sex marriage were responding to the High Court's imminent resolution of the controversy. One of the people interviewed for the piece was Gerald N. Rosenberg, who "said his former predictions of a wider, lasting backlash to marriage rulings had been overtaken by the 'sea change in public opinion'" (Eckholm 2015a). That brief statement amounts to an enormously respected scholar's having publicly to eat his own published words.

In the 1980s, Gerald Rosenberg and I were graduate students in Yale University's Department of Political Science. Our time spent studying in New Haven overlapped, and we have talked together at political science conferences and otherwise interacted substantially since then. In truth, I have long considered him to be a friend in academe, and my earlier mentioned curricular allegiance to the first edition of *The Hollow Hope* affirms my immense esteem for his erudition. Nonetheless, I cannot avoid rubbing salt in what must be a festering professional wound.

Two items from the last chapter are crucially important to this discussion of judicial efficacy and warrant recapitulation here. First is the recognition that even lower federal courts achieved the advent of legal same-sex marriage in numerous American jurisdictions. In October 2014, when the Supreme Court declined to accept state appeals from the Fourth, Seventh, and Tenth Circuits, and also when the Ninth Circuit followed its sister circuits, the number of marriage-equality jurisdictions leapt nearly overnight from nineteen to thirty-five – all without the substantive intervention of the Supreme Court itself. Hence, securing meaningful social change in sixteen states did not require the active involvement of any court of last resort. District and circuit courts were adequate for the task, something *The Hollow Hope*, with its focus on the Supreme Court, would impart to be unfathomable.

The second matter from Chapter 6 worthy of repetition here involves my temporal projections about when Congress and the states would have fully embraced marriage equality if those representative bodies had been permitted to pursue, solely through the democratic political process itself, the expansion of civil marriage to include gay and lesbian pairs. The earliest conceivable date for the congressional repeal of DOMA would have been 2023 (ten years after *Windsor* struck down the federal law), while the fiftieth state (presumptively Mississippi) voluntarily to join the marriage-equality fold would have acted sometime in the early twenty-second century (generations after *Obergefell*).

Another important scholar who has questioned the wisdom of the LGBT movement's heavy reliance on litigation as a mechanism for meaningful social change is Michael J. Klarman in *From the Closet to the Altar: Courts, Backlash, and the Struggle for Same-Sex Marriage* (2013). I had the good fortune to evaluate this volume for the *Law and Politics Book Review*[22] and gave it exceptionally high praise, as indicated by the review's opening paragraph:

Michael J. Klarman is the Great Synthesizer. A gifted and tenacious historian, he vacuums up terabytes of data from untold primary and secondary sources and then adeptly weaves the assembled knowledge into an irresistible narrative tapestry. Best known for the Bancroft-Prize-winning *From Jim Crow to Civil Rights: The Supreme Court and the Struggle for Racial Equality* [2004], Klarman has turned his ample talents for collecting and analyzing information toward chronicling the modern American gay rights movement in *From the Closet to the Altar: Courts, Backlash, and the Struggle for Same-Sex Marriage*. The result is wondrous. (Pinello 2013, 330)

My single cavil with Klarman's otherwise "magnificent historical achievement" (Pinello 2013, 333) was his commentary on judicial efficacy.

Near the end of the book, Klarman explores at length the familiar debate between courts as either facilitators of social change or fomenters of political backlash, and concludes that "[o]n balance, litigation has probably advanced the cause of gay marriage more than it has retarded it" (p. 218). No disagreement there, especially after the U.S. Supreme Court's recent invalidation of Section 3 of the federal Defense of Marriage Act (DOMA) in *United States* v. *Windsor*. Yet Klarman's next sentence is "But such litigation has also probably impeded the realization of other objectives of the gay rights movement [like banning workplace discrimination and penalizing hate crimes], and it has had significant collateral effects on politics." The grounds for at least the first half of that assertion are far more speculative.

For example, he states that "[w]ere it not for the [1993 Hawaii Supreme Court] *Baehr* [v. *Lewin*] litigation, DOMA probably would not exist" (p. 212). That's a remarkable statement in light of the rest of his astute political examination, because the congressional passage of DOMA was only a question of when, not if. Surely there's no doubt that the Hawaii litigation triggered a national backlash. But any such notable first step by a state judiciary (or legislature), whether in Hawaii, Massachusetts, Vermont, or another place, would have prompted the same political response in the nation's capitol. *Baehr* itself was not a necessary condition for DOMA.

More importantly, Klarman presumes that, without the same-sex-marriage litigation, American public opinion on gay rights issues would have continued to advance at the same breath-taking rates since the 1990s, noting, for instance, that "[b]efore 2009, the annual rate of increase in support for gay marriage was about 1.5 percentage points, but since then it has been closer to 4 percentage points" (pp. 196–97). In light of Klarman's own convincing argument that the many marriage cases over two decades moved lesbians and gay men to come out of the closet in droves, he cannot sustain a concomitant claim that public opinion in support of, say, the prohibition of sexual-orientation discrimination would have necessarily accrued at the same rate, because the increased visibility of gay people was an essential ingredient for the public support of all their rights.[23]

---

[22] Published by the Law and Courts Section of the American Political Science Association.
[23] See also Lewis and Rogers (1999); Bellafante (2006); Lewis (2011); and Reynolds (2013).

With regard to assessing judicial impact, Klarman invites consideration of experiences elsewhere: "In other countries, where courts typically play a less central role on issues of social reform, gay rights progress has occurred more incrementally through legislatures and has generated less political backlash" (p. 167). But more nuanced attention to cross-national comparisons provides a different understanding than what *From the Closet to the Altar* offers. For example, Miriam Smith proved in her masterful *Political Institutions and Lesbian and Gay Rights in the United States and Canada* [2008] how the porous American political system facilitates grass-roots retrenchments in civil rights.[24] A system of federalism that places at the subnational level the most important governmental powers touching minority rights, coupled with democratic checks such as referenda and citizen initiatives to amend subnational constitutions, necessarily produce the most opportunities for the political backlash that Klarman abhors. Whereas, in a country like Canada, where governmental power is concentrated at the national level in a Westminster parliamentary system among numerous competitive national political parties, the occasions for the suppression of minority rights are vastly reduced. Thus, as Smith highlighted, Canada's parliament decriminalized consensual sodomy nationwide as long ago as 1969, thereby removing the criminal stigma surrounding gay Canadians that might later have retarded their civil rights advances. Yet it took until the 2003 ruling by the Supreme Court in *Lawrence* v. *Texas* to invalidate all sodomy laws here. And the 34-year lag between the two actions is not unparalleled. The Canadian parliament in 2005 legalized marriage for all same-sex couples there, whereas only about one-third of gay and lesbian pairs in the United States may legally wed eight years later, and with nationwide marriage equality nowhere reliably in sight. As Smith clearly demonstrated, these dissimilar gay rights outcomes are not attributable at all to cultural or social differences between the two countries. Rather, political structure is the key explanatory variable. Accordingly, it's no wonder gay people in the United States turned to courts for civil rights remedies. Legal tribunals provided them the only meaningful hope for enduring reform. *And the inevitable backlash that is guaranteed by America's institutional organization should not have surprised – or unduly alarmed – any knowledgeable observer.* (Pinello 2013, 332–33, emphasis added)[25]

After all, as Judge Posner – author of dozens of books, including *Sex and Reason* (1994) – observed in *Baskin* v. *Bogan* (2014), "[H]omosexuals are among the most stigmatized, misunderstood, and discriminated-against minorities in the history of the world," and he made no brief for American exceptionalism from that generalization. Chapter 5 recalls that other minorities who were at least equally despised were people of color in the United States before the 1970s and Jews in Nazi-occupied Europe. And from a contemporary worldwide perspective, Posner's assessment is well established. In 2015, the International Lesbian, Gay, Bisexual, Trans and Intersex Association listed more than seventy-five countries with criminal laws against sexual activity by LGBT

---

[24] See also Rayside (2007) and Wilson (2013).

[25] The legal and political science literatures on judicial efficacy are enormous and include other instructive contributions from Andersen (2005); Keck (2009, 2014); Howard and Steigerwalt (2011); Eskridge (2013); Gash (2015); and Grossman and Swedlow (2015). Cf. D'Emilio (2007).

people, including eight nations with the death penalty for same-sex intimacy ("Erasing 76 Crimes" 2015).

Consequently, same-sex couples and their supporters were absolutely correct to seek relief in Hawaii state courts in the early 1990s. Then they were spot on to turn to the Vermont judiciary for vindication later that decade. And approaching the Massachusetts bench for a remedy made perfectly logical sense a few years thereafter. And so on and so forth. As Bishin et al. (2015) persuasively demonstrated, "[G]roups pursuing rights should not be dissuaded by threats of backlash that will set their movement back in the court of public opinion."[26]

No other avenue for the comprehensive consummation of *this* meaningful social change was elsewhere on the U.S. policy-making horizon during the late twentieth and early twenty-first centuries, nor in the foreseeable future. There was simply no viable hope for marriage equality in the United States other than through the judiciary. And the denouement of more than two decades of reliance on the bench for deliverance from the war on same-sex couples and their families was the 2013–15 tsunami of golden court rulings. In addition, those judgments were "consumer-choice" (Canon 1998, 221–23), or essentially self-implementing. So compliance on the ground was virtually immediate and universal (Eckholm and Fernandez 2015; "Federal Judges' Rulings Clear Hurdles to Same-Sex Marriages" 2015; "Louisiana: Marriage Barrier Falls" 2015; Johnson 2015b; cf. Mura and Pérez-Peña 2015). Thus, by July 2015, *all* American lesbian and gay pairs could get legally married *in their homes states*, proving that their advocates' strategic convictions had been empirically sound, and *not* hollow.

As Judge Posner succinctly reminded us, "Minorities trampled on by the democratic process have recourse to the courts; the recourse is called constitutional law" (*Baskin* 2014, 671).

---

[26] See also Kreitzer, Hamilton, and Tolbert (2014).

APPENDIX A

The Texts of Super-DOMAs

GEORGIA'S QUESTION 1 OF NOVEMBER 2004

This state shall recognize as marriage only the union of man and woman. Marriages between persons of the same sex are prohibited in this state. No union between persons of the same sex shall be recognized by this state as entitled to the benefits of marriage. This state shall not give effect to any public act, record or judicial proceeding of any other state or jurisdiction respecting a relationship between persons of the same sex that is treated as a marriage under the laws of such other state or jurisdiction. The courts of this state shall have no jurisdiction to grant a divorce or separate maintenance with respect to any such relationship or otherwise to consider or rule on any of the parties' respective rights arising as a result of or in connection with such relationship.

MICHIGAN'S PROPOSAL 2 OF NOVEMBER 2004

To secure and preserve the benefits of marriage for our society and for future generations of children, the union of one man and one woman in marriage shall be the only agreement recognized as a marriage or similar union for any purpose.

NORTH CAROLINA'S AMENDMENT 1 OF MAY 2012

Marriage between one man and one woman is the only domestic legal union that shall be valid or recognized in this State.

OHIO'S ISSUE 1 OF NOVEMBER 2004

Only a union between one man and one woman may be a marriage valid in or recognized by this state and its political subdivisions. This state and its political subdivisions shall not create or recognize a legal status for relationships of unmarried individuals that intends to approximate the design, qualities, significance or effect of marriage.

TEXAS'S PROPOSITION 2 OF NOVEMBER 2005

Marriage in this state shall consist only of the union of one man and one woman. This state or a political subdivision of this state may not create or recognize any legal status identical or similar to marriage.

WISCONSIN'S REFERENDUM 1 OF NOVEMBER 2006

Only a marriage between one man and one woman shall be valid or recognized as a marriage in this state. A legal status identical or substantially similar to that of marriage for unmarried individuals shall not be valid or recognized in this state.

Protocol of Interview Questions for Same-Sex Couples

BACKGROUND

What is your age?
Do you work outside the home?
What kind of work do you do?
You're a couple, right? How long have you been together?
How long has each of you lived in [name of state]?
Do you have any children? If so, what are their gender and age?

RELATIONSHIP RECOGNITION

Have you had any ceremony to celebrate your relationship?
Are you interested in getting married to each other? Why, or why not?
Would you go to another state or country to get married?
Does a civil union or domestic partnership interest you? Why, or why not?
Would some form of government recognition of your relationship benefit you
    or your family? How so?

[NAME OF SUPER-DOMA]

Are you familiar with [name of state]'s [name of Super-DOMA]?
What did the passage of [name of Super-DOMA] mean to you?
Has [name of Super-DOMA] affected you or your family in some direct way?

CHILDREN

Does [child(ren)'s name]'s school recognize [the same-sex partner of the biolog-
    ical parent] as a guardian or family member of [child(ren)'s name]?

If [child(ren)'s name]'s school needed a parent's signature on a school form, would school officials accept the signature of [the same-sex partner]?

If there were a medical or other emergency at school, would school officials allow [the same-sex partner] to make health care or other choices on [child(ren)'s name]'s behalf?

HOSPITALS

If one of you were hospitalized, would the local hospital permit the other to visit?

If one of you were unable to make medical-care decisions for yourself, would the local hospital allow the other to make such choices?

Do local hospitals recognize as family the same-sex partners of the biological parents of child patients?

BENEFITS

Have you or your family been denied any benefits because of [name of Super-DOMA]?

Health insurance? Property or inheritance issues? Taxation?

Have you done anything to try to overcome the denial of these benefits? What?

Have you drawn up, or will you draw up, wills or execute other legal documents like powers of attorney because of [name of Super-DOMA]? Health care proxies? Hospital visitation authorizations? Living wills?

Did you hire a lawyer to do so? How much did it cost?

Are you confident that these documents will be honored when needed?

Has the passage of [name of Super-DOMA] affected your senses of security or well-being? How?

Do you know of any other practical, grassroots effects of [name of Super-DOMA]?

RESISTANCE/PLAYING THE SYSTEM

Have you engaged, or will you engage, in any acts of resistance with regard to [name of Super-DOMA]?

For example, do you ever impersonate each other when dealing with third parties in order to achieve goals made more simple by such pretense?

Have you ever presented yourselves as siblings? At a hospital or other health care facility?

What about tax advantages achieved through deductions of child expenses or mortgage expense?

RELOCATION

Have you ever thought of leaving [name of state] for another state that was
   more legally welcoming of your relationship?
What legal or political events might prompt you to move to another state?
What is the likelihood that you would relocate?

OTHER COUPLES

Other than what you've said about yourselves, do you know of any other same-
   sex couples in [name of state] who have been directly affected by [name of
   Super-DOMA]? How so?
Do you know of any couples who have in fact left [name of state] because of
   [name of Super-DOMA]?
Do you know of any couples who are thinking of leaving [name of state]?
Do you know of any couples who have not relocated to [name of state] from
   another place because of [name of Super-DOMA]?

CONCLUSION

Is there anything else involving [name of Super-DOMA] that you'd like to add?

Case References

Adoption of Tammy. 1993. 416 Mass. 205, 619 N.E. 2d 315.
Advisory Opinion to the Attorney General re: Florida Marriage Protection Amendment. 2006. 926 So. 2d 1229.
Angel Lace M. v. Terry M. 1994. 184 Wis. 2d 492, 516 N.W. 2d 678.
Appling v. Walker. 2014. 2014 WI 96, 358 Wis. 2d 132, 853 N.W. 2d 888.
Baehr v. Lewin. 1993. 74 Haw. 645, 852 P.2d 44.
Baskin v. Bogan [District Court]. 2014. 12 F. Supp. 3d 1144.
Baskin v. Bogan [Court of Appeals]. 2014. 766 F. 3d 648.
Bassett v. Snyder. 2014. 59 F. Supp. 3d 837.
Bishop v. Smith. 2014. 760 F. 3d 1070.
Bishop v. United States ex rel. Holder. 2014. 962 F. Supp. 2d 1252.
Bond v. United States. 2011. 564 U.S. 211.
Boseman v. Jarrell. 2010. 364 N.C. 537, 704 S.E. 2d 494.
Bostic v. Rainey. 2014. 970 F. Supp. 2d 456.
Bostic v. Schaefer. 2014. 760 F. 3d 352.
Bourke v. Beshear. 2014. 996 F. Supp. 2d 542.
Bowers v. Hardwick. 1986. 478 U.S. 186.
Boy Scouts of America v. Dale. 2000. 530 U.S. 640.
Brandon-Thomas v. Brandon-Thomas. 2015. 163 So. 3d 644.
Brenner v. Scott. 2014. 999 F. Supp. 2d 1278.
Brinkman v. Miami University. 2007. 2007-Ohio-4372, 2007 Ohio App. LEXIS 3910.
Burns v. Hickenlooper. 2014. 2014 U.S. Dist. LEXIS 100894.
Campaign for Southern Equality v. Bryant. 2014. 64 F. Supp. 3d 906.
Citizens United v. Federal Election Commission. 2010. 558 U.S. 310.
City of Atlanta v. McKinney. 1995. 265 Ga. 161, 454 S.E. 2d 517.
City of Atlanta v. Morgan. 1997. 268 Ga. 586, 492 S.E. 2d 193.

Cleveland Taxpayers v. *Cleveland*. 2010. 2010-Ohio-4685, 2010 Ohio App. LEXIS 3981.

Conde-Vidal v. *Garcia-Padilla*. 2014. 54 F. Supp. 3d 157.

DeBoer v. *Snyder* [District Court]. 2014. 973 F. Supp. 2d 757.

DeBoer v. *Snyder* [Court of Appeals]. 2014. 772 F. 3d 388.

De Leon v. *Perry*. 2014. 975 F. Supp. 2d 632.

De Sylva v. *Ballentine*. 1956. 351 U.S. 570.

Elane Photography, LLC v. *Willock*. 2013. 309 P. 3d 53.

Fisher-Borne v. *Smith*. 2014. 14 F. Supp. 3d 695.

Geiger v. *Kitzhaber*. 2014. 994 F. Supp. 2d 1128.

Goodridge v. *Department of Public Health*. 2003. 440 Mass. 309, 798 N.E. 2d 941.

Goodson v. *Castellanos*. 2007. 214 S.W. 3d 741.

Griswold v. *Connecticut*. 1965. 381 U.S. 479.

Hamby v. *Parnell*. 2014. 56 F. Supp. 3d 1056.

Harmon v. *Davis*. 2010. 2010 Mich. App. LEXIS 2566.

Henry v. *Himes*. 2014. 14 F. Supp. 3d 1036.

Hollingsworth v. *Perry*. 2013. 570 U.S. ___, 133 S. Ct. 2652.

In re Adoption of Jane Doe. 1998. 130 Ohio App. 3d 288; 719 N.E. 2d 1071.

In re Adoption of K.R.S. 2012. 109 So. 3d 176.

In re Bonfield. 2002. 97 Ohio St. 3d 387, 2002-Ohio-6660, 780 N.E.2d 241.

In re Divorce of Naylor and Daly. 2011. 330 S.W. 3d 434.

In re Hadaway. 2008. 290 Ga. App. 453, 659 S.E.2d 863.

In the Matter of the Marriage of J.B. and H.B. 2010. 326 S.W. 3d 654.

Jernigan v. *Crane*. 2014. 64 F. Supp. 3d 1261.

Kitchen v. *Herbert* [District Court]. 2013. 961 F. Supp. 2d 1181.

Kitchen v. *Herbert* [Court of Appeals]. 2014. 755 F. 3d 1193.

Langbehn v. *Public Health Trust of Miami-Dade County*. 2009. 661 F. Supp. 2d 1326.

Latta v. *Otter* [District Court]. 2014. 19 F. Supp. 3d 1054.

Latta v. *Otter* [Court of Appeals]. 2014. 771 F. 3d 456.

Lawrence v. *Texas*. 2003. 539 U.S. 558.

Lawson v. *Kelly*. 2014. 58 F. Supp. 3d 923.

Loving v. *Virginia*. 1967. 388 U.S. 1.

Matter of Jacob. 1995. 86 N.Y. 2d 651, 660 N.E. 2d 397, 636 N.Y.S. 2d 716.

McConkey v. *Van Hollen*. 2010. 2010 WI 57, 326 Wis. 2d 1, 783 N.W. 2d 855.

McKettrick v. *McKettrick*. 2015. 2015-Ohio-366, 2015 Ohio App. LEXIS 342.

National Pride at Work, Inc. v. *Governor of Michigan*. 2008. 481 Mich. 56, 748 N.W. 2d 524.

Nevada Dep't of Human Res. v. *Hibbs*. 2003. 538 U.S. 721.

Obergefell v. *Hodges*. 2015. ___ U.S. ___, 135 S. Ct. 2584.

Obergefell v. *Wymyslo*. 2013. 962 F. Supp. 2d 968.

Ohio ex rel. Popovici v. *Agler*. 1930. 280 U.S. 379.

Perdue v. *O'Kelley*. 2006. 280 Ga. 732, 632 S.E. 2d 110.

Ralph v. *City of New Orleans*. 2009. 4 So. 3d 146.

Robicheaux v. *Caldwell*. 2014. 2 F. Supp. 3d 910.

Romer v. *Evans*. 1996. 517 U.S. 620.

Rosenbrahn v. *Daugaard*. 2015. 61 F. Supp. 3d 862.

Ross v. *Goldstein*. 2006. 203 S.W. 3d 508.

Rowell v. *Smith*. 2012. 133 Ohio St. 3d 288, 2012-Ohio-4313, 978 N.E. 2d 146.

Searcey v. *Strange*. 2015. 2015 U.S. Dist. LEXIS 7776.

Shelby County v. *Holder*. 2013. 570 U.S. ___, 133 S. Ct. 2612.

South Carolina v. *Katzenbach*. 1966. 383 U.S. 301.

Stankevich v. *Milliron*. 2013. 2013 Mich. App. LEXIS 1684.

State v. *Carswell*. 2007. 114 Ohio St. 3d 210, 2007 Ohio 3723, 871 N.E. 2d 547.

Tanco v. *Haslam*. 2014. 7 F. Supp. 3d 759.

Texas v. *Naylor and Daly*. 2015. 2015 Tex. LEXIS 581, 58 Tex. Sup. J. 1216.

T.M.H. v. *D.M.T.* 2011. 79 So. 3d 787.

United States v. *Windsor*. 2013. 570 U.S. ___, 133 S. Ct. 2675.

Waters v. *Ricketts*. 2015. 48 F. Supp. 3d 1271.

Wheeler v. *Wheeler*. 2007. 281 Ga. 838, 642 S.E.2d 103.

Whitewood v. *Wolf*. 2014. 992 F. Supp. 2d 410.

Wolf v. *Walker*. 2014. 986 F. Supp. 2d 982.

Zablocki v. *Redhail*. 1978. 434 U.S. 374.

References

"261 DADT discharges in 2010." 2011. www.advocate.com. March 25.

adams, jimi, and Ryan Light. 2015. "Scientific Consensus, the Law, and Same Sex Parenting Outcomes." *Social Science Research* 53:300.

American Psychological Association. 2009. *Report of the Task Force on Therapeutic Responses to Sexual Orientation.* Washington, DC: American Psychological Association.

Andersen, Ellen Ann. 2005. *Out of the Closets and into the Courts: Legal Opportunity Structure and Gay Rights Litigation.* Ann Arbor, MI: University of Michigan Press.

Andersen, Ellen Ann. 2009. "The Gay Divorcée: The Case of the Missing Argument." In Scott Barclay, Mary Bernstein, and Anna-Maria Marshall (eds.), *Queer Mobilizations: LGBT Activists Confront the Law.* New York: New York University Press, 281–302.

"Anti-Gay Adoption Bill Another Shameful Moment for Michigan." 2015. *Detroit Free Press* Editorial Board. June 12.

Associated Press. 2014. "Judges Take Tough Tone at Gay Marriage Hearing." *New York Times.* August 26.

Associated Press. 2015a. "Kentucky Taxpayers Owe $2.3 Million in Fees in Same-Sex Marriage Case." August 25.

Associated Press. 2015b. "Ohio to Pay $1.3 Million in Same-Sex Marriage Attorneys' Fees." November 2.

Badgett, M. V. Lee, and Christy Mallory. 2014. "The *Windsor* Effect on Marriages by Same-Sex Couples." Los Angeles: Williams Institute, the Law School of the University of California at Los Angeles.

Bai, Matt. 2004. "Who Lost Ohio?" *New York Times Magazine.* November 21.

Barth, Jay, L. Marvin Overby, and Scott H. Huffmon. 2009. "Community Context, Personal Contact, and Support for an Anti-Gay Rights Referendum." *Political Research Quarterly* 62:355.

Becker, Amy B., and Dietram A. Scheufele. 2011. "New Voters, New Outlook? Predispositions, Social Networks, and the Changing Politics of Gay Civil Rights." *Social Science Quarterly* 92:324.

Bell, Dawson. 2009. "Michigan Voters Shifting Views on Gay Couples." *Detroit Free Press.* June 7.

Bellafante, Ginia. 2005. "Surrogate Mothers' New Niche: Bearing Babies for Gay Couples." *New York Times.* May 27.

Bellafante, Ginia. 2006. "In the Heartland and out of the Closet." *New York Times.* December 28.

Bernard, Tara Siegel. 2011. "The Extra Hoops Gay Parents Must Jump Through." *New York Times.* March 24.

Bernard, Tara Siegel. 2012. "A Family With Two Moms, except in the Eyes of the Law." *New York Times.* July 21.

Bernard, Tara Siegel. 2015. "Same-Sex Parents' Right May Be Unresolved." *New York Times.* June 15.

Beyerlein, Kraig, and Christopher J. Eberle. 2014. "Who Violates The Principles of Political Liberalism?: Religion, Restraint, and the Decision to Reject Same-Sex Marriage." *Politics and Religion* 7:240.

Biblarz, Timothy J., and Judith Stacey. 2010. "How Does the Gender of Parents Matter?" *Journal of Marriage and Family* 72:3.

Biegel, Stuart. 2010. *The Right to Be Out: Sexual Orientation and Gender Identity in America's Public Schools.* Minneapolis, MN: University of Minnesota Press.

Biggers, Daniel R. 2014. *Morality at the Ballot: Direct Democracy and Political Engagement in the United States.* New York: Cambridge University Press.

Bishin, Benjamin G., Thomas J. Hayes, Matthew B. Incantalupo, and Charles Anthony. 2015. "Opinion Backlash and Public Attitudes: Are Political Advances in Gay Rights Counterproductive?" *American Journal of Political Science.* doi: 10.1111/ajps.12181

Biskupic, Joan. 2015. "As U.S. gay-marriage battle looms, attorneys fight over fees." www.reuters.com. April 16.

Bluemke, Jessica. 2012. "Pastor calls for electrified fence to corral and exterminate gays." www.patheos.com. May 24.

Bobic, Igor. 2013. "Boehner calls ENDA 'unnecessary.'" www.talkingpointsmemo.com. November 14.

Bosman, Julie. 2015. "One Couple's Unanticipated Journey to Center of Landmark Gay Rights Case." *New York Times.* January 24.

Bowe, John. 2006. "Gay Donor or Gay Dad?" *New York Times Magazine.* November 19.

Brekke, Kira. 2014. "Gay widower shares heartbreaking story of why he's suing Alabama." www.huffingtonpost.com. August 6.

Brennan, Bryna. 1989. "'Boarder Babies': Abandoned by Addicted Mothers, and Still Unwanted." *Los Angeles Times.* July 30.

Bruni, Frank. 2015. "The G.O.P.'s Assertive God Squad." *New York Times.* Opinion. February 25.

Bumiller, Elisabeth. 2004. "Bush Says His Party Is Wrong to Oppose Gay Civil Unions." *New York Times.* October 26.

Burger, Timothy J. 2014. "Inside George W. Bush's closet." *Politico Magazine.* www.politico.com. July/August.

Button, James W., Barbara A. Rienzo, and Kenneth D. Wald. 2000. "The Politics of Gay Rights at the Local and State Level." In Craig A. Rimmerman, Kenneth D. Wald, and

Clyde Wilcox (eds.), *The Politics of Gay Rights*. Chicago: University of Chicago Press, 269–89.

Cahill, Sean. 2005. "The Symbolic Centrality of Gay Marriage in the 2004 Presidential Election." In H. N. Hirsch (ed.), *The Future of Gay Rights in America*. New York: Routledge, 47–80.

Cahill, Sean. 2007. "The Anti-Gay Marriage Movement." In Craig A. Rimmerman and Clyde Wilcox (eds.), *The Politics of Same-Sex Marriage*. Chicago: University of Chicago Press, 155–91.

Cahn, Peter S. 2013. "The Campus Climate for Gay Faculty." *Chronicle of Higher Education*. June 14.

Campbell, David C., and Carin Robinson. 2007. "Religious Coalitions for and against Gay Marriage: The Culture War Rages on." In Craig A. Rimmerman and Clyde Wilcox (eds.), *The Politics of Same-Sex Marriage*. Chicago: University of Chicago Press, 131–54.

Campbell, David E., John C. Green, and J. Quin Monson. 2014. *Seeking the Promised Land: Mormons and American Politics*. New York: Cambridge University Press.

Campbell, David E., and J. Quin Monson. 2008. "The Religion Card: Gay Marriage and the 2004 Presidential Election." *Public Opinion Quarterly* 72:399.

Canon, Bradley C. 1998. "The Supreme Court and Policy Reform: The Hollow Hope Revisited." In David A. Schultz (ed.), *Leveraging the Law: Using the Courts to Achieve Social Change*. New York: Peter Lang, 215–49.

Cason, Mike. 2014. "Paul Hard, plaintiff in marriage recognition lawsuit, describes pain of being treated with indifference." blog.al.com. February 13.

Chaffee, Nadine. 2007. "One Son's Choice: Love or Country?" *Newsweek*. February 5.

Chibbaro, Lou, Jr. 2013. "D.C. court expands staff after increase in gay weddings." www.washingtonblade.com. September 16.

Conley, Dalton. 2007. "Spread the Wealth of Spousal Rights." *New York Times*. Opinion. May 20.

Cosentino, Lawrence. 2011. "State of tarnished pride." www.lansingcitypulse.com. June 8.

"Court Decision Prompts Domestic Partner Policy Revision." 2009. *Blueprint* 11 (2):3. Detroit: Blue Cross Blue Shield of Michigan.

Crampton, Thomas. 2004. "Using the Courts to Wage a War on Gay Marriage." *New York Times*. May 9.

D'Amico, Francine. 2000. "Sex/uality and Military Service." In Craig A. Rimmerman, Kenneth D. Wald, and Clyde Wilcox (eds.), *The Politics of Gay Rights*. Chicago: University of Chicago Press, 249–65.

Dao, James. 2004a. "Same-Sex Marriage Issue Key to Some G.O.P. Races." *New York Times*. November 4.

Dao, James. 2004b. "Flush with Victory, Grass-Roots Crusader against Same-Sex Marriage Thinks Big." *New York Times*. November 26.

Davey, Monica. 2014. "Twinned Cities Now Following Different Paths." *New York Times*. January 13.

Davey, Monica. 2015. "Gay Rights Battle in Indiana Moves to Local Level." *New York Times*. October 1.

D'Emilio, John. 2000. "Cycles of Change, Questions of Strategy: The Gay and Lesbian Movement after Fifty Years." In Craig A. Rimmerman, Kenneth D. Wald, and Clyde

Wilcox (eds.), *The Politics of Gay Rights*. Chicago: University of Chicago Press, 31–53.

D'Emilio, John. 2007. "Will the Courts Set Us Free? Reflections on the Campaign for Same-Sex Marriage." In Craig A. Rimmerman and Clyde Wilcox (eds.), *The Politics of Same-Sex Marriage*. Chicago: University of Chicago Press, 39–64.

Dillender, Marcus. 2014. "The Death of Marriage? The Effects of New Forms of Legal Recognition on Marriage Rates in the United States." *Demography* 51:563.

Doan, Long, Annalise Loehr, and Lisa R. Miller. 2014. "Formal Rights and Informal Privileges for Same-Sex Couples: Evidence from a National Survey Experiment." *American Sociological Review* 79:1172.

Dominus, Susan. 2004. "Growing up with Mom and Mom." *New York Times Magazine*. October 24.

Dorf, Michael C., and Sidney Tarrow. 2014. "Strange Bedfellows: How an Anticipatory Countermovement Brought Same-Sex Marriage into the Public Arena." *Law and Social Inquiry* 39:449.

Dyck, Joshua J., and Shanna Pearson-Merkowitz. 2012. "The Conspiracy of Silence: Context and Voting on Gay Marriage Ballot Measures." *Political Research Quarterly* 65:745.

Eckholm, Eric. 2015a. "Opponents of Gay Marriage Ponder Strategy as Issue Reaches Supreme Court." *New York Times*. April 22.

Eckholm, Eric. 2015b. "Next Fight for Gay Rights: Bias in Jobs and Housing." *New York Times*. June 28.

Eckholm, Eric. 2015c. "Mormon Church Will Keep Ties with Boy Scouts despite Objecting to Gay Leaders." *New York Times*. August 27.

Eckholm, Eric, and Manny Fernandez. 2015. "Falling in Line in the South with Ruling on Marriage." *New York Times*. June 30.

Egan, Patrick J., Nathaniel Persily, and Kevin Wallsten. 2008. "Gay Rights." In Nathaniel Persily, Jack Citrin, and Patrick J. Egan (eds.), *Public Opinion and Constitutional Controversy*. New York: Oxford University Press, 234–66.

Elder, Janet. 2007. "Those Young People, They're So Unpredictable." *New York Times*. April 22.

Ellis, Lindsay. 2015. "Supreme Court's Gay-Marriage Ruling Allows Something Else: Gay Divorce." *Wall Street Journal*. August 14.

Ellison, Christopher G., Gabriel A. Acevedo, and Aida I. Ramos-Wada. 2011. "Religion and Attitudes toward Same-Sex Marriage among U.S. Latinos." *Social Science Quarterly* 92:35.

Engel, Stephen M. 2015. "Developmental Perspectives on Lesbian and Gay Politics: Fragmented Citizenship in a Fragmented State." *Perspectives on Politics* 13:287.

Ensley, Michael J., and Erik P. Bucy. 2010. "Do Candidate Positions Matter? The Effect of the Gay Marriage Question on Gubernatorial Elections." *American Politics Research* 38:142.

"Erasing 76 Crimes" 2015. "79 Countries Where Homosexuality Is Illegal." 76crimes .com July 9.

Eskridge, William N., Jr. 1994. "GayLegal Narratives." *Stanford Law Review* 46:607.

Eskridge, William N., Jr. 2013. "Backlash Politics: How Constitutional Litigation Has Advanced Marriage Equality in the United States." *Boston University Law Review* 93:275.

Eskridge, William N., Jr. 2015. "It's Not Gay Marriage vs. the Church Anymore." *New York Times*. April 26.

Fausset, Richard. 2015. "Unlikely Allies in a Gay Rights Battle in Georgia." *New York Times*. March 7.

"Federal Judges' Rulings Clear Hurdles to Same-Sex Marriages." 2015. *New York Times*. July 2. National Briefing.

Fenno, Richard F., Jr. 1986. "Observation, Context, and Sequence in the Study of Politics." *American Political Science Review* 80:3.

Flegenheimer, Matt. 2015. "In Manhattan, a Happy Union of Matrimony and Bureaucracy." *New York Times*. September 1.

Gamble, Barbara S. 1997. "Putting Civil Rights to a Popular Vote." *American Journal of Political Science* 41:245.

Garretson, Jeremiah J. 2014. "Changing with the Times: The Spillover Effects of Same-Sex Marriage Ballot Measures on Presidential Elections." *Political Research Quarterly* 67:280.

Gash, Alison L. 2015. *Below the Radar: How Silence Can Save Civil Rights*. New York: Oxford University Press.

Gates, Gary J. 2013. "LGBT Parenting in the United States." Los Angeles: Williams Institute, the Law School of the University of California at Los Angeles.

Gates, Gary J. 2015. "Demographics of Married and Unmarried Same-Sex Couples: Analyses of the 2013 American Community Survey." Los Angeles: Williams Institute, the Law School of the University of California at Los Angeles.

Gates, Gary J., and Abigail M. Cooke. 2011a. "Ohio Census Snapshot: 2010." Los Angeles: Williams Institute, the Law School of the University of California at Los Angeles.

Gates, Gary J., and Abigail M. Cooke. 2011b. "United States Census Snapshot: 2010." Los Angeles: Williams Institute, the Law School of the University of California at Los Angeles.

Gates, Gary J., and Frank Newport. 2012. "Special report: 3.4% of U.S. adults identify as LGBT." www.gallup.com. October 18.

Gates, Gary J., and Frank Newport. 2015. "An estimated 780,000 Americans in same-sex marriages." www.gallup.com. April 24.

Gates, Gary J., and Jason Ost. 2004. *The Gay & Lesbian Atlas*. Washington, DC: Urban Institute Press.

"Gay state workers in Michigan lose DP benefits." 2004. www.advocate.com. December 3.

Gelman, Andrew, Jeffrey Lax, and Justin Phillips. 2010. "Over Time, a Gay Marriage Groundswell." *New York Times*. August 22.

Gilgoff, Dan. 2007. *The Jesus Machine: How James Dobson, Focus on the Family, and Evangelical America Are Winning the Culture War*. New York: St. Martin's Griffin.

Goldberg, Abbie E., Nanette K. Gartrell, and Gary Gates. 2014. "Research Report on LGB-Parent Families." Los Angeles: Williams Institute, the Law School of the University of California at Los Angeles. July.

Goodstein, Laurie. 2015. "Mormons Sharpen Stand against Same-Sex Marriage." *New York Times*. November 7.

Gordon, Elizabeth Ellen, and William L. Gillespie. 2012. "The Culture of Obedience and the Politics of Stealth: Mormon Mobilization against ERA and Same-Sex Marriage." *Politics and Religion* 5:343.

Gossett, Charles W. 2009. "Pushing the Envelope: Dillon's Rule and Local Domestic-Partnership Ordinances." In Scott Barclay, Mary Bernstein, and Anna-Maria Marshall (eds.), *Queer Mobilizations: LGBT Activists Confront the Law*. New York: New York University Press, 158–86.

Green, John C. 2000. "Antigay: Varieties of Opposition to Gay Rights." In Craig A. Rimmerman, Kenneth D. Wald, and Clyde Wilcox (eds.), *The Politics of Gay Rights*. Chicago: University of Chicago Press, 121–38.

Greenberger, Scott S. 2004. "Gay-Marriage Ruling Pushed Voters; Mobilized Bush, Left Kerry Wary." *Boston Globe*, November 7.

Grossmann, Matt, and Brendon Swedlow. 2015. "Judicial Contributions to U.S. National Policy Change since 1945." *Journal of Law and Courts* 3:1.

Grummel, John A. 2008. "Morality Politics, Direct Democracy, and Turnout." *State Politics and Policy Quarterly* 8:282.

Haider-Markel, Donald P., and Mark R. Joslyn. 2008. "Beliefs about the Origins of Homosexuality and Support for Gay Rights." *Public Opinion Quarterly* 72:291.

Haider-Markel, Donald P., and Mark R. Joslyn. 2013. "Politicizing Biology: Social Movements, Parties, and the Case of Homosexuality." *Social Science Journal* 50:603.

Hanson, David W. 2010a. "How to Be Welcoming: Here's a List of Strategies to Recruit and Retain Top Gay and Lesbian Job Candidates." *Chronicle of Higher Education*. January 29.

Hanson, David W. 2010b. "Adoption Advice for Gay and Lesbian Employees." *Chronicle of Higher Education*. March 23.

Hawes, Jennifer Berry. 2015. "Judge orders S.C. attorney general to pay $135,276 in gay marriage attorneys' fees." www.postandcourier.com. August 10.

Healthcare Equality Index. 2009. www.hrc.org/issues/hei.asp.

Healy, Jack. 2015. "States Weigh Gay Marriage, Rights and Cake." *New York Times*. July 8.

Healy, Jack, Michael D. Shear, and Erik Eckholm. 2014. "Scenes of Exultation in Five States as Gay Couples Rush to Marry." *New York Times*. October 7.

Herman, Didi. 2000. "The Gay Agenda Is the Devil's Agenda: The Christian Right's Vision and the Role of the State." In Craig A. Rimmerman, Kenneth D. Wald, and Clyde Wilcox (eds.), *The Politics of Gay Rights*. Chicago: University of Chicago Press, 139–60.

Hesse, Monica. 2015. "Deeply Conservative Oklahoma Adjusts to Sudden Arrival of Same-Sex Marriage." *Washington Post*. January 24.

Hinch, Jim. 2014. "Evangelicals Are Changing Their Minds on Gay Marriage." *Politico Magazine*. www.politico.com. July 7.

Hirsch, H. N. 2005. "Liberal with a Twist: Queering Marriage." In H. N. Hirsch (ed.), *The Future of Gay Rights in America*. New York: Routledge, 285–96.

Howard, Robert M., and Amy Steigerwalt. 2011. *Judging Law and Policy: Courts and Policymaking in the American Political System*. New York: Routledge.

Huffington Post. 2012. "North Carolina Pastor Sean Harris: Parents should 'punch' their effeminate children." www.huffingtonpost.com. May 1.

Huffington Post. 2013. "Divorce rate by state: how does your state stack up?" www.huffingtonpost.com. September 5.

Hull, Kathleen E. 2006. *Same-Sex Marriage: The Cultural Politics of Love and Law*. New York: Cambridge University Press.

Hulse, Carl. 2004. "Senate Republicans Split on Wording Gay-Marriage Ban." *New York Times*. July 13.

Hulse, Carl. 2006. "Senate Emphasis on Ideology Has Some in G.O.P. Anxious." *New York Times*. June 7.

Hume, Robert J. 2013. *Courthouse Democracy and Minority Rights: Same-Sex Marriage in the States*. New York: Oxford University Press.

Innis, Michelle. 2015. "Australian Ruling Party Split over Legalizing Gay Marriage." *New York Times*. September 6.

Janofsky, Michael. 2005. "Gay Rights Battlefields Spread to Public Schools." *New York Times*. June 9.

Johnson, Chris. 2015a. "Michigan governor signs religious freedom adoption bills." www.washingtonblade.com. June 11.

Johnson, Chris. 2015b. "Eighth Circuit deals finishing blows to state marriage bans." www.washingtonblade.com. August 11.

Johnson, Kirk. 2006. "Gay Marriage Losing Punch as Ballot Issue." *New York Times*. October 14.

Jones, Marian Moser. 2013. "Will Same-Sex Marriage Rulings Lead to an LGBT Brain Drain in Some States?" *Chronicle of Higher Education*. June 27.

Kaplan, Marion A. 1998. *Between Dignity and Despair: Jewish Life in Nazi Germany*. New York: Oxford University Press.

Karimi, Faith. 2012. "North Carolina's ban on same-sex marriage sparks cheers, jeers." www.cnn.com May 9.

Katz, Jonathan M. 2015. "North Carolina Officials Can Now Cite Religion as Basis to Refuse Marriage Duties." *New York Times*. June 12.

Keck, Thomas M. 2009. "Beyond Backlash: Assessing the Impact of Judicial Decisions on LGBT Rights." *Law and Society Review* 43:151.

Keck, Thomas M. 2014. *Judicial Politics in Polarized Times*. Chicago: University of Chicago Press.

Kendall, Kate. 2010. "Sonoma County CA separates elderly gay couple and sells all of their worldly possessions." www.bilerico.com. April 17.

Kirkpatrick, David D. 2004. "Warily, a Religious Leader Lifts His Voice in Politics." *New York Times*. May 13.

Klarman, Michael J. 2004. *From Jim Crow to Civil Rights: The Supreme Court and the Struggle for Racial Equality*. New York: Oxford University Press.

Klarman, Michael J. 2013. *From the Closet to the Altar: Court, Backlash, and the Struggle for Same-Sex Marriage*. New York: Oxford University Press.

Klein, Ethel D. 2005. "The Anti-Gay Backlash?" In H. N. Hirsch (ed.), *The Future of Gay Rights in America*. New York: Routledge, 81–91.

Koppelman, Andrew. 2006. *Same Sex, Different States: When Same-Sex Marriages Cross State Lines*. New Haven, CT: Yale University Press.

Kreitzer, Rebecca J., Allison J. Hamilton, and Caroline J. Tolbert. 2014. "Does Policy Adoption Change Opinions on Minority Rights? The Effects of Legalizing Same-Sex Marriage." *Political Research Quarterly* 67:795.

Kusserow, Richard P. 1990. "OIG [Office of the Inspector General of the U.S. Department of Health and Human Services] Management Advisory Report: 'Boarder Babies.'" June 28. oig.hhs.gov/oei/reports/oei-03-89-01541.pdf.

Langbein, Laura, and Mark A. Yost, Jr. 2009. "Same-Sex Marriage and Negative Externalities." *Social Science Quarterly* 90:292.

Lannutti, Pamela J. 2011. "Examining Communication about Marriage Amendments: Same-Sex Couples and Their Extended Social Networks." *Journal of Social Issues* 67:264.

Lax, Jeffrey R., and Justin H. Phillips. 2009. "Gay Rights in the States: Public Opinion and Policy Responsiveness." *American Political Science Review* 103:367.

Lee, Mark. 2014. "We're here. There aren't many of us. Get used to it." www .washingtonblade.com. August 6.

Leonhardt, David. 2015. "A Geographic Divide on Family Life in America." *New York Times*. June 11.

Lewin, Tamar. 2015a. "Final Holdout on Same-Sex Adoption." *New York Times*. August 13.

Lewin, Tamar. 2015b. "Egg Donors Want Room to Name Their Price." *New York Times*. October 17.

Lewis, Daniel C. 2013. *Direct Democracy and Minority Rights: A Critical Assessment of the Tyranny of the Majority in the American States*. New York: Routledge.

Lewis, Daniel C., Frederick S. Wood, and Matthew L. Jacobsmeier. 2014. "Public Opinion and Judicial Behavior in Direct Democracy Systems: Gay Rights in the American States." *State Politics and Policy Quarterly* 14:367.

Lewis, Gregory B. 2009. "Does Believing Homosexuality Is Innate Increase Support for Gay Rights?" *Policy Studies Journal* 37:669.

Lewis, Gregory B. 2011. "The Friends and Family Plan: Contact with Gays and Support for Gay Rights." *Policy Studies Journal* 39:217.

Lewis, Gregory B., and Marc A. Rogers. 1999. "Does the Public Support Equal Employment Rights for Gays and Lesbians?" In Ellen D. B. Riggle and Barry L. Tadlock (eds.), *Gays and Lesbians in the Democratic Process: Public Policy, Public Opinion, and Political Representation*. New York: Columbia University Press, 118–45.

Lipka, Sara. 2010. "Support for Gay Marriage Is Greater among College Freshmen than Americans at Large." *Chronicle of Higher Education*. March 16.

Liptak, Adam. 2004. "Bans on Interracial Unions Offer Perspective on Gay Ones." *New York Times*. March 17.

Liptak, Adam. 2010. "Justices, 5–4, Reject Corporate Spending Limit." *New York Times*. January 21.

Liptak, Adam. 2013. "Supreme Court Invalidates Key Part of Voting Rights Act." *New York Times*. June 25.

Liptak, Adam. 2014. "Supreme Court Delivers Tacit Win to Gay Marriage." *New York Times*. October 7.

Liptak, Adam. 2015. "The Case Against Gay Marriage: Top Law Firms Won't Touch It." *New York Times*. April 12.

Livengood, Chad. 2015. "Gay Marriage Case a Race with Time for Michigan Couple." *Detroit News*. April 25.

Lofton, Katie, and Donald P. Haider-Markel. 2007. "The Politics of Same-Sex Marriage versus the Politics of Gay Civil Rights: A Comparison of Public Opinion and State Voting Patterns." In Craig A. Rimmerman and Clyde Wilcox (eds.), *The Politics of Same-Sex Marriage*. Chicago: University of Chicago Press, 313–40

"Louisiana: Marriage Barrier Falls." 2015. *New York Times*. July 3. National Briefing.

Lovett, Ian. 2013. "After 37 Years of Trying to Change People's Sexual Orientation, Group to Disband." *New York Times*. June 21.

Lupia, Arthur, Yanna Krupnikov, Adam Seth Levine, Spencer Piston, and Alexander Von Hagen-Jamar. 2010. "Why State Constitutions Differ in Their Treatment of Same-Sex Marriage." *Journal of Politics* 72:1222.

Maisel, Natalya C., and Adam W. Fingerhut. 2011. "California's Ban on Same-Sex Marriage: The Campaign and its Effects on Gay, Lesbian, and Bisexual Individuals." *Journal of Social Issues* 67:242.

Mallory, Christy. 2015. "Estimating the Economic Impact of Marriage for Same-Sex Couples after *Obergefell*." Los Angeles: Williams Institute, the Law School of the University of California at Los Angeles.

"Marriage and Politics." 2004. *New York Times*. October 29. Editorial.

"Married People Are Healthier, Study Finds." 2004. *New York Times*. December 16. National Briefing.

Martin, J. A., B. E. Hamilton, M. J. K. Osterman, S. C. Curtin, and T. J. Mathews. 2015. "Births: Final Data for 2013: Supplemental Table I-4: Births to Unmarried Women." *National vital statistics reports*, 64(1). Hyattsville, MD: National Center for Health Statistics.

Marusic, Kristina. 2015. "These states spent millions fighting marriage equality – and now they're having trouble paying." www.mtv.com. September 11.

McKinnon, Mark. 2015. "We Republicans lost on gay rights. That's a good thing." www .politico.com. June 1.

Metz, Tamara. 2010. *Untying the Knot: Marriage, the State, and the Case for Their Divorce*. Princeton, NJ: Princeton University Press.

Miller, Claire Cain, and David Leonhardt. 2015. "Where Gay Americans Choose to Live and Why." *New York Times*. March 22.

Movement Advancement Project, Family Equality Council, and Center for American Progress. 2011. *All Children Matter: How Legal and Social Inequalities Hurt LGBT Families*. www.lgbtmap.org

Mura, John, and Richard Pérez-Peña. 2015. "Marriage Licenses Are Issued, but the Debates Continue." *New York Times*. September 5.

Murphy, Dean E. 2004. "Some Democrats Blame One of Their Own." *New York Times*. November 5.

Neely, Melissa B. 2008. "Indiana's Proposed Defense of Marriage Amendment: What Will It Do and Why Is It Needed?" *Indiana Law Review* 41:245.

Oliphant, Thomas. 2004. "The Gay Marriage Deception." *Boston Globe*. November 7.

"One Step Closer to Marriage Equality." 2014. *New York Times*. Editorial. October 7.

Oosting, Jonathan. 2014. "Michigan political points: Voters split on prospect of gay marriage amendment as courts review ban." www.mlive.com. October 4.

Pappas, Christine, Jeanette Mendez, and Rebekah Herrick. 2009. "The Negative Effects of Populism on Gay and Lesbian Rights." *Social Science Quarterly* 90:150.

Parker-Pope, Tara. 2009. "Kept From a Dying Partner's Bedside." *New York Times*. May 19.

Parker-Pope, Tara. 2010. "In Sickness and in Health, regardless of Gender." *New York Times*. April 20.

Paulson, Michael. 2015. "Churches Grapple with New Era." *New York Times*. June 29.

Pew Forum and Research Center. 2009. "Most Still Oppose Same-Sex Marriage; Majority Continues to Support Civil Unions." The Pew Forum on Religion and Public Life, and the Pew Research Center for the People and the Press. October 9.

Philipps, Dave. 2015. "Ousted as Gay, Aging Veterans Are Battling again for Honorable Discharges." *New York Times*. September 7.

Pierceson, Jason. 2013. *Same-Sex Marriage in the United States: The Road to the Supreme Court*. Updated edition. Lanham, MD: Rowman & Littlefield Publishers.

Pinello, Daniel R. 1995. *The Impact of Judicial-Selection Method on State-Supreme-Court Policy: Innovation, Reaction, and Atrophy*. Westport, CT: Greenwood Press.

Pinello, Daniel R. 2003. *Gay Rights and American Law*. New York: Cambridge University Press.

Pinello, Daniel R. 2005. "Is Supreme Court Justice Antonin Scalia a homophobe?" www .danpinello.com.

Pinello, Daniel R. 2006. *America's Struggle for Same-Sex Marriage*. New York: Cambridge University Press.

Pinello, Daniel R. 2013. "Review of *From the Closet to the Altar: Courts, Backlash, and the Struggle for Same-Sex Marriage* by Michael J. Klarman." *Law and Politics Book Review* 23:330.

Posner, Richard A. 1994. *Sex and Reason*. Cambridge, MA: Harvard University Press.

Posner, Richard A., and Eric J. Segall. 2015. "Scalia's Majoritarian Theocracy." *New York Times*. December 3. Op-Ed.

Powell, Richard J. 2013. "Social Desirability Bias in Polling on Same-Sex Marriage Ballot Measures." *American Politics Research* 41:1052.

Preston, Julia. 2013. "Green Card Is Approved for Gay Men in Florida." *New York Times*. July 1.

Rayside, David. 2007. "The United States in Comparative Context." In Craig A. Rimmerman and Clyde Wilcox (eds.), *The Politics of Same-Sex Marriage*. Chicago: University of Chicago Press, 341–64.

Reynolds, Andrew. 2013. "Representation and Rights: The Impact of LGBT Legislators in Comparative Perspective." *American Political Science Review* 107:259.

Rich, Frank. 2006. "Mary Cheney's Bundle of Joy." *New York Times*. Opinion. December 17.

Richman, Kimberly D. 2009. *Courting Change: Queer Parents, Judges, and the Transformation of American Family Law*. New York: New York University Press.

Riggle, Ellen D. B., and Sharon S. Rostosky. 2007. "The Consequences of Marriage Policy for Same-Sex Couples' Well Being." In Craig A. Rimmerman and Clyde Wilcox (eds.), *The Politics of Same-Sex Marriage*. Chicago: University of Chicago Press, 65–84.

Riggle, Ellen D. B., Sharon S. Rostosky, and Robert A. Prather. 2006. "Advance Planning by Same-Sex Couples." *Journal of Family Issues* 27:758.

Riggle, Ellen D. B., and Barry L. Tadlock. 1999. "Gays and Lesbians in the Democratic Process: Past, Present, and Future." In Ellen D. B. Riggle and Barry L. Tadlock (eds.), *Gays and Lesbians in the Democratic Process: Public Policy, Public Opinion, and Political Representation*. New York: Columbia University Press, 1–21

Rimmerman, Craig A. 2000. "Beyond Political Mainstreaming: Reflections on Lesbian and Gay Organizations and the Grassroots." In Craig A. Rimmerman, Kenneth D.

Wald, and Clyde Wilcox (eds.), *The Politics of Gay Rights*. Chicago: University of Chicago Press, 54–78.

Rivkin, David B., Jr., and Lee A. Casey. 2006. "Conservatives: Keep Gay Marriage out of the Courts." *New York Times*. Opinion. November 17.

Roberts, Sam. 2010. "Study Finds Wider View of 'Family.'" *New York Times*. September 15.

Rosenberg, Gerald N. 2008. *The Hollow Hope: Can Courts Bring about Social Change?* 2nd ed. Chicago: University of Chicago Press.

Saad, Lydia. 2005. "Gay rights attitudes a mixed bag." www.gallup.com. May 20.

Sack, Kevin. 2010. "In Hospital Decision, Obama Finds Safe Ground on Gay Rights." *New York Times*. April 17.

Salvato, Albert. 2004. "Ohio: More Opposition to Ban on Same-Sex Marriage." *New York Times*. September 29. National Briefing.

Sanner, Ann. 2014. "Ohio's Gay Marriage Debate Goes beyond Courtroom." Associated Press. August 2.

Saulny, Susan. 2012. "Young in G.O.P. Erase the Lines on Social Issues." *New York Times*. August 9.

Scheiber, Noam. 2015. "U.S. Agency Rules for Gays in Workplace Discrimination." *New York Times*. July 18.

Schwartz, John. 2011. "When Same-Sex Marriages End." *New York Times*. July 3.

Selten, Eric. 2012. "Name change happy ending for same-sex marriage." www.eznamechange.com. December 29.

Severson, Kim. 2011. "New Law Provides Fodder for Both Sides of Marriage Debate: Atlanta Closer in Distance than in Philosophy." *New York Times*. June 27.

Shear, Michael D. 2015. "Obama Calls for End to 'Conversion' Therapies for Gay and Transgender Youth." *New York Times*. April 8.

Shear, Michael D., and John Schwartz. 2011. "Law Firm Quits G.O.P. Effort over Defense of Marriage Act." *New York Times*. April 26.

Sherkat, Darren E., Kylan Mattias De Vries, and Stacia Creek. 2010. "Race, Religion, and Opposition to Same-Sex Marriage." *Social Science Quarterly* 91:80.

Sherrill, Kenneth. 1996. "The Political Power of Lesbians, Gays, and Bisexuals." *PS: Political Science and Politics* 29:469.

Sherrill, Kenneth. 2005. "Same-Sex Marriage, Civil Unions, and the 2004 Presidential Vote." In H. N. Hirsch (ed.), *The Future of Gay Rights in America*. New York: Routledge, 37–46.

Shorto, Russell. 2005. "What's Their Real Problem with Gay Marriage? It's the Gay Part." *New York Times Magazine*. June 19.

Smith, Daniel A., Matthew DeSantis, and Jason Kassel. 2006. "Same-Sex Marriage Ballot Measures and the 2004 Presidential Election." *State and Local Government Review* 38:78.

Smith, Gilia C. 2011. "Same-Sex Marriage Bans' Effects on Public Universities' Benefits." *Chronicle of Higher Education*. July 24.

Smith, Miriam. 2008. *Political Institutions and Lesbian and Gay Rights in the United States and Canada*. New York: Routledge.

Sommer, Udi, Victor Asal, Katie Zuber, and Jonathan Parent. 2013. "Institutional Paths to Policy Change: Judicial versus Nonjudicial Repeal of Sodomy Laws." *Law and Society Review* 47:409.

Stacey, Judith, and Timothy J. Biblarz. 2001. "(How) Does the Sexual Orientation of Parents Matter?" *American Sociological Review* 66:159.

Sterett, Susan M. 2009. "Parents and Paperwork: Same-Sex Parents, Birth Certificates, and Emergent Legality." In Scott Barclay, Mary Bernstein, and Anna-Maria Marshall (eds.), *Queer Mobilizations: LGBT Activists Confront the Law*. New York: New York University Press, 103–19.

Stewart, James B. 2012. "The Costs of a Stand for Gay Marriage." *New York Times*. May 26.

Stolberg, Sheryl Gay. 2010. "Obama Alters Hospital Rules for Gay Rights." *New York Times*. April 16.

Stolberg, Sheryl Gay. 2015. "Gay Rights Case Caps Transition for Cincinnati." *New York Times*. April 26.

Stone, Amy L. 2012. *Gay Rights at the Ballot Box*. Minneapolis, MN: University of Minnesota Press.

Strasser, Mark. 2007. "State Marriage Amendments and Overreaching: On Plain Meaning, Good Public Policy, and Constitutional Limitations." *Law and Inequality* 25:59.

Sullivan, Andrew. 2004. "The Impact on Gays." *The Dish*. www.dish.andrewsullivan.com November 3.

Suri, Manil. 2015. "Why Is Science So Straight?" *New York Times*. September 5.

Tavernise, Sabrina. 2011. "Adoptions Rise by Same-Sex Couples, despite Legal Barriers." *New York Times*. June 14.

Taylor, Jami K., Daniel C. Lewis, Matthew L. Jacobsmeier, and Brian DiSarro. 2012. "Content and Complexity in Policy Reinvention and Diffusion: Gay and Transgender-Inclusive Laws against Discrimination." *State Politics and Policy Quarterly* 12:75.

Taylor, Verta, Katrina Kimport, Nella Van Dyke, and Ellen Ann Andersen. 2009. "Culture and Mobilization: Tactical Repertoires, Same-Sex Weddings, and the Impact on Gay Activism." *American Sociological Review* 74:865.

Tillman, Zoe. 2015a. "Oklahoma Judges Awards $300K in Legal Fees in Gay Marriage Case." *National Law Journal*. May 5.

Tillman, Zoe. 2015b. "Judge Slashes Fees for Lawyers in West Virginia Same-Sex Marriage Case." *National Law Journal*. July 17.

Tillman, Zoe. 2015c. "Michigan Pays $1.9M in Legal Fees in Same-Sex Marriage Case." *National Law Journal*. October 8.

Tinsley, Anna M. 2015. "2,500 same-sex couples get marriage licenses in Texas." www.star-telegram.com. September 12.

Toner, Robin. 2004. "Cheney Stakes out His Own Position on Gay Marriages." *New York Times*. August 25.

Wald, Kenneth D. 2000. "The Context of Gay Politics." In Craig A. Rimmerman, Kenneth D. Wald, and Clyde Wilcox (eds.), *The Politics of Gay Rights*. Chicago: University of Chicago Press, 1–28.

Weigel, David. 2014. "Rick Santorum endorsed the judge who just legalized gay marriage in Pennsylvania." www.slate.com. May 20.

Whitehead, Andrew L. 2010. "Sacred Rites and Civil Rights: Religion's Effect on Attitudes toward Same-Sex Unions and the Perceived Cause of Homosexuality." *Social Science Quarterly* 91:63.

Whitehead, Andrew L. 2014. "Politics, Religion, Attribution Theory, and Attitudes toward Same-Sex Unions." *Social Science Quarterly* 95:701.

Wieder, Ben. 2012. "Do Gay Rights Affect Tourism?" *Stateline*. Pew Charitable Trusts. www.pewtrusts.org. July 12.

Wikipedia. 2015. "Texas Proposition 2 (2005)." www.wikipedia.org (accessed July 28, 2015).

Wilcox, Clyde, Paul R. Brewer, Shauna Shames, and Celinda Lake. 2007. "If I Bend This Far I Will Break? Public Opinion about Same-Sex Marriage." In Craig A. Rimmerman and Clyde Wilcox (eds.), *The Politics of Same-Sex Marriage*. Chicago: University of Chicago Press, 215–42.

Wilcox, Clyde, and Robin Wolpert. 2000. "Gay Rights in the Public Sphere: Public Opinion on Gay and Lesbian Equality." In Craig A. Rimmerman, Kenneth D. Wald, and Clyde Wilcox (eds.), *The Politics of Gay Rights*. Chicago: University of Chicago Press, 409–32.

Wilkerson, Isabel. 2010. *The Warmth of Other Suns: The Epic Story of America's Great Migration*. New York: Random House.

Wilson, Angelia R. 2013. *Why Europe is Lesbian and Gay Friendly (and Why America Never Will Be)*. Albany, NY: State University of New York Press.

Witkowski, D'Anne. 2004. "Granholm: Proposal 2 Goes Too Far." *Between The Lines News*. October 28.

Wolfson, Evan. 2015. "Gay Rights: What Comes Next." *New York Times*. Opinion. June 27.

Zernike, Kate. 2004. "Groups Vow Not to Let Losses Dash Gay Rights." *New York Times*. November 14.

Index

ABC News, 235
Abilene, Texas, 176
ACLU of Georgia, 56, 138, 158
ACLU of Michigan, 48, 49
Adam and Sam, 134
Adelman, David, 89
adoption and foster care of children, 116, 117,
    146, 198, 263
  anticipated restrictions on, 119, 134, 178
  availability of after *Obergefell v. Hodges*,
    254
  bans on by LGBT people in Arkansas and
    Florida, 117
  costs of, 264
  incidence of, 107, 264
  joint adoptions, 53, 178
  limited by Super-DOMAs, 138, 177
  polling data on, 23, 246, 247
  see also second-parent adoption of children
    and same-sex couples *and* surrogacy
Adoption Assistance, 135, 263
Adoption of Tammy, 53
adultery
  as original legal ground for divorce, 269
  laws against not enforced, 271
  no constitutional amendments against,
    273
*Advisory Opinion to the Attorney General re:
    Florida Marriage Protection Amendment*,
    53
Affordable Care Act, 242
African Americans
  compared to same-sex couples, 155, 197

migrating from the American South, 152,
    197
Agnes and Rosemary, 163, 218, 219
  married in Northampton, 163
AIDS, 273, 280
Akron, Ohio, 152
Alabama, 4, 35, 220, 225
  as unlikely to embrace same-sex marriage
    for a very long time, 250
  hospital-visitation denials in, 78
  low cost of living in, 163
  no sexual-orientation-discrimination ban in,
    106
Alabama Court of Civil Appeals, 53
Alan and Larry, 171, 172
Alaska, 5, 233
  as unlikely to embrace same-sex marriage
    for a very long time, 250
  high rate of divorce in, 259
  no sexual-orientation-discrimination ban in,
    106
Albert and Harry, 272
Alger, Horatio, 222
Alice and Julie, 201
Alito, Samuel, 225, 230, 232, 234, 237, 241,
    245, 246, 248, 249, 251, 252
  advocacy of for the democratic process, 241,
    245, 246, 248
  hypocrisy of, 251, 252
  problems with democratic-process thesis of,
    246, 249, 250, 252
Alliance Defense Fund, 30, 67
Amanda and Joyce, 83, 127

Amendment 1, 7, 8, 20, 21, 23, 54, 57, 60, 63,
    81, 82, 86–88, 93, 95, 108, 109, 143, 147,
    197, 198, 201, 208–213, 222, 266, 268,
    271, 285
  absence of business community
    participation in debate over, 8
  dehumanizing the LGBT community, 271
  funded by Roman Catholic Church, 23, 266
  impact of on biological-family ties, 86, 88
  impact of on children raised by same-sex
    couples, 108
  impact of on closeted LGBT people, 147
  impact of on LGBT migration, 198
  inhibiting personal relationships, 143
  legal burdens of on nonbiological parents,
    143
  legislative deliberation over, 7, 211
  making LGBT people homeless, 93
  organized opposition to, 21
  political campaign surrounding, 20
  prompting public bigotry, 268
  size of popular majority of, 6
  suppressing immigration into North
    Carolina, 201, 208, 209, 211–213
  text of, 5, 285
  triggering LGBT migration, 197
  see also North Carolina
American Airlines, 207
American Bar Association, 258
American Family Association, 30
American Political Science Association, 279,
    282
  Law and Courts Section of, 279, 282
America's Struggle for Same-Sex Marriage, 3,
    11, 24, 279, 280
Amish, 32
Amy and Brenda, 177, 179, 180, 263
  discrimination against in Georgia as foster
    parents, 178, 263
  exceptional nature of, 180
Andrea and Louise, 132, 136
Andrew and Raymond, 135
Angel Lace M. v. Terry M., 52, 112
Angela and Jessica, 65, 128, 129, 136, 205
Ann Arbor, Michigan, 10, 71, 156, 177,
    182–186, 205, 266, 267
  arboretum in, 182
  lacking bubble effect, 186
  LGBT-friendly hospitals in, 71
  progressive on LGBT rights, 50, 205
Anthony and Ronald, 197, 198
Appleton, Wisconsin, 10, 66, 97, 257

Appling v. *Walker*, 35, 50, 54
  compared with *National Pride at Work, Inc.*
    v. *Governor of Michigan*, 52
  upholding domestic-partner registry, 50
Appling, Julaine, 51
Archer, Phillip D., 219, 221
Arizona, 5, 212, 233
  amount of same-sex couples' attorney's fees
    paid for by, 265
  no sexual-orientation-discrimination ban in,
    106
Arkansas, 4, 9, 33, 189, 225
  amount of same-sex couples' attorney's fees
    paid for by, 265
  ban on adoptions by LGBT people in, 117
  low cost of living in, 163
  no sexual-orientation-discrimination ban in,
    106
Athens-Clark County, Georgia
  second-parent adoption in, 120
Atlanta, 7, 10, 14, 16, 21, 22, 54–57, 59, 70,
    77, 79, 89, 102, 119–121, 123, 125, 132,
    133, 135–137, 144, 146, 157–159, 161,
    170–172, 178, 179, 202, 203, 214, 254,
    256, 263, 273
  2009 mayor's race in, 157
  domestic-partner benefits in, 57
  less progressive than Des Moines, 202
  LGBT loyalty for, 161
  LGBT-friendly hospitals in, 72
  Morningside area of, 134, 159
  Perimeter of, 157–159
Atlanta Stonewall Democrats, 119
Atlanta-Fulton Public Library System, 202,
    204
Augusta, Georgia, 123
Austin, Texas, 7, 36, 53, 58, 116

Badger Care, 176, 255
Baehr v. *Lewin*, 249, 282
Bai, Matt, 25
Baltimore, 183–185
Bank of America, 8
Barbara and Jane, 72, 78, 95
Baskin v. *Bogan*, 233, 279, 283
  setting the gold standard for measuring
    court decisions, 278
Bassett v. *Snyder*, 247
Belanger, Katie, 19, 24, 96, 112, 152
Ben and Ted, 114, 145, 146, 175
  playing the system, 175
Berean Baptist Church, 268

Berg, Alvin, 150
Bertie and Olive, 76, 135, 160, 174
  playing the system, 174
Bertram and Leonard, 171
Betty and Sandra, 156
Between Dignity and Despair, 152, 173,
  269; *see also* Kaplan, Marion A.
Beverly and Kelly, 90, 146
Biden, Joe, 235
Biggers, Daniel R., 1
bigotry
  definition of, 268, 275
  egregious examples of against LGBT people,
    268, 269
  motivating Super-DOMA sponsors, 267,
    269–276
Bipartisan Campaign Reform Act of 2002, 252
Bishop v. *Smith*, 232
Bishop v. *United States ex rel. Holder*, 233,
  236, 240
Black, Timothy S., 232, 239
Blackwell, Kenneth, 32
Bloom, Daniel A., 89, 137, 273
  experience of as a family-court judge, 273
Blue Cross and Blue Shield, 47, 70
boarder babies, 13
Bonasera, Michael D., 42
Bond v. *United States*, 229
Boseman v. *Jarrell*, 112
Bostic v. *Rainey*, 233
Bostic v. *Schaefer*, 233
Boston Globe, 273
Boston Public Library, 202
Bourke v. *Beshear*, 233
Bowers v. *Hardwick*, 227, 238
Bowling Green, Ohio
  nondiscrimination ordinance in, 105
Bowman, A. Lynne, 26, 27, 68, 266
Boy Scouts of America, 146
  antigay policies of, 272
Boy Scouts of America v. *Dale*, 272
Brandon-Thomas v. *Brandon-Thomas*, 53
Brenda, *see* Amy and Brenda
Brenner v. *Scott*, 233
Brett and Lloyd, 63–65
Brigham Young University
  not rejecting sexual-orientation
    discrimination in employment, 272
Brinkman v. *Miami University*, 67
Brinkman, Jr., Thomas E., 67
Brooks, Douglas L., 59, 157
Brown University, 215

bubble effect, the, 156–160, 192; *see also*
  LGBT migration
Burch, Lorie L., 71, 95, 220, 221
Burns v. *Hickenlooper*, 233
Burress, Phil, 17, 24, 25, 29–32, 37, 39, 67,
    149, 266, 271, 273, 275, 276
  acknowledging non-Super-DOMA
    techniques to fortify marriage, 270
  as a general in the war against same-sex
    couples, 276
  believing that LGBT people need to be
    repaired, 275
  bigotry of, 274–276
  declining to make premarital counseling
    more readily available, 271
  explaining his motivations as Super-DOMA
    sponsor, 269
  explaining the basis of homosexuality, 275
  influence of on 2004 presidential election,
    25
  opposed to lesbians having children, 274
  profiled by the *New York Times*, 25, 273
  prominent public role of, 273, 275
  refusing to make the law harder for people
    to divorce, 271
  service of on the board of Exodus
    International, 274
  voluntary participation of in interview, 276
  see also Citizens for Community Values *and*
    Issue 1
Bush, George W., 6, 25–27, 30, 55, 85, 185,
    186, 206, 243, 250, 277
  Ohio's 2004 margin of victory for, 32
business community
  absence of in Super-DOMA debates, 8
  as progressive on LGBT issues, 202, 207

Calgary, Alberta, Canada, 203
California, 5, 95, 105, 137, 144, 160, 163,
    187–189, 201, 204, 209, 225, 240, 255,
    266
  domestic partnerships of for same-sex
    couples, 267
  high cost of living in, 221
  LGBT migration from, 191, 209, 221
  LGBT migration to, 204, 207, 266
  outlawing "conversion" or "reparative"
    therapies, 274
  placing both same-sex-partner names on
    child-adoption decrees, 115
Campaign for Southern Equality v. *Bryant*,
  233

Canada, 2, 9, 13, 14, 26, 64, 91, 95, 137, 185, 203, 227, 260, 283
  as progressive on LGBT issues, 203, 283
  legalizing same-sex marriage, 283
  LGBT migration to, 2, 204
Carl and Henry, 115–117
Carol and Donna, 124, 156, 159
Carolinas Medical Center, 170
Carolyn and Stephanie, 117, 191, 193–196, 198
  crying when their marriage was bureaucratically acknowledged, 196
Casebook on Sexual Orientation and the Law, 279
Catherine and Frances, 215–217
Catholic Church, *see* Roman Catholic Church
CBS News, 277
Cecil, Jason A., 119, 248
Census Bureau, 258
Census, U.S., 150
  determining the number of same-sex unmarried partners, 150
  of 2010, 243, 261
  of 2020, 243
Centers for Disease Control and Prevention, 77, 258
Chapel Hill, North Carolina, 8, 10, 200, 210, 211, 213
  real-estate market in, 208, 213
  zoning in and housing discrimination, 82
Charles and Joseph, 164
Charlotte, North Carolina, 10, 20, 86, 93, 108, 170, 211
Cheney, Dick, 6
Cheryl and Mildred, 69
Chicago, 192, 195, 196
  LGBT migration to, 194
Christian Citizens Alliance, 6
Christian Coalition of Georgia, 21
Christine and Marian, 91
Christopher and Juan, 79, 162, 163, 176
  playing the system, 176
Chronicle of Higher Education, 199
Cincinnati, Ohio, 6, 17, 29, 32, 67, 82, 83, 152, 218, 266, 270
  charter-amendment campaign in, 29
  hostility to LGBT rights in, 43, 159
Citizens for Community Values, 6, 17, 28, 29, 32, 37, 57, 67, 82, 149, 266, 271
  declining to make premarital counseling more readily available, 271

  described as mean, 69
  enforcing Issue 1, 57
  refusing to make the law harder for people to divorce, 271
  resources of, 28
  see also Burress, Phil *and* Issue 1
Citizens for the Protection of Marriage, 6, 44, 50
Citizens United v. *Federal Election Commission*, 252
City of Atlanta v. *McKinney*, 57
City of Atlanta v. *Morgan*, 57
Civil Rights Act of 1871, 265
Civil Rights Attorney's Fees Award Act, 265
civil unions
  closeted LGBT people's ignorance of, 168
  polling data on, 19, 23, 46, 55, 246, 276, 277
Clayton County, Georgia
  second-parent adoption in, 123
Cleveland Heights, Ohio
  domestic-partner registry in, 219
Cleveland Indians, 91
Cleveland Taxpayers v. *Cleveland*, 53, 67
Cleveland, Ohio, 10, 27, 32, 39, 43, 65, 67, 68, 74, 88, 105, 111, 128, 130, 145, 160, 163, 174, 200, 219
  domestic-partner registry of, 67
  LGBT migration to, 219
  LGBT parents group in, 151
Clinton, William Jefferson, 3, 29, 227
Cobb County, Georgia
  second-parent adoption in, 120, 123, 124
COBRA, 100
Colorado, 5, 62, 233
  amount of same-sex couples' attorney's fees paid for by, 265
Columbus Education Association, 68
Columbus, Ohio, 10, 23, 26–29, 32, 36, 41–43, 63, 68, 72, 76, 84, 90, 95, 105, 127, 131, 145, 156, 160, 174, 181, 204, 218
Concerned Women for America, 30
Conde-Vidal v. *Garcia-Padilla*, 233
Connecticut, 136, 163, 185, 206, 214, 225, 249
  LGBT migration to, 218
Connie and Tracy, 147
consensual-sodomy statutes
  civil effects of, 15, 283
Crews, Ronald, 276
Cuyahoga County, Ohio, 68
Czuba, Richard, 246

Dade County, Florida, 78
Dallas, 10, 35, 71, 79, 95, 115–118, 135, 161,
    162, 165, 176, 192, 195, 199, 207, 208,
    221, 257
  closeted couples in, 168, 255
  gay tolerant v. gay friendly, 220
  LGBT migration to, 207, 221
  real-estate market in, 206, 219
Dallas Visitors Bureau, 220
David and Harold, 161, 162
Dawn and Rita, 82
Dayton, Ohio, 105, 152
De Leon v. *Perry*, 233
De Sylva v. *Ballentine*, 228
DeBoer v. *Snyder*, 233, 241, 278
DeBoer, April, 278
Deborah and Gladys, 91, 94, 267
Debra and Martha, 168–170, 255
Decatur, Georgia, 89, 124, 159, 167
  having high proportion of same-sex couples,
    159
Defense of Marriage Act, 103, 227, 229–231,
    238, 242, 243, 254, 270, 281, 282
  as an aggressive indignity transformed into
    virtuous benevolence, 269
  Baehr v. *Lewin* not a necessary condition
    for, 282
  certainty of congressional passage of, 282
  impact of invalidation of, 189, 195, 254,
    255, 258
  passage of, 4
  probability of congressional repeal of, 243,
    281
  size of congressional majorities for, 251
  struck down by *United States* v. *Windsor*, 16
  see also Mini-DOMAs *and* Super-DOMAs
DeKalb County, Georgia, 70, 79, 104, 120,
    122, 124, 126, 157
  as LGBT friendly, 157
  importance to same-sex couples of living in,
    126
  offering domestic-partner benefits, 119
  second-parent adoption in, 120–124
Delaware, 6, 189, 190, 225, 249
  LGBT migration to, 188
Democratic Party, 27, 225, 234, 235, 242, 243,
    250
  and congressional control, 243
  support of for same-sex marriage, 235
democratic process, the, 281
  blind faith in, 244
  clearest example of, 250

  judicial advocacy for, 241–245
  Michigan as a case study of, 245–247
  political context of, 242
  rate of change under toward same-sex
    marriage, 249, 250
  skewing of by gerrymandering, 243
Denise and Tammy, 113
Department of Health and Human Services
  regulating hospitals to be more LGBT
    friendly, 75
Des Moines, Iowa, 257
  as more progressive than Atlanta, 202
Detroit, 10, 82, 199, 215
  having no LGBT-friendly hospitals, 71
Detroit Free Press, 19, 246, 247
DeWine, Mike, 6
Diana and Paula, 111, 142, 143
Dictionary.com, 268
dissenting-opinion strategy
  a natural experiment to measure the
    effectiveness of, 237
District of Columbia, 244, 249
  as a same-sex-marriage destination, 262
  legalizing same-sex marriage, 244
  LGBT migration to, 139
  marriage bureau of, 262
Doerfer, Sue, 68, 86, 104, 130, 135, 151, 200
  experiencing hospital-access denial, 74
DOMAs
  number of states adopting, 30
  see also Defense of Marriage Act,
    Mini-DOMAs, *and* Super-DOMAs
domestic relations
  power to regulate, 4
domestic-partner benefits
  availability of after *Obergefell* v. *Hodges*,
    254
  availability of in California, 267
  denial of in Michigan, 247
  expanded by "other qualified adult"
    programs, 246
  importance of to same-sex couples, 216
  limitations on in Georgia, 248
  polling data on, 23, 46, 246
  see also Super-DOMA effects
Donna, *see* Carol and Donna
"Don't Ask, Don't Tell," 159, 242
  involuntary discharges under, 4
  passage of, 3
  repeal of, 242
Doris and Ruth, 174
Dorothy and Lisa, 13, 22, 85, 95, 137, 161

Doster, Eric E., 45
Downing, Timothy J., 39, 47
Doyle, Jim, 66, 98
DuBois, Blanche, 109
Due Process Clause, 226, 227, 229, 232, 238
Duke Power, 8
Duke University
  antigay employment discrimination at, 81
Duluth, Minnesota, 150
Durham County, North Carolina, 111
Durham, North Carolina, 10, 60, 78, 81, 111,
  157, 210
D'Emilio, John, 173

East Grand Rapids, Michigan, 247
East Lansing, Michigan, 10
Edward and Steven, 211–213, 217, 221
Eichner, Maxine, 7
Elizabeth and Jennifer, 2, 149, 154
Elwell, Marlene, 45
Emma and Joan, 82
Emory Healthcare, 72
Emory University, 125
EPIC-MRA, 247
Episcopal Church, 206
Equal Protection Clause, 226, 230, 232
  protecting marriage as a fundamental
    federal right, 227
Equality Ohio, 26, 27, 68, 74, 75, 104, 130,
  151, 200, 266
  emergence of, 62
equitable partition
  as an alternative to divorce, 104
Eric and Scott, 66
Esther and Sheila, 114
Evelyn and Gloria, 99–101
Exodus International, 274
  apology of to the LGBT community, 274
  demise of, 274

Facebook, 86, 92
Fair Wisconsin, 19, 24, 96, 98, 112, 152
Falk, Michael, 182–186, 191, 197, 266
  as archetypical refugee, 186
Family Policy Councils, 30, 31
Family Research Council, 30, 32
  paying for the expenses of Ohio's Issue 1,
    266
Family Research Institute of Wisconsin, 51
Farmers Branch, Texas, 165
Fayette County, Georgia
  second-parent adoption in, 123

Fayetteville, North Carolina, 268
federal courts, 224–241
  explaining decisions of in favor of same-sex
    marriage, 233–235
  impact of, 224–226
  impact of political party on, 234, 235
  lower courts' invalidating half of the
    nation's Super-DOMAs, 226
Federal Marriage Amendment, 224
federalism
  effects of, 4, 228, 229, 234, 283
Federalist Society, 48
Feldman, Martin L.C., 241
Fey, Carol Ann, 36, 40
Fifth Amendment, 229, 230
First Amendment, 252
Fisher-Borne v. *Smith*, 233
Fitzgerald, Scott, 19, 51
Fitzgerald, Tami, 17, 20, 24, 25, 271, 276
  as a general in the war against same-sex
    couples, 276
  bigotry of, 271, 275, 276
  calling domestic partners "sex partners",
    271
  favoring heterosexism, 271
  refuted by Albert and Harry, 272
Flint, Michigan
  having no LGBT-friendly hospitals, 71
Florence, 7, 275
  refuting that sexual orientation is mutable,
    275
Florida, 4, 10, 17, 35, 53, 73, 78, 109, 171, 221
  antigay hospital episode in, 78
  ban on adoptions by LGBT people in, 117,
    178
  no sexual-orientation-discrimination ban in,
    106, 109
Florida Court of Appeals, 53
Foreman, Matt, 27
Forsyth County, Georgia
  second-parent adoption in, 123
Fort Worth, Texas, 10, 168, 208
foster care of children, *see* adoption and foster
  care of children
Fourteenth Amendment, 224, 226, 229, 230,
  232, 233, 237, 238, 245, 265
Frances, *see* Catherine and Frances
Frank and Jeff, 92, 162
Franklin County Court of Common Pleas, 41
Franklin County, Ohio, 41–43, 58, 85
Free Dictionary, The, 268
Friedman, Bernard A., 278

From Jim Crow to Civil Rights, 282; *see also* Klarman, Michael J.
From the Closet to the Altar, 281, 283; *see also* Klarman, Michael J.
Fulton County, Georgia, 56, 70, 79, 89, 104, 120, 122–124, 126, 157
  as LGBT friendly, 157
  importance to same-sex couples of living in, 126
  offering domestic-partner benefits, 203
  second-parent adoption in, 120–122, 124

Gabbard, Mike, 29
Gallup Organization, 235
Gary and Herman, 100
Gay & Lesbian Atlas, The, 150
Gay and Lesbian Advocates and Defenders, 27
Gay and Lesbian Medical Association, 71
Gay Rights and American Law, 34, 58, 234
Gayellow Pages, 11, 14
Geiger v. *Kitzhaber*, 233
General Mills, 8
geography
  importance of to same-sex couples, 126
George and Kenneth, 175, 176, 255
  playing the system, 175
Georgia, 4, 6, 10, 13, 18–20, 22, 53–59, 70–72, 77, 79, 83, 85, 89, 95, 102–104, 107, 118–126, 132–138, 144–146, 152, 156, 158, 159, 161, 163, 166, 167, 170–173, 178–180, 199, 202, 203, 214, 221, 223, 248–250, 254, 256, 260, 261, 263, 264, 273, 277
  as unlikely to embrace same-sex marriage for a very long time, 250
  attempts to limit adoption and foster care of children in, 248
  complete language of Super-DOMA not on the ballot of, 18, 277
  considering ban on adoptions by LGBT parents, 134
  dealing with homophobia in, 155
  establishing legal parentage in, 120
  inability to divorce in, 102
  interviewing people of color in, 14
  judicial-selection method in, 121
  law regarding guardianship of children, 144
  LGBT avoidance of, 202, 203
  LGBT loyalty for, 157
  LGBT migration from, 170, 171, 178, 179
  LGBT-friendly hospitals in, 71

lost revenues in, 260, 262–264
low cost of living in, 163
no sexual-orientation-discrimination ban in, 80, 106
number of interviews conducted in, 12
political probability in for
  same-sex-relationship recognition, 248
second-parent adoption in, 118–126
selection of for Super-DOMA study, 9
see also *specific cities and counties and Question 1*
Georgia Christian Coalition, 55
Georgia Department of Driver Services, 144
Georgia Division of Family and Children Services
  lobbying to prevent bans on adoptions by LGBT parents, 119
Georgia Equality, 18, 54, 55, 119, 152, 248
Georgia Power Company, 256
Georgia Psychological Association, 8
Georgia Stonewall Democrats, 248
Georgia Supreme Court, 57, 203
Germany, 152, 153, 155, 160, 163, 165, 181, 269
  bubble effect in, 156
  Jewish loyalty to in the 1930s, 155
  Jewish migration from during Nazi era, 152
  see also Kaplan, Marion A.
gerrymandering, 243
Ginsburg, Ruth Bader, 245
Gladys, *see* Deborah and Gladys
Glengariff Group, 19, 246, 247
Gloria, *see* Evelyn and Gloria
Goodridge v. *Department of Public Health*, 279, 280
  bringing about enormous social change, 280
  radicalizing and coalescing the gay community, 280
Goodson v. *Castellanos*, 53
Grady Health Systems, 54, 72
Graham, Jeff, 18, 20, 54, 55, 119, 152, 248
Grand Rapids, Michigan
  having no LGBT-friendly hospitals, 71
Granholm, Jennifer, 6, 66
Great Lakes Science Center, 200
Great Recession, 101, 243
Greensboro, North Carolina, 10, 20, 222
Greenville, North Carolina, 147
Gregory and Josh, 101
Griswold v. *Connecticut*, 227
Gundrum, Mark D., 51
Gwinnett County, Georgia, 159

Hamby v. Parnell, 233
Hamilton County, Ohio, 82
Harmon v. Davis, 53
Harold, *see* David and Harold
Harris, Sean
  advocating violence against nonconforming
    children, 268
Harry, *see* Albert and Harry
Harvard Business School, 211
Hawaii, 29, 30, 133, 225, 249, 280, 282,
  284
  effect of on rest of nation, 29, 280, 282
Hawaii Supreme Court, 249, 282
health insurance
  cost of, 69, 100
  see also Super-DOMA effects
Heather and Teresa, 97–99, 101, 257, 258
Helen and Lee, 26, 27, 61, 63, 69, 82, 90
Helms, Jesse, 209
Hemphill, Kristina, 45
Henry, *see* Carl and Henry
Henry County, Georgia, 121
  second-parent adoption in, 121, 123
Henry v. Himes, 232
Herman, *see* Gary and Herman
Hitler, Adolf, 152, 155, 162
Hollingsworth v. Perry, 240
Hollow Hope, The, 279–281
  assessing judicial impact on same-sex
    marriage, 280
  focusing on supreme courts, 281
  second edition of, 280
homosexuality
  immutability of, 278
homosexuals
  among the most discriminated-against
    minorities in the world, 278, 283
Hood County, Texas
  amount of same-sex couples' attorney's fees
    paid for by, 265
hospitals
  federal regulation of to be more LGBT
    friendly, 75
Houston, 53, 125
  anti-gay-parent episode in, 125
Human Rights Campaign, 27, 28, 160

Idaho, 4, 150, 233
  amount of same-sex couples' attorney's fees
    paid for by, 265
  as unlikely to embrace same-sex marriage
    for a very long time, 250

  low cost of living in, 163
  no sexual-orientation-discrimination ban in,
    106
If These Walls Could Talk 2, 73
Illinois, 100, 150, 195, 196, 225, 249, 266
  legislative debates on same-sex marriage in,
    195
  LGBT migration to, 194
  recognizing out-of-state marriages, 196
In re Adoption of Jane Doe, 111
In re Adoption of K.R.S., 53
In re Bonfield, 111
In re Divorce of Naylor and Daly, 36
In re Hadaway, 138, 158
In the Life Atlanta, 14
In the Matter of the Marriage of J.B. and H.B.,
  35
Indiana, 194, 233, 272, 278
  arguing straight couples are sexually
    irresponsible, 279
  judicial invalidation of anti-same-sex-
    marriage statute of, 278
  no sexual-orientation-discrimination ban in,
    106
inheritance rights
  polling data on, 23, 246
initiatives, 283
  bypassing legislatures, 6
  definition of, 5
  impact of compared with referenda, 57
interest groups
  sponsoring initiatives, 6
  see also Citizens for Community Values *and*
    Vote for Marriage NC
International Lesbian, Gay, Bisexual, Trans
  and Intersex Association, 283
interviews, 9–15, 73, 151, 153, 168, 200, 260,
  261, 263, 276, 287
  archived by Yale University, 276
  as optimally situated to test for
    Super-DOMA effects, 15
  completed before federal-court action, 10
  described by age, 12
  described by ceremonies celebrating
    relationships, 13
  described by duration, 12
  described by education and employment, 15
  described by ethnicity and race, 14
  described by gender, 12
  described by length of residence in states, 13
  described by native-born interviewees, 13
  described by parents raising children, 12

expressing interest in legal marriage benefits,
14
many interviewees affiliated with colleges
and universities, 200
methodology of, 9–11
not being fully representative of the
population of interest, 14, 15, 168, 200,
260, 263
number of, 10, 11
protocol for, 11, 73, 151, 153, 154, 287
research challenges of, 11, 15
Iowa, 105, 149, 150, 157, 193, 206, 214, 228,
249, 255, 257, 266
LGBT migration to, 206
Iowa Supreme Court, 193
Irene and Marilyn, 113, 114
Issue 1, 6, 17, 26–29, 31, 32, 36–44, 46, 47,
54, 57, 58, 61, 63–65, 67, 68, 73–76,
83–86, 88, 90, 91, 94, 95, 104, 105,
128–131, 136, 149–151, 155, 175, 200,
204, 206, 218, 219, 239, 241, 248, 266,
267, 270, 271, 274, 285
and same-sex divorce, 41
author of, 31
denying full citizenship to LGBT people, 89
facilitating discrimination, 75, 95
facilitating violence, 136
Family Research Council funding of, 32, 266
funding for the defeat of, 266
getting on the ballot, 31
hampering economic activity, 267
Human Rights Campaign donation to the
fight against, 28
impact of churches on, 31, 32
impact of newspapers on, 31, 32
impact of on 2004 presidential election, 26
impact of on child-custody disputes, 41, 274
impact of on closeted LGBT people, 94
impact of on estate and financial planning,
42
impact of on health care, 73, 76
impact of on legal documents, 90, 274
impact of on LGBT migration, 149
impact of on physical safety, 91
impact of on schools, 130, 131
impact of on widows and widowers, 84
implemented by threat of legal action, 67
judicial invalidation of, 239
judicial validation of, 241
LGBT people's ignorance of real threat
from, 155
made palatable to Ohioans, 47

meaning of, 36, 38, 270
meaning of limited by *State* v. *Carswell*, 39
message of to LGBT families, 130, 135, 136
no legislative history for, 37
political campaign surrounding, 28, 31
polling data on, 30
positive impacts of, 63
prompting conservatives to vote in 2004, 25
size of popular majority of, 6, 32, 248
sponsor's strategy to enforce, 68
sponsored by Citizens for Community
Values, 17
suppressing immigration into Ohio, 204,
206
text of, 26, 36, 285
triggering LGBT migration, 150, 151
see also Ohio

Jackson Memorial Hospital
antigay episode at, 78
James and John, 21, 80
Jane, *see* Barbara and Jane
Janet and Marie, 204
Janice and Judy, 93, 94, 108
Jason and Kevin, 199
Jeff, *see* Frank and Jeff
Jennifer, *see* Elizabeth and Jennifer
Jernigan v. *Crane*, 233
Jerry and Walter, 124, 125
Jessica, *see* Angela and Jessica
Jeter, Mildred, 226
Joan, *see* Emma and Joan
John, *see* James and John
Johns Hopkins University, 183–185, 266
Johnson, Lyndon B., 250
Jones, John E., III, 277
Joseph, *see* Charles and Joseph
Josh, *see* Gregory and Josh
Joyce, *see* Amanda and Joyce
Juan, *see* Christopher and Juan
judicial impact, 34, 35, 38–40, 43, 44, 46–50,
52–54, 58, 279, 281–284
courts not being hollow hopes, 279
lower federal courts granting same-sex
marriage, 281
Judy, *see* Janice and Judy
Julie, *see* Alice and Julie

Kansas, 4, 63, 233
low cost of living in, 163
no sexual-orientation-discrimination ban in,
106

Kaplan, Jay, 48
Kaplan, Marion A., 152, 153, 155, 156, 160,
     162–165, 173, 181, 269; *see also Between
     Dignity and Despair*
Kathleen and Pamela, 166, 167
Katz, Barbara E., 70, 79, 102, 120, 124,
     125
Kelly, *see* Beverly and Kelly
Kennedy, Anthony, 226–229, 234, 236, 237,
     249, 253
   as a consistent supporter of LGBT rights,
     236
   as an advocate for same-sex marriage,
     241
   majority opinions of not paragons of
     doctrinal clarity, 237
Kenneth, *see* George and Kenneth
Kentucky, 4, 9, 33, 150, 225, 265
   amount of same-sex couples' attorney's fees
     paid for by, 265
   attorney's fees paid by to defend
     Super-DOMA, 265
   low cost of living in, 163
   no sexual-orientation-discrimination ban in,
     106
Kern, Terence C., 236, 240
Kerry, John, 25, 26, 31, 32
Kevin, *see* Jason and Kevin
Kimberly and Shirley, 135, 161, 263
King, Martin Luther, 256
Kitchen v. Herbert, 232, 233, 238–240
Klarman, Michael J., 281–283
   as the Great Synthesizer, 282
Kreller, Jaye J., 208, 210, 213
Kristallnacht, 155, 156, 165, 181

LaCrosse County, Wisconsin, 96
LaCrosse, Wisconsin, 112, 114, 115
   permitting second-parent adoption in, 112,
     114
Lambda Legal, 56, 133
*Langbehn v. Public Health Trust of
     Miami-Dade County*, 78
Langbehn, Janice, 78
Langdon, David, 40, 41, 57, 69, 82, 274
   as author of Issue 1, 31
   representing a lesbian in court, 275
Lansing, Michigan, 10
   having no LGBT-friendly hospitals, 71
Larry, *see* Alan and Larry
Latta v. Otter, 233
Laura and Sarah, 157

Law and Politics Book Review, 282
Lawrence v. Texas, 226, 227, 231–234,
     236–239, 283
   dissents of, 227, 232, 237, 239, 240
Lawson v. Kelly, 233
Lee, *see* Helen and Lee
legal documents
   challenges regarding execution of, 79
   costs of, 90
   limitations of, 77–80, 154
   see also Super-DOMA effects
legislative history
   as means for interpreting constitutional
     amendments, 37
   importance of, 52
Leonard, *see* Bertram and Leonard
LexisNexis, 57
LGBT communities
   politically unprepared in 2004, 32
LGBT Community Center of Greater
     Cleveland, 75, 130, 151
LGBT instruction manual or user's guide, 125,
     126
LGBT migration, 149–223
   analogies to German Jews and African
     Americans in the South, 152, 153, 197,
     222
   benefits of, 191
   deprivations arising from, 179, 190
   estimate of migrants from Super-DOMA
     states, 150–152, 222
   exceptional nature of couples who migrated,
     179, 180, 186, 187, 198
   impact on of age, 186, 197, 217, 223
   impact on of bubble effect, 156–159, 197,
     223
   impact on of economic issues, 163–165,
     192–195, 221–223
   impact on of education, 193, 197–199, 217,
     223
   impact on of expected legal or political
     redemption, 162, 163, 197, 223
   impact on of family ties, 160, 161, 193–195,
     197, 212, 213, 218, 221, 223
   impact on of internalized homophobia,
     168–173, 223
   impact on of marketable skills and portable
     jobs, 186, 191, 197, 223
   impact on of same-sex couples' ability to
     pass, 173, 174
   impact on of same-sex couples' playing the
     system, 173, 175–177, 223

impact on of traditionally gendered
relationship roles, 165–168
knowledge and appreciation of threat to
well being, 153–155, 186, 197
loyalty to country or state, 155, 156, 186,
197, 223
migrants to Super-DOMA states, 217–221
motivated by only the harshest forms of
government mistreatment, 181
partial migrations by same-sex couples,
177–180
permanent migrations by same-sex couples,
181–199
retirement as common strategy for, 188
LGBT population
size of, 3
Lillian and Robin, 138–141
Linda and Patricia, 1–3, 11, 149, 154, 187
as archetypical refugees, 187
Lisa, *see* Dorothy and Lisa
Lloyd, *see* Brett and Lloyd
Lois and Ruby, 107, 133, 144, 145
Los Angeles Public Library, 202
Louise, *see* Andrea and Louise
Louisiana, 4, 9, 32, 35, 225, 241, 248
as unlikely to embrace same-sex marriage
for a very long time, 250
defending Super-DOMA of, 241
no sexual-orientation-discrimination ban in,
106
size of Super-DOMA popular majority in,
248
Louisiana Court of Appeal, 53
Loving v. Virginia, 226, 233, 236
Loving, Richard, 226

Maddow, Rachel, 189
Madison, Wisconsin, 7, 9, 10, 22, 66, 92, 100,
101, 113
Maiden, North Carolina, 268
Maine, 208, 225, 244, 249
legalizing same-sex marriage, 244
Manchester, New Hampshire, 199
Maria and Margaret, 86, 87, 177
playing the system, 177
Margaret, *see* Maria and Margaret
Marian, *see* Christine and Marian
Marie, *see* Janet and Marie
Marilyn, *see* Irene and Marilyn
Mark and Paul, 170, 171, 173, 213–215,
217
Marquette University, 97

marriage
as a fundamental federal constitutional
right, 227
as a religious institution, 23
benefits of, 5
conferring respectability on sexual
relationships, 278
costs of, 261
direct ways of defending and protecting,
269, 270, 273
expansion of the definition of by the
political process, 244
fortified by non-Super-DOMA techniques,
270
fortified for heterosexual couples, 25, 258
importance of to children raised by
same-sex couples, 103, 114, 115, 137, 256
legal grounds for the dissolution of, 269
not fortified by Super-DOMAs, 260
polling data on, 235
social status of, 93
solidifying and clarifying intrafamily
relationships, 136, 137
marriage penalty, 255, 256
definition of, 255
marriage-evasion statute, 9, 187, 226
Marshall, Thurgood, 227
Martha, *see* Debra and Martha
Maryland, 150, 163, 183, 185, 197, 198, 225,
249
allowing names of both parents on birth
certificates, 135
high cost of living in, 197
LGBT migration to, 139, 183, 185, 186
Mason-Dixon line, 43, 170
Massachusetts, 5, 13, 14, 24, 30, 92, 105, 126,
149, 157, 163, 170, 172, 178, 180, 185,
193, 203, 204, 206, 214, 215, 225, 249,
257, 260, 282, 284
high cost of living in, 193, 214
LGBT migration from, 219, 221
LGBT migration to, 150, 193, 201, 203,
204, 214, 215, 218
second-parent adoption permitted in, 112
Massachusetts Family Institute, 276
Massachusetts Supreme Judicial Court, 52,
279
Massucci, LeeAnn M., 23, 40, 131
Matter of Jacob, 53
McCain-Feingold Act, 252
McConkey v. Van Hollen, 53
McKettrick v. McKettrick, 53

mean value
  definition of, 12
Measure 36, 5, 16, 33
median value
  definition of, 12
Medicaid, 135, 175, 263
Memphis, Tennessee, 29
Miami, 78, 99
  antigay hospital episode in, 73, 78
Miami University, 67
Michael and Robert, 21, 49
Michelle and Sharon, 61, 157
Michigan, 1, 2, 4, 6, 9, 10, 13, 16, 18, 19, 21,
    35, 43–50, 52, 54–59, 61, 66, 69, 71, 82,
    99, 111, 115, 152, 154, 161, 177,
    181–186, 194, 199, 203, 205, 215–218,
    223, 225, 241, 245–248, 250, 254, 258,
    260, 261, 263–266, 278
  amount of same-sex couples' attorney's fees
    paid for by, 265
  as a case study for the democratic process,
    245–247
  as aggressively opposed to the civil rights of
    same-sex couples, 247
  judicial-selection method in, 35
  lack of LGBT loyalty for, 186
  LGBT avoidance of, 205
  LGBT expectation of reasonableness in,
    162
  LGBT loyalty for, 156, 161
  LGBT migration from, 1, 2, 149, 154,
    182–185, 266, 267
  LGBT migration to, 218
  LGBT-friendly hospitals in, 71
  limitations in on adoption and foster care of
    children, 247
  lost revenues in, 260, 262–264
  low cost of living in, 163, 216
  no sexual-orientation-discrimination ban in,
    80, 106
  number of interviews conducted in, 12
  "other qualified adult" programs in,
    246
  Public Employee Domestic Partner Benefit
    Restriction Act of, 247
  public-opinion changes in, 246, 247
  second-parent adoption denied in, 111
  selection of for Super-DOMA study, 9
  see also specific cities and counties and
    Proposal 2
Michigan Christian Citizens Alliance, 44
Michigan Civil Service Commission, 246

Michigan Court of Appeals, 53
Michigan State University, 47
Michigan Supreme Court, 19, 35, 43, 46–49,
    52, 58, 183, 203, 246, 268
Mildred, see Cheryl and Mildred
Milwaukee County, Wisconsin, 96, 227
Milwaukee Journal Sentinel, 51
Milwaukee Public Schools, 113
Milwaukee, Wisconsin, 9, 10, 61, 62, 97, 100,
    113, 157, 226
Mini-DOMAs, 33
  definition of, 5
  objectives of, 5
  see also Defense of Marriage Act and
    Super-DOMAs
Minneapolis, 194
Minnesota, 2, 150, 192, 194, 225, 249
  defeat of same-sex-marriage ban in, 8,
    194
  LGBT migration to, 193
Miriam and Naomi, 83, 146, 158, 221
  experience of changing surnames, 83
Mississippi, 5, 33, 189, 220, 225, 248
  among last states voluntarily to embrace
    same-sex marriage, 194, 281
  no sexual-orientation-discrimination ban in,
    106
  size of Mini-DOMA popular majority in,
    248
Missouri, 5, 33, 225
  amount of same-sex couples' attorney's fees
    paid for by, 265
  no sexual-orientation-discrimination ban in,
    106
Modern Family, 145
Monroe, North Carolina, 201
Montana, 5, 33, 233
  no sexual-orientation-discrimination ban in,
    106
Montreal, Quebec, Canada, 203
Mormon Church, 272
  sponsoring the Boy Scouts of America, 272
Music Man, The, 272

Nantucket Island, Massachusetts, 16
Naomi, see Miriam and Naomi
Nashif, Tim, 276
National Organization for Marriage, 272
National Pride at Work, Inc. v. *Governor of
    Michigan*, 35, 43, 47–50, 54, 55, 57, 66,
    246, 268
  compared with *Appling* v. *Walker*, 52

Nazis, 152, 153, 155, 156, 162, 173, 181, 269
  making the abnormal seem normal, 269
  mislabeling anti-Jewish measures as sensible,
    269
NBC News, 235
Nebraska, 4, 150, 225
  having first Super-DOMA, 9
  low cost of living in, 163
  no sexual-orientation-discrimination ban in,
    106
Nelson, Vincent, 150
Nevada, 5, 103, 233
Nevada Dep't of Human Res. v. Hibbs,
    239
Nevins, Gregory, 56, 57
New Hampshire, 199, 225, 228, 244,
    249
  legalizing same-sex marriage, 244
New Jersey, 163, 218, 225, 249
  civil unions for same-sex couples in, 218
  LGBT migration to, 204, 218
  low rate of divorce in, 259
  outlawing "conversion" or "reparative"
    therapies, 274
  second-parent adoption permitted in,
    218
New Mexico, 225, 249
New York City, 178, 181, 211, 215
  marketing itself as a same-sex-marriage
    destination, 262
  marriage bureau of, 262
New York Court of Appeals, 53
New York State, 157, 163, 180, 194, 195, 209,
    212–215, 225, 227–229, 244, 249, 263
  ease of foster parenting in, 178
  high cost of living in, 216
  legalizing same-sex marriage, 244, 262
  legislative debates on same-sex marriage in,
    92
  LGBT migration from, 209
  placing both same-sex-partner names on
    child-adoption decrees, 178, 263
  recognizing out-of-state marriages, 227
  second-parent adoption permitted in, 112
New York Times, 25, 150, 205, 222, 259, 273,
    277, 281
  profiling Phil Burress, 25, 273
North Carolina, 4, 6, 10, 13, 20, 21, 23, 54,
    57–61, 82, 86–88, 93, 95, 108–112, 138,
    143, 147, 152, 170, 177, 197–201,
    208–213, 222, 223, 233, 250, 254, 260,
    261, 263, 264, 266, 268, 271, 275

  as unlikely to embrace same-sex marriage
    for a very long time, 250
  having the last Super-DOMA campaign, 17
  last state in the Southeast without a
    constitutional DOMA, 211
  LGBT avoidance of, 201, 208, 209
  LGBT loyalty for, 157
  lost revenues in, 260, 262–264
  low cost of living in, 163
  no sexual-orientation-discrimination ban in,
    80, 106
  number of interviews conducted in, 12
  right-to-work state, 147
  second-parent adoption denied in, 112,
    198
  selection of for Super-DOMA study, 9, 10
  sexual-orientation discrimination in,
    170
  *see also specific cities and counties and
    Amendment 1*
North Carolina Supreme Court, 112
North Dakota, 2, 4, 9, 33, 225
  amount of same-sex couples' attorney's fees
    paid for by, 265
  low cost of living in, 163
  no sexual-orientation-discrimination ban in,
    106
Northampton, Massachusetts, 163, 219

Oakland University, 199
  antigay housing discrimination at, 82
Obama, Barack, 235, 242, 243
Obergefell v. Hodges, 224, 225, 233, 236, 246,
    247, 249, 251, 262, 265, 273, 281
  appendix of, 232, 237
  counterfactual outcomes to from dissenters'
    approach, 250
  determining gay people's fundamental right
    to marry, 224
  dissents of, 225, 244, 245, 252, 267
  effects of, 254, 256, 257
  estimate of revenues generated by, 262
  invalidating half of the nation's
    Super-DOMAs, 225
  legal precedents for, 226, 227
  majority opinion of, 253
  predating nationwide embrace of same-sex
    marriage by a century, 250, 281
  preordained outcome of, 234
  tax benefits and penalties of, 254, 255
  ways of formally disturbing, 224, 225
Obergefell v. Wymyslo, 232, 233, 239

Ohio, 4, 6, 9, 10, 13, 24–32, 35–44, 47, 54,
    56–59, 61, 63–65, 67–69, 73–76, 83, 84,
    86, 88–92, 94, 95, 100, 105, 106, 111,
    114, 126–132, 135, 136, 145, 146, 149,
    151, 152, 159, 160, 164, 175, 194, 199,
    201, 204, 206, 218, 219, 223, 225, 232,
    239, 241, 248, 250, 254, 260, 261,
    263–267, 271, 273
  amount of same-sex couples' attorney's fees
    paid for by, 265
  domestic violence law of, 38
  Equal Housing and Employment Act of,
    105
  funding for and against Issue 1, 266
  importance of in 2004 presidential election,
    25
  judicial-selection method in, 35
  LGBT avoidance of, 193, 200, 204,
    206
  LGBT migration from, 150, 151, 156,
    204
  LGBT migration to, 219
  lost revenues in, 260, 262–264, 267
  low cost of living in, 145, 163
  media markets in, 28
  no sexual-orientation-discrimination ban in,
    80, 106
  number of interviews conducted in, 12
  number of same-sex couples living in,
    151
  organizing the LGBT community in, 26, 27
  polling data from on same-sex relationships,
    23, 248
  ritual of public hazing in, 83, 84
  second-parent adoption denied in, 111
  selection of for Super-DOMA study, 9
  shared-custody agreements in, 111, 131
  statutory DOMA of, 30
  surname changes in, 82
  see also specific cities and counties and
    Issue 1
Ohio Campaign to Protect Marriage, 31
Ohio Court of Appeals, 41, 53
Ohio ex rel. Popovici v. Agler, 228
Ohio Freedom to Marry, 27
Ohio State University, 95
Ohio Supreme Court, 37, 39–41, 44, 46, 47, 82
Oklahoma, 4, 9, 32, 201, 233, 236, 240
  amount of same-sex couples' attorney's fees
    paid for by, 265
  defending Super-DOMA of, 236
  LGBT migration from, 186, 201

  low cost of living in, 163
  no sexual-orientation-discrimination ban in,
    106
Oklahoma City, Oklahoma, 201
Olive, *see* Bertie and Olive
Olson, Theodore, 240
Oregon, 5, 24, 33, 62, 163, 225
  amount of same-sex couples' attorney's fees
    paid for by, 265
  ease of obtaining civil-union certification
    from, 70
  having many state and local LGBT
    initiatives, 62
Oregon Family Council, 276
O'Connor, Sandra Day, 227

Page, Bob, 222
  profiled by the *New York Times*, 222
Palmieri, Jennifer, 25
Pamela, *see* Kathleen and Pamela
Patricia, *see* Linda and Patricia
Paul, *see* Mark and Paul
Paula, *see* Diana and Paula
Paulding County, Georgia
  second-parent adoption in, 123
Pell grants, 177
Pennsylvania, 277
  amount of same-sex couples' attorney's fees
    paid for by, 265
  judicial invalidation of anti-same-sex-
    marriage statute of, 277
  no sexual-orientation-discrimination ban in,
    106
Perdue v. O'Kelley, 53
Perimeter, The, *see* Atlanta
Perkins, Tony, 30
Perry, Rick, 220
Petro, Jim, 6
Philadelphia, 189
Phoenix, Terri, 79, 94, 271
Piedmont Hospital, 72
Pinello, Daniel R., 280
Political Institutions and Lesbian and Gay
    Rights in the United States and Canada,
    283
Pond, Lisa, 78
Portland, Oregon, 280
Posner, Richard A., 278, 279, 283, 284
  setting the gold standard for measuring
    court decisions, 278
precedent
  importance of legal, 236, 237

Proposal 2, 1, 6, 19, 43–50, 52, 55, 57, 58, 66,
   70, 71, 82, 155, 177, 183, 185, 199, 205,
   215–217, 241, 245–247, 278, 285
   compared to Question 1, 55
   cynical wording of, 19
   eliminating second-parent adoptions, 47
   enforced by the American Family
      Association of Michigan, 57
   facilitating housing discrimination, 82
   impact of on domestic-partner benefits, 47,
      216
   impact of on legal documents, 48, 50
   interpreted as broadly as possible, 48
   interpreted by Michigan Supreme Court, 35,
      44
   judicial invalidation of, 278
   judicial validation of, 241
   length of time in effect, 246
   LGBT people's ignorance of real threat
      from, 155
   meaning of, 45, 46, 216, 217
   memorializing hostile political climate, 247
   passive voice of, 49
   political campaign surrounding, 45
   polling data on, 19, 23, 247
   scuttling domestic-partnership provisions,
      66
   size of popular majority of, 6, 245
   sponsored by Michigan Christian Citizens
      Alliance, 44
   suppressing immigration into Michigan,
      199, 205, 215–217
   text of, 18, 35, 285
   triggering LGBT migration, 182–186
   see also Michigan
Proposition 2, 57, 80, 95, 115, 156, 206, 207,
   266, 286
   emotional loss from, 95
   favoring biological kin, 80
   funding of, 266
   not suppressing immigration into Texas,
      220, 221
   size of popular majority of, 6, 248
   suppressing immigration into Texas,
      206–208
   text of, 36, 286
   see also Texas
Proposition 8, 5, 16, 144, 240
Providence Road Baptist Church, 268
Providence, Rhode Island, 215
pseudonyms
   use of, 3

Public Employee Domestic Partner Benefit
   Restriction Act, 247

Question 1, 22, 54–57, 59, 70, 77, 85, 102,
   104, 119, 134, 135, 137, 138, 146, 152,
   155, 157, 158, 166, 171, 172, 178–180,
   202, 203, 214, 221, 248, 273, 277, 285
   amount of fundraising against, 20
   compared to Proposal 2, 55
   complete language of not on the ballot, 17,
      277
   impact of, 54, 157
   impact of on foster parenting, 178
   impact of on health care, 132
   impact of on inheritance and taxation, 85
   impact of on schools, 132, 133
   increasing costs of raising children, 134,
      135
   interpreted to mean same-sex couples may
      not adopt children, 158
   legislative deliberation over, 8
   LGBT people's ignorance of real threat
      from, 155
   limiting adjudication of rights, 104, 137, 138
   meaning of, 59
   political probability for repeal of, 248
   size of popular majority of, 6, 248
   suppressing immigration into Georgia, 202,
      203, 214
   text of, 5, 285
   triggering LGBT migration, 180
   voters not understanding, 18
   see also Georgia

Rachel and Veronica, 73, 88, 160
Raleigh, North Carolina, 7, 10, 21, 80
Ralph v. City of New Orleans, 53
Raymond, see Andrew and Raymond
Reagan, Ronald, 236, 277, 278
Rebecca and Virginia, 186–191, 197
   emotional when their marriage was
      bureaucratically acknowledged, 191
Redhail, Roger, 226
Reed, Kasim, 157
referenda, 283
   definition of, 5
   impact of compared with initiatives, 57
   nature of legislative deliberation over, 6
Referendum 1, 20, 22, 50, 52, 57, 61, 62, 66,
   92, 97, 99–101, 113, 114, 187, 188, 191,
   245, 246, 278, 286
   being just about marriage, 20

Referendum 1 (*cont.*)
  effects of alleviated by domestic-partner
    registry, 101
  emotional and psychological damage of, 92
  impact of on health care, 97, 100
  impact of on parents raising children, 113
  interpreted by Wisconsin Supreme Court, 35
  judicial invalidation of, 278
  legislative history of, 50
  political campaign surrounding, 19, 24
  polling data on, 24
  size of popular majority of, 6, 245
  sponsored by Wisconsin legislature, 50
  supported by Roman Catholic Church, 22
  text of, 35, 286
  triggering LGBT migration, 187, 188
  see also Wisconsin
Rehnquist, William, 227
religion
  impact on the passage of Super-DOMAs, 22
  see also Mormon Church *and* Roman
    Catholic Church
Replacements, Ltd., 222
Republican Party, 27, 55, 63, 105, 120, 199,
    220, 224, 225, 235, 236, 243, 246, 250,
    277, 278
  2012 platform of, 243
  and congressional control, 243
  gerrymandering by, 243
  not steadfastly prejudiced against LGBT
    people, 277
research methods, 9–11, 152, 173, 204, 206,
    208, 211, 217
  limitations of, 11, 152
  measuring non-immigration to
    Super-DOMA states, 204, 206, 211, 217
  sampling same-sex couples, 11, 173
Research Triangle Park, North Carolina, 209,
    210
Rhode Island, 225, 249
Richard and Tim, 76, 84
Rita, *see* Dawn and Rita
Robert, *see* Michael and Robert
Roberts, John, 225, 230, 232, 234, 237, 241,
    244–246, 248, 249, 251, 252, 267, 269,
    273, 276
  advocacy of for the democratic process, 241,
    244–246, 248
  condemning characterizations of
    Super-DOMA supporters as bigoted, 267,
    268, 273, 276
  hypocrisy of, 251, 252

overlooking state-supreme-court assaults on
    the democratic process, 249
  problems with democratic-process thesis of,
    246, 249, 250, 252
Robicheaux v. *Caldwell*, 233, 241
Robin, *see* Lillian and Robin
Roe v. *Wade*, 245
Rogers, Jim, 8
Roman Catholic Church, 23, 97, 145, 272
  funding Super-DOMAs, 23, 266
  opposition of to same-sex relationships, 22
  refusal of to recognize divorce, 270
Romer v. *Evans*, 236
Ronald, *see* Anthony and Ronald
Rosemary, *see* Agnes and Rosemary
Rosenberg, Gerald N., 279, 280
  arguing courts are severely limited to help
    disadvantaged people, 280
  assessing judicial impact on same-sex
    marriage, 280
  publicly eating his own published words,
    281
Rosenbrahn v. *Daugaard*, 233
Ross v. *Goldstein*, 53
Roswell, Georgia, 89
Rowell v. *Smith*, 41
Rowse, Jayne, 278
Ruby, *see* Lois and Ruby
Ruth, *see* Doris and Ruth

Sam, *see* Adam and Sam
same-sex couples
  affecting local opinion on same-sex
    relationships, 21
  and prior marriages to opposite-sex
    partners, 93
  as foster parents, 107, 116, 117, 119, 177,
    178, 263, 264
  as pro-marriage, 20
  average age of in sample, 250
  basic rights of necessary to look after one
    another, 96
  better off legally in the Deep South, 54
  characterized by Indiana as model parents
    and citizens, 279
  correctly seeking same-sex marriage through
    judicial action, 284
  costs of in raising children, 134, 135
  demeaned and stigmatized by
    Super-DOMAs, 268
  desiring public recognition of their
    relationships, 261

employment discrimination involving, 80,
81
entering into partnership agreements,
103
estimate of male pairs, 263
estimate of marrying out of state, 261
experiences of compared with race, 21
fearing rural areas, 62, 74, 159
federal courts rescuing, 224–226
having legal documents, 73, 74, 77–79, 154,
187
housing discrimination affecting, 81, 82
in the closet, 169, 171–173, 255, 256
life changes to from federal-court decisions,
254
not expecting to be able to get legally
married during their lifetimes, 250
not seeking marriage, 260
number of in each state, 261
number of legally married, 226
number of raising children, 107
permanent migrations by, 181–198
playing the system, 161, 174–177
problems of regarding wills, 79, 90, 91, 102,
127, 154
raising adopted children of color, 12,
145
raising adopted children with special needs,
13, 115, 120, 135, 263
seeking common surnames, 82–84, 117,
132, 133, 195, 196
seeking divorce, 36, 41, 103, 104
seeking full legal status for both partners as
parents, 108, 127, 129
temporary migrations by, 177–180, 260,
261
see also adoption and foster care of children
and second-parent adoption of children
and surrogacy
San Antonio, Texas, 116, 118
permitting second-parent adoption in, 116,
192
San Francisco, 200, 221, 280
Sandra, *see* Betty and Sandra
Santorum, Rick, 277
Sarah, *see* Laura and Sarah
Savannah, Georgia, 120
Scalia, Antonin, 227, 231, 237–246, 248, 249,
251, 252
advocacy of for the democratic process,
241–243, 245, 246, 248
as a double agent, 237–241

as a judicial friend of the American LGBT
community, 241
as an ineffective strategic actor, 241
death of, 225
heralding nationwide marriage equality,
232, 234, 238–241
hypocrisy of, 251, 252
problems with democratic-process thesis of,
246, 249, 250, 252
Schiavo, Terri, 98
Scott, *see* Eric and Scott
Seagraves, Debbie, 56, 138, 158
Searcey v. Strange, 233
second-parent adoption of children, 53
availability of after *Obergefell v. Hodges*,
254
availability of in Super-DOMA states,
110–114, 116, 118–125
costs of, 114, 118, 120, 125, 192
effects from failure to achieve, 123, 124,
130, 131, 133, 141, 144, 147
importance of to same-sex couples,
126–130, 198
states permitting, 110
see also adoption and foster care of children
and same-sex couples *and* surrogacy
Section 1983, 265
Section 1988, 265
Sex and Reason, 283
sexual-orientation discrimination
based on belief that sexual orientation is
mutable, 275
no legal protections against, 3, 106,
170
refusal of Congress to ban, 243
Shaker Heights, Ohio, 219
Sharon, *see* Michelle and Sharon
Sheila, *see* Esther and Sheila
Shelby County v. Holder, 251
dissents of, 251, 252
Shelby, Robert J., 238
Sherrill, Kenneth, 173
Shirley, *see* Kimberly and Shirley
Sierra Club, 190
Small Town, Ohio, 129
Smith College, 219
Smith, Miriam, 283
Snyder, Richard, 246, 247
implacable hostility of to LGBT rights,
247
Social Security benefits, 14, 78, 97, 103, 128,
164

South Carolina, 4, 35, 233
    among last states voluntarily to embrace
        same-sex marriage, 194
    amount of same-sex couples' attorney's fees
        paid for by, 265
    as unlikely to embrace same-sex marriage
        for a very long time, 250
    no sexual-orientation-discrimination ban in,
        106
South Carolina v. *Katzenbach*, 250
South Dakota, 4, 225
    low cost of living in, 163
    no sexual-orientation-discrimination ban in,
        106
southern states
    having influx of LGBT people, 13
Spainhour, Andrew, 20
Springfield, Illinois, 196
Spyer, Thea, 227
Stankevich v. *Milliron*, 53
state courts
    deciding LGBT-rights claims more favorably
        than federal courts, 34
State v. *Carswell*, 37, 38, 40, 44, 47
Stephanie, *see* Carolyn and Stephanie
Sterling Heights, Michigan
    having no LGBT-friendly hospitals, 71
Steven, *see* Edward and Steven
Stewart and William, 84, 218, 221
    returning to Ohio, 217
Sullivan, Andrew, 63
Super-DOMA effects, 15, 16, 59–96, 101–110,
    113–115, 118, 125–138, 141, 144–147
    alienation from family and friends, 64,
        86–89, 198
    book as history of, 16
    complicating relationships with children of
        same-sex couples, 113, 145–147, 174
    denial of access to funeral homes, 2, 154
    denial of adoption rights, 138
    denial of compassion and respect, 94
    denial of domestic-partner benefits, 66, 68
    denial of domestic-violence protective
        orders, 94
    denial of family-medical-leave benefits, 76
    denial of health care, 69–76
    denial of legal recognition to both parents,
        107, 110, 141, 142
    denial of partner notification in time of
        emergency, 2, 90, 154
    denial of partner's pension, 2, 154
    denial of retirement benefits, 70

denial of standing to sue for partner's
    wrongful death, 2, 154
derogating the place of marriage in
    American culture, 136
disrupting business relationships, 89
divorce rates not reduced, 259
employment discrimination, 80
fear, insecurity, and emotional loss, 89–94
financial losses to states, 260–267
hazing ritual when changing surnames, 83,
    84
hospital denials of authority and visitation,
    71, 98
housing discrimination, 81
inability to divorce, 101–104
increasing parenting costs, 134, 135
interviews as optimally situated to test for,
    15
lack of in Georgia, 16
limiting employment opportunities, 76, 77
messages to children of same-sex couples,
    135, 136
not alleviated by money, 212, 221, 222
not fortifying heterosexual marriage, 260,
    272
number of children born out of wedlock not
    reduced, 259
on aging and end-of-life care, 73
on business agreements, 49, 138, 139
on disputes between same-sex couples, 49
on employment benefits, 47
on wills, 48
positive impacts, 62–65
rates of two-parent households not
    increased, 259
reducing states' attractiveness as retirement
    locations, 201
suppressing immigration into Super-DOMA
    states, 199–217, 223
tax penalties, 84, 85
see also Super-DOMAs
Super-DOMA sponsors, 17, 19, 20, 24, 25,
    267, 269–276
    acknowledging non-Super-DOMA
        techniques to fortify marriage, 270, 271
    bigotry of, 271–276
    denying antigay animus, 17
    mislabeling antigay measures as sensible,
        269
    motivations of, 24, 25, 267–276
    not worthy of universal, unalloyed scorn,
        276

Super-DOMA states
  costs to from LGBT migration, 184, 223
  economic losses to, 260–264, 266
  list of, 4
  low costs of living in, 163
  obligation of to pay plaintiffs' attorney's
    fees, 265
  population of, 4
  selection of for study, 9
Super-DOMAs
  alleged to be just about marriage, 277
  as impediments to change, 66–69
  complicating end-of-life planning, 80
  cumulative campaign costs of, 266
  definition of, 4
  denying couples basic rights to look after
    one another, 96
  emotional and psychological tolls of, 59, 97
  enforcement of in Michigan and Ohio, 56
  facilitating discrimination, 71, 95
  having little organized opposition against,
    20
  how added to state constitutions, 5
  impact of invalidation of, 254–258
  impact of on couples raising children,
    107–110
  intangible costs to states of, 266
  interpreted by state courts, 35, 54
  judicial invalidation of, 253
  lawyers declining to defend amendments in
    court, 205
  legal burdens of on nonbiological parents,
    143
  motivated by sponsor bigotry, 267–276
  not increasing rates of two-parent
    households, 259
  not reducing divorce rates, 259
  not reducing the number of children born
    out of wedlock, 259
  objectives of, 5, 258–260
  objectives of not achieved, 260
  popular majorities of, 32
  repulsing young, well-educated people, 223,
    266
  texts of, 5
  unfulfilled objectives of, 258, 260
  voters not understanding, 277
  see also Defense of Marriage Act *and*
    Mini-DOMAs *and* Super-DOMA effects
Superior, Wisconsin, 150
surrogacy
  choice of for having children, 134

  costs of, 134, 262, 263
  estimate of number of male couples
    choosing, 263
  for overcoming unavailability of
    second-parent adoption, 135
  see also adoption and foster care of children
    and same-sex couples *and* second-parent
    adoption of children
Szabo, John F., 202–204

T.M.H. v. D.M.T., 53
Taft, Bob, 6, 30, 63
Tammy, *see* Denise and Tammy
Tampa Bay, Florida, 203
Tanco v. Haslam, 233
Ted, *see* Ben and Ted
Tennessee, 5, 161, 225
  as unlikely to embrace same-sex marriage
    for a very long time, 250
  no sexual-orientation-discrimination ban in,
    106
Teresa, *see* Heather and Teresa
Tester, Patrick, 206–208, 219
Texas, 4, 6, 13, 54, 57–59, 71, 95, 115–118,
    135, 152, 160, 163, 165, 168–170,
    192–197, 199, 206, 219, 220, 223, 225,
    227, 238, 248, 250, 254, 255, 260, 261,
    263, 264, 266
  "absent-parent" form of, 118
  among last states voluntarily to embrace
    same-sex marriage, 194
  as unlikely to embrace same-sex marriage
    for a very long time, 250
  considering referendum to ban adoptions by
    LGBT parents, 117
  lacking LGBT-friendly hospitals, 71
  LGBT avoidance of, 206–208
  LGBT migration from, 192–194
  LGBT migration to, 220, 221
  lost revenues in, 260, 262–264
  low cost of living in, 163, 192, 221
  no personal income tax in, 195
  no sexual-orientation-discrimination ban in,
    80, 106
  number of interviews conducted in, 12
  recruiting lesbian and gay parents, 115
  same-sex divorce in, 36
  second-parent adoption in, 115, 119, 192
  selection of for Super-DOMA study, 9
  surname changes in, 195
  see also *specific cities and counties and*
    Proposition 2

Texas Child Protective Services, 115
recruiting gay and lesbian parents , 116
Texas Court of Appeals, 35, 53, 58
Texas Department of Motor Vehicles
refusal of to accept out-of-state marriage
certificates, 195
Texas Supreme Court, 36
Texas v. *Naylor and Daly*, 36
Thomas, Clarence, 225, 227
Thomasville, Georgia, 221
Thompson, Sharon, 111
Tifton, Georgia, 72
Tim, *see* Richard and Tim
Toledo, Ohio, 152
Toronto, Ontario, Canada, 203
Tracy, *see* Connie and Tracy

U.S. Courts of Appeals, 232–234, 240, 265,
278, 281
relevant same-sex-marriage decisions of, 233
U.S. Department of Homeland Security, 258
U.S. District Courts, 232–234
relevant same-sex-marriage decisions of, 233
U.S. Supreme Court, 16, 34, 57, 163, 164, 170,
188, 189, 191, 195, 198, 224–226,
230–234, 236, 238, 239, 241, 243, 246,
247, 250, 252–254, 257, 260, 262, 265,
272, 281–283
impact of good fortune on, 236
joining a national transformation on
same-sex marriage, 233
letting lower-court same-sex-marriage
judgments go into effect, 233
LGBT faith and trust in, 163
rescuing same-sex couples, 224
United States v. *Windsor*, 16, 188, 226, 227,
230–232, 236, 238, 239, 243, 278, 281,
282
ambiguous majority opinion of, 228–230,
234
counterfactual outcomes to from dissenters'
approach, 250
decision of based on Due Process and Equal
Protection clauses, 230, 238
decision of based on federalism, 228, 229,
241
dissents of, 230–232, 234, 237–242, 245,
251, 252
effects of, 254, 257
impact of on binational couples, 258
invalidating DOMA ten years before
Congress could have, 281

lower federal courts' lopsided
interpretations of, 232–234, 236
majority opinion of, 228–230, 253
prompting same-sex couples to marry out of
state, 257, 262
providing a natural experiment on the
strategy of dissent, 237
tax benefits and penalties of, 254, 255
University of Georgia, 120
University of Michigan, 47, 69, 71, 156, 177,
182, 184, 216, 266
committed to guaranteeing domestic-partner
benefits, 185, 216
cost to of losing Michael Falk, 184, 266
University of Michigan Medical School, 205
University of North Carolina, 79, 209, 211,
213, 271
antigay employment discrimination at, 80
public condemnation of LGBT people at,
200
University of Notre Dame
not rejecting sexual-orientation
discrimination in employment, 272
University of Wisconsin, 99
Urban Libraries Council, 203
USA Today, 45
Utah, 4, 9, 33, 233, 238, 239, 272
amount of same-sex couples' attorney's fees
paid for by, 265
as unlikely to embrace same-sex marriage
for a very long time, 250
defending Super-DOMA of, 238, 239
low cost of living in, 163

Valdosta, Georgia, 72
Vancouver, British Columbia, Canada, 2, 137
Vermont, 26, 30, 78, 91, 126, 149, 163, 167,
177, 199, 204, 214, 215, 225, 228, 244,
249, 282, 284
legalizing same-sex marriage, 244
LGBT migration to, 204
low cost of living in, 214, 215
Vermont-style civil union, 19, 39
Vernor's ginger ale, 216
Veronica, *see* Rachel and Veronica
Virginia (person), *see* Rebecca and Virginia
Virginia (state), 4, 5, 17, 18, 35, 56, 138–142,
150, 226, 233
amount of same-sex couples' attorney's fees
paid for by, 265
as unlikely to embrace same-sex marriage
for a very long time, 250

House Bill 751, 138
legal burdens of on nonbiological parents, 141, 142
LGBT migration from, 186
no sexual-orientation-discrimination ban in, 106
prohibition of against interracial marriage, 226, 236
same-sex domestic violence in, 56
Virginia Highlands Festival, 180
Voinovich, George, 6
Vote for Marriage NC, 17, 20, 271
voters, 17–20, 22–24, 276, 277
distinguishing motivations of, 17, 24
lacking animus toward LGBT people, 23, 276, 277
Voting Rights Act of 1965, 250
size of congressional majorities for 2006 reauthorization of, 251

Wald, Kenneth, 173
Walmart, 165
Walter, *see* Jerry and Walter
war, 1, 3–9, 150, 181–198, 224, 253, 258–267, 276
archetypical refugees of, 182
as expensive, 260–267
battleground of, 1
declarations of, 3–9
end of, 253
final battle of, 224
five-star generals of, 276
refugees from, 150, 181–199
unfulfilled objectives of, 258
Warmth of Other Suns, The, 149; *see also* Wilkerson, Isabel
Warren, Earl, 226
Warren, Michigan
having no LGBT-friendly hospitals, 71
Washington County, Wisconsin, 112
Washington State, 78, 150, 163, 225, 228, 249
Washington, DC, 214, 226
Waters v. Ricketts, 233
Waukesha County, Wisconsin, 62
Webster's Dictionary, 44, 48, 268
West Virginia, 233
amount of same-sex couples' attorney's fees paid for by, 265
no sexual-orientation-discrimination ban in, 106
Wheeler v. Wheeler, 121, 123
Whitewood v. Wolf, 233, 277

Wilkerson, Isabel, 149, 152, 153, 173, 197, 222
Williams College, 214
Williams Institute
estimate of for revenues generated by *Obergefell* v. *Hodges,* 262
estimate of for the mean cost of weddings, 261
estimate of on number of same-sex couples in states, 151
estimate of on number of same-sex couples raising children, 107
Williamstown, Massachusetts, 214, 215
Wilmington, Delaware, 189
Windsor, Edith, 227, 229
Winnipeg, Manitoba, Canada, 2, 149
Winston-Salem, North Carolina, 10, 63, 90, 272
Wisconsin, 4, 6, 10, 13, 19, 24, 35, 50–52, 54, 57–59, 61, 66, 92, 96–101, 112–115, 152, 162, 163, 175, 176, 180, 187–191, 199, 223, 226, 233, 245, 250, 254, 255, 258, 260, 261, 263–265, 278
amount of same-sex couples' attorney's fees paid for by, 265
as exceptional Super-DOMA state, 9
as unlikely to embrace same-sex marriage for a very long time, 250
domestic-partner registry of, 9, 24, 96–101, 112
judicial-selection method in, 35
lacking animus toward LGBT people, 24
LGBT expectation of reasonableness in, 162
LGBT loyalty for, 157, 162
LGBT migration from, 150, 187
lost revenues in, 260, 262–264
low cost of living in, 163
marriage-evasion statute, 9, 187
number of interviews conducted in, 12
only Super-DOMA state with sexual-orientation-discrimination ban, 80
second-parent adoption in, 112, 119
selection of for Super-DOMA study, 9
see also specific cities and counties and Referendum 1
Wisconsin Education Association Council, 66
Wisconsin Family Action, 19
Wisconsin State Journal, 51
Wisconsin Supreme Court, 35, 50, 52, 112
Wolf v. Walker, 233
Women in Medicine, 204
World War II, 269

Worley, Charles
  advocating concentration camps for LGBT
    people, 268
Wyoming, 233
  no sexual-orientation-discrimination ban in,
    106

Yale University, 281
  archiving LGBT interviews, 276
YMCA, 95

Zablocki v. *Redhail*, 226, 236
Zablocki, Thomas, 226